CONVENTIONAL FORCE REDUCTIONS

CONVENTIONAL FORCE REDUCTIONS

A Dynamic Assessment

Joshua M. Epstein

THE BROOKINGS INSTITUTION
Washington, D.C.

Library of Congress Cataloging-in-Publication Data

Epstein, Joshua M., 1951-
     Conventional force reductions : a dynamic assessment / Joshua M.
     Epstein.
          p.   cm.
     ISBN 0-8157-2462-4 (alk. paper) — ISBN 0-8157-2461-6
     (pbk. : alk. paper)
     1. Europe—Defenses. 2. Europe—Armed Forces. 3. Warfare, Con-
     ventional. 4. Arms control.   I. Title.
     UA646.E59   1990
     355'.03304—dc20   90-31523
                                                                               CIP

9 8 7 6 5 4 3 2 1

THE BROOKINGS INSTITUTION

The Brookings Institution is an independent organization devoted to nonpartisan research, education, and publication in economics, government, foreign policy, and the social sciences generally. Its principal purposes are to aid in the development of sound public policies and to promote public understanding of issues of national importance.

The Institution was founded on December 8, 1927, to merge the activities of the Institute for Government Research, founded in 1916, the Institute of Economics, founded in 1922, and the Robert Brookings Graduate School of Economics and Government, founded in 1924.

The Board of Trustees is responsible for the general administration of the Institution, while the immediate direction of the policies, program, and staff is vested in the President, assisted by an advisory committee of the officers and staff. The by-laws of the Institution state: "It is the function of the Trustees to make possible the conduct of scientific research, and publication, under the most favorable conditions, and to safeguard the independence of the research staff in the pursuit of their studies and in the publication of the results of such studies. It is not a part of their function to determine, control, or influence the conduct of particular investigations or the conclusions reached."

The President bears final responsibility for the decision to publish a manuscript as a Brookings book. In reaching his judgment on the competence, accuracy, and objectivity of each study, the President is advised by the director of the appropriate research program and weighs the views of a panel of expert outside readers who report to him in confidence on the quality of the work. Publication of a work signifies that it is deemed a competent treatment worthy of public consideration but does not imply endorsement of conclusions or recommendations.

The Institution maintains its position of neutrality on issues of public policy in order to safeguard the intellectual freedom of the staff. Hence interpretations or conclusions in Brookings publications should be understood to be solely those of the authors and should not be attributed to the Institution, to its trustees, officers, or other staff members, or to the organizations that support its research.

For
Lucy, Joey, Sam,
Melissa, and Elaine

FOREWORD

A REVOLUTION in East-West military relations is under way in Europe; never has Western strategy been in such a state of flux. An early sign of dramatic change came on December 7, 1988, when, in his United Nations address, General Secretary Mikhail Gorbachev announced that the Soviet armed forces would be unilaterally reduced by half a million, a pledge quickly followed by announcements of unilateral cuts by East European nations. More momentous was the arms control proposal offered by the Soviet Union on March 6, 1989, at the opening of the Conventional Forces in Europe (CFE) talks in Vienna: the Soviets accepted NATO's demand that each side reduce the number of ground weapons to equal ceilings slighty below NATO's existing levels, an asymmetrical agreement that would impose vast reductions on the numerically predominant Warsaw Treaty Organization in return for comparatively minor Western cuts. Precisely because the Western reductions would be so limited, however, the CFE agreement is expected to produce insignificant savings in the West. With the opening of the Berlin Wall on November 9, 1989, and the upheavals in Eastern Europe that followed, there are even more widespread political and economic pressures for conventional force reductions beyond CFE.

Using a dynamic model of warfare he has developed, Joshua M. Epstein analyzes the current balance and demonstrates how Western security would progressively improve with the implementation of the Soviet and East European unilateral reductions, the CFE agreement, and a CFE II agreement under which NATO and the WTO would reduce forces to equal levels 50 percent below the levels specified in CFE I. Indeed, Epstein argues that the improvement under such a CFE II agreement would be sufficient to permit the United States to make further reductions unilaterally without detriment to Western security.

The author, a senior fellow in the Brookings Foreign Policy Studies program, acknowledges the valuable suggestions of John D. Steinbruner, director of that program. For their insightful reviews of the manuscript, he thanks Robert Axelrod, John Nicholas Beldecos, Richard K. Betts, Stephen D. Biddle, Jonathan Dean, and William Durch. The book benefited from numerous discussions with Paul B. Stares and Bruce G. Blair. The author also thanks Raymond L. Garthoff for his comments. A special acknowledgement of Ethan Gutmann's contributions appears on a separate page.

The author is grateful to James R. Schneider who edited the manuscript and to Ann M. Ziegler who provided word processing. He also thanks Lisa B. Mages for preliminary research assistance and Vernon L. Kelley for verifying the book's factual content. Susan Woollen prepared the manuscript for publication.

Funding for the book was provided by the Carnegie Corporation of New York and the John D. and Catherine T. MacArthur Foundation. The author and Brookings are grateful for that support.

The views expressed in this study are those of the author and should not be ascribed to the persons or foundations whose assistance is acknowledged above, or to the trustees, officers, or other staff members of the Brookings Institution.

BRUCE K. MACLAURY
President

January 1990
Washington, D.C.

Author's Special
Acknowledgment

THE COMPREHENSIVENESS of this study is due in no small measure to the indispensable contributions of Ethan Gutmann. He prepared the Warsaw Treaty Organization (WTO) and NATO mobilization schedules used in assessing the current conventional balance (tables C-1 and C-3); he prepared a meticulous accounting of the WTO's annnounced unilateral reductions by unit and systematically converted these into armored division equivalents (table C-6); he helped project WTO and NATO mobilization schedules under the prospective CFE agreement (tables C-8 and C-10) and under the proposed CFE II agreement (tables C-12 and C-14), in which connections he developed a "TO&E expansion factor" to count spare weaponry. He drafted the footnotes to tables in appendix C, and helped estimate budgetary savings associated with CFE and deeper reductions; he spent untold hours executing computer simulations and devising efficient ways to display numerical assumptions and results; the pie charts showing the restructuring of WTO forces implicit in CFE I and CFE II are his creations. He helped develop numerical inputs for the multisectoral feint attack (table C-5); and he contributed to the empirical analysis of tank exchange ratios in appendix B.

For his tireless and expert assistance, I am profoundly grateful.

CONTENTS

Tables

Appendix C tables begin on p. 110

Figures

CHAPTER ONE

INTRODUCTION

Two of the more dramatic initiatives in postwar East-West relations were taken by the Soviet Union in late 1988 and early 1989. First, on December 7, 1988, in an address to the United Nations, Soviet General Secretary Mikhail Gorbachev announced a plan to reduce unilaterally the size of the Soviet armed forces by half a million, with cuts of particular relevance to NATO falling on Soviet divisions stationed in Eastern Europe. The East Europeans followed suit early in 1989, announcing plans for unilateral reductions of their own to be implemented, like the Soviet cuts, by 1991.

Next, on March 6, 1989, at the opening of the Conventional Forces in Europe (CFE) negotiations in Vienna, Soviet Foreign Minister Eduard Shevardnadze presented an arms control proposal under which NATO and the Warsaw Treaty Organization would each reduce conventional forces to common ceilings far below the WTO's current levels. Indeed, the Soviets accepted NATO's proposal for deep asymmetrical reductions to 20,000 tanks and 28,000 armored personnel carriers on each side in the Atlantic-to-the-Urals (ATTU) region.

While much of the Western debate revolves around the political and economic motivations that may or may not underlie these Soviet actions, this study focuses on their *military* implications. Specifically, it begins by addressing two fundamental questions. First, assuming they are implemented, what will be the *military* effect on the current conventional balance of the unilateral reductions announced by the Soviets and East Europeans? Second, what would be the military effect of implementing the CFE agreement now under negotiation in Vienna?[1]

1. Core features of the CFE agreement are settled. Aspects not finalized at the time of this writing are treated by adopting what, for NATO, are the most conservative assumptions—for example, that the Soviet proposals for outstanding weaponry (for instance, artillery) are adopted. See chapter 4. Troop reductions, per se, are not modeled in this book. The weapon reductions that are explicitly modeled, however, would obviously entail substantial troop reductions.

Whatever its final details, the CFE agreement, while dramatically reducing the Warsaw Treaty Organization's forces, would have only a marginal effect on NATO's force structures and, notably, NATO's defense budgets. Yet any such agreement, especially following the WTO's unilateral cuts, is likely to solidify an enduring change in Western perceptions of the threat and to produce strong pressures to reduce forces further. It is therefore important to formulate and examine reduction plans that go beyond the initial CFE agreement (CFE I). A third goal of this book, accordingly, is to set forth and examine a number of post–CFE I regimes.

Organization of the Book

To gauge the effect on the European conventional balance of the WTO's unilateral initiatives, of the CFE agreement, and of reductions beyond CFE, it is necessary to begin with an assessment of the current balance itself. This is set forth in chapter 2. The aim of that chapter is to establish a conservative base case from which to gauge the *change in* NATO's security that would result from these prospective alterations. In a sense, this study is one huge sensitivity analysis. I believe the base case provides a conservative assessment of the current conventional balance in Europe, and I present my argument to that effect.

I do not claim to have a crystal ball, however. There are other plausible assumptions and other plausible assessments. But whether one accepts my assessment or not, let us fix on the larger, comparative issue: is NATO better off or is it worse off under the postulated alterations? Those who would prefer to begin that comparison with a different base case are free to do so. But one need not accept my base case to accept the overall *comparative* judgments developed here.

With the base case in hand (chapter 2), the same "test scenarios" are rerun under the WTO's announced unilateral reductions in chapter 3. They are then rerun assuming implementation of the prospective CFE agreement in chapter 4. And they are rerun under a range of post-CFE reductions and restructurings in chapter 5, where the important issue of "force to space" is addressed. Overall conclusions are given and discussed in chapter 6.

Conclusions

In summary, the conclusions are that NATO's security would progressively improve with the implementation of (1) the WTO's unilateral reductions; (2) the CFE agreement; and (3) a CFE II agreement under which NATO and the WTO reduce forces to equal levels 50 percent below the levels specified in CFE I. Indeed, for reasons explained in chapter 5, the improvement (over the current balance) under CFE II would be sufficient to permit the United States to make further, unilateral, reductions without endangering NATO's security.

Political Context

Even more dramatic than Gorbachev's announcement of unilateral reductions and the Soviets' initiatives at CFE were the Soviets' decision to permit the effective dismantling of the Berlin Wall on November 9, 1989, and the sweeping transformations in Eastern Europe that followed. Without question, these events represent a political watershed and hold out the prospect of eventually dismantling the Central European military confrontation.

Under the circumstances, a book analyzing war scenarios might seem anachronistic. Those who believe so are welcome to interpret this book as a work of contemporary analytical history, marking the Central European military balance as it was when the cold war ended. To my mind, the book could not be more timely or essential. Those who would resist progress in arms control (for instance, out of bureaucratic or vested interest) are likely to dismiss proposals for deep reductions, arguing that the recent upheavals in Eastern Europe and the apparent demise of Soviet control are—like Gorbachev's revolution itself—"reversible." Arms control, the argument runs, must be based not on intentions, but on capabilities, on "cold military realities," which have only begun to change.

This book's argument for deep reductions cannot be dismissed on those grounds. The analyses were conducted before the Wall's political demise and proceed on the hyperconservative assumption of unified WTO aggression against NATO. Even on that assumption, the book recommends mutual reductions 50 percent below CFE with unilateral U.S. reductions beyond.

Obviously, if one is prepared to relax that hyperconservative political assumption, then even more dramatic reductions become tenable. The image of East Germans fighting West Germans is already farfetched. It seems only a matter of time before Soviet forces leave Eastern Europe and the WTO dissolves as a unified military threat to the West. At that point, with a CFE agreement in place, the rationale for a U.S. military presence in Central Europe would come into serious question. If, in addition to reducing their forces under CFE and withdrawing their residual forces in Eastern Europe, the Soviets were to restructure for defense in depth beginning at the Soviet border, the rationale for a U.S. military presence based on large-scale military threats to West Germany would all but evaporate.

If the CFE agreement is implemented, and the East Europeans consolidate their independence, and the Soviets withdraw, how much U.S. force, if any, should remain in Europe? And precisely whom would it be protecting against what? With CFE I (or CFE II) in place, should the United States agree to Soviet proposals that both superpowers withdraw all forces from Europe?

Such questions will obviously command attention. And, though its immediate goals are more limited, this book provides all the data and all the analytical tools needed to examine a wide range of possible future security arrangements in Europe.

Methodology

Indeed, while addressing questions of practical importance, the book's most enduring contributions are, in my view, methodological; it seeks to set a standard of explicitness and analytical rigor for the field.

The technique of dynamic analysis is employed in this study. An explicit mathematical model is used to simulate the mutual attrition of engaged ground and air forces, the flow of reinforcing units into battle, and the movement of battle fronts over time, under a range of clearly specified test scenarios.[2] The approach is entirely general, and remains applicable to other military balances even if—as hoped—the NATO-WTO military confrontation "withers away." The specific equations employed are an extended version of the adaptive dynamic model. This is presented and discussed in appendix A, which seeks to advance the mathematical theory

---

2. The alternative, static, approaches—reliance on bean counting and rules of thumb—are patently inadequate to the task at hand, as I have argued elsewhere. See Joshua M. Epstein, "Dynamic Analysis and the Conventional Balance in Europe," *International Security*, vol. 12 (Spring 1988), pp. 154–65; and Epstein, "The 3:1 Rule, the Adaptive Dynamic Model, and the Future of Security Studies," *International Security*, vol. 13 (Spring 1989), pp. 90–127. See also, Epstein, *Measuring Military Power: The Soviet Air Threat to Europe* (Princeton, 1984), pp. xix–xxx.

of combat in its own right.[3] Analogies to theoretical ecology—predator-prey modeling in particular—and to cybernetics are exploited.

To run my model and simulate combat in the scenarios of interest, a number of numerical assumptions concerning technical and behavioral factors are required. Beyond the mobilization capabilities of each side, these concern such variables as casualty-exchange ratios for ground forces and daily sortie rates (missions per day) for close air support planes. These detailed assumptions have been cleared from the general reader's path but are fully and explicitly presented for expert scrutiny in appendix B. Here, original empirical research is presented and brought to bear in estimating key model parameters. All mobilization assumptions are given, along with their sources, in appendix C. A number of sensitivity analyses on the important casualty-exchange ratio are given in appendix D.

In short, one may dispute the results. But, because all assumptions and methods are openly stated, those results are *replicable*.

Many important and interesting questions are not taken up in this study. Verification and NATO's nuclear modernization are among them. Simi-

---

3. The advantages of the original adaptive dynamic model over Lanchester models and the attrition-FEBA expansion model have been set forth elsewhere. On deficiencies of Lanchester's equations and their contemporary extensions, see Joshua M. Epstein, *The Calculus of Conventional War: Dynamic Analysis without Lanchester Theory* (Brookings, 1985); and Epstein, "Dynamic Analysis and the Conventional Balance in Europe," pp. 159–62. Shortcomings of the attrition-FEBA expansion model are set forth in Epstein, "Dynamic Analysis and the Conventional Balance in Europe," p. 160 and pp. 160–61, note 11; and in Epstein, "The 3:1 Rule, the Adaptive Dynamic Model, and the Future of Security Studies," pp. 123–24, note 84. As I wrote in the latter article, my equations "are not perfect or all-encompassing; but are they *better*? I believe so. Can they be improved further? Of course" (p. 124). In appendix A some improvements are offered. Those who resist mathematical modeling per se, should consider the following argument:

> Anyone who has an opinion on the balance has made implicit judgments about the most important factors, or variables, and about the ways in which those variables would interact in time and space. In short, they have a model. And to close one's eyes and imagine a Soviet romp across Germany or an adept NATO repulse is in fact to run that model of war. The only difference between a so-called "modeler" and the rest of the field is the former's willingness to systematically explicate his or her assumptions. But this difference is critical. No real progress is possible without clear, *explicit* hypotheses about the dynamics of combat. Indeed, without some explicit theoretical framework, it will not even be clear what to measure; what data to collect. Any hope of a *testable*—and ultimately *tested*—theory will be lost."

Epstein, "The 3:1 Rule, the Adaptive Dynamic Model, and the Future of Security Studies," p. 118. On quantification generally, see, in addition to the above writings, Epstein, *Measuring Military Power: The Soviet Air Threat to Europe* (Princeton University Press, 1984), pp. xix–xxx.

larly, outcomes would vary depending on the Soviet Navy's success in interdicting NATO's sea line of communication and NATO's success in interdicting reinforcements from the Soviet Union, neither of which campaigns is explicitly modeled here. This is a partial analysis focused on what I believe to be the core military capabilities that would be altered by the WTO's unilateral cuts and by deeper reductions in the ground and tactical air forces of NATO and the WTO.

CHAPTER TWO

THE CURRENT CONVENTIONAL BALANCE IN NATO'S CENTRAL REGION: THE BASE CASE

BECAUSE warfare is a dynamic process including many factors beyond sheer numbers, a static enumeration of forces does not constitute an assessment of the balance. While accounting is not sufficient, it is certainly necessary.

As an essential first step in the analysis, complete ground force mobilization and deployment schedules for NATO and the Warsaw Treaty Organization must be postulated. One may dispute endlessly whether or not particular countries, such as France, should be included, and for how long. Such questions cannot be answered definitively. Participation could well depend on the specific constellation of political events that precipitate the war, and on politics during the war. To assess the sensitivity of military outcomes to changes in such political assumptions, one can, of course, run the analysis with selected countries of each alliance omitted or by having them drop out—or even defect—during the war.[1] But to get an analysis under way at all, some set of assumptions must be made. For the base case analysis, standard assumptions are used. For instance, France is included. Turkey, Greece, and Spain are not. The United States is assumed to withhold forces for Korea, the Persian Gulf, and lesser contingencies outside Europe. The Soviet forces assumed to be withheld are identified in the notes to table C-1 of appendix C. Tables C-1 and C-3 of that appendix provide detailed country-by-country lists of all forces included and their potential arrival times at the central front. These mobilization schedules are the wartime reinforcement schedules, assuming no interdiction by either side.

---

1. For modeling purposes, dropping out might be treated as negative reinforcement.

The forces of each side are scored in a *modified version* of the Weapon Effectiveness Index/Weighted Unit Value III (WEI/WUV III) system recently declassified by the U.S. Army.[2] For example, helicopters are taken out and treated separately in the close air support component of the modeling, as are air defenses. This scoring system, which can itself be subjected to sensitivity analysis, permits the conversion of disparate opposing forces into common numerical units called armored division equivalents (ADEs), which are shown on the vertical axes of figures 2-1 and 2-2. The WEI/WUV system has many of the strengths and weaknesses of other aggregate indexes, such as gross national product, which collapse into one aggregate homogeneous measure a heterogeneous collection of things. Gross national product is useful for purposes of economic modeling. The modified ADE figures are also useful when taken not as conclusive in their own right but as inputs to dynamic models.[3]

Close air support can have a substantial impact on the battlefield and must be included in a thorough assessment. The forces assumed for each side are shown in table 2-1.

2. U.S. Army, Concepts Analysis Agency, *Weapons Effectiveness Indices/Weighted Unit Values III (WEI/WUVIII)*, CAA-SR-79-12 (Bethesda, Md., November 1979). Modifications are specified in the notes to table C-1.

3. Some have objected to the use of ADEs in dynamic models on the ground that, as one critic put it, "the WEI/WUV-ADE methodology was not developed for use in dynamic models of combat"; see Charles A. Kupchan, "Setting Conventional Force Requirements: Roughly Right or Precisely Wrong," *World Politics*, vol. 61 (July 1989), p. 548. Of course, group theory was not developed for use in physics, calculus was not developed for use in economics, and the laser was not developed for use in eye surgery. Yet, in each case, and in countless others, the entity in question turns out to be invaluable in applications not anticipated by the developer. So, too, in this case. The main choice, at bottom, is between a disaggregated (heterogeneous) model in which diverse weapon interactions (antitank versus tank, artillery versus infantry) are separately modeled, and an aggregate (homogeneous) model in which a single index, such as an ADE, is used. The advantage of heterogeneous models is their detail; but detail comes at the expense of mathematical transparency and requires a large number of judgments concerning the allocation of the disparate fires across disparate possible targets. Homogeneous aggregate models lack the detail of heterogeneous models but permit one to revealingly capture primary dynamics with relatively simple mathematics, while avoiding a swamp of fire-allocation decisions. *Any* aggregate model requires that weapons be (a) categorized (for example, tanks, artillery), (b) weighted by category (since a pistol should count for less than a tank in armored war), (c) scored by weapon (since an M-1 tank is better than a T-55), and (d) summed over the unit (such as a division) in question. Basically, if one chooses a simple aggregate model, there is no alternative to using some index of this sort. And any index of this sort is going to look—algebraically—very much like an ADE. One can debate the *numerical* judgments made in assigning category weights or weapon effectiveness scores. And one can conduct sensitivity analyses on those values. But it is scientifically naive to assert that because X was "not developed for" application A, it cannot be successfully employed in that capacity.

FIGURE 2-1. **Arrival of WTO Reinforcements at Central Front**

Armored division equivalents

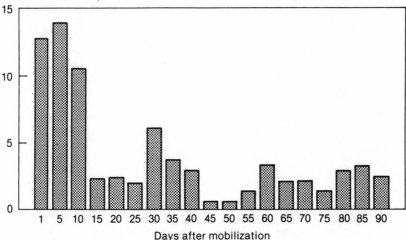

Days after mobilization

Source: appendix C.

FIGURE 2-2. **Arrival of NATO Reinforcements at Central Front**

Armored division equivalents

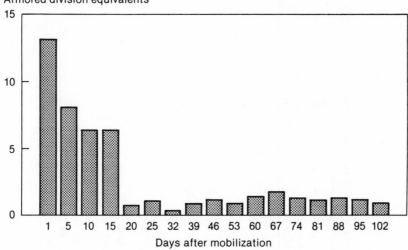

Days after mobilization

Source: appendix C.

TABLE 2-1. NATO and WTO Close Air Support (CAS) and Battlefield Air Interdiction (BAI) Forces at Mobilization and M+10 Days

| | NATO | | | | | WTO | | | |
| | CAS | | BAI | | | CAS | | BAI | |
Country & weapon	M day	M+10	M day	M+10	Country & weapon	M day	M+10	M day	M+10
United States					USSR				
F-111			140	220	MIG-21			45	45
A-10	108	520			MIG-27			405	405
F-16A/B			240	461	SU-17			180	225
A-7				252	SU-24			45	45
F-4			24	386	SU-25	90	240		
Apache AH-64	264	380			MI-24 HIND	630	1,050		
AH-15	208	408			Czechoslovakia				
Belgium					MIG-21			30	30
Mirage 5BA	25	25	25	25	MIG-23			40	40
F-16A/B			36	61	SU-7			50	50
Alpha Jet	32	32			SU-25	25	25		
Canada					GDR				
CF-18			36	36	SU-22			40	40
Denmark					MIG-23			24	24
F-16A/B			30	30	Poland				
Draken	16	16			MIG-17			80	80
PAH-1		12			SU-7			30	30
					SU-22			120	120
					Total	745	1,315	1,089	1,134

France				
Mirage F-III			73	73
Mirage F-5F			30	30
Jaguar-A		15	24	101
Alphajet	40	40		
SA-342	35	70		
SA-341	13	13		
Germany				
F-104G			80	80
F-4F			60	60
Tornado	20	20	83	124
Alphajet	80	80	73	91
PAH-1	105	105		
Netherlands				
F-16A/B			68	68
F-5	49	70	68	68
UK				
Tornado			108	180
Harrier	31	51		
Jaguar		24	48	84
Lynx AH-1	55	120		
Total	1,081	2,001	1,178	2,362

Sources: David C. Isby and Charles Kamps, Jr., *Armies of NATO's Central Front* (London: Jane's, 1985); "USAF Almanac," *Air Force Magazine*, vol. 71 (May 1988); "Defence in Canada," special issue 1, *NATO's Sixteen Nations*, vol. 33 (1988); Robert Jackson, *NATO Air Power* (Novato, Calif.: Presidio Press, 1987); "NATO Center Region Military Balance Study, 1978–1984," Office of the Assistant Secretary of Defense for Program Analysis and Evaluation, July 13, 1977; Michael Skinner, *U.S.A.F.E.: A Primer of Modern Air Combat in Europe* (Novato, Calif.: Presidio Press, 1983); John Collins and Bernard C. Victory, *U.S./Soviet Military Balance: Statistical Trends, 1987–1988*, 87-745-8 (Congressional Research Service, September 1, 1987); Congressional Budget Office, *U.S. Ground Forces and the Conventional Balance in Europe* (June 1988); and International Institute for Strategic Studies, *The Military Balance, 1986–1989* (London, 1988).

Most analyses prudently assume some lag between the Warsaw Pact's mobilization day (Pact M-day) and NATO's. NATO might not have unambiguous warning of WTO mobilization. And even if it did, the alliance's response could be sluggish due to political inertia, the fear that overreaction might provoke attack, or other factors. The exact lag has always been debatable, and cannot be predicted. Of course, if one assumes NATO would never react, then questions of force structure—of material adequacy—become moot. A recently declassified Pentagon analysis of the balance assumes a 5-day lag in NATO's mobilization.[4] This means that if the WTO were to attack after 90 days of mobilization (Pact M + 90), NATO would have had 85 days (NATO M + 85) of mobilization. This assumption can be relaxed in sensitivity analyses. Assuming the 5-day lag, the WTO and NATO ground force mobilization schedules are directly compared in figure 2-3. Each curve simply cumulates the incremental ADEs given in figures 2-1 and 2-2, assuming a 5-day gap. The *ratio* of WTO ground forces to NATO ground forces at each point in this mobilization race is shown in figure 2-4. It is interesting, though hardly conclusive, to notice that on these assumptions, the WTO would never acquire a theaterwide edge exceeding 1.8 to 1 and that were both military establishments fully mobilized, the WTO's theaterwide preponderance would settle at around 1.65 to 1.

At what point in its mobilization might the WTO launch an attack? In war, the choice of attack time is one important prerogative of the aggressor. Because it is highly uncertain, one must examine a spectrum of possibilities. This study uses four. They are shown in table 2-2. At one end of the range (scenario I) is a short-mobilization attack on NATO's in-place forces by selected Soviet units deployed in Eastern Europe, with WTO and NATO reinforcing echelons flowing into the ongoing battle. In the base case simulations, reinforcements are assumed to arrive on the schedules given in tables C-1 and C-3 of appendix C, which are plotted in figure 2-3. At the opposite end of the attack time spectrum is scenario IV, an attack after virtually full mobilization by both sides. Scenarios II and III represent intermediate possibilities. All four assume the 5-day NATO lag noted above, and include the close air support forces listed in table 2-1.

At the theater level of warfare, attackers have the initial advantage of

4. Office of the Assistant Secretary of Defense for Program Analysis and Evaluation, "NATO Center Region Military Balance Study, 1979–1984," Department of Defense, July 13, 1979, p. I-25.

FIGURE 2-3. **WTO versus NATO Mobilization Schedules, 1989**

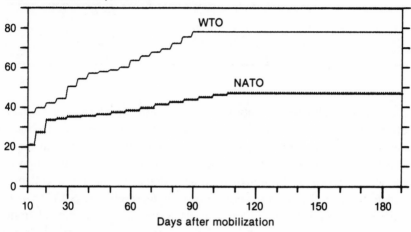

Armored division equivalents

Days after mobilization

Source: appendix C.

FIGURE 2-4. **Ratio of WTO Forces to NATO Forces during Mobilization, 1989**

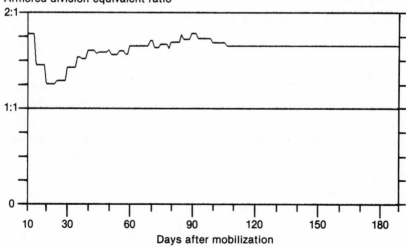

Armored division equivalent ratio

Days after mobilization

Source: appendix C.

TABLE 2-2. **Base Case Scenarios, Days of Mobilization before Attack**

Scenario	WTO	NATO
I	10	5
II	30	25
III	60	55
IV	90	85

being able to choose not only the *time* but also the *place* of their main efforts. In a Central European war, the Soviets would be expected to focus concentrations of force on particular sectors of NATO's front in hopes that the local preponderance, combined with aggressive prosecution of the attack, could be exploited to produce defensive paralysis, collapse, penetration, or defeat in detail. To counter these efforts, NATO would have to exhibit dexterity in applying its forces across the central front. By "dexterity" I mean the ability to *detect* evolving concentrations, *decide* what countering units are needed and where they should come from, *communicate* (securely) those decisions in the form of orders to the chosen units, and *move* those units to the threatened area, all of this before it is too late. The Soviets would doubtless attempt to interfere with each of these steps, and NATO would try to counter those efforts at interference, which efforts, in turn, the Soviets would seek to thwart, and so on, in a welter of measures, countermeasures, and counter-countermeasures.

One's assessment of the balance depends heavily on one's assumptions concerning NATO's dexterity in this sense.

Simulations Assuming Perfect Dexterity

If one assumes perfect dexterity on NATO's part—that is, that the proportional distribution of NATO's force up and down the front equals the WTO's at all times—then the current balance is very good. Applying the mobilization assumptions of appendix C and performance assumptions of appendix B in the extended adaptive dynamic model in appendix A, the Western alliance comes from behind to thwart the WTO in each of the four basic attacks without loss of West German territory.[5]

5. In discussing simulation results, two issues must constantly be kept distinct: attrition and territorial sacrifice. These processes are related in the adaptive dynamic model, which makes no judgment as to the definition of "victory." In the model it is possible to overtake the adversary

This is shown in figures 2-5 to 2-8. While intimidating at first glance, these simulation graphs are straightforward and will repay study. For instance, figure 2-5 simulates attack scenario I. Because on the day of attack (D-day) the WTO has mobilized for 10 days and NATO has mobilized for 5, the development is referred to as a "10/5 scenario." At the outset, the WTO attacks with nearly 40 ADEs (where the WTO curve intercepts the vertical, ADE, axis). NATO defends initially with 21. Over time, shown on the horizontal axis, each side reinforces as it fights. The jagged spikes represent points at which reinforcements enter the fray (from figures 2-1 and 2-2). These reinforcements, a moderately favorable ground-to-ground casualty-exchange ratio (1.7 attackers killed for each defender killed),[6] and a more effective close air operation permit NATO to prevail. On the assumptions employed here (see appendix B for full details) there is no territorial sacrifice by NATO. Similar tales are told by figures 2-6, 2-7, and 2-8.

In all cases, NATO comes from behind to win the attrition war without loss of territory. The longer the mobilization, the less spikey these curves become, since the later the attack the fewer the remaining reinforcements. In scenario IV (figure 2-8) for example, virtually all the WTO and NATO forces are included at the outset, so very few reinforcement spikes remain.

The main point is clear. *With perfect dexterity*, NATO wins the attrition war without losing territory. *With imperfect dexterity*, NATO can do poorly.

Simulations Assuming Imperfect Dexterity

As the simplest possible illustration of the problem of imperfect dexterity, let us reconsider the least complicated of the basic scenarios—the fully mobilized attack—under somewhat different assumptions about the spatial distribution of forces. Specifically, rather than the perfect coun-

---

in the attrition sense after sacrificing 500 kilometers of territory; it is far from clear that one should classify such an outcome as a "win" for NATO. Rather than burden the text with constant reminders of the distinction, I freely use phrases like "thwart the WTO without losing territory" on the understanding that "thwart," or words like it, will here be read as applying strictly to the attrition war. Each reader is free to decide whether a given attrition/movement outcome constitutes an overall "victory" or overall "defeat" for NATO, the WTO, for both, or for neither (the latter two being understudied possibilities).

6. This estimate is discussed at length in appendix B.

FIGURE 2-5. **Scenario I (10/5), Mutual Attrition**

Armored division equivalents

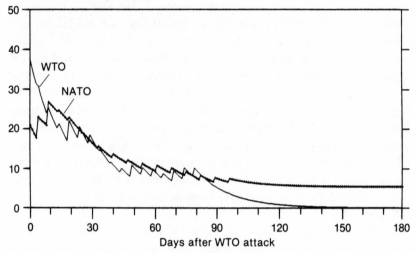

Days after WTO attack

Sources: appendixes A, B, and C.

FIGURE 2-6. **Scenario II (30/25), Mutual Attrition**

Armored division equivalents

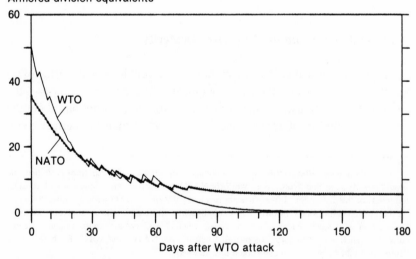

Days after WTO attack

Sources: appendixes A, B, and C.

FIGURE 2-7. **Scenario III (60/55), Mutual Attrition**

Armored division equivalents

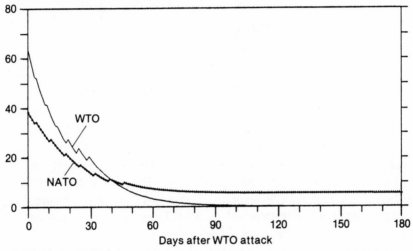

Days after WTO attack

Sources: appendixes A, B, and C.

FIGURE 2-8. **Scenario IV (90/85), Mutual Attrition**

Armored division equivalents

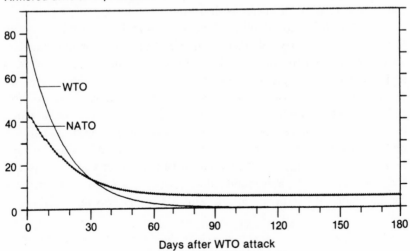

Days after WTO attack

Sources: appendixes A, B, and C.

FIGURE 2-9. **Theater-Level Misallocation**

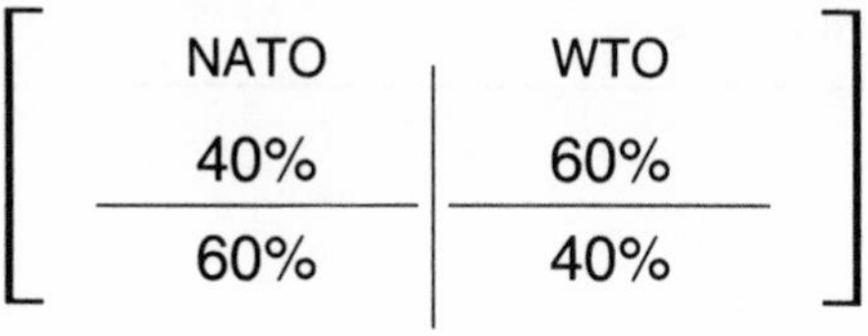

$$
\begin{bmatrix}
\dfrac{\text{NATO}}{40\%} & \dfrac{\text{WTO}}{60\%} \\[2ex]
60\% & 40\%
\end{bmatrix}
$$

terconcentration assumed in the previous simulations, imagine that the WTO allocates 60 percent of its forces to NATO's northern half and 40 percent to NATO's southern half, and that NATO does just the reverse, as illustrated in figure 2-9. If all other assumptions are left exactly as they were in the previous cases, the effect of this failure to counterconcentrate efficiently is dramatic, as shown in figures 2-10 and 2-11. Figure 2-11 simply plots total kilometers lost by NATO (on the vertical axis) against time in days (on the horizontal axis).

NATO does not come from behind to win in the north; it is badly defeated. Moreover, if—to be evenhanded—the WTO is credited with the same defensive advantages (relative concealment and preparation of firing positions) in the south as NATO is assumed to enjoy in the north, and if it is credited with the same casualty-exchange ratio, then NATO cannot successfully counterattack in the south. NATO's northern withdrawal rate (its rate of retreat) climbs to 20 kilometers a day, and the cumulative territorial sacrifice is disastrous.

Now, for NATO to permit a 60:40 versus 40:60 overall misallocation to develop over nearly full mobilization and then to maintain that misallocation through the first ten days of a conventional war would be a major blunder.[7] This gross misallocation is, to be sure, a worst case, but will nonetheless prove a revealing test case for conventional arms control.

While a 60:40 versus 40:60 asymmetry after nearly full mobilization (scenario IV) is of debatable plausibility, the same asymmetry early in mobilization is worrisome because of NATO's peacetime maldeployment problem.[8] Specifically, a 60:40 versus 40:60 asymmetry at the outset of scenario I (the 10/5 short-mobilization attack) is a reasonable surrogate for the canonical ''surprise'' attack. This is a second way in which NATO

---

7. NATO is assumed to correct to 60:40 at D+10, ten days after war begins. Close air support is assumed to track the ground allocations on both sides.

8. NATO's most powerful forces are in the south.

FIGURE 2-10. **Scenario IV, 60:40 versus 40:60 Initial NATO Misallocation, Mutual Attrition in the North**

Armored division equivalents

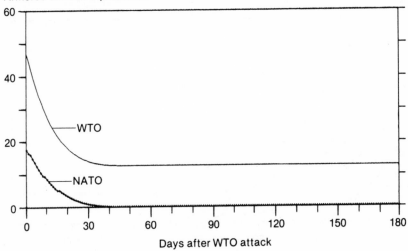

Days after WTO attack

Sources: appendixes A, B, and C.

FIGURE 2-11. **Scenario IV, 60:40 versus 40:60 Initial NATO Misallocation, Movement of the Front in the North**

Kilometers lost by NATO

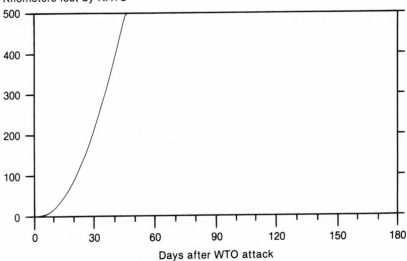

Days after WTO attack

Sources: appendixes A, B, and C. Although the adaptive dynamic model imposes no upper limit on territory lost in principle, a practical upper limit of 500 kilometers is assumed in this book.

FIGURE 2-12. **Scenario I, 60:40 versus 40:60 Initial NATO Misallocation, Mutual Attrition in the North**

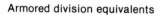
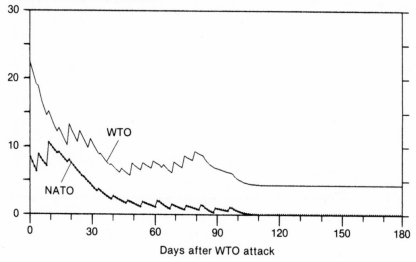

Sources: appendixes A, B, and C.

FIGURE 2-13. **Scenario I, 60:40 versus 40:60 Initial NATO Misallocation, Movement of the Front in the North**

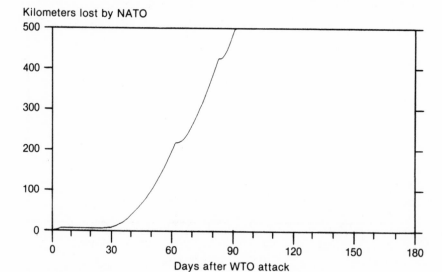

Sources: appendixes A, B, and C.

could plausibly lose, even assuming a fairly dextrous correction by NATO. Figure 2-12 assumes that NATO corrects to 60:40 itself after 10 days of combat (on D + 10). As shown, this correction is not sufficient to produce an attrition stalemate (NATO never quite catches up); and, vast territory is still lost in this contingency. This scenario provides a second test case for arms control.

One might conclude from these computer runs that the answer is simply to correct NATO's peacetime maldeployment and be done with it. Of course that would help, but it solves the problem only if one assumes the attack plan employed above; the WTO always bashes ahead with 60 percent here and 40 percent there. In reality there are eight corps sectors (figure 2-14). And notwithstanding such critical terrain obstacles as the Harz Mountains, there are many areas where concentration could occur. While I find implausible the sophisticated dance of veils that some have hypothesized, a classic multisectoral attack with feints cannot be ruled out. This case is often referred to as "large-scale offensive action." The idea would be to trick NATO into reinforcing the wrong corps sectors, then penetrate elsewhere. NATO's eight corps sectors are shown in figure 2-14.

Malcolm Hoag colorfully formulated the problem: "Suppose the Pact plan were designed to generate the impression that each of NATO's eight corps was being hit with at least one main attack, if only to capitalize upon the political point that each of NATO's Central Front governments will be made to fear that 'their' army was vitally threatened at one or more places. Suppose, however, that only three of the eight Pact attacks (say upon NATO's II, IV, and VII Corps) were main attacks, while the remaining five were fixing attacks designed to look like main attacks." In the fixing attacks, or feints, for instance, WTO forces might be instructed to prosecute the attack ferociously and to absorb heavy losses

to maximize the "noise level." In the inevitable "fog of war," that might all too convincingly look like a main attack to a defender. . . . [Since] each of eight NATO ground corps commanders worries about his sector being chosen by the enemy for a main attack and trains his forces for this eventuality, in wartime he may mistake a fixing attack for a main attack. NATO's commander will have good reason to worry about the availability of intelligence in such a situation. His nightmare is that each of the eight corps commanders will simultaneously be requesting all the help that he can get, with

FIGURE 2-14. **NATO's Eight Corps Sectors**

each request appearing to be equally valid. If he apportions his air and other resources uniformly among the corps, in despair about obtaining better intelligence about the ground battle in time, he knows that he is moving toward that enemy-preferred uniform allocation that will waste his precious resources. Yet if he withholds

FIGURE 2-15. **Multisectoral WTO Attack with Feints**

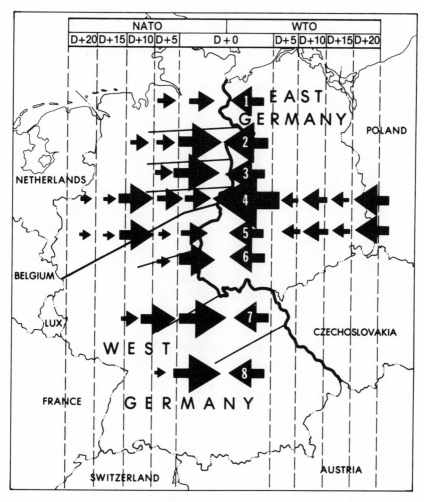

his support until the situation becomes clearer, he may withhold it too long and be faced with enemy breakthroughs.[9]

This is the realm of theater strategy; there is no fixed allocation of defensive force that would manage the problem. NATO would have to adapt during

9. Malcolm W. Hoag, *Strengthening NATO Capabilities: A "Hi-Lo" Ground Force Mix for Area Defense*, R-2039-AF (Santa Monica, Calif.: Rand Corp., 1977), p. 5. For a demanding definition of the term "breakthrough," see T. N. Dupuy and others, *A Study of Breakthrough Operations*, DNA 41245 (Fairfax, Va.: Historical Evaluation and Research Organization, 1976), p. 1.

the war—when its adaptive apparatus would be attacked—and unless its dexterity were high, it might not fare well.

From the hundreds of attacks that might be constructed, no one can predict *the* multisectoral, multiecheloned attack plan the Soviets would select, nor at this juncture can anyone predict the efficiency with which any plan selected would be countered by NATO. It is possible, however—indeed it is essential—to construct paradigmatic cases to gauge the effect of *changes* in force structure, notably those that would be produced by arms control. One such case is represented in figure 2-15. The NATO and WTO arrows are proportional in size to the number of armored division equivalents involved in the action depicted. Corps sectors are listed in the large arrow heads. The days on which attacking and defending forces arrive in each corps sector are indicated across the top. The exact reinforcement schedule (the actual ADE numbers) by corps sector for NATO and the WTO is given in full in appendix C, table C-5. Essentially, the WTO sets up a big threat to corps sector IV; and NATO goes for it, allocating most of its reinforcement to that sector. The real breakthrough then occurs in the now underreinforced corps sector V, despite the fact that the WTO's follow-on forces are equal in sectors IV and V. Indeed, the result is a blowout in corps sector V, as shown in figures 2-16 and 2-17.

Figure 2-18 interprets this movement graph in the theater context, giving the front's "traces" over time for this contingency.

Summarizing the results thus far, if NATO's dexterity is perfect, the conventional balance is fine. If NATO's dexterity is imperfect, the alliance could find itself in rather desperate straits over a range of scenarios. Theater-level dexterity, in short, would appear to be the linchpin of NATO's conventional defense. If the demand for dexterity is high, what can be said of the supply?

Need for a Dexterity Net Assessment

First and foremost, this is a topic deserving much more attention than it has received, or will receive here. Indeed, I will do little beyond pointing out the uncertainties surrounding the four fundamental components of counterconcentration that were noted earlier: detection, decision, communication, and movement.

FIGURE 2-16. **Multisectoral Feint Attack with Imperfect NATO Dexterity, Attrition History in Corps Sector V**

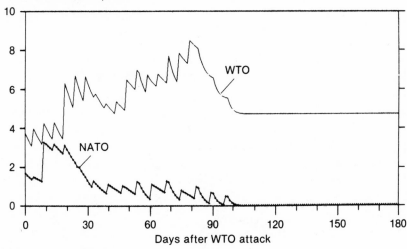

Armored division equivalents

Sources: appendixes A, B, and C.

FIGURE 2-17. **Multisectoral Feint Attack with Imperfect NATO Dexterity, Movement of the Front in Corps Sector V**

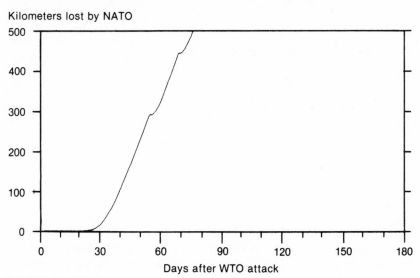

Kilometers lost by NATO

Sources: appendixes A, B, and C.

FIGURE 2-18. **The Front during Multisectoral Feint Attack, Imperfect NATO Dexterity**

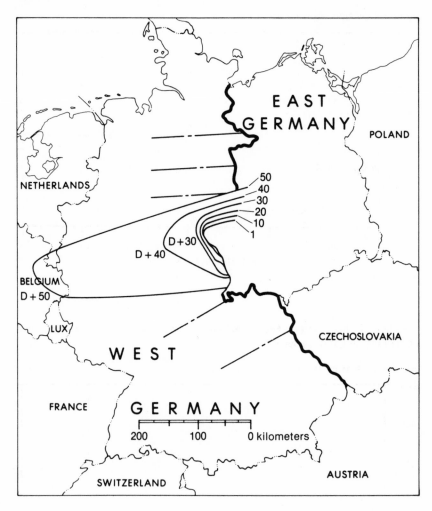

Detection

The sine qua non of dexterity is, of course, detection. NATO would have to identify evolving WTO concentrations on the ground, and the information would have to be available to NATO commanders in time to matter. NATO has recognized the problem for a long time, and has spent heavily on intelligence satellites, remotely piloted vehicles, and aircraft such as the reconnaissance version of the F-4 (the RF-4) and TR-1, to pick up WTO ground concentrations. The joint surveillance/target attack radar system (JSTARS) is designed to track armored movements deep behind enemy lines and, unlike its predecessors, it is designed to do so in real time. But according to the Office of Technology Assessment, to see deep, JSTARS must operate close to the forward line of NATO's own troops where it would be potentially vulnerable. The air force argues that the system can be operated from 150 kilometers behind NATO's lines. In any case JSTARS would be a very bright emitter of radio signals and a high-value target, deserving and probably receiving considerable attention from the Soviet Air Force.[10] Moreover, it is not yet clear whether, or by what procedures, JSTARS's imagery would be distributed to non-U.S. corps sectors.[11]

NATO's ability to detect concentration efforts is generally regarded as good, but a rigorous assessment would estimate the theater reconnaissance system's susceptibility to electronic countermeasures (jamming, deception) and its physical vulnerability (while airborne and while on its bases, for aircraft) to attack.

Decision

Just as in the prewar phase, warning is one thing, response is another. Once sensors have detected a concentration of armor on the move, their data must be successfully transmitted to high-echelon command posts. There, information from diverse sources must be processed and presented to authorities in a format facilitating informed choices among tactical alternatives. Is the armor concentration a feint? If it is a true main breakthrough effort (or a follow-on force designed to exploit an imminent penetration), what forces should be applied to counter it, and where should they come from—neighboring corps sectors or operational reserves? NATO's lead in computers and information processing is obviously valuable here. But, again, is one prepared to assume errorless and timely decisionmaking?

10. Office of Technology Assessment, *New Technology for NATO: Implementing Follow-On Forces Attack*, OTA-ISC-309 (June 1987), pp. 9–10.

11. I am grateful to Paul B. Stares for this information.

Communication

Next, decisions must be communicated to the units whose fire is to be brought to bear in the threatened area. Orders from high echelons down to corps commanders are the most secure since they can be transmitted over land lines (the microwave towers used in peace are vulnerable), by satellite, or ultimately, by helicopter. Communications at the tactical level— among the units affected—are more vulnerable, though much more redundant. Field radios can be subjected to point and barrage jamming, as was shown in the 1973 Arab-Israeli war. The problem has, of course, been recognized, and NATO would attempt to counter WTO jamming with electronic counter-countermeasures. But the likely outcome of that competition is hard to judge.[12]

Deployment

Assuming that NATO decides to counter a WTO concentration, the countering units, having received their orders, would have to deploy to the threatened area, in time to take up prepared positions affording them traditional defensive advantages. Just as in the command and control area, NATO has spent heavily on logistics for precisely this reason, and therefore a degree of optimism is surely warranted. Certainty, however, is not. While Soviet airpower has very serious limitations, it could make a challenging problem harder by degrading the command and control and logistical infrastructure needed to counterconcentrate and by attacking NATO's reinforcing units as they move. Even if one penalizes Soviet tactical airpower harshly for technological backwardness and operational rigidity, it could damage NATO's dexterity, as could other WTO weapons.

It seems to me that, until more research is done, there will be significant uncertainties in the detection, decision, communication, and deployment chain that constitutes NATO's theater-level dexterity.[13] Pending a more

---

12. Many of these issues and other questions of command and control, are examined in Paul B. Stares, *Command Performance: The Neglected Dimension of European Security* (Brookings, forthcoming).

13. Moreover, even if one considers each "link" in the detection-decision-communication-deployment chain to be highly reliable, the overall probability of at least one failure is notable. For example, if the independent probabilities of successful detection, decision, communication, and deployment are all 95 percent, the overall probability of a successful chain is $(0.95)^4$, or 81 percent. And, for three simultaneous breakthrough efforts the probability of at least one failure would be nearly 50 percent. I thank Bruce G. Blair for this point.

definitive resolution of this question, it seems prudent to relax the assumption of perfect dexterity and consider the contribution of unilateral WTO reductions and negotiated mutual asymmetrical cuts to the solution of the three idealized test cases constructed earlier.

Test 1: Initial 60:40 versus 40:60 NATO misallocation in scenario I (10/5).

Test 2: Initial 60:40 versus 40:60 misallocation in scenario IV (90/85).

Test 3: NATO misallocation under a multisectoral feint attack.

To begin, which, if any, of these problems would be solved by the unilateral cuts recently announced by Gorbachev and the East Europeans?

CHAPTER THREE

THE UNILATERAL WTO CUTS

ON December 7, 1988, Mikhail Gorbachev announced at the United Nations that by 1991 the Soviet Union would unilaterally reduce its overall troop strength by 500,000, of which 50,000 would come from Central Europe. There, 6 tank divisions would be cut and, in the Atlantic-to-the-Urals region overall, 10,000 tanks, 8,500 artillery pieces, and 800 combat aircraft would be cut. This dramatic announcement was followed by East European pledges to reduce their forces unilaterally. As reported by Moscow, the overall reductions are shown in table 3-1. Since these announcements, sufficient details concerning the units affected have become available to permit the translation of these cuts into the ADE scores used in the analyses here.[1] The detailed accounting of WTO reductions by unit and the computations converting those reductions into ADEs are presented fully in tables C-6 and C-7 of appendix C. Table 3-2 summarizes the results.

With all else fixed, the implementation of these reductions would have a significant impact on the WTO's mobilization capability, as shown in figure 3-1. NATO, the bottom curve, is held at its current (1989) level. Clearly, the WTO mobilization curve shifts downward upon institution of the reductions. Notice that it shifts down *early* in mobilization, reflecting the concentration of Soviet reductions on units stationed in Eastern Europe proper. The reductions' effect on the WTO-to-NATO force *ratio* over the course of mobilization is also illuminating. This is shown in figure 3-2. Whereas today, the ratio levels off at 1.65 to 1, the unilateral reductions would depress the advantage to 1.4 to 1.

---

1. In this analysis, and in the analyses of CFE I and CFE II below, weaponry reduced is generally assumed to be destroyed. Technically, it might be sold rather than destroyed. In any case, it is assumed never to reenter the ATTU region.

TABLE 3-1. **Projected Reduction of Armed Forces and Military Budgets in Warsaw Pact Countries as of 1991**

Countries	Troops	Tanks	Armored vehicles	Guns and mortars	Combat aircraft	Military budget (percent)
Bulgaria[a]	10,000	200	0	200	20	12
Hungary	9,300	251	30	430[b]	9	17
GDR	10,000	600	0	0	50	10
Poland	15,000	0	0	0	0	7.7–5.5[c]
Romania[d]	0	0	0	0	0	0
Czechoslovakia[e]	12,000	850	165	0	51	15
Total (except USSR)	56,300	1,901	195	630[b]	130	0
USSR forces in Europe[f]	240,000	10,000	0	8,500	800	14.2
Total in Europe	296,300	11,901	195	9,130[b]	930	0
USSR forces in Asia	200,000	0	0	0	0	0
USSR forces in the south	60,000	0	0	0	0	0
Grand total	556,300	11,901	195	9,130[g]	930	0

Source: From "Warsaw Pact Forces, Budget Reduction Figures" (in Russian), *Argumenty I Fakty* , no. 6 (February 1989), p. 8.
a. Five warships also cut.
b. Includes 180 antitank weapons.
c. Of the state budget.
d. In 1986 Romania reduced its military budget and arms by 5 percent.
e. Divisional and regimental tactical training sessions are being reduced by 50 percent and combat fire by 25 to 30 percent.
f. Production of military equipment and arms is being reduced by 19.5 percent.
g. Includes 540 antitank weapons.

While these reductions are obviously a step in the right direction, their operational military significance for specific scenarios of interest cannot be gauged by comparisons of combat *inputs*. What effect do these reductions have on combat *outcomes*—mutual attrition and the movement of battle fronts over time—in the scenarios of interest? Specifically, which, if any, of the three test cases developed in chapter 2 are remedied by the unilateral initiatives?

TABLE 3-2. **Projected Unilateral Reductions Scored in ADEs**

Country	1989	WTO reductions	1991
USSR	61.3	8.1	53.2
GDR	4.0	0.5	3.5
Czechoslovakia	6.4	0.8	5.6
Poland	6.5	2.7	3.8
Total WTO	78.1	12.1	66.1

Source: appendix C. Totals may not add due to rounding.

FIGURE 3-1. **WTO versus NATO Mobilization Capabilities before and after Unilateral WTO Reductions**

Armored division equivalents

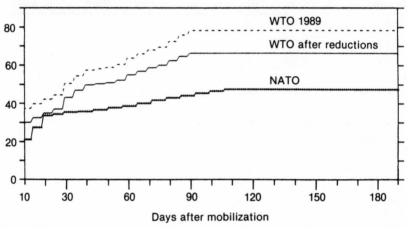

Days after mobilization

Source: appendix C.

FIGURE 3-2. **Ratio of WTO Forces to NATO Forces during Mobilization before and after Unilateral WTO Reductions**

Armored division equivalent ratio

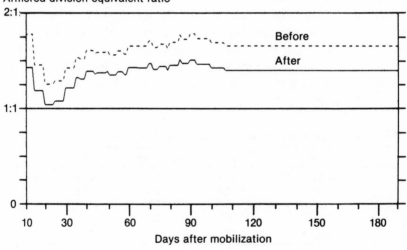

Days after mobilization

Source: appendix C.

FIGURE 3-3. **Scenario IV with 60:40 versus 40:60 Initial Misallocation, Attrition in the North before and after Unilateral WTO Reductions**

Armored division equivalents

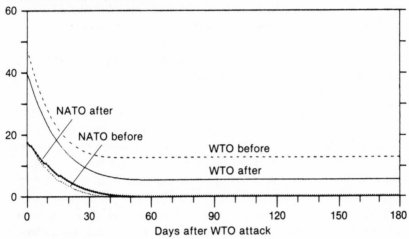

Days after WTO attack

Sources: appendixes A, B, and C.

FIGURE 3-4. **Scenario IV with 60:40 versus 40:60 Initial Misallocation, Movement of the Front in the North before and after Unilateral WTO Reductions**

Kilometers lost by NATO

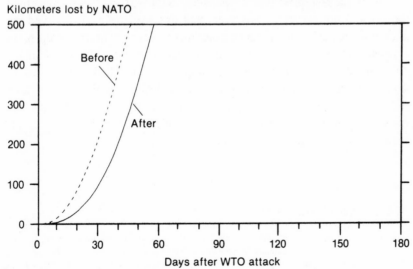

Days after WTO attack

Sources: appendixes A, B, and C.

The second of the imperfect dexterity test cases was a 60:40 versus 40:60 misallocation in scenario IV (90/85)—the fully mobilized case—with a NATO correction 10 days after attack (D + 10). The WTO's unilateral cuts, unfortunately, do not save the day. Indeed, they do not come close to solving this problem, as shown in figures 3-3 and 3-4.

Similarly, the unilateral cuts alone do not reverse the outcome in test case 3, the multisectoral feint attack. Leaving all other assumptions as they were in chapter 2, the unfortunate course of events in corps sector V is virtually unchanged, as shown in figures 3-5, 3-6 and 3-7.

The unilateral reductions *would* have a big impact on the "surprise attack" problem, idealized here as test case 1, an aggregate NATO misallocation of 60:40 versus 40:60 in a short-mobilization (10/5) scenario with a NATO correction at D + 10 (that is, ten days into the conflict). Under the unilateral cuts, NATO now comes from behind to win in the attrition sense, as shown in figure 3-8. In the adaptive dynamic model, as in real war, it is possible to "win" in the attrition sense, but to lose vast territory before overtaking the adversary.[2] Fortunately, the unilateral reductions have the additional benefit of stabilizing the front without territorial sacrifice in this scenario. Before, matters were quite different, as shown in figure 3-9.

I thus find myself in broad agreement with the Central Intelligence Agency's assessment that the unilateral reductions would go a long way to solving the "surprise attack" problem that has, for so long, concerned the West. I am skeptical, however, that this scenario ever deserved the attention it received. Intelligence assessments recently reported in the press suggest that the problem has been seriously overblown for some time.[3] And, in any event, other important cases are not handled by these reductions, beneficial as they certainly are. In conclusion, the WTO's unilateral reductions are militarily significant, but not revolutionary. I am not sure the same qualification applies to the Conventional Forces in Europe agreement under negotiation in Vienna.

2. See chapter 2, note 5.
3. In November 1989, the *Washington Post* reported that "The U.S. intelligence community, in a fundamental reassessment of the military balance in Europe, has concluded that for the past several years the Soviet Union and its Warsaw Pact allies have been incapable of quickly launching a massive attack against the West. . . ." Patrick E. Tyler and R. Jeffrey Smith, "Study Finds NATO War Plans Outdated," *Washington Post*, November 29, 1989, p. 1.

FIGURE 3-5. **Multisectoral Feint Attack with Imperfect NATO Dexterity, Attrition in Corps Sector V before and after Unilateral WTO Reductions**

Armored division equivalents

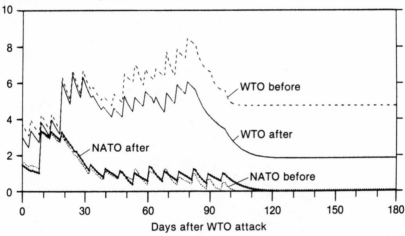

Sources: appendixes A, B, and C.

FIGURE 3-6. **Multisectoral Feint Attack with Imperfect NATO Dexterity, Movement of the Front in Corps Sector V before and after Unilateral WTO Reductions**

Kilometers lost by NATO

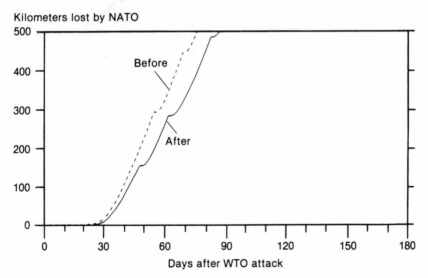

Sources: appendixes A, B, and C.

FIGURE 3-7. **The Front during Multisectoral Feint Attack, with Imperfect NATO Dexterity after Unilateral WTO Reductions**

FIGURE 3-8. **Scenario I with 60:40 versus 40:60 Initial NATO Misallocation, Attrition in the North before and after Unilateral WTO Reductions**

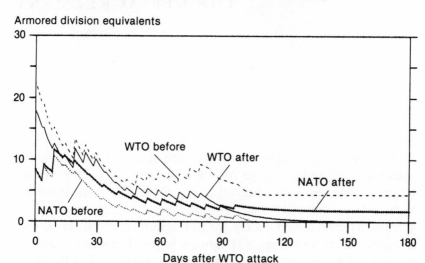

Armored division equivalents

Days after WTO attack

Sources: appendixes A, B, and C.

FIGURE 3-9. **Scenario I with 60:40 versus 40:60 Initial NATO Misallocation, Movement of the Front in the North before and after Unilateral WTO Reductions**

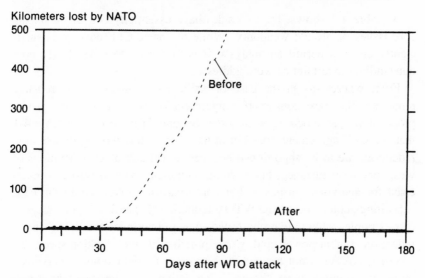

Kilometers lost by NATO

Days after WTO attack

Sources: appendixes A, B, and C.

CHAPTER FOUR

THE CFE AGREEMENT

AT THE TIME of this writing, both sides had agreed to the principle of equal numerical ceilings in the Atlantic-to-the-Urals (ATTU) region for six force categories, with subceilings on (a) the overall levels deployable by any one country and (b) the levels any country could deploy outside its national territory. Numerically, the CFE agreement would impose deep asymmetrical reductions on WTO ground forces. Regarding weaponry, the terms of the agreement and differences outstanding as of December 1989 are shown in table 4-1.

Assessing CFE: The Ground Balance

As table 4-1 shows, the two sides have essentially converged on the core issues of ground weaponry. While the basic CFE concept is sufficiently clear to permit an analysis, it is important to state clearly how outstanding uncertainties were addressed.

First, where—as in the case of artillery—a *numerical* discrepancy remained, the most conservative interpretation was adopted; the Soviet proposal was assumed to be in force. Second, it is clear from table 4-1 that the CFE agreement does not at the time of this writing dictate how reductions are to be apportioned between newer and older generations of weaponry—for instance, tanks. Some judgment must therefore be exercised for analytical purposes. For conservatism's sake, within the CFE subceilings noted above, the WTO's reductions for each weapon category (for example, tanks) are orchestrated so as to maximize the WTO's post-reduction combat power, and, where possible, its mobilization speed. By contrast, NATO is not assumed to apportion its reductions to maximize on an alliancewide basis. Rather, each nation is assumed to take a per-

TABLE 4-1. **NATO and WTO Weapon Ceilings under the CFE Agreement**

Weapon category[a]	NATO	WTO
Tanks		
Each alliance	20,000	20,000
Any one country	12,000	14,000
Outside of national territory	3,200	4,500
Artillery pieces		
Each alliance	16,500	24,000
Any one country	10,000	17,000
Outside of national territory	1,700	4,000
Armored personnel carriers		
Each alliance	28,000	28,000
Any one country	16,800	18,000
Outside of national territory	6,000	7,500
Aircraft		
Each alliance	4,600	1,500
Any one country	. . .	1,200
Outside of national territory	. . .	350
Helicopters		
Each alliance	2,200	1,700
Any one country	. . .	1,350
Outside of national territory	. . .	600

Source: "European Arms Control after the NATO Summit," *Arms Control Today* (June-July 1989), p. 5.
a. There are differences in the ways these categories are defined by NATO and the WTO.

centage cut equal to the percentage cut imposed on the alliance at large, and to maximize its own national combat power (and, where possible, its mobilization speed). Clearly, the sum of these national maxima is less than the alliancewide maximum attainable in principle. For example, the CFE agreement calls for roughly a 10 percent cut in NATO's tanks deployed in the ATTU. It is assumed that Germany would cut the worst 10 percent of its tanks and that Turkey would cut the worst 10 percent of its tanks. But, the alliance as a whole would be better off if it were to take the entire reduction from Turkey's tanks alone. For purposes of modeling, then, within the CFE's sublimits, the WTO was assumed to maximize power in this fashion, alliancewide, while NATO was assumed to maximize by nation only.

From NATO's standpoint, this effect is more than offset by the size and asymmetry of the reductions. Indeed, if one confines attention to the forces traditionally considered in assessments of the central front balance, excluding Soviet forces opposite China, U.S. forces in Korea, and so forth, the numerical effect of the CFE agreement is stunning: *after* mobilization, NATO would outnumber the WTO in tanks, artillery, and armored vehicles.[1] The explanation of this remarkable effect is straightforward. The CFE agreement covers the ATTU region only. This includes virtually all the WTO forces of relevance to the central front. But it excludes very substantial NATO reinforcements from the continental United States (CONUS). NATO is permitted this margin from *outside* the ATTU after parity under CFE is imposed *inside* the ATTU. The Soviets have no comparable reinforcement from outside the ATTU. For example, *after* full mobilization of both sides, NATO would outnumber the WTO by some 3,500 tanks.[2]

Once a reasonable accounting has been achieved, it remains to translate the proposed numerical reductions into the combat scoring system one is using, in this case modified ADEs. All quantitative and qualitative accounting details and the computations converting the reductions into ADEs are explicitly provided in appendix C. Interpreted in this conservative fashion, the CFE agreement would lead to the comparative mobilization capacity shown in figure 4-1.

The WTO's fully mobilized ADE score is 45, down a notable 33 ADEs from its pre-CFE level of 78. This represents a reduction of over 42 percent. The effect of CFE on the WTO's mobilization capacity is strikingly depicted in figure 4-2.

NATO's fully mobilized ADE score falls by only 8 percent, largely because most of the American contribution to NATO—the CONUS-based reinforcement—lies outside the ATTU and, hence, is unaffected by CFE.

---

1. Soviet forces opposite China have generally been omitted from assessments of the Central Front balance for some time. And, as previously noted, they are omitted here. First, Soviet far eastern forces are being reduced unilaterally. Second, the Soviets remain concerned with their Chinese border and are unlikely to leave it undefended. Third, the forces opposite China are, overwhelmingly, classified as category III, the lowest readiness status, indicating obsolescent equipment and low levels of manning and training. Fourth, the single railroad (the trans-Siberian) available for the redeployment of these forces to Europe could be interdicted with high confidence. Soviet intertheater mobility beyond the trans-Siberian railroad—airlift and trucks—is limited and, to my knowledge, no such redeployment has ever been practiced. The forces, moreover, might well be difficult to integrate into combat operations in Europe, for example, given language differences. For a Pentagon assessment omitting these Soviet forces, see Office of the Assistant Secretary of Defense for Program Analysis and Evaluation, "NATO Center Region Military Balance Study, 1978–1984," Department of Defense, July 13, 1979.

2. NATO would not necessarily outnumber the WTO in ADEs, however, since ADEs include weapons not covered by CFE (for example, small arms, some types of mortars, and important types of antiarmor weapons).

FIGURE 4-1. **WTO versus NATO Mobilization after CFE**

Armored division equivalents

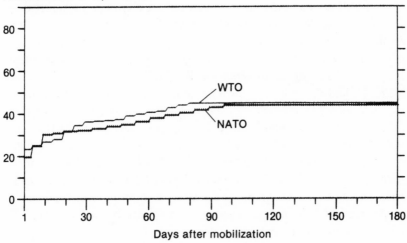

Days after mobilization

Source: appendix C.

FIGURE 4-2. **WTO Mobilization before and after CFE**

Armored division equivalents

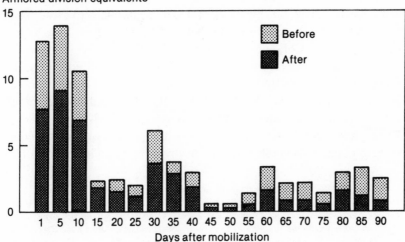

Days after mobilization

Source: appendix C.

The highly asymmetrical agreement would produce a marked change in force *ratios* during mobilization, as shown in figure 4-3.

As noted earlier, ratio comparisons do not constitute meaningful assessments of the conventional balance before arms control or after. What do the CFE numbers mean in dynamic operational terms? Specifically, what effect would these cuts have on the two test cases outstanding from chapter 3, the gross 60:40 versus 40:60 misallocation at nearly full mobilization and the multisectoral feint attack case? *Both problems are effectively solved by the CFE agreement.* Figure 4-4 shows NATO's gross misallocation scenario under the projected CFE reductions. NATO comes from behind to "win" in the north without loss of territory. Finally, consider the previously disastrous case of NATO misallocation under a multisectoral WTO attack with feints. Under the CFE agreement NATO wins the attrition war and holds the WTO to a 15 kilometer advance in corps sector V.[3] These results are given in figures 4-5 and 4-6. The CFE reductions reverse the previous outcomes.

Now, some analysts may find these misallocation scenarios too pessimistic to begin with. To them, CFE simply improves on a good situation. Other, more pessimistic, analysts will find these scenarios quite plausible. But then they should be *even more* enthusiastic about CFE than the optimists since it fundamentally improves a bad situation. Indeed, even the most pessimistic have for decades conceded that NATO's qualitative advantages compensate *to some degree* for the WTO's quantitative preponderance. Under the CFE agreement, the Soviets would sacrifice their numerical advantage *and* permit NATO to retain its qualitative lead. Those who hold the WTO to be superior before CFE must grant that, by their own criteria, the CFE agreement reverses the balance.

In summary, under a conservative reading of the CFE reductions, they dramatically improve NATO's security. One may accept or reject my base case assessment of the current balance. But it is hard to imagine any convincing case in which the CFE cuts would leave NATO *worse off*. The change—the "delta," as it were—will be positive regardless of one's starting point, as suggested by the sensitivity analyses in appendix D.

3. This outcome satisfies reasonable definitions of forward defense. For instance, it falls well within the Rand Corporation's stalwart defense criterion (stalemate and loss of no more than 40 kilometers). James A. Thomson and Nanette C. Gantz, *Conventional Arms Control Revisited: Objectives in the New Phase*, N-2697-AF (Santa Monica, Calif.: Rand Corp., 1987), p. 6. In this analysis, close air support (CAS) is assumed to be reduced to a common ceiling 15 percent below the WTO CAS level given in table 2-1.

FIGURE 4-3. **Ratio of WTO to NATO during Mobilization after CFE**

Armored division equivalent ratio

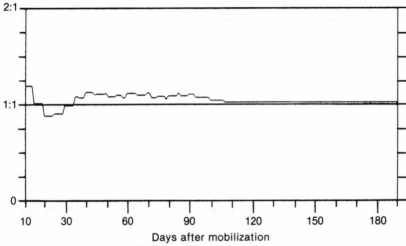

Days after mobilization

Source: appendix C.

FIGURE 4-4. **Scenario IV with 60:40 versus 40:60 Initial NATO Misallocation, Mutual Attrition in the North after CFE**

Armored division equivalents

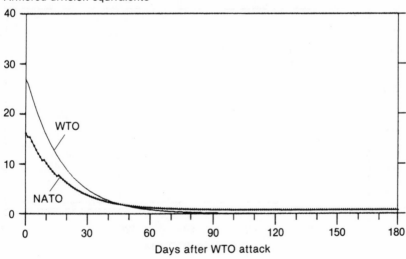

Days after WTO attack

Sources: appendixes A, B, and C.

FIGURE 4-5. **Multisectoral Feint Attack with Imperfect NATO Dexterity, Mutual Attrition in Corps Sector V after CFE Reductions**

Armored division equivalents

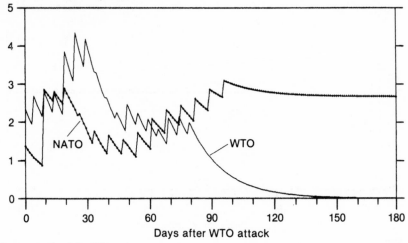

Days after WTO attack

Sources: appendixes A, B, and C.

FIGURE 4-6. **Multisectoral Feint Attack with Imperfect NATO Dexterity, Movement of the Front in Corps Sector V after CFE Reductions**

Kilometers lost by NATO

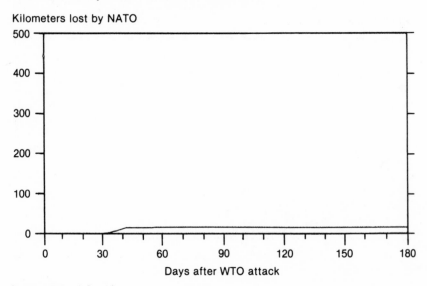

Days after WTO attack

Sources: appendixes A, B, and C.

Air Power: The Burden of Proof

The above simulations take account of close air support on both sides. Neither NATO's nor the WTO's CFE proposal would prohibit close air operations at the levels simulated in the analysis. The WTO's negotiating position on aircraft is currently in flux but appears to be gravitating toward NATO's more permissive overall ceiling for combat-capable aircraft on each side. It may be that the Soviets will in time accede completely to NATO's position. However, if Western intransigence on air power were to jeopardize the rest of CFE, especially its revolutionary benefits on the ground, a historic blunder will have been made. First, depending on how aircraft are counted, the WTO might be forced to endure larger numerical cuts than NATO en route to the equal ceilings proposed by the West. Moreover, those equal ceilings apply to *inputs*; but equality in inputs does not mean equality in *output*. By all accounts, NATO enjoys a substantial technological lead in aircraft. Further, NATO pilots fly more than twice as much as their Soviet counterparts, and the training is far more realistic. Historically, such qualitative factors have loomed larger than mere numbers in determining outcomes. Indeed, air-to-air combat is the prime example, as shown in table 4-2.

In World War II, American pilots in the Pacific theater lost only one plane for every ten Japanese planes they shot down—an exchange ratio of 10:1. In the Middle East war of 1967 (the Six-Day War), the Israelis scored a ratio of 20:1; in the Yom Kippur War of 1973, the ratio was 40:1; in Lebanon in 1982, it was over 85:1. These disparities are explained by technological advantages and above all by differences in pilot skill,

TABLE 4-2. **Exchange Ratios in Aerial Warfare**

Theater	Contestants	Winner[a]	Exchange ratio[b]
Pacific (World War II)	United States, Japan	United States	10:1
Korea (1950–53)	United States, North Korea	United States	10:1
Vietnam (1965–68)	United States, North Vietnam	United States	2.3:1
Vietnam (1970–73)	United States, North Vietnam	United States	12.5:1
Middle East (1967)	Israel, Arab states	Israel	20:1
Middle East (1973–74)	Israel, Arab states	Israel	40:1
Lebanon (1982)	Israel, Syria	Israel	86:1[c]

Source: Joshua M. Epstein, *Measuring Military Power: The Soviet Air Threat to Europe* (Princeton University Press, 1984), pp. 110–12.
a. The term "winner" is understood to apply only to the air war in the Vietnam cases.
b. Loser's planes lost to each one of winner's planes lost.
c. 86 Syrian planes shot down with no Israeli losses.

neither of which would be compromised by the Soviet proposal. Even if NATO would achieve a combat exchange ratio of 2:1 (worse than its performance in Vietnam before the U.S. Navy began the high-intensity TOPGUN air-to-air combat training program), that translates into a distinct advantage, even at numerical equality in the air.[4]

Moreover, nothing in the Soviet proposal prevents NATO from improving its air defenses through increased sheltering for NATO aircraft, improvements in runway hardening and repair, improved electronic deception, higher readiness and sortie rates so fewer aircraft are sitting on the ground, and more flying and simulator hours to ensure greater combat effectiveness when aloft. Much more importantly, as for shooting down WTO air attackers, the Soviet proposal places no limit on ground-based air defense missiles of any kind—from Stinger to Patriot. Even if a convincing case could be made that CFE would nullify NATO's real operational advantage in air-to-air combat, there are other ways to shoot down a plane, none of which would be limited.

The same point applies to deep-interdiction attacks on WTO air bases. Militarily, it matters little whether a Soviet fighter-bomber is destroyed from the air while sitting on its airstrip or is blown out of the sky as it crosses into West German airspace. Moreover, even if a compelling case could be made for destroying WTO planes on their air bases, one could use conventional missiles rather than piloted aircraft for the mission.

As for follow-on-forces attack (FOFA), most of the Soviets' follow-on forces (FOFs) themselves would disappear under the prospective CFE agreement. What imperative exists for FOFA if the FOF's themselves can be negotiated away? Or, to put it differently, why should NATO invest heavily to kill Soviet ground reinforcements with aircraft when it can get a ''sure kill'' with a pen—at the negotiating table? The issue is not whether NATO's FOFA force will shrink in absolute terms under CFE. The issue is whether the ratio of NATO FOFA platforms to WTO FOFs themselves would be seriously compromised. That is, rather than mechanically requiring that numbers of aircraft be equalized, one might ask that an agreement not reduce the FOFA-to-FOF ratio; that is, that it satisfy the inequality,

$$\frac{\text{NATO FOFA After CFE}}{\text{WTO FOFs After CFE}} \geq \frac{\text{NATO FOFA Before CFE}}{\text{WTO FOFs Before CFE}}.$$

4. TOPGUN was instituted during the bombing pause, 1968–70.

Equivalently, this requires that

$$\frac{\text{NATO FOFA After CFE}}{\text{NATO FOFA Before CFE}} \geq \frac{\text{WTO FOFs After CFE}}{\text{WTO FOFs Before CFE}}.$$

The right-hand side, however, equals 21.4 ADEs After divided by 40.9 ADEs Before, which is to say that the CFE agreement cuts the WTO follow-on forces by nearly 50 percent. But not even the Soviets' *initial* position on numbers of aircraft would have required NATO to reduce its FOFA capability (the left-hand side) by this amount. The Soviets' emerging *final* position on aircraft will afford even more latitude for a reasonable bargain. Moreover, this entire point rests on acceptance of FOFA as a strategy. It is at least debatable on grounds of stability and on grounds of military cost-effectiveness.[5] After all, there are other ways and other places to destroy follow-on forces.

In summary, while the Soviets appear to be willing to compromise, Western intransigence on air power would be imprudent, given the unregulated means of accomplishing air missions and given the revolutionary impact on the crucial ground balance of the main provisions of the CFE agreement.

5. See Joshua M. Epstein, *The 1987 Defense Budget* (Brookings, 1986), pp. 39–41.

CHAPTER FIVE

REDUCTION AND RESTRUCTURING BEYOND CFE

BY THE DYNAMIC measures applied in the preceding chapters, the prospective CFE agreement will improve NATO's security dramatically. Even after the CFE agreement, however, Western Europe will remain by far the world's most heavily armed camp. At the same time, reciprocal fears of premeditated aggression will be at a postwar low. Political and economic pressures for reductions and restructuring beyond CFE will be correspondingly high. In the United States many will question, and justifiably, the need to continue spending roughly $300 billion a year on defense after the principal threat to America's main security interest has been reduced asymmetrically by over 40 percent, as it would be under CFE. The brute fact is that CFE alone will not save much money in the United States.[1] If there are reductions beyond CFE that save money without degrading stability, they should be pursued.

Equal Reductions in the ATTU

The CFE agreement produces a condition of premobilization numerical equality in the ATTU for tanks, armored vehicles, and artillery. Having

---

1. The CFE I reductions are estimated to produce direct savings of approximately $1.8 billion per year in 1990 dollars (in U.S. Army forces alone). This estimate is based on the U.S. Army ground unit costs given in Barry M. Blechman with the assistance of Ethan Gutmann, "A $100 Billion Understanding," in Simon Serfaty, ed., *The Future of U.S.-Soviet Relations: Twenty American Initiatives for a New Agenda* (Lanham, Md.: University Press of America, 1989), pp. 366–67, and price deflators from Office of the Assistant Secretary of Defense (Comptroller), *National Defense Budget Estimates for FY 1990/1991* (Department of Defense, March 1989),

attained this numerical equality, the two alliances might proceed with a further equal reduction in the ATTU region. What would be the effect of a CFE II agreement under which both sides reduce weapon systems in the ATTU to a common ceiling 50 percent below the level under CFE I? Figure 5-1 projects the WTO-to-NATO force ratio, in ADEs, over the course of mobilization under such a CFE II.

The CFE II reductions, of course, would magnify the asymmetrical effect of the CFE agreement, producing a force ratio curve even more favorable to NATO. This is because the same U.S. reinforcement from the continental United States—that is, from outside the ATTU—looms ever larger proportionally as the numerically equal forces (tanks, artillery, and armored vehicles) within the ATTU are reduced.

The dynamic effect, in turn, is quite predictable. The reduction improves the simulated outcomes. Figures 5-2 and 5-3 chart the results, in attrition and movement terms, in the most demanding scenario, the multisectoral feint attack with imperfect NATO dexterity: the corps sector V front is effectively stationary and NATO's margin of victory is improved over CFE I.[2]

Unilateral U.S. Reductions beyond CFE II

Indeed, if this CFE II agreement were in force, the United States could unilaterally eliminate the 3 National Guard divisions, 1 independent armored brigade, and 15 independent artillery battalions listed in table 5-1 and still do as well as under CFE I in the most demanding scenarios—the 60:40 versus 40:60 misallocation in scenario IV and the multisectoral feint attack with imperfect NATO dexterity.[3] These unilateral reductions would be taken from the end of the U.S. reinforcement schedule; they are the last units to arrive at the front. The reductions were derived iteratively, by cutting slightly from the reinforcement list, checking the resulting dynamic outcomes, and then cutting some more until the—quite

p. 50. Including air power, the Congressional Budget Office estimates the direct savings at slightly over $2 billion a year in 1990 dollars. CBO, "Budgetary Effects of the President's Conventional Arms Proposal," Staff Working Paper, June 1989.

2. NATO loses 5 kilometers in this case, as against 15 kilometers in CFE I. Under CFE II, close air support is assumed to be reduced to a common ceiling 50 percent below the ceiling assumed under CFE I.

3. When I say that NATO does "as well as under CFE I," I mean that NATO does no worse in terms of movement of the front and still wins the attrition war.

FIGURE 5-1. **Ratio of WTO to NATO during Mobilization under CFE II Reductions in the ATTU to levels 50 Percent below CFE I**

Armored division equivalent ratio

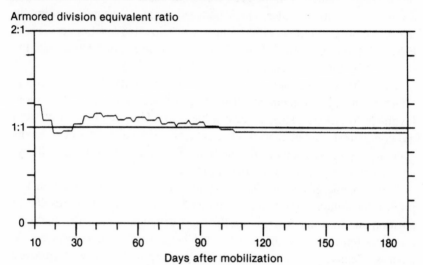

Days after mobilization

Source: appendix C.

FIGURE 5-2. **Multisectoral Feint Attack with Imperfect NATO Dexterity, Corps Sector V Attrition Assuming Reductions to levels 50 Percent below CFE I**

Armored division equivalents

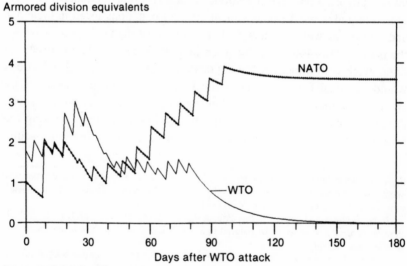

Days after WTO attack

Sources: appendixes A, B, and C.

FIGURE 5-3. **Multisectoral Feint Attack with Imperfect NATO Dexterity, Corps Sector V Movement of the Front Assuming Reductions to Levels 50 Percent below CFE I**

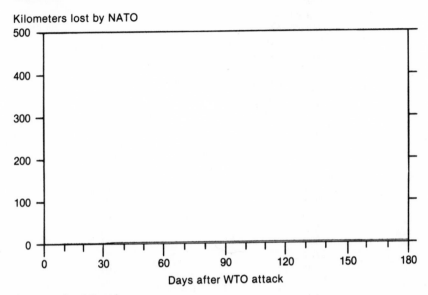

Kilometers lost by NATO

Days after WTO attack

Sources: appendixes A, B, and C.

satisfactory—CFE I outcomes were restored.[4] The idea was to arrive at a regime that, with respect to CFE I, could be termed the "equal risk/ lower cost" regime.[5] Even further NATO cuts would be possible if one were willing to assume greater dexterity than is assumed in the test scenarios or if NATO were assumed to implement obstacle plans of the sort discussed below.

Force-to-Space Rules of Thumb

Despite NATO's *relative* growth under CFE II, *all* reductions beyond CFE I in the ATTU have been vigorously opposed in some Western

4. Concerning the term "restored," see preceding note.
5. The CFE II reductions plus the unilateral reductions listed in table 5-1 are estimated to produce direct savings of approximately $16.8 billion per year in 1990 dollars (in U.S. Army forces alone). This estimate is based on the U.S. Army ground unit costs given in Blechman and Gutmann, "A $100 Billion Understanding," pp. 366–67, and price deflators from Office

TABLE 5-1. **National Guard Units to Eliminate after CFE II**

Units	ADEs
Divisions	
50th armored	.91
49th armored	.91
42nd infantry (2 brigades)	.63
Independent brigades	
31st armored	.26
Independent artillery battalions	
113th	.04
115th	.04
118th	.04
135th	.04
138th	.04
142d	.04
196th	.04
197th	.04
209th	.04
147th	.04
151st	.04
169th	.04
227th	.04
163d	.04
631st	.04
Total	3.35

Source: Units removed from the reinforcement schedule given in appendix C. Sum of rounded entries may not agree with total, which is the rounded sum of unrounded entries.

military and academic circles based on so-called force-to-space rules of thumb.[6] Two assumptions underlie this position. The first assumption is that there is some *absolute* minimum number of defensive ground forces per kilometer, a minimum ground-unit density, that is necessary for suc-

of the Assistant Secretary of Defense (Comptroller), *National Defense Budget Estimates for FY1990/1991*, p. 50. Using this method, the savings from CFE I were estimated at $1.8 billion per year (see chap. 5, note 1 above). At $16.8 billion per year, the net saving of CFE II plus the unilateral cuts in table 5-1 is thus $15 billion per year. If air power is included in CFE II, further direct savings would accrue. See CBO, *Budgetary and Military Effects of a Treaty Limiting Conventional Forces in Europe* (January 1990).

6. See, for example, John J. Mearsheimer, "Numbers, Strategy, and the European Balance," *International Security*, vol. 12 (Spring 1988), pp. 184–85. Some who previously opposed deep cuts on force-to-space grounds may have abandoned their opposition in light of recent political developments in Eastern Europe. I cannot say; and it is irrelevant. My argument here is methodological and concerns the *analytical merit* of long-standing force-to-space rules of thumb as such, rules which endure as conventional wisdom and which may yet loom large in future European and non-European contexts.

cessful defense, and that this minimum cannot be violated no matter what. The second assumption is that reductions beyond CFE would push NATO below this absolute minimum. Statements of the rule vary, but they seem to cluster around a value of one division per 25 kilometers of front.[7] Sometimes one "equivalent division" per 25 kilometers, or other standardized division, is employed. For explanatory purposes, it matters little which version is adopted.

In fact, a host of unsupported assumptions—about queuing, about dexterity, and about combat dynamics—are implicit in these rules of thumb. An attempt to formalize the conventional wisdom will demonstrate what some of those assumptions are and how little analytical support there is for the force-to-space objections to arms control. (None of this discussion denies the obvious point that there are physical limits on the number of vehicles that can be crammed into a given sector of front. The discussion concerns minimum defensive *requirements,* not maximum physical constraints.)

First, it is absurd to speak of defensive force-to-space requirements independent of an adversary; ultimately, it is force-to-force relationships that matter. While most would concede this point, few pursue it. Let us pursue it. Suppose that in an initial round of asymmetrical cuts, NATO and the WTO had both reduced forces to the canonical "defensive minimum" density of one division per 25 kilometers. Is there *no* further WTO reduction that would permit NATO to go lower safely, say to one division per 30 kilometers? Surely if the WTO went to zero divisions, NATO could safely reduce. What if the WTO went to 10 or 15 divisions total? It is incumbent on those who reject *equal* reductions below the canonical minimum to specify the *unequal* reductions that would permit NATO to go safely below those densities. Implicitly, there must be acceptable, even if highly asymmetrical, terms of trade. For the sake of illustration, for instance, for NATO to reduce from 1 division per 25 kilometers to 0.75 divisions per 25 kilometers, one might require that the WTO reduce from 1 division per 25 kilometers to 0.50 divisions per 25 kilometers. The first point, in any case, is that *force-to-space requirements are not adversary-*

7. See for example, Stephen J. Flanagan and Andrew Hamilton, "Arms Control and Stability in Europe: Reductions Are Not Enough," *Survival,* vol. 30 (September–October 1988), p. 463, note 20; and James A. Thomson and Nanette C. Gantz, *Conventional Arms Control Revisited: Objectives in the New Phase,* N-2697-AF (Santa Monica, Calif.: Rand Corp., December 1987), p. 12. For variants, see John J. Mearsheimer, "Why the Soviets Can't Win Quickly in Central

independent; ceteris paribus, there are, in principle acceptable terms of trade.

A second point is also often neglected and deserves analysis. Those who posit inviolable density "floors" for the defense never seem to mention analogous floors for the attacker. Let us grant for the moment that as the defense thins out, the attacker can more easily penetrate locally. Pursuing this logic, if, over the entire central region, both sides were reduced to a single division, a penetration would be virtually assured! But, of course, with a single division, the penetration could not be exploited to any lasting effect; *no consolidation of military control would be possible* over any appreciable area. If one is to posit defensive force-to-space "minima," then one should also posit offensive minima—densities below which no penetration (however easy) is worth its salt. Once the attacker is below those minimum consolidation densities, equal reductions are once again acceptable to the defense.

Simply for heuristic purposes, imagine that this "consolidation minimum" is reached when forces fall to an average density of 1 division per 100 kilometers—or 0.25 divisions per 25 kilometers. This line of reasoning suggests a *curve of acceptability,* sketched in figure 5-4. Problems begin when NATO falls to (suspending disbelief) 1 division per 25 kilometers. If NATO is to reduce further, to say 0.75 divisions per 25 kilometers, it requires that the WTO fall by more, say to 0.50 divisions per 25 kilometers; *a given NATO cut requires a larger WTO cut in this region* (see arrows). The terms of trade are harsher for the WTO the larger (in absolute terms) its forces, since a penetration has worse consequences for NATO the more assuredly the WTO can consolidate gains. However, as the WTO falls toward its minimum consolidation level (illustratively set at 0.25 divisions per 25 kilometers), the terms of trade ease; indeed, below that WTO density, equality—or, in principle, less than equality— suffices for NATO, as shown. Assuming for the moment that negotiated reductions would, beyond some phase, force both sides to move on the equality curve (E), the question for the defense would be whether the gap between the acceptability curve (A) and the equality curve (E) could be filled by means not constrained by agreement, for instance, by increasing

Europe," *International Security,* vol. 7 (Summer 1982), pp. 24, 25, 27; and Barry R. Posen, "Measuring the European Conventional Balance: Coping with Complexity in Threat Assessment," *International Security,* vol. 9 (Winter 1984–85), pp. 74–78.

FIGURE 5-4. **The Curve of Acceptability**

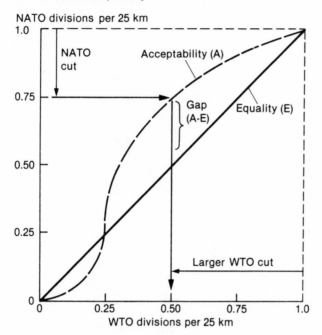

use of long-range delivery systems, mines, rapidly emplaceable obstacles, and preparation of terrain.

It will prove useful to generalize slightly. Rather than pick a particular number as the defensive minimum, let us call the value d_{min}. Obviously, NATO's d_{min} could differ from the WTO's due to various factors, but let us use d_{min} for both sides for expository purposes. And, instead of positing some specific minimum consolidation level, let us likewise assume a common value c_{min}. Then the picture is as shown in figure 5-5. In terms of this commonsensical formulation, the force-to-space objection to reductions beyond CFE embodies three claims:

—Further reductions would depress NATO to below d_{min}, while leaving the WTO level well above c_{min};

—Since negotiated reductions are *equal*, NATO will be bound politically to the equality (E) curve, where it will fall significantly short of militarily acceptable levels (the A curve) in divisions; and

—There is no way to bridge the gap between A and E within the terms of a post-CFE agreement.

FIGURE 5-5. **The Curve of Acceptability Generalized**

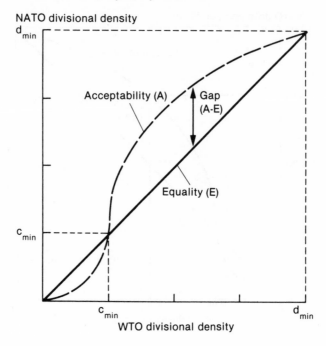

NATO divisional density

WTO divisional density

The force-to-space opponents of deeper reductions have not begun to make a convincing case that even one of these claims is true. Moreover, for deeper cuts to make sense, *only one* of the claims must be false.

First, regarding d_{min}, the "forward density," or actual ratio of force to space one computes for NATO, depends on the scenario: the density would be different after 90 days of mobilization than after 5 days. It also depends on how much of NATO's front—how much "space"—is included in the computation; can the Harz Mountains be partially subtracted, for instance? Finally, the forward density after arms control depends on the forces assumed to be affected by a treaty: the ATTU region, after all, encompasses many forces with little bearing on *forward* densities, such as Turkish, Spanish, and Soviet Central Reserve divisions. Those who hold that NATO's densities "would be inadequate" should set forth clearly what they think NATO's density "would be" and *how they calculate it*.

Suppose that were done and that, for the scenarios and forces of interest, the calculated force density along the front was less than 1 division per

25 kilometers. Does that put NATO below d_{min}? Certainly, the available data does not endow any particular density with much significance. The U.S. Army Concepts Analysis Agency (CAA) has recently published data from 189 battles from 1939 to 1982.[8] These data "display extreme variability inconsistent with the notion of a 'magic' density necessary for (or even associated with) stalemate."[9] See table 5-2.

Assertions that d_{min} equals 1 division (or 1 "equivalent division," or 1 ADE) per 25 kilometers are suspect as generalizations. None of this proves that for a *next* war in Europe there is no rule of thumb worth observing. What it suggests, however, is that any such guideline will have to be arrived at analytically, "from the ground up," as it were. Conceptual issues, therefore, are probably more important than empirical ones at this point. Indeed, the logical starting point for this force-to-space debate would be an existence theorem: a tight argument that d_{min} *exists*.

Speaking rigorously, d_{min} is that point at which equal numerical reductions drive NATO below acceptable force levels, the point at which the A and E curves diverge. This is the point at which, with no air power and setting the two forces equal in all other respects, a given cut in NATO would call for a *larger* cut in the WTO, the point where without compensatory action an equal cut yields a gap. Now, why is there *any* point at which a militarily significant gap arises? The answer, it seems to me, is fairly complex and ultimately involves assumptions about attacker queuing, defender dexterity, and the relationships among battle *durations*, attrition *rates*, and force *ratios*.

Playing devil's advocate, the best argument I can construct for a force-to-space concern at reduced force levels runs as follows.[10] The attacker can concentrate his forces wherever he wants and can concentrate up to some maximum level before stacking up, or queuing (a point allegedly dictated by yet other rules of thumb) occurs. The defender does not know where the attacker will concentrate, and accordingly (!?) distributes his forces evenly across the front.[11] The defending force thus has the same

8. Robert McQuie, *Historical Characteristics of Combat for Wargames (Benchmarks)*, CAA-RP-87-2 (Bethesda, Md.: U.S. Army Concepts Analysis Agency, July 1988).

9. John Patrick Elwood, "Conventional Wisdom: Force-to-Space Considerations and Conventional Arms Control in Europe," Senior thesis, Princeton University, 1989, p. 28.

10. I am grateful to Stephen Biddle for his help in articulating a coherent formulation of the force-to-space concern and for numerous discussions of the question.

11. A defender might not do this. He might deploy a light screening force along the front, and withhold the bulk of his force as a mobile reserve. If so, the redeployment times (t_1 and t_2) defined below would be reinterpreted as redeployment times from reserve areas, rather than from nearby corps sectors proper.

TABLE 5-2. **Average Densities Associated with Stalemate and Withdrawal**[a]

Category	Mean[b]	Standard deviation	Median
Initial personnel ratio			
Stalemate	1.7	.6	. . .
Withdrawal	1.5	.7	. . .
Troops per kilometer			
Attacker			
Stalemate	2904.2	2975.0	2126.5
Withdrawal	3027.3	2999.8	2410.0
Defender			
Stalemate	1691.6	1706.1	1191.7
Withdrawal	1896.7	1774.3	1491.0
Tanks per kilometer			
Attacker			
Stalemate	19.6	26.3	14.4
Withdrawal	22.8	25.6	23.4
Defender			
Stalemate	10.0	12.9	6.0
Withdrawal	12.4	21.0	13.9
Artillery per kilometer			
Attacker			
Stalemate	22.6	31.6	14.7
Withdrawal	21.0	28.5	24.4
Defender			
Stalemate	14.8	18.4	9.6
Withdrawal	12.5	16.3	14.0
CAS sorties per kilometer per day			
Attacker			
Stalemate	5.9	10.0	2.0
Withdrawal	7.2	17.9	6.3
Defender			
Stalemate	3.2	8.4	0.1
Withdrawal	1.1	3.9	0.9

Source: John Patrick Elwood, "Conventional Wisdom: Force-to-Space Considerations and Conventional Arms Control in Europe," Senior thesis, Princeton University, 1989, p. 28, based on data in Robert McQuie, *Historical Characteristics of Combat for Wargames (Benchmarks)*, CAA-RP-87-2 (Bethesda, Md.: U.S. Army, Concepts Analysis Agency, July 1988).

a. Those 91 battles involving withdrawal of 0–4 kilometers were considered stalemates while those 51 involving withdrawal of 10–120 kilometers were considered withdrawal battles.

b. Mean indicates geometric mean for initial personnel ratio and arithmetic mean for all other measures. See appendix B for a discussion of the geometric mean's preferability over the arithmetic mean for samples involving ratios of this sort. All numbers have been rounded.

average density in every sector. This average obviously falls as forces are reduced equally on both sides. However, the attacker can still concentrate the maximum feasible level on any chosen sector.[12] In that sector the

12. Obviously, this fails once the attacker's total force is less than the per sector maximum. For expository purposes this discussion assumes the attacker exceeds that level.

initial force ratio will equal *the attacker's maximum over the defender's average.* This ratio grows and presumably gives the attacker an increasing probability of penetrating in the chosen sector as forces decline initially.

To put some analytical meat on these heuristic bones, consider a specific numerical example. Let us make the following six basic assumptions: (1) the theater has three sectors; (2) the maximum that can be packed into any sector is 100 units; (3) the defender has zero information on the attacker's point of attack, until the attack occurs. In the face of that uncertainty, (4) the defender apportions forces equally among sectors; (5) the attacker focuses all his force on one sector of his choosing (leaving all others undefended); (6) the attacker-defender casualty-exchange ratio is $\rho = 1$. Let us confine attention to ground forces only and imagine that each side has 300 units. The defense deploys forces equally among sectors at 100 units each. The attacker focuses all force on sector 1. He has 300 units; but because of the force-to-space maximum of 100 units, a queue results. The offense must engage his forces in sequence. The issue is clear, and is illustrated in figure 5-6.

Let D_1 denote the duration of the opening battle between the attacker's first echelon of 100 units and the defender's 100 in sector 1. Let t_1 denote the time required by the defender's 100 units in sector 2 to redeploy to sector 1. Clearly, this defensive reinforcement arrives in the nick of time if $t_1 = D_1$. In that case the defender's 100 units from sector 2 arrive in time to fight the attacker's second echelon. Let the duration of that (second) battle be D_2. Pursuing the same reasoning, the defender's 100 units in sector 3 will arrive just in time to meet the attacker's third echelon if that defender force can redeploy before the second battle ends, at time $D_1 + D_2$. If t_2 is the redeployment time from sector 3, this reinforcement also arrives in the nick of time if $t_2 = D_1 + D_2$.

Retaining all six basic assumptions, a perfect stalemate results if $t_1 = D_1$ and $t_2 = D_1 + D_2$. Obviously, if $t_1 < D_1$ and $t_2 < D_1 + D_2$, the defender has time to spare, or excess dexterity. However, if $t_1 > D_1$, the defender's first reinforcement is too late; if $t_2 > D_1 + D_2$, the defender's second reinforcement is too late. For simplicity's sake, let us say that a catastrophic rupture occurs if either is too late. Hence, we have a formal catastrophe condition (C1) for world 1:

(C1) $t_1 > D_1$ or $t_2 > D_1 + D_2$

Leaving all assumptions intact, let us now move to world 2, in which forces fall equally to 100 units versus 100 units. Then the picture is given

FIGURE 5-6. **World 1: 300 Defense Units versus 300 Attack Units**

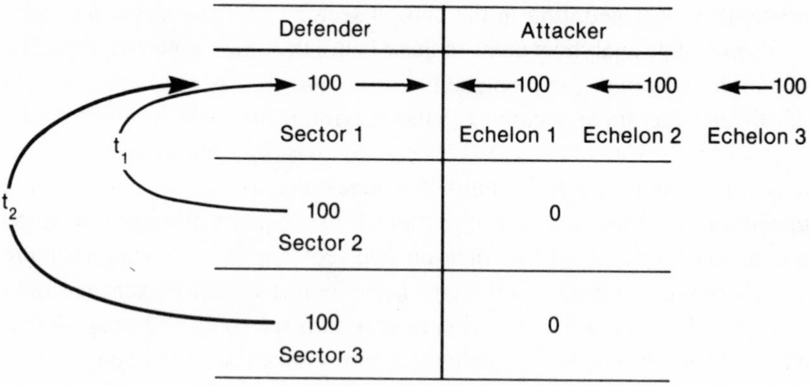

Defender		Attacker		
100 →		←—100	←—100	←—100
Sector 1		Echelon 1	Echelon 2	Echelon 3
100		0		
Sector 2				
100		0		
Sector 3				

in figure 5-7. Now if the attacker concentrates all his force on sector 1, he can amass a 3:1 ratio there, whereas before, the force-to-space maximum of 100 held him to a 1:1 ratio. This is the arithmetical phenomenon of interest: the ratio of the attacker's sectoral *maximum* to the defender's sectoral *average* begins to *grow* as the defender's force falls below a

FIGURE 5-7. **World 2: 100 Defense Units versus 100 Attack Units**

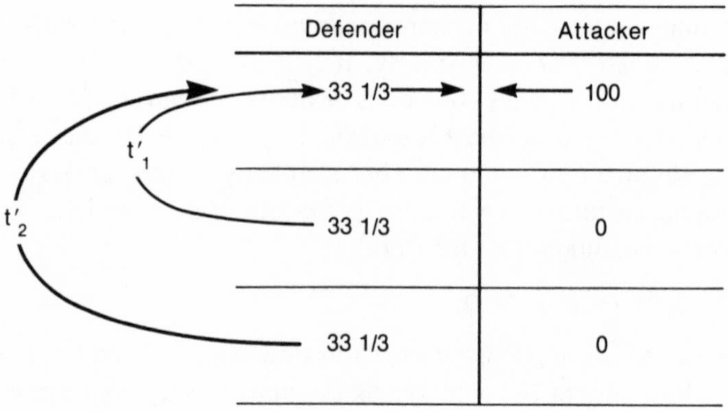

Defender		Attacker
33 1/3 →		← 100
33 1/3		0
33 1/3		0

certain level, in this example, 300.[13] At or below 100 per side, it should be noted, the attacker cannot improve on 3:1.[14]

These, I believe, are the micromechanics people tacitly have in mind when they express a force-to-space concern over low equal levels. And there is obviously a legitimate issue here, one deserving much more research.[15] Indeed, nothing can be concluded from figures 5-6 and 5-7 alone. There are four questions outstanding.

First, under what conditions is world 2 in fact worse for the defender than world 1? Second, when is either world unacceptable, or catastrophic, to the defender? Third, is there any evidence that, if NATO did nothing to compensate, reductions beyond CFE would put it in an unacceptable position? And, finally, even on the as yet unsupported assumption that such reductions would create an unacceptable situation, couldn't restructuring be designed to provide compensatory measures, restoring the original benefit of those reductions?[16]

Now, a complete mathematical characterization of the conditions under which world 2 is worse for the defender than world 1 is complex. However, it will prove useful to specify a clearly sufficient condition for world 2 to be worse than world 1, accepting for the moment the six basic assumptions elaborated earlier. Returning to world 2 (figure 5-7), let D_1' be the time required by the attacker to eat through the defender's 33 1/3 units in sector 1. Defense catastrophe results if this occurs before the defender's reinforcements arrive from sector 2; let t_1' denote the redeployment time required. If D_2' is the time required by the attacking force surviving the first engagement to eat through these reinforcements, then for the defender's reinforcement from sector 3 to arrive just in time, we must have $t_2' = D_1' + D_2'$. These redeployment times might be shorter than in world 1 because the defending forces are smaller and perhaps more mobile

13. Obviously, in the *n*-sector case, the number is *n* times the per sector maximum.

14. Since the attacker (*A*) equals the defender (*D*), if *A* is less than or equal to the sectoral maximum, then concentration of all attacker forces there yields an initial attacker-defender ratio of $A/(D/n) = A/(A/n) = n$, the number of sectors.

15. For a theoretically advanced treatment of force to space and of the optimum spatial distribution of defending forces under uniform and nonuniform probability densities for the point of attack, see Raj Gupta, "The Calculus of Conventional Force Structure: Force Optimization and Its Implications for Deep Arms Reductions," Senior thesis, Department of Electrical Engineering and The Woodrow Wilson School, Princeton University, May 1989.

16. Assuming that reductions would create a gap and that compensation is feasible, economic efficiency would require also that the cost of compensating not exceed the savings resulting from the reductions that created the gap. This standard should not be difficult to meet, since the

as a result. Once again, perfect stalemate occurs if $t_1' = D_1'$ and if $t_2' = D_1' + D_2'$. Likewise, catastrophe results if the attacker can burn through the immediate defense before reinforcements arrive. Hence, catastrophe occurs in world 2 if

(C2) $t_1' > D_1'$ or $t_2' > D_1' + D_2'$.

Still holding to the six basic assumptions (notably that $\rho = 1$), world 2 is certainly worse than world 1 if the differences between reinforcement times and battle durations are greater in world 2 than in world 1, that is, if

(C3) $(t_1' - D_1') > (t_1 - D_1)$ and $t_2' - (D_1' + D_2') > t_2 - (D_1 + D_2)$.

This follows if sector 1 battle durations fall (as force ratios grow) faster than redeployment times fall as defensive forces shrink. Implicit in judgments that world 2 is worse than world 1 are unstated hypotheses concerning the effect of force ratios on battle durations and the effect of force size on defense dexterity.[17]

Now, even if world 2 were shown to be worse than world 1 in the above comparative sense (C3), the defender might still be perfectly *adequate* in world 2, or to put it succinctly, (C3) does *not* imply (C2). At $\rho = 1$ the defense is still adequate so long as (a) the defender's first redeployment time, t_1', is less than the time, D_1', needed by the attacker to annihilate the 33 1/3 defenders initially deployed in sector 1, *and* (b) t_2' is less than the sum of D_1' and D_2' (the total time needed by the attacker to annihilate the initial defenders plus those redeployed from sector 2).

Even under all the simplifying assumptions set forth at the outset, an argument would still need to be made that world 2 is catastrophic for the defense, an *argument* involving attrition *rates* and redeployment *times* that condition $C2$ obtains.

Without even touching the six basic assumptions listed above, it should be obvious that judgments about the probability of catastrophe rest on all

---

savings accruing from CFE II and the unilateral reductions of table 5-1 are substantial (see chap. 5, note 5 above), while the costs associated with the main compensatory measures (obstacle systems and terrain modification) are quite modest. For some representative costs, see Joshua M. Epstein, *The 1987 Defense Budget* (Brookings, 1986), note 30.

17. Although no empirical or theoretical basis has yet been provided for it, even if one believes the rule of thumb that, ceteris paribus, a 3:1 ratio in some measurement units would guarantee breakthrough (however one defines that term), does it guarantee it in an hour, a day, a week, or a month? Does it happen before reinforcements arrive or not?

sorts of implicit claims about battle *durations* and attrition *rates* as functions of force *ratios* engaged and claims about dexterity—reaction and movement times (t_1 and t_2), given different intersector *distances* and relative *velocities* of attacker and defender reinforcements.[18] When one then relaxes those six basic, and *quite implausible*, simplifying assumptions, admitting that the defender's information is not zero, that the defender need not allocate equal forces to all sectors or hold zero in reserve, that the attacker might not leave entire sectors undefended from counterattack, and, most notably, that the casualty-exchange ratio need not equal 1.0 or even be a constant, matters become terribly complex.

Where is the analysis showing that, when these complex dynamics are taken into account in the current NATO context, the catastrophe condition (which should be stated clearly) is met when NATO equals 1 ADE per 25 kilometers? Nowhere. Until some analysis—a serious argument using serious numbers—is presented to that effect, there will be no analytical basis for assuming that d_{min} = 1 division per 25 kilometers or 1 ADE per 25 kilometers or any other rule of thumb.

In considering NATO specifically, moreover, there are two further factors that make the idealized example above even more farfetched. First, even after CFE II and the unilateral U.S. cuts proposed here, NATO would retain 20 ADEs at the start of mobilization. The image of a defense so thin that an attacker could simply zip through the holes unopposed is unrealistic. And, as is discussed below, defensive restructuring after CFE could make it even more unrealistic.

A second point to ponder in considering NATO specifically is this: assuming equal totals and exchange ratios of 1.0 or more, the entire force-to-space argument collapses if the defender is assumed to have adequate dexterity. By definition, the defender could counterconcentrate adequate numbers in that case. Hence, for NATO to be worse off at lower equal levels than at higher equal levels, one or both of the following conditions must hold: (1) the demand for defensive dexterity grows as equal forces decline in size; or (2) NATO's dexterity falls—the "supply" of dexterity falls—as equal forces decline in size.

The first proposition was discussed earlier and follows if, ceteris paribus, battle durations fall as force ratios rise. Even if this is true, however, the second is arguably false. Indeed, the opposite might well obtain. Small

---

18. For a more general and thorough treatment of these relationships, see Gupta, "Calculus of Conventional Force Structure."

forces might well enhance dexterity. In an already densely packed ballroom, a dozen people huddling are hard to detect; yet the same dozen people huddling are set into sharp relief if the ballroom floor is nearly empty. Likewise, a concentration (the "signal") should be easier, not harder, for NATO to detect as the overall WTO theater force population (the "noise") falls. The detection (and hence decision) components of NATO's theater-level dexterity should be aided by deep reductions. Mobility might also be easier for NATO's smaller force, which could inherit a bigger logistics tail per weapon as a result of weapon cuts. In any case, nothing in the Soviet proposal constrains the acquisition of more theater surveillance or theater mobility assets. There is no reason, in short, why NATO's dexterity should fall. Indeed, it might well grow. It is important to recall that, in any event, the test scenarios used in assessing CFE II, and the unilateral reductions beyond it, already assume *poor* NATO dexterity. To the extent that defensive force-to-space requirements are surrogates for dexterity, I have already imposed serious "force-to-space penalties" on NATO in my analyses. Even on those demanding assumptions, NATO wins the attrition war without significant territorial sacrifice after CFE II and the unilateral cuts presented here.

In summary, a great deal of basic research (on the dynamics of combat and on theater-level dexterity and queuing) remains to be done before someone identifies a particular defensive force-to-space density—d_{min}— below which equal reductions are prejudicial to NATO, the level where, ceteris paribus, sharply asymmetrical reductions would be required on force-to-space grounds.

Moreover, the entire discussion thus far has been cast in terms of ground units alone. Even if, in ground units, a post-CFE gap between acceptability and equality were established, there are in principle ways to bridge it.

What is "Force"?

For instance, even if deploying a division is one way to defend 25 kilometers, why assume it is the only way? What about two-thirds of a division and 500 close air support planes? Or one-third of a division, 300 close air support planes, and 10,000 rapidly scatterable mines? In principle, there is obviously a trade-off between divisions on the ground and other means of delivering fire (figure 5-8).[19] One way to bridge the alleged

---

19. On the distinction between firing platforms (inputs) and delivered fire (output) in this context, see Joshua M. Epstein, "The 3:1 Rule, the Adaptive Dynamic Model, and the Future of Security Studies," *International Security*, vol. 13 (Spring 1989), note 84.

FIGURE 5-8. **Illustrative Alternative Means of Delivering a Given Division's Worth of Fire into a 25 Kilometer Sector of Front**

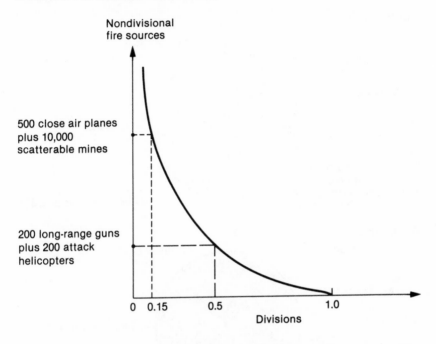

gap between equality and acceptability would be by restructuring forces, substituting nondivisional means for ground units and moving up this trade-off curve, as it were.

Restructuring

A second way of mitigating the problem of counterconcentration at low equal force levels would be to restructure forces to reduce their capacity for rapid armored penetration. To a significant extent, this would be accomplished by the deep armor (tank, armored vehicle, and artillery) reductions of CFE I and CFE II, as indicated by the pie charts shown in figure 5-9. The tank-heaviness of WTO forces (the percent of total ADE score attributable to tanks) would decrease from nearly 40 percent before CFE to 21 percent after CFE II. The Soviets claim to have further substantial plans along these lines. Measures that would be consistent with the defensive restructuring of divisions would include the substitution of air defense and antitank guided weaponry for remaining tanks and other armored fighting vehicles, the withdrawal of forward ammunition stocks,

FIGURE 5-9. **WTO Force Composition on Central Front under Alternative Reductions**

Before CFE I

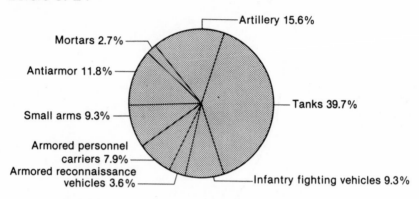

Artillery 15.6%
Mortars 2.7%
Antiarmor 11.8%
Small arms 9.3%
Armored personnel carriers 7.9%
Armored reconnaissance vehicles 3.6%
Tanks 39.7%
Infantry fighting vehicles 9.3%

After CFE I

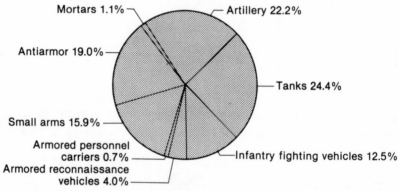

Mortars 1.1%
Artillery 22.2%
Antiarmor 19.0%
Tanks 24.4%
Small arms 15.9%
Armored personnel carriers 0.7%
Armored reconnaissance vehicles 4.0%
Infantry fighting vehicles 12.5%

After CFE II[a]

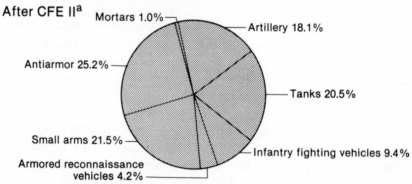

Mortars 1.0%
Artillery 18.1%
Antiarmor 25.2%
Tanks 20.5%
Small arms 21.5%
Armored reconnaissance vehicles 4.2%
Infantry fighting vehicles 9.4%

a. Previous reductions have eliminated armored personnel carriers.

and the elimination of assault-bridging and mine-clearing capabilities, for example.

Further limits on the geographical distribution of forces—zonal constraints—might be pursued in (or after) CFE. Through its sublimits on forces deployed outside of national territory and on forces permissible for any one country, the CFE agreement would implicitly establish crude zones in the ATTU. While these affect proximity to the West German border, they impose no further limit on the distribution of forces up and down the front. And yet, the discussions of dexterity above demonstrate that this north-south dimension is every bit as critical as the east-west one. The attacker's capacity to rapidly concentrate forces undetected could be severely hampered by arms control provisions limiting the north-south distribution of forces. If such zonal schemes were bolstered with strict exit and entry provisions and monitoring, they would provide nearly unambiguous warning in the worst case.

Finally, NATO can restructure its own force in a way that results in higher-confidence forward defense if deterrence fails and in greater stability in crisis. A defense distributed in greater depth with greater reliance on forward obstacle systems would advance both ends even if the Soviets did not restructure defensively themselves. If both sides restructured along such lines, the likelihood of crises escalating to war would be even further reduced.

Obstacle Systems

As defined by the U.S. Army, an obstacle is "any obstruction that stops, delays, diverts, or restricts movement."[20] First, as a general proposition, NATO could undertake a concerted program of terrain enhancement. Simple, inexpensive, and unobtrusive alterations can turn existing terrain features and transportation infrastructure into significant obstacles to armored advance. For instance, one way to bolster the obstructing effect of canals is to build "a reinforced concrete step at the top of the slope out of the water on the friendly side of the canal." According to the army, this would "prevent any Warsaw Pact bridging equipment from articulating from the water surface to the top of the step and deny exit from a

20. Lyle G. Suprise and others, *Peacetime Defensive Preparations in Europe*, R-82-3 (U.S. Army Engineer Studies Center, March 1982), p. D-2.

float bridge or raft."[21] Tank steps on the friendly sides of levees, streams, and rivers would present barriers to snorkeling or fording armored vehicles.[22] Such unilateral measures would reinforce limits on assault bridging equipment itself.

Roads and rail lines running north-south could be altered to obstruct east-west movement. In the army's view, their shoulders "should be modified to form a triangular tank ditch on the enemy side of the road. . . . This concept of a reinforced tank ditch could be one of the most economical and socially acceptable of any of the postulated terrain enhancements." For autobahns, concrete median strips "could be incorporated into a highway divider system and need only be 1 meter in height to have a decisive effect against armored vehicles."[23]

Other basic terrain modifications could include building earthen barriers (mogul belts), creating rock- and boulder-strewn fields in open terrain (used extensively in Korea), reinforcing existing stone fences, building cross-country terracing, converting firebreaks in forests to tank ditches, and selectively cutting timber to create log barriers. In peacetime, bridges and roads could be—and to a remarkable extent are—prechambered to accept explosives in a crisis. Their demolition in wartime could bring armored columns to a halt.

Perhaps the best of the nonlethal obstacles is instant antitank ditching. It is unobtrusive, inexpensive, safe, and highly flexible and effective. "These instant antitank ditches consist of plastic pipe buried seven feet in the ground—below every farmer's plow—and liquid explosive stored elsewhere. In a crisis the liquid explosive can be placed in the pipes in a few hours. If the crisis disappears the liquid explosive can be removed from the pipes and put back in storage. In the event of attacks, instant antitank ditches, impassable to armored vehicles, can be created as enemy tanks approach."[24]

Finally, there are obstacles that do more than delay. Mines are comparatively inexpensive and historically have proved to be effective antiarmor weapons. Minefields need *not* be emplaced in peacetime. According to the army, "it is within the range of current technology to create mine-

21. Suprise and others, *Peacetime Defensive Preparations*, p. E-15.
22. On artificial flooding, see Suprise and others, *Peacetime Defensive Preparations*, pp. E-10, E-15.
23. Suprise and others, *Peacetime Defensive Preparations*, pp. E-16–E-17.
24. John Tillson, "Preparing To Defend," unpublished manuscript, August 20, 1986, p. 8.

fields over days or within seconds."[25] Scatterable mines can be stocked at preselected sites for emplacement on tactical warning.

The primary function of obstacles—even minefields—is not to directly kill advancing armor but to delay or stop attacking forces, maximizing their exposure to defensive fire. As a rule, the slower a target is moving the easier it is to hit. According to army analyses, at a range of 2,000 meters, the hit probabilities of U.S. M-1 and M-60A3 tanks against reference targets improve from 0.22 to 0.54 when target velocities fall from 10 kilometers per hour to 2 kilometers per hour.[26] Obstacles, therefore, can increase the effectiveness of defensive ground fire dramatically. The same applies to the defender's close air support effectiveness.

While maximizing the attacker's exposure to defensive fire, an optimal defense will also minimize the defender's exposure to the attacker's fire. Although the obstacle system must be covered by fire, the defender's antitank missile and armor positions can be carefully dug in, well concealed, lightly fortified, and connected to alternative positions by sunken roads.[27] None of this would look at all like the Maginot Line.

In 1975 the army analyzed the effect of obstacles and prepared positions on exchange ratios—attackers killed per defender killed—for various types of direct-fire weapons over a range of force ratios. The obstacle produces three changes in the tactical situation: "first, assuming defender observation of the obstacle, the attacker's arrival there will assure a positive detection; second, the attacker's movement is halted for the specific period of time it requires to breach the obstacle; and, third, keeping the attacker stationary at the obstacle accrues a higher kill probability (P_k) to defender weapons than would apply if the attacker were a moving target."[28] In addition to a base case (no obstacles) and an obstacle case, the army considered a combined case in which, in addition to having obstacles, defenders operated from protected positions. While obstacles increase the attacker's exposure and raise the defender's P_k, the protected positions

25. Gerald E. Cooper, *Battlefield Obstacles—An Appraisal of the State of the Art in Measuring Obstacle Effectiveness* (Engineer Studies Group, Department of the Army, distributed by Defense Technical Information Center, Defense Logistics Agency, September 1976), p. 45.

26. Suprise and others, *Peacetime Defensive Preparations*, p. D-11.

27. Office of the Assistant Secretary of Defense for Program Analysis and Evaluation, "NATO Center Region Military Balance Study 1978–1984," Department of Defense, July 13, 1979, p. I-51.

28. Engineer Studies Group, Department of the Army, *Measuring Obstacle Effectiveness: A Fresh Perspective*, vol. 1 (Fort Belvoir, Va., March 1975), p. 7.

TABLE 5-3. **Effect of Obstacles and Prepared Positions on Exchange Ratios**

Weapon	Exchange ratio	Improvement over base case (percent)
Force ratio 1:1 [a]		
M60A1 tank		
Base case	2.6	. . .
Obstacle case	6.9	165
Combined case	17.4	569
TOW antitank missile		
Base case	20.8	. . .
Obstacle case	249.0	1,097
Combined case	499.0	2,299
Force ratio 2:1 [a]		
M60A1 tank		
Base case	1.3	. . .
Obstacle case	4.1	215
Combined case	10.1	677
TOW antitank missile		
Base case	15.1	. . .
Obstacle case	163.5	983
Combined case	329.7	2,083
Force ratio 3:1 [a]		
M60A1 tank		
Base case	0.9	. . .
Obstacle case	2.4	167
Combined case	6.1	578
TOW antitank missile		
Base case	8.8	. . .
Obstacle case	33.4	280
Combined case	91.1	935

Source: Engineer Studies Group, Department of the Army, *Measuring Obstacle Effectiveness: A Fresh Perspective*, vol. 1 (Fort Belvoir, Va., March 1975), p. 20. The attacker is always assumed to use T-62 medium tanks (p. 6).
a. Attackers to defenders.

reduce the defender's exposure, reducing the attacker's P_k by up to 65 percent.[29]

The effects of obstacles and prepared defensive positions on attacker-defender exchange ratios in these experiments was startling, as shown in table 5-3. At a 3:1 ratio of attackers to defenders, the improvement in exchange ratio due to obstacles was 167 percent for the M60A1 tank and 280 percent for the TOW antitank guided missile. When combined with protected firing positions for the defense, the numbers rose to 578 percent

29. Engineer Studies Group, *Measuring Obstacle Effectiveness*, p. 9.

FIGURE 5-10. **The Effect of Dummy Antitank Positions on Breakthroughs**

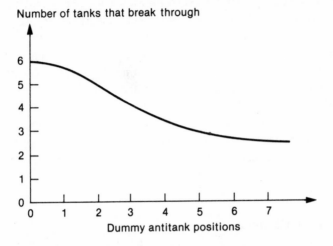

Number of tanks that break through

Dummy antitank positions

Source: P. N. Tkachenko, "Matematicheskie Modeli Boevykh Destvii," Sovetskoe Radio (Moscow 1969), reproduced in H. F. Stoekli, *Soviet Tactical Planning: Overcoming Anti-Tank Defences* (Sandhurst, England: Soviet Studies Research Center, January 1986), p. 27.

and 935 percent, respectively.[30] A host of other army studies supports the general proposition that obstacles and prepared positions have a sharp beneficial effect on exchange ratios. For instance, one study found that "prepared positions for the defending force allowed the U.S. forces to increase the vehicle loss exchange ratio by 140 percent."[31]

Dummy defensive positions and other simple modes of deception can enhance the effect of prepared defenses. Interestingly, Soviet models suggest that the number of tanks able to penetrate a given antitank defense falls as the number of dummy antitank positions increases (figure 5-10).

By squandering fire on dummy defenses, the attacker reduces his firing efficiency (actual defenses engaged per time period) while increasing his exposure to defensive fire. Fake muzzle flashes from the defensive zone can further confound an attacker. Even dummy minefields have been

30. These runs assumed a single defender at the obstacle. With multiple defenders, the improvements increased further, almost doubling. Engineer Studies Group, *Measuring Obstacle Effectiveness*, p. 32.

31. Eugene Ehrlich and G. Leslie Geiger, *Survivability—The Effort and the Payoff* (Engineer Studies Center, Department of the Army, distributed by Defense Technical Information Center, Defense Logistics Agency, June 1981), pp. 21–22. See also, Boyd A. Jones, *The Influence of Obstacles on Anti-Armor Weapon System Effectiveness* (Carlisle Barracks, Pa.: U.S. Army War College, 1983), p. 21.

employed successfully.[32] As one U.S. Army study put it, "surprise may also be achieved by making every location look like a real minefield whether it is or not." The issue of surprise is important because prepared defenses are portrayed in drab terms. The army study continues, "Not too long ago obstacle-related combat implied unsurprising, undistinguishable barriers to most people. Obviously, it need not and probably should not. People should get used to thinking about obstacles and surprise at the same time."[33] An obstacle system can desynchronize an attack, throw a wrench into its gears, and present it with sudden uncertainties. In the Soviet case, where flexibility, initiative, and innovation appear to be scarce, a forced breakdown of, or departure from, the plan could be highly disruptive.

Attack Clarification

Regarding the critical issue of counterconcentration and theater-level dexterity, the main benefit of a defense prepared in depth would be informational. By "filtering out" the feints from the true main axes of attack, a forward zone of prepared defenses reduces the defender's uncertainty about the attacker's true concentration points. NATO commanders could, in consequence, "allocate little or none of their mobile reserves and airpower to the sectors where enemy penetration of the zone is shallow. Instead, they can husband these resources for application almost solely to the sectors of main attack, where they will be needed by NATO's hard-pressed ground defenders."[34]

William Kaufmann has eloquently described the obstacle system's informational benefits and the way in which these could permit NATO to counterconcentrate more efficiently.

With perfect information and a frictionless response to the Pact concentrations, the NATO commander could deal with this tactic as

---

32. "This point is driven home by an example of a small action in Tunisia in early 1943. Four German tanks stopped at the wire marking a dummy minefield and all four were destroyed. 'They had taken the wire at its face value and had become sitting shots for antitank guns waiting for them.'" Howard E. Boone, "The Feasibility of Estimating the Contribution of Artificial Obstacles to Force Performance," Thesis, Army Command and General Staff College, Ft. Leavenworth, Kans., 1975, p. 22.

33. Cooper, *Battlefield Obstacles*, p. 45.

34. Malcolm Hoag, *Strengthening NATO Capabilities: A "Hi-Lo" Ground Force Mix for Area Defense*, R-2039-AF (Santa Monica, Calif.: Rand Corp., 1977), p. vii.

readily as with a steamroller assault undertaken uniformly all along the front. But conditions of perfect information and absence of friction are rarely met. Barriers could help to deal with these dangers in two ways—by compelling the attacker to concentrate his forces even more heavily if he is to achieve his breakthrough within a short time, and by permitting the defender to man the front more lightly and hold a larger proportion of his mobile forces in reserve. Barriers thus would ease the defending commander's uncertainty and facilitate his decision to reallocate his units and commit the reserve forces at his disposal.[35]

Of course, the combination of attack clarification and delay produces the opportunity for efficient air attacks on whatever queues are produced by obstacles.[36] The shallow cross-corps sector application of long-range attack systems could also make sense under these circumstances.

Test

Numerous specific architectures for a defense in depth have been proposed. They have in common a forward zone of densely obstacled and enhanced terrain inlaid with a connected system of prepared defensive positions, or strongpoints. A certain amount of the defender's armor is held in reserve as a *masse de maneuvre* designed to contain penetrations and counterattack to regain lost territory. In his impressive study, Malcolm Hoag proposed a 30-kilometer-deep checkerboard of 1,260 strongpoints manned primarily by militia, with up to a half of NATO's tank-heavy armored force held in reserve as a *masse de maneuvre*.[37] John Tillson has outlined other proposals, as have a number of Europeans.[38]

---

35. William W. Kaufmann, "Nonnuclear Deterrence," in John D. Steinbruner and Leon V. Sigal, eds., *Alliance Security: NATO and the No-First-Use Question* (Brookings, 1983), p. 68.

36. According to a recently declassified Pentagon analysis, the delay could be substantial. See "NATO Center Region Military Balance Study, 1978–84," table I-29 and p. I-51. See also Congressional Budget Office, *U.S. Ground Forces and the Conventional Balance in Europe* (June 1988), pp. 38–43.

37. Hoag, *Strengthening NATO Capabilities*.

38. Tillson, "Preparing To Defend." The principal Europeans are discussed in Jonathan Dean, "Alternative Defense—Answer to NATO's Post-INF Problems?" *International Affairs*, vol. 64 (Winter 1987–88), pp. 61–82.

In a discussion of this length, I cannot hope to resolve such issues as the optimal depth of the forward defensive zone or size of the mobile armored reserve. I would not recommend that maneuver forces be held west of the Weser River (an average of 60 kilometers from the front)[39] for obvious reasons (such as bridge interdiction); and a forward zone much shallower than 30 kilometers might prove too thin to impose the delay or extract the information desired from the system.

More as a call for further research than as a claim to a solution, it is possible to test a generic defense using dynamic methods. Let us return to the base case in which NATO grossly misallocates after virtually full mobilization—this is the 60:40 versus 40:60 case in scenario IV. Rather than deploy all 40 percent of NATO's forces forward in the Northern Army Group (NORTHAG) zone, as was assumed before, let us distribute them in three equal layers. One-third of its ADEs would be deployed at the inter-German border, the second third at the 20 kilometer mark; and the final third at 40 kilometers. For the first layer, let the ground-to-ground casualty-exchange ratio, ρ, be 1.7:1 as in the base case. Certainly, by comparison with the army's own studies, in which obstacles raise ρ by hundreds of percent, it is not overly optimistic to raise ρ by 10 percent in the second zone (from 20 to 40 kilometers deep) and by 25 percent in the third (from 40 to 60 kilometers deep).[40] To be conservative, let us not raise NATO's close air effectiveness above the level assumed in the base case, though one could argue that it should be raised as well.

How does this hypothetical defense perform in the misallocated (60:40 versus 40:60) case that proved so catastrophic to NATO, even after the WTO's unilateral cuts? The results are given in figures 5-11 and 5-12. In sharp contrast to the no-barrier base case in which NATO was crushed and lost 500 kilometers, here NATO comes from behind to win the attrition war and loses 42 kilometers. Isn't this defense in depth a *better forward defense* in fact? Yes.

39. See "NATO Center Region Military Balance Study, 1978–1984," table I-2.

40. The casualty-exchange ratio is assumed to grow as the attacker progresses from zone to zone because the defenders arrayed in successive zones have progressively more time to prepare their positions, greater familiarity with the terrain, and intelligence gained from the attacker's engagements in the preceding zone. Unlike the defender's, moreover, the attacker's lines of communication and his flanks are progressively more extended and vulnerable the more deeply he presses through the sequence of prepared zones.

FIGURE 5-11. **Scenario IV, Initial 60:40 versus 40:60 NATO Misallocation, Attrition in North with Barrier System and Distributed Defense**

Armored division equivalents

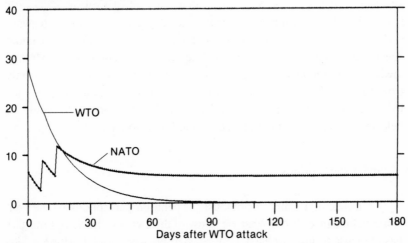

Days after WTO attack

Sources: appendixes A, B, and C.

FIGURE 5-12. **Scenario IV, Initial 60:40 versus 40:60 NATO Misallocation, Movement of the Front with Barrier System and Distributed Defense**

Kilometers lost by NATO

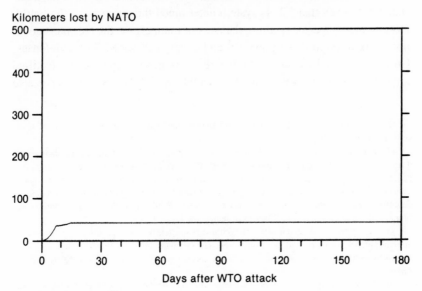

Days after WTO attack

Sources: appendixes A, B, and C.

From Forward Deployment to Forward Defense

The goal of forward defense is to minimize territory lost. It is not at all clear, and has never been clear, that the goal of forward *defense* is best served by forward *deployment*. Indeed, by locking forces forward early, NATO is *more* vulnerable to feints and penetrations than under deeper, barrier-bolstered, distributed defensive configurations.[41] Moving toward such architectures is *not* a departure from forward *defense*—only from forward *deployment*. Indeed, forward *defense* could be strengthened by such innovations, and so could stability, since more force would be held in reserve rather than poised forward as if to attack.[42]

Soviet Perceptions

Deterrence and stability obviously depend on perceptions of the conventional balance. From what we know of their views, the Soviet military has immense respect for barriers. First, barriers were crucial to the Soviets' own July 1943 success in the Battle of Kursk, the turning point of the war on the eastern front and a battle that looms large in current Soviet discussions of stability in Europe. "The Soviets built one of the most elaborate systems of field fortifications around Kursk."[43] It is no overstatement to say that "This system determined the outcome of the battle. Despite their superiority along the axes of main effort, the Germans could not break through these powerful and deeply echeloned Soviet defenses. Counter attacked by strong Soviet reserves in the depth of the fortified area, the Germans were forced to withdraw."[44] The Soviets have also

41. On optimal configurations under various assumptions, see Gupta, "Calculus of Conventional Force Structure."

42. This discussion is not meant either (a) to imply that NATO's current defense plans afford it no depth whatsoever or (b) to endorse any particular version of mobile defense or "alternative defense." Rather, it is intended to demonstrate rigorously that, on defensible assumptions about casualty-exchange ratios, a layered defense can sacrifice *less* ground than one in which the same defensive force is deployed as far forward as possible. While NATO's current posture is not literally of the latter kind, it is closer to it than to the layered idea.

43. The system "included nearly 6,000 kilometers of trenches, strongpoints, 1 million mines, antitank ditches, and wire and other obstacles. The Germans could not break through and were forced by counterattack to withdraw." Ehrlich and Geiger, *Survivability—The Effort and the Payoff*, p. 7.

44. Trevor N. Dupuy and others, *The Value of Field Fortifications in Modern Warfare*, vol. 1, DNA-5054F-1 (Dunn Loring, Va.: Historical Evaluation and Research Organization, 1979), p. 14.

observed the effectiveness of prepared defenses in the Middle East. Regarding the October 1973 war, "the fortifications and obstacles on the Golan Heights helped to dilute the effects of the Syrian surprise attack and were the principal reason the Syrians were unable to penetrate into Galilee."[45]

Some NATO military factions might resist increased reliance on obstacle systems because, while slowing an attack, they could also limit the defender's maneuverability. This argument has tragic precedents. Speaking of the fall of France, Liddell Hart wrote that "there had also been ample time beforehand to block the German approach routes with mines, or even by the simple device of felling the trees along the forest roads through the Ardennes to the Meuse—a proposal that was urged on the French High Command but rejected on the ground of keeping the routes clear for their own cavalry's advance!"[46] Malcolm Hoag asks, "as one pertinent example of overvaluing one's own full capability to maneuver, what can match the spectacle of the German parade to the defeat of France in World War II, headlights visible all the way from Cologne to the Meuse, with nothing put in their path from either the air or the ground?"[47]

Moreover, it is not necessarily true that obstacles limit maneuver. Both Rommel and Montgomery made extensive use of obstacles in their North African war of mobility.[48] Indeed, obstacles can produce economy of force, freeing units for mobile action that would otherwise be fixed guarding unprepared terrain. "In the Battle of the Bulge, the hasty defenses, blocks, and minefields installed along the entire front of the [U.S.] 4th division beginning on 17 December facilitated the use of Economy of Force along the southern four-fifths of the Division Sector, and the massing of about half the division in about one-fifth of the sector, opposite the only serious German threat." Related to the issue of dexterity, "the key factor is the capability of the defender to allocate his forces to meet a developing situation at the critical points. To support that allocation other areas must be defended by reduced elements (economy of force) or the attacker must be significantly delayed."[49] Obstacle systems help in both respects.

45. Dupuy and others, *Value of Field Fortifications in Modern Warfare*, vol. 1, p. 17.

46. B. H. Liddell Hart, *Deterrent or Defense* (Praeger, 1960), p. 104.

47. Hoag, *Strengthening NATO Capabilities*, p. 66.

48. Montgomery exploited natural obstacles, ensuring that false maps fell into Rommel's hands, leading the latter into areas of soft ground bad for armor.

49. Boone, "Feasibility of Estimating the Contribution of Artificial Obstacles to Force Performance," pp. 18–19.

This, it is worth noting, was France's greatest blunder. The French deployed a third of their army *behind* the Maginot Line, which was never breached, when the entire point of the Line was to free ground units for action in other areas such as the Ardennes.

Now, in fact, NATO militaries by and large do not evidence strong resistance to barriers, which it must be stressed would bear no resemblance to the Maginot Line in any case. The U.S. Army refers to "stockpiles containing several hundred thousand mines and tens of thousands of tons of other barrier materials. In addition, U.S. Army Europe plans for the use of a significant portion of the deployed force to execute extensive barrier plans in the event of a Warsaw Pact attack on NATO forces in Central Europe."[50] The NATO militaries, moreover, are signatories to the secret 1979 Central Region Barrier Agreement, which presumably mandates preparations of the sort just alluded to, preparations mentioned in other Pentagon documents declassified since that time.[51]

Europeans and Depth

As I argued earlier, an obstacle-bolstered distributed defense in greater depth would provide higher confidence of forward *defense* than NATO's current doctrine of forward *deployment*. In minimizing the probability of a catastrophic penetration and massive territorial loss, the essential problem is to have adequate forces in the right places at the right times; counterconcentration or dexterity is the main issue. Forward *deployment*— by locking units forward into inactive or feint sectors—can exacerbate the problem by requiring complex disengagements and lateral redeployments that might be avoided if thinner forces were deployed forward in an obstacle system (affording them higher exchange ratios by all accounts) and main maneuver forces were held in operational reserve. The likelihood that deep penetrations would occur, or that any ground would be permanently lost, would actually fall, and with it, the attractiveness of attack in the first place.

50. Boone, "Feasibility of Estimating the Contribution of Artificial Obstacles to Force Performance," p. 1.

51. While the agreement is classified, its existence is not. The full citation is North Atlantic Treaty Organization, Allied Forces, Central Europe, *Central Region Barrier Agreement (CRBA) (U)*, Brunssum, Netherlands, August 31, 1979 (NATO-Secret), and is given in Suprise and others, *Peacetime Defense Preparations*, p. G-8.

Here too, doctrinal realities seem to be changing. In the 1988 British *Statement on the Defence Estimates* we read that

Forward defence does not necessarily imply a static defence. . . . In order to take advantage of force improvements, such as recent developments in anti-armour capability, Northern Army Group (NORTHAG) has adopted a more mobile operational concept that acknowledges the possibility of initially having to yield ground. Reconnaissance forces would identify the main axes of attack and a quick reacting covering force would, if necessary, delay the enemy to allow the main forces to prepare defensive positions. Ground defence forces, supported by air forces, would then exploit obstacles and minefield barriers to break up and reduce invading forces, while mobile reserves (including air-mobile forces) would attack the flanks and the rear of enemy spearheads.[52]

While the military operational details of "alternative defense" require clarification, the very fact that these concepts have a significant audience in Germany attests to the growing acceptability of defenses distributed in depth. Finally, political acceptability always depends on presentation. Obviously, if this type of defensive restructuring is presented as a Maginot Line suggesting the division of Germany, it will be politically unacceptable. If, however, it is presented as a precautionary infrastructure for a post–cold war world, a way to increase stability while reducing force levels—and hence German personnel and spending requirements—it might fare better.

Indeed, looking beyond CFE I and CFE II—indeed, looking beyond the NATO-WTO confrontation—obstacle-bolstered defenses distributed in depth might well prove to be the sinews of collective security in Europe. If all major potential adversaries were to adopt such defenses, the likelihood of crises between any two such actors escalating to war would almost surely be reduced.

Stability

Under any of the CFE agreements outlined earlier, a Soviet leader contemplating aggression against NATO would face an awesome array of

52. *Statement on the Defence Estimate 1988*, vol. 1, presented to the British Parliament by the British Secretary of State for Defense (London, 1988), p. 16.

deterrents: powerful conventional forces backed by thousands of theater-based (including naval) nuclear weapons, augmented by the "strategic" forces of Britain and France, all buttressed by the intercontinental nuclear forces of the United States. Even if, in the face of powerful evidence to the contrary, one posits a Soviet inclination to engage in it, premeditated, calculated aggression against Western Europe under these circumstances seems implausible.

It seems more plausible that, if war comes, it will come out of a crisis in which the mobilization efforts of each side are read as threatening by the other, resulting in an escalation spiral in which preemption, rightly or wrongly, comes to be seen as attractive. The perception that the opponent's mobilization is offensive in cast might well generate such spirals. Accordingly, if mobilization took each military establishment into unequivocally defensive postures, the act of mobilization would be less provocative and escalatory than it might otherwise be. Of course, there is no hard and fast way to distinguish a defensive posture from an offensive one, technically. But ambiguity can be vastly reduced. A posture in which the forward and first line of defense is a system of obstacles and prepared defenses with mobile armored reserves to the rear should be less provocative—and more effective—than one in which armored forces are glowering at each other across a border.

NATO might unilaterally increase stability by moving in this direction. If the Soviets are as interested in restructuring for nonoffensive defense as they say, they can reciprocate and the world might be an even safer place. And if they do not reciprocate, NATO will, in fact, be better prepared for the worst.

CHAPTER SIX

SUMMARY AND CONCLUSIONS

The Current Balance

If one uses the extended adaptive dynamic model presented in appendix A, the performance assumptions presented and discussed in appendix B, and the mobilization assumptions given in appendix C, NATO stalemates the WTO without losing territory in all four base case scenarios, so long as a high degree of theater-level dexterity is assumed. However, if NATO's dexterity is poor and it fails to counterconcentrate efficiently, it could lose badly and quickly. That proposition is demonstrated by three test scenarios:

Test 1: Initial 60:40 versus 40:60 misallocation in scenario I (10/5).
Test 2: Initial 60:40 versus 40:60 misallocation in scenario IV (90/85).
Test 3: Misallocation under a multisectoral feint attack.

Under the current balance and the given assumptions, NATO fails each test.

The Unilateral Reductions

If the unilateral reductions announced by Gorbachev and the East Europeans were implemented as detailed in appendix C, then test 1, a surrogate for the canonical surprise attack, is passed. Leaving all other assumptions as they were in the base case, NATO wins in attrition without losing territory. Since those unilateral reductions are concentrated on the WTO units that would lead such an attack, a significant impact on the early attack (10/5) case is to be expected. NATO still fails tests 2 and 3 under the unilateral reductions.

The CFE Agreement

Implementation of the CFE agreement, as interpreted in chapter 4, would permit NATO to pass test 2 completely (NATO wins the attrition war without territorial sacrifice) and test 3 almost completely (NATO wins the attrition war but loses around 15 kilometers).

Given these sharp improvements, Western intransigence on reductions in air power seems unreasonable. As far as air defense is concerned, the prospective CFE agreement would leave NATO with an air-to-air force at least as capable as the WTO's, if reasonable credit is taken for NATO's technological and training advantages. Moreover, nothing in the CFE agreement would constrain acquisition of ground-based air defenses or passive improvements in NATO's air force survivability. As far as air-to-ground operations are concerned, NATO is concerned primarily with a degradation in its follow-on-forces attack (FOFA) capabilities. Impressive interdiction capabilities would, in fact, remain after the CFE agreement. Moreover, the case for FOFA, debatable even now, would be seriously undercut by the agreement itself, which drastically reduces the Soviets' follow-on forces.

CFE II

While improving NATO's relative military position dramatically, the CFE agreement will still leave Central Europe the most heavily armed camp in the world, and will produce negligible savings in the U.S. defense budget. As a first step beyond CFE, which equalizes forces at near NATO's levels in the ATTU, equal CFE II reductions of 50 percent should be attractive to the West. Simulated outcomes improve across the board under such an agreement.[1]

CFE II Plus Unilateral U.S. Cuts

Such reductions would confer on NATO a numerical preponderance (after mobilization) even greater than that produced by CFE I. This nu-

---

1. Ground lost in test 3 falls from 15 kilometers in CFE I to 5 kilometers in this case.

merical edge is not necessary for a successful NATO defense. With CFE II in place, if the United States were to eliminate unilaterally the late-arriving reinforcements listed in table 5-1, NATO would still do as well militarily as under CFE I.

Sensitivity Analysis

Recognizing that warfare is an uncertain process and that key assumptions can be challenged, the entire series of simulations was done under six different assumptions concerning the ground-to-ground casualty-exchange ratio, ρ. Beyond the base case, five different constant ρ-values were examined (1.2, 1.3, 1.5, 1.85, 2.0). A nonconstant (force-ratio dependent) ρ was also tested using the extended model given in the appendix. The results are summarized in appendix D. In some cases, the absolute outcomes differ sharply from those produced by the ρ-value of 1.7 used in the base cases (the value is developed in appendix B). But, as was stressed in the introduction, the central issue is relative, not absolute. With that in mind, select any scenario. Then for any ρ-value greater than or equal to 1.3, four claims apply to the computer simulations.

—NATO is better off under the WTO's unilateral cuts than under the current balance. The image of a leaner, meaner threat is not supported by this analysis.

—NATO is better off under CFE I than under the WTO's unilateral cuts alone.

—NATO is better off under CFE II than under CFE I.

—If, with CFE II in force, the United States were to eliminate unilaterally three National Guard divisions, one independent armored brigade, and fifteen independent artillery battalions (see table 5-1) from the tail of the reinforcement list, NATO would do as well as under CFE I, and the U.S. defense burden would be lower than it is today or under CFE I. Obviously, the improvement over the current balance would still be vast.

While the main issue is relative not absolute, it is worth stating outright that the simulations offered in the text represent a conservative assessment. The conservatism and empirical plausibility of the parameter values employed is established in appendix B. Beyond these, the test scenarios themselves seem quite demanding. Some may even feel they are unduly demanding, unrealistically complimentary to the Soviets, whose simulated performance in orchestrating theater-level offensive operations (for example, in the multisectoral feint case) would rival the most virtuosic attacks in history.

Overall, it thus seems warranted to assert that the CFE II agreement followed by the U.S. reductions I suggest would not only leave NATO much *better off* than it is at present but would leave NATO very *well off* from a security standpoint, a position that could be further reinforced by nonprovocative unilateral and negotiated means.

Force-to-Space Rules of Thumb

No convincing analytical case has yet been marshalled to support the force-to-space opposition to such reductions. Moreover, even if such a case could be made, NATO could use arms control and restructuring to ameliorate the problem. In addition to boosting unilaterally its own capacity to counterconcentrate fire through improved theater surveillance, mobility, and long-range precision delivery systems, NATO could move to an obstacle-bolstered defense distributed in greater depth and, as a precondition for reductions, it could insist on a less threatening spatial distribution of WTO forces as well. The crucial north-south disposition of equal reduced forces might be enforced through zonal arrangements with exit and entry provisions and monitoring procedures specified in an agreement. Reciprocal adoption of dispersed defenses distributed in depth and bolstered by unobtrusive or rapidly emplaceable obstacle systems would improve forward defensive capacity and should increase stability.

Rather than simply reject deep reductions, NATO should attempt to work out and explicate the concrete provisions that would make deep cuts beneficial. If those provisions cannot be agreed to, then so be it. But they should at least be identified. There is something bizarre about the proposition that nearly forty-five years after World War II, when neither side has any incentive for calculated aggression, each must continue to devote vast resources to the maintenance of huge military establishments for war in Central Europe. Particularly in the wake of recent developments in Eastern Europe, there is a growing sense that the military confrontation is fast becoming, if it is not already, an expensive and dangerous political anachronism. The real challenge is to chart a stable course out. I suspect the challenge can be met analytically. Whether it can be met politically remains to be seen.

EXTENDING THE ADAPTIVE
DYNAMIC MODEL

In this appendix an extended version of the original adaptive dynamic model is presented. First, the model's variables are defined. Then the extended equations are presented. The original equations have been published and discussed elsewhere.[1] Hence, a basic familiarity with the original adaptive dynamic model is assumed in this appendix.

Variables

Ground Forces

$A_g(t)$ Attacker's ground lethality surviving at start of tth day.[2]

$RA_g(t)$ Attacker's ground lethality reinforcement at start of tth day.

$\alpha_g(t)$ Attacker's ground prosecution rate per day, $0 \leq \alpha_g(t) \leq 1$.

$\alpha(t)$ Attacker's ground-to-ground lethality attrition rate per day (no-airpower case), $0 \leq \alpha(t) \leq 1$.[3]

$\alpha_a(t)$ Attacker's total ground lethality attrition rate per day (air- and ground-induced), $0 \leq \alpha_a(t) \leq 1$.

---

1. Joshua M. Epstein, *The Calculus of Conventional War: Dynamic Analysis without Lanchester Theory*, (Brookings, 1985); and Epstein, *Strategy and Force Planning: The Case of the Persian Gulf* (Brookings, 1987), appendix C.

2. For my current work on European security issues, ground lethality is measured in a modified version of the U.S. Army's recently declassified Weapons Effectiveness Index/Weighted Unit Value (WEI/WUV) III system. Modifications are specified in the notes to table C-1.

3. This is the ground attrition rate due only to defensive ground fire.

α_{aT} Attacker's threshold, or equilibrium, attrition rate; the value of $\alpha_a(t)$ the attacker seeks to achieve and sustain, $0 < \alpha_{aT} \leq 1$.

$D_g(t)$ Defender's ground lethality surviving at start of tth day.

$RD_g(t)$ Defender's ground-lethality reinforcement at start of tth day.

α_{dT} Defender's threshold attrition rate; the value above which withdrawal begins, $0 \leq \alpha_{dT} < 1$.

$\alpha_d(t)$ Defender's total ground-lethality attrition rate per day (air- and ground-induced), $0 \leq \alpha_d(t) \leq 1$.

$W(t)$ Defender's rate of withdrawal in kilometers per day.

W_{max} Defender's maximum rate of withdrawal.

t Time in days, $t = 1, 2, 3, \ldots$.

Exchange-rate Components

λ_d Parameter reflecting the defender's capacity to concentrate fire in engagements (interpreted as a measure of predation efficiency below).

λ_a Analogous parameter reflecting the attacker's capacity to concentrate fire in engagements.

$\rho(t)$ Exchange ratio (attacker ground lethality killed per defender ground lethality killed) due to ground fires as a function of time.

Close Air Support Forces

$D_a(t)$ Defender's close air support (CAS) aircraft surviving at start of tth day.

$RD_a(t)$ Defender's CAS reinforcement at start of tth day.

α_{da} Defender's CAS aircraft attrition rate per sortie, $0 \leq \alpha_{da} \leq 1$.[4]

S_d Defender's CAS daily sortie rate.

K_d Attacker's armored fighting vehicles (AFVs) killed per defender CAS sortie.

$A_a(t)$ Attacker's CAS aircraft surviving at start of tth day.

$RA_a(t)$ Attacker's CAS reinforcement at start of tth day.

α_{aa} Attacker's CAS aircraft attrition rate per sortie, $0 \leq \alpha_{aa} \leq 1$.

---

4. In yet more elaborate versions of the model, these attrition rates would themselves be functions of the density and effectiveness of air defenses whose performance and suppression would be modeled.

K_a Defender's AFVs killed per attacker CAS sortie.

S_a Attacker's CAS daily sortie rate.

V AFVs per division equivalent (DE).[5]

L Lethality points per DE.

$ACAS(t)$ Defensive ground lethality killed by attacker's CAS on the tth day.

$DCAS(t)$ Attacking ground lethality killed by defender's CAS on the tth day.

Equations

The general equations for battle are simply

$$(\text{A-1}) \quad A_g(t) = A_g(t - 1)[1 - \alpha(t - 1)] - DCAS(t - 1) + RA_g(t),$$

and

$$(\text{A-2}) \quad D_g(t) = D_g(t - 1) - \frac{\alpha(t - 1)}{\rho(t - 1)} A_g(t - 1)$$
$$- ACAS(t - 1) + RD_g(t).$$

Notice that, with all variables as defined above, equations A-1 and A-2 are accounting identities. They become a true model when specific functional forms are given. Proceeding,

$$(\text{A-3}) \qquad \alpha(t) = \alpha_g(t)\left(1 - \frac{W(t)}{W_{\max}}\right),$$

and

$$(\text{A-4}) \quad W(t) = \begin{cases} 0 & \text{if } \alpha_d(t-1) \leq \alpha_{dT} \\ W(t-1) + \left(\dfrac{W_{\max} - W(t-1)}{1 - \alpha_{dT}}\right)(\alpha_d(t-1) - \alpha_{dT}) & \text{if } \alpha_d(t-1) > \alpha_{dT} \end{cases}$$

---

5. Assumed to include self-propelled and towed artillery.

with

$$\text{(A-5)} \qquad \alpha_d(t) = \frac{D_g(t) - [D_g(t+1) - RD_g(t+1)]}{D_g(t)}.$$

We set $W(1) = 0$. On the attacker's side,

$$\text{(A-6)} \quad \alpha_g(t) = \alpha_g(t-1) - \left(\frac{\alpha_{aT} - \alpha_g(t-1)}{\alpha_{aT}}\right)(\alpha_a(t-1) - \alpha_{aT}),$$

with

$$\text{(A-7)} \qquad \alpha_a(t) = \frac{A_g(t) - [A_g(t+1) - RA_g(t+1)]}{A_g(t)}.$$

We set $\alpha_g(1)$ equal to some initial value $[\alpha_g(1) < \alpha_{aT}]$.[6] The ground-induced exchange ratio is given by

$$\text{(A-8)} \qquad \rho(t) = \rho_0 \frac{D_g(t)^{\lambda_d}}{A_g(t)^{\lambda_a}},$$

where ρ_0 is a constant which can be interpreted in a number of ways taken up below.

The tactical air terms are symmetrical with respect to offense and defense. Forces available at the start of day t are

$$\text{(A-9)} \qquad D_a(t) = D_a(t-1)[1 - \alpha_{da}]^{S_d} + RD_a(t),$$

and

$$\text{(A-10)} \qquad A_a(t) = A_a(t-1)[1 - \alpha_{aa}]^{S_a} + RA_a(t).$$

In turn,

$$\text{(A-11)} \qquad DCAS(t) = aD_a(t), \text{ where}$$

$$a = \frac{LK_d}{V}\left[\frac{1 - (1 - \alpha_{da})^{S_d+1}}{\alpha_{da}} - 1\right]$$

6. Technically, one could set $\alpha_g(1) = \alpha_{aT}$. But in that case the model degenerates into one in which the defender is adaptive but the attacker is not. Or, one might let the first value be

$$\alpha_g(1) = \frac{A_g(1) - [A_g(1) - P_d(T)P_d(H|T)P_d(K|H)D_g(1)^{\lambda_d} - DCAS(1)]}{A_g(1)},$$

if the defender's target acquisition, conditional hit, and conditional kill probabilities—$P_d(T)$, $P_d(H|T)$, and $P_d(K|H)$—are known.

and

(A-12) $ACAS(t) = bA_a(t)$ where

$$b = \frac{LK_a}{V}\left[\frac{1 - (1 - \alpha_{aa})^{S_a + 1}}{\alpha_{aa}} - 1\right].$$

Discussion

The main extensions of the original adaptive dynamic model are the inclusion of ground and close air support reinforcements and a generalized ground-to-ground casualty-exchange ratio, $\rho(t)$.[7]

Leaving airpower aside, and leaving aside for the moment the particular functional form for $\rho(t)$ given in equation A-8, the accounting identities A-1 and A-2 alone reveal a general fact about warfare that may be stated as a simple—and perhaps not completely intuitive—theorem: *Warfare achieves stasis if the exchange ratio equals the reinforcement ratio.* By stasis, I mean the conditions

[a] $A_g(t) = A_g(t - 1)$ and

[b] $D_g(t) = D_g(t - 1)$.

Attacker and defender force levels on Tuesday equal their respective levels on Monday; mutual attrition continues, but, due to reinforcement, there is no net change in the engaged forces of either side. If one thought of reinforcements as births, and engaged forces as populations of competing species, these would be the zero population growth, or equilibrium, conditions. Ecological parallels are, in fact, enriching, and they will be exploited in this discussion. Proceeding with a proof of the simple theorem, it was noted that equations A-1 and A-2 are, taken alone—with all variables defined in general—a pair of accounting identities. The conditions [a] and [b] can be written

$$A_g(t) - A_g(t - 1) = 0, \text{ and}$$

$$D_g(t) - D_g(t - 1) = 0.$$

7. These extensions were first published in Joshua M. Epstein, "The 3:1 Rule, The Adaptive Dynamic Model, and the Future of Security Studies," *International Security*, vol. 13 (Spring 1989), pp. 112–13, note 56, and p. 114, note 59.

From equations A-1 and A-2, these are equivalently

$$\alpha(t - 1)A_g(t - 1) = RA_g(t), \text{ and}$$

$$\frac{\alpha(t - 1)}{\rho(t - 1)}A_g(t - 1) = RD_g(t).$$

Dividing the first by the second yields the theorem:

$$\rho(t - 1) = \frac{RA_g(t)}{RD_g(t)}.$$

The exchange ratio equals the reinforcement ratio in equilibrium (the point at which rates of change in attacker and defender are zero). The competing species are replenishing in a ratio equal to that in which they are killing one another off: "birth" balances "death," as it were.

Obviously, one would not generally assume that condition in setting up an analysis. For practical purposes, the exchange ratio must be independently specified. In the original adaptive dynamic model, $\rho(t)$ was taken to be constant. When the original model was published, I noted that extensions were worth pursuing.[8] And two are offered below. But before proceeding, it should be pointed out that the constancy assumption is, in truth, quite rich, and embeds *density dependencies* of considerable complexity in a plausible and efficient manner. In discussing the casualty-exchange ratio in this light, a useful point of departure is the simple Lanchester square system with no movement. Movement will be discussed below.

Density Dependence

The Lanchester square relations are

[1] $\dfrac{dR}{dt} = -bB$, and

[2] $\dfrac{dB}{dt} = -rR$.

In this framework, increasing force density is a *pure benefit*. If the red force, R, grows, a greater volume of fire is focused on the blue force, B,

---

8. See Epstein, *Calculus of Conventional War*, p. 22, note 44.

and in equation [2], the blue attrition rate, *dB/dt*, grows proportionally. At the same time, however, *no penalty* is imposed on red in equation [1] when, in fact, if the battlefield is crowded with reds, the blue target acquisition problem is eased and red's attrition rate, *dR/dt*, should grow.

In warfare, each side is at once *both predator and prey*. Increasing density is a benefit for an army as predator, but it is a cost for that same army as prey. The Lanchester square system captures the predation benefit but completely ignores the prey cost of density. The latter, moreover, is familiar to us all. For instance, if a hunter fires his gun into a sky black with ducks, he is bound to bring down a few. Yet if a single duck is flying overhead, it takes extraordinary accuracy to shoot it down. To ducks, considered as prey, density carries costs.

The so-called Lanchester linear variant is much more plausible in this, ecological, light. Here,

$$[3] \quad \frac{dR}{dt} = (-bB)R, \text{ and}$$

$$[4] \quad \frac{dB}{dt} = (-rR)B.$$

In parentheses are the Lanchester square terms reflecting the "predation benefit" of density, but they are now multiplied by a term (the prey force level) reflecting "prey costs," as it were. The red attrition rate, *dR/dt*, in equation [3] slows as the red population goes to zero, reflecting the fact that, as the prey density falls, the predator's search ("foraging") requirements for the next kill increase. Equivalently, red's attrition rate grows if, like the ducks in the analogy, its density grows. In summary, a density cost is present to balance the density benefit reflected in the parenthesized term.

Now, at first glance, this mathematical structure would appear to be far richer than the simple constant casualty-exchange ratio used in the original adaptive dynamic model. Remarkably, however, the constant casualty exchange ratio is capturing precisely these complex density dependencies.

How can this be? The casualty-exchange ratio is, by definition, *dR/dB*; it is the instantaneous change in red per change in blue. Observe that equations [3] and [4] imply

$$[5] \quad \frac{dR}{dB} = \frac{(-bB)R}{(-rR)B} = \frac{b}{r}.$$

But this is precisely a constant casualty-exchange ratio. The original adaptive dynamic model's constant value is not simply an impoverished default, but embeds a complex balance of density dependencies.

A constant casualty-exchange ratio is used for the base case simulations and for most of the runs discussed in this book. Two extensions, however, are explored. In describing the first of these, a useful point of departure is, once more, Lanchester theory.

Time and Force Ratio Dependence

First, as presented in *The Calculus of Conventional War*,[9] a highly general form of Lanchester's equations is

$$[6] \quad \frac{dR}{dt} = -bB^{c_1}R^{c_2} \quad \text{and}$$

$$[7] \quad \frac{dB}{dt} = -rR^{c_3}B^{c_4}.$$

The corresponding casualty-exchange ratio is

$$[8] \quad \frac{dR}{dB} = \frac{b}{r} \frac{B^{c_1 - c_4}}{R^{c_3 - c_2}}.$$

Clearly, from equation [6], c_1 is blue's predation benefit from increasing density while from equation [7], c_4 is blue's prey cost of increasing density.[10] Hence the exponent $c_1 - c_4$ might be thought of as the *net predation benefit of increasing density*, which is net concentration capacity in Lanchester's sense. The red exponent, $c_3 - c_2$ is analogously interpreted. Let us therefore define

$$\lambda_b = \text{Blue's net predation benefit} = c_1 - c_4, \text{ and}$$

$$\lambda_r = \text{Red's net predation benefit} = c_3 - c_2$$

Then,

$$[9] \quad \frac{dR}{dB} = \frac{b}{r}\left(\frac{B^{\lambda_b}}{R^{\lambda_r}}\right).$$

9. See Epstein, *Calculus of Conventional War*, p. 2, note 2.
10. All c values are in the closed interval [0,1].

This generalization produces *attrition stalemate* conditions equivalent to the Lanchester square case if λ_b and λ_r both equal 1 (pure predation benefit), the Lanchester linear case if λ_b and λ_r both equal zero (no *net* predation benefit), and mixed cases for other values of λ_b and λ_r, which of course need not equal one another and need not be integer-valued.

In the sensitivity analyses of appendix D, an extended version of the adaptive dynamic model is run. The casualty-exchange ratio is, in algebraic form, equivalent to [9]. I use

$$[10] \quad \rho(t) = \rho_0 \frac{D_g(t)^{\lambda_d}}{A_g(t)^{\lambda_a}} \,.$$

Clearly, $D_g(t)$ and λ_d play the roles of $B(t)$ and λ_b; $A_g(t)$ and λ_a are the analogues of $R(t)$ and λ_r; and ρ_0 is the twin of b/r. This term may also be thought of as the ratio of certain probability products.[11]

In appendix D, ρ_0 is assigned the weighted geometric mean of historical tank casualty-exchange ratios, a value computed in appendix B. The exponents are set at $\lambda_d = 0.100$ and $\lambda_a = 0.075$, a slight asymmetry intended to credit NATO for its relatively greater investment in target acquisition, information processing, and associated technologies of "predation" in engagements.

Notice that equation [10], in making $\rho(t)$ depend on the force ratio makes it depend on reinforcements, which in turn provides one possible rational for withdrawal (to buy time for reinforcements), a topic discussed below.

The entire discussion thus far has concerned attrition stalemate only. Traditionally, however, warfare has concerned not just attrition, but also territory. When one speaks of a military "outcome," it is crucial to specify whether one defines outcomes in terms of attrition, territory, or some combination. In any case, the two are strictly distinct.

Combat Dynamics and Movement of Battle Fronts

In particular, two sides might fight to an attrition stalemate in a war lasting one week in which no movement of the battle front occurs. Or those same two forces might fight to the same attrition stalemate in a war lasting four years in which vast territories are sacrificed. The mere fact of attrition stalemate does *not* determine a combat's dynamics: the pace

---

11. See Epstein, "The 3:1 Rule," pp. 112–13, note 56.

of attrition, the duration of the war, or the amount of territory that is gained or lost. In the real world, these depend on behavioral and strategic factors, like the rates of attrition the belligerents are prepared to endure to achieve their aims, that may differ radically across *identical* force structures. Yet, in Lanchester theory, there is no way to represent such key factors; force structure (force levels and firing effectiveness) strictly determine dynamics.

In the original adaptive dynamic model (and of course this version), by contrast, there is a way to represent these factors. The key variables are the equilibrium attrition rates, α_{dT} and α_{aT}. The first, α_{dT}, is defined as the daily attrition rate the defender is willing to suffer in order to hold territory. The second, α_{aT}, is defined as the daily attrition rate the attacker is willing to suffer in order to take territory.

War, in addition to being a contest of target-servicing technologies, is a contrast of wills. So it is not outlandish to posit basic levels of pain (attrition) that each side comes willing to suffer to achieve its aims on the ground. If the defender's attrition rate is less than or equal to α_{dT}, he remains in place. If his attrition rate exceeds this "pain threshold," he withdraws, in an effort to restore attrition rates to tolerable levels, an effort that may fail dismally depending on the adaptations of the attacker. If the attacker's attrition rate exceeds tolerable levels, he cuts the pace at which he prosecutes the war; if his attrition rate is below the level he is prepared to suffer, he increases his prosecution rate.[12]

It is the interplay of the *two adaptive systems*, each searching for its equilibrium, that produces the observed dynamics, the actual movement that occurs and the actual attrition suffered by each side.[13]

---

12. If one thought of the battlefield as a "death market," then the market would "clear" when each side's actual attrition rate equals its equilibrium rate. Neither side demands—or will tolerate—a higher rate of attrition than the other is supplying at the moment. To pursue the economic analogy, α_{dT} and α_{aT} are the equilibrium "blood prices" in this market.

13. The model is adaptive in a second, and more subtle, respect. Suppose that on Monday, the defender's attrition rate exceeds his threshold, α_{dT}, by some amount, X. In response, the defender withdraws at a rate $W(t)$ on Tuesday. Suppose, however, that—because his own attrition rate on Monday was below his threshold, α_{aT}—the attacker increases his prosecution rate on Tuesday, and that as a result, the defender's attrition rate on Tuesday again exceeds his threshold by the same amount, X. Only a defender unable to learn would withdraw at $W(t)$ again, since that rate *already failed* to solve his problem. A more deeply adaptive defender would withdraw at a rate greater than $W(t)$; and, in the original (and, of course, the extended) adaptive dynamic model, he does. This makes sense. If walking slowly away from a swarm of attacking bees does not reduce the sting rate, we try jogging. If jogging doesn't reduce the sting rate, we run, and

While the ecological literature on density-dependent predator-prey dynamics is directly relevant to the modeling of mutual attrition, once defensive withdrawal (movement) and offensive prosecution enter the picture, the cybernetic literature, which concerns itself with error control through feedback and adaptation, becomes applicable.[14] Indeed, in its most basic form, withdrawal might be thought of as an attrition regulatory servomechanism. The pain thresholds, α_{dT} and α_{aT} play the roles of homeostatic targets, in other words.

One apparent misconception about these "pain" thresholds should be dispelled. I do not claim, nor does my model imply, that battlefield commanders are necessarily aware of the numerical values of α_{dT} and α_{aT}. I was led to equations A-4 and A-6 by the patently anomalous character of defensive withdrawal in Lanchester theory, and by the fact that the trading of space for time—a fundamental military tactic—is mathematically precluded by that theory.[15] The introduction of these thresholds struck me—and still strikes me—as the most direct mathematical way to *permit* defensive withdrawal to affect attrition, and thus to permit the trading of space for time. Their introduction also generates the fertile analogy between armies and a broad array of goal oriented, feedback-control (cybernetic) systems.

To posit an error-controlling feedback system, however, does not imply a conscious awareness (on the part of that system) of the *numerical* parameter settings against which the error is measured, as countless biological examples attest. For instance, before the advent of the thermometer, humans were not *aware* that their bodies adapted around a threshold, or

---

so on, until we're running as fast as we can (W_{max}). Of course, in the bee case, we actually are free to take something close to W_{max} as the first "trial retreat rate" because we are not concerned with territorial sacrifice. Analogous points apply to the attacker and his learning behavior in adjusting his prosecution rate ($\alpha_g(t)$).

14. On predator-prey modeling, interested readers might begin with Robert M. May, "Models for Two Interacting Populations" in Robert M. May, *Theoretical Ecology: Principles and Applications* (London: Blackwell Scientific Publications, 1981), pp. 78–104. See also May, *Stability and Complexity in Model Ecosystems* (Princeton University Press, 1974). For an advanced treatment, see Morris W. Hirsch and Stephen Smale, *Differential Equations, Dynamical Systems, and Linear Algebra* (Academic Press, 1974), pp. 258–73. Classic works on cybernetics are Norbert Wiener, *Cybernetics* (John Wiley, 1948); and W. Ross Ashby, *An Introduction to Cybernetics* (Methuen, rpt. 1984).

15. For this critique, see Epstein, *Calculus of Conventional War*, and Epstein, "Dynamic Analysis and the Conventional Balance in Europe," *International Security*, vol. 12 (Spring 1988), pp. 159–62.

"target," temperature of 98.6°F, by shivering (to increase heat) when below it and by sweating (to decrease heat) when above it. But, that threshold *existed* nonetheless. Similarly, the use of α_{dT} and α_{aT} does not imply a conscious awareness of their numerical values, or even of their existence as such.

These same parameters do *allow* one to reflect certain strategic decisions affecting the way in which given forces are applied. Specifically, with a given force, an attacker may prosecute the offensive at a ferocious pace, virtually unresponsive to losses. The British at the Somme in 1916 come to mind. Or, an attacker may operate *the same forces* at a more restrained pace. A high value of α_{aT} will produce the former type of attack; a low value of α_{aT} will generate the latter.

Similarly, the tactical defender may be more or less stalwart in holding his positions. Guerrilla defenders may withdraw—"disappear"—when even slight attrition is suffered. For such tactical defenders, the withdrawal-threshold attrition rate, α_{dT}, is very close to zero. At Verdun, by contrast, no attrition rate was high enough to dislodge the defenders from their entrenched positions. Petain's famous order, "Ils ne passeront pas!" effectively set α_{dT} equal to one.

These strategic and human realities are captured—however crudely— in the adaptive dynamic model. And they are captured by a mechanism that permits movement to affect attrition, a feedback that simply is not possible in any version of Lanchester's equations, in the attrition-FEBA expansion framework, or obviously in any static methods.[16]

Position Dependence

As noted above, I stated in *The Calculus of Conventional War* that "more elaborate extensions of the present model could allow ρ to vary in time or space or both (for example, as a function of the position of the front, to reflect a sequence of progressively improving, or worsening, defensive positions prepared in depth)."[17]

Such effects can easily be reflected by substituting $\hat{\rho}(t)$ for $\rho(t)$ in equation A-8 above, where

---

16. On relevant shortcomings of the large model, TACWAR, see Robert E. Kuenne, "The Computation and Use of Weapons' Effects in TACWAR: An Exposition and Motivation," draft paper, Institute for Defense Analyses, February 17, 1987, p. 45.

17. Epstein, *Calculus of Conventional War*, p. 22, note 44.

(A-13) $\hat{\rho}(t) = \beta(q)\rho(t)$, $\beta(q) > 0$.

Here $\beta(q)$ is a position-dependent step function that is greater than one if the defender's new position is better than his initial one, and less than one if it is worse. The idea is simple. Let q be the front's position at any time (obviously, the sum of $W(t)$s). And, for expository purposes, assume that the defense of some sector is prepared in depth; imagine three swaths lying between 0 and x_1 kilometers, x_1 and x_2 kilometers, and x_2 and x_3 kilometers. Then $\beta(q)$ is simply

$$\beta(q) = \begin{cases} 1 & \text{if } 0 \leq q \leq x_1 \\ a_1 & \text{if } x_1 < q \leq x_2 \\ a_2 & \text{if } x_2 < q \leq x_3 \end{cases}$$

If the terrain is worse for the defender between x_1 and x_2 than it is between x_2 and x_3, then $a_1 < a_2$, and so on. Clearly a_1 and a_2 are $\rho(t)$ multipliers; $a_1, a_2 > 0$. This extension is employed in assessing the impact of barriers in chapter 5.[18]

The entire theater (corps sector by corps sector, for example) would be "coded" in the above fashion in the most elaborate form, as is done in some larger models.

Analogous extensions are obviously possible for air, making its per sortie effectiveness (or its sortie rate) "adapt" to differences in the front's position,[19] and making it depend on target densities.[20]

---

18. This extension was first published in Epstein, "The 3:1 Rule," p. 112, note 55.

19. For instance, let $\hat{K}_d = \beta'_d(q)\hat{K}_d$ where $\beta'_d(q)$ is the defender's air analogue to $\beta(q)$ above: $\beta'_a(q)$ would be the attacker's. Obviously, air multipliers (the a_is) would in general be different from the ground multipliers. Notice that $\beta'_a(q)$ might rise while $\beta'_a(q)$ falls over some sectors (but not, obviously, if the defender's bases are overrun).

20. A natural approach would be to let

$$K(s) = K_{\max}[1 - e^{-cT(s)}], \text{ where}$$

$K(s)$ is the kill rate per sortie s, with $K_{\max}$ being the maximum feasible rate; $T(s)$ is the target density; the constant c "tunes" the function for search adeptness. Clearly, as target density grows, $K(s)$ approaches $K_{\max}$; as target density falls, $K(s)$ approaches zero. Attackers and defenders would, in general, have different constants, initial target densities, and so forth. For an interesting ecological parallel in the predator-prey literature, see Robert M. May, *Stability and Complexity in Model Ecosystems*, p. 82. With P and H representing predators and prey, respectively, May discusses a net predation rate of $kP[1 - e^{-cH}]$. He writes that "this net predation rate has the natural feature of being proportional to H for small prey populations, but saturating to a constant k per predator for large H" (p. 82).

Time-varying λs

A further generalization, under development, makes each side's capacity to concentrate ground fire in engagements—its λ, or net predation benefit from increased density—a function of time. It would appear that a principal objective in warfare is to maximize one's capacity to concentrate fire while degrading the adversary's. Passive means (such as cover, deception, dispersal, and maneuver) and active means (such as direct suppression of enemy command, control, communications, and intelligence, C^3I, systems) are employed to bring about asymmetries in the capacity to concentrate fire.

Purely Illustrative Assumptions

For illustrative purposes only, and simply to get a feel for the colorful trajectories possible under time-varying λs, it is useful to examine the case where each side's λ-value declines from some initial value by a fixed rate per day. That is,

$$\lambda_d(t) = \lambda_d(t - 1)(1 - c_d) = \lambda_d(1)(1 - c_d)^t, \text{ and}$$

$$\lambda_a(t) = \lambda_a(t - 1)(1 - c_a) = \lambda_a(1)(1 - c_a)^t,$$

where $\lambda_d(1)$ and $\lambda_a(1)$ are the defender's and attacker's (possibly different) initial fire concentration capacities and c_d and c_a are their constant degradation rates per day. (Here, $0 \leq c_d, c_a \leq 1$.)

Learning occurs in various processes. And it often occurs in war. The efficiency of predation may grow as experience—in search, analysis, and coordination—is gained. Such learning could produce growth in the capacity to concentrate fire, growth that would be reflected in rising $\lambda(t)s$. Negative c-values will produce that mathematical effect, and may be interpreted as growth, or learning, in the capacity to concentrate fire.[21] More directly, the same effect may result from increases in the volume of physical resources dedicated to the maximization of concentration capacity.

Of course, it may happen that one side's fire concentration capacity rises as the other's falls. Setting $c_d > 0$ and $c_a < 0$ will produce that interesting case.

---

21. Here, I assume a ceiling of $\lambda = 1$.

Evolving Concentration Capacity

Concentration capacity (the $\lambda(t)$s) need not decline, or grow, at constant rates, as assumed above. Rather, that capacity might depend on certain physical assets—target sensors, data processing, fire allocation, communication, and other C^3I resources—whose destruction or electronic nullification (and regeneration) may be quite irregular or jagged and may, in turn, produce a complicated pattern of changing concentration capacities (λs) over time. To convincingly model *the evolution of each side's capacity to concentrate*, therefore, a number of steps are necessary.

First, one must identify and enumerate the (targetable) entities—such as reconnaissance and damage assessment devices, headquarters, and C^3 transmitters—whose physical destruction will bring about a reduction in the capacity to concentrate fire. Second one must postulate how that capacity (that is, the $\lambda(t)$s) changes as these concentration-supporting targets are destroyed and replenished; what is the *shape* of the curve? Third, one must model the campaign(s) against those concentration-supporting target systems. Each step faces significant empirical challenges. I, certainly, do not claim to have solved this problem. But, it does strike me as an interesting, and potentially important, line of research.

NUMERICAL ASSUMPTIONS FOR THE PERFORMANCE PARAMETERS IN THE ADAPTIVE DYNAMIC MODEL

Use of the adaptive dynamic model requires one to specify numerical values for the model's performance parameters. All the numerical assumptions used here are listed in table B-1 and then discussed in turn.

TABLE B-1. **Performance Assumptions**

Variable[a]	Assumed value	Variable[a]	Assumed value
ρ	1.70	S_a	2.00
α_{aT}	0.06	K_d	0.50
α_{dT}	0.06	K_a	0.25
W_{max}	20.00	$W(1)$	0.00
α_{da}	0.05	L	99,314
α_{aa}	0.05	V	1200.00
S_d	3.00	$\alpha_g(1)$	0.03

a. All these variables are fully defined in appendix A.

The Casualty-Exchange Ratio, ρ

With the publication of the August 1986 CHASE study, and the publication in July and October 1988 of Robert McQuie's analyses of 189 battles from 1939 to 1982, a large body of historical battle data has come into our possession.[1] The data permit statistical research on historical

---

1. Robert L. Helmbold and Aqeel A. Khan, *Combat History Analysis Study Effort (CHASE): Progress Report for the Period August 1984–June 1985* (Requirements and Resources Directorate, U.S. Army Concepts Analysis Agency, August 1986); Robert McQuie, *Historical Characteristics of Combat for Wargames (Benchmarks)*, CAA-RP-87-2 (U.S. Army Concepts Analysis Agency, July 1988); and McQuie, *A Set of Templates for Evaluating Wargames (Benchmarks)* (U.S. Army Concepts Analysis Agency, October 1988).

casualty-exchange ratios in various units—personnel, tanks, artillery, and numerous weighted and unweighted combinations of these. Thorough statistical treatment—some of which should include multiple regression analyses—will take years, and will doubtless reveal much about exchange ratios and other factors in battle.

Two preliminary observations are nonetheless relevant. The historical exchange ratio data exhibit great variability; they are not tightly clustered around a central value. Second, the central value itself is lower than one might expect; it is certainly lower than I expected when I began this empirical research.

To begin, in what units should we examine ρ for purposes of constructing a base case? I use tank loss data. It is a better rough surrogate for the units used in the analysis (modified ADEs) than personnel. There may be better surrogates still. But, as a first approximation, tanks are defensible units.

Now, one could simply calculate the *arithmetic* mean of the historical ρ values: over all 132 battles in which tanks were lost, one would calculate

$$M = \frac{1}{132} \sum_{i=1}^{132} \left(\frac{\text{Attacker tanks lost}}{\text{Defender tanks lost}} \right)_i.$$

This is *not* the appropriate statistic to use. To see why, imagine two battles. In battle one, suppose ρ was 10 (ten attackers were killed per each defender killed). In battle two, suppose ρ was 1/10 (ten defenders were killed for each attacker killed)—just the reverse. The right "average" ρ—the one reflecting the obvious symmetry—would be 1.0. But the *arithmetic* mean would be

$$M = \frac{1}{2} \left(10 + \frac{1}{10} \right) = 5.05,$$

which is clearly inappropriate. The appropriate statistic is the geometric mean. For n values, ρ_i, the *geometric mean* is defined as

$$GM = \sqrt[n]{\rho_1 \times \rho_2 \times \cdots \times \rho_n}.$$

For the example just given,

$$GM = \sqrt{10 \times \frac{1}{10}} = 1, \text{ which is what we want.}$$

Now, it is easy to prove that

$$GM = e^{\frac{1}{n}\sum_{i=1}^{n} \ln \rho_i},$$

where e is Euler's number, the base of the natural logarithms (ln). This formula says that GM equals Euler's number raised to the arithmetic mean of the natural logs of the computed ρs.

This is an improvement over the arithmetic mean, but has a significant shortcoming; it assigns the same weight to a battle involving 5 tanks as to one involving 5,000. If one were gauging "public opinion," one would not accord the same weight to a sample of 60 from a tiny hamlet in Utah to a sample of 600,000 from Manhattan. Likewise, some weighting scheme seems reasonable here. Obviously, there are options. And, in a longer study, they could be examined. For our base case purposes, I will weight by the total number of tanks.

For the ith battle in the sample, let tot_i equal the total attacker tanks plus the total defender tanks. Then, the weighted geometric mean, WGM, we define as follows:

$$WGM = e^{\left(\dfrac{\sum\limits_{i=1}^{n} tot_i \ln(\rho_i)}{\sum\limits_{i=1}^{n} tot_i} \right)}.$$

This has the elegant property of reducing to the geometric mean (GM) if all weights are set at 1.0.

The computed value of this variable over all 132 relevant battles is a rather sobering 1.18.[2] This statistic does not bode well for any especially powerful empirically based theory of an inherent defensive advantage. While various factors such as training and command can push the value up or down from case to case, *merely being the defender* would appear to confer around a 20 percent edge. If one believes NATO should take no credit whatever for its disproportionate effort in those areas, then one's "best estimate" would be $\rho = 1.2$.

Now, superiority in these areas weighs at least as heavily on exchange ratios as does being the defender—the Israeli's and Germans' very high exchange ratios *as attackers* shows this clearly. These happen to be two areas in which NATO has invested disproportionately. According to the

---

2. Computed from the tank battle data given in McQuie, *Historical Characteristics of Combat*, pp. D1–D12. In subsequent discussion, this is rounded to 1.2.

Pentagon's declassified "NATO Center Region Military Balance Study," "NATO maintains about 3.5 C^{3}I/support personnel per weapon operator, which is double the Pact's 1.77 ratio."[3] Similarly, NATO as a whole trains much more and the training is, by and large, a good deal more realistic. Regarding the United States specifically, "U.S. combat troops receive from two-and-a-half to ten times as much combat weapons training per year, and serve three times as long."[4] Given the inherent variability of the data, and the uncertainty surrounding the combat returns to be assumed for these efforts of NATO's, a wide range of ρ-values are plausible, as suggested in the table below.

TABLE B-2. A Spectrum of ρ- Values

Weighted geometric mean	1.20	1.20	1.20	1.20	1.20
C^{3}I/support multiplier	1.00	1.10	1.20	1.25	1.30
Training multiplier	1.00	1.10	1.20	1.25	1.30
Overall ρ- value	1.20	1.50	1.70	1.88	2.00

It seems unduly pessimistic to insist that NATO take literally *no* credit for its relatively greater effort in these areas; 1.2 seems implausibly low. In my previous work on the balance, I have used 1.85, a value consistent with the assignment of 25 percent multipliers for C^{3}I and training.[5] This remains a plausible value, as are others. Simply to test the *change in* outcomes under different arms control regimes, *any one of these values might have been used in the base case.*

In all candor, the historical tank exchange ratio is lower than I had

3. Office of the Assistant Secretary of Defense for Program Analyses and Evaluation, "NATO Center Region Military Balance Study, 1978–1984" (July 1979), p. I-22–I-24. C^{3}I stands for command, control, communications and intelligence. Support includes maintenance and engineers, for example. Engineers figure in exchange ratios, according to the study, by providing "a greater capability to . . . prepare the terrain for defense" (p. I-22).

4. Carl Levin, *Beyond the Bean Count: Realistically Assessing the Conventional Military Balance in Europe*, 2d ed. (July 1988). p. 49.

5. Barry Posen has argued that a C^{3}I/support multiplier of up to 1.5 is plausible. See "Measuring the European Conventional Balance: Coping with Complexity in Threat Assessment," *International Security*, vol. 9, (Winter 1984–85), p. 69. Many of these C^{3}I and support personnel have to do with corps-level activities related more to dexterity at theater level than to lethality in engagements. Hence, at the level of ρ, I find a 1.5 multiplier to be overly optimistic. Since, in the attrition-FEBA expansion model used by Posen, the attackers killed (in the no-airpower case) is the product $D\rho$, where D is the defender's ADE score, it is clear that the 1.5 could be interpreted either as an ADE-boost or a ρ-boost: obviously, $(1.5D)\rho = D(1.5\rho)$. For analyses using 1.85, see Joshua M. Epstein, *The 1987 Defense Budget* (Brookings, 1986), p. 38; and Epstein, *The 1988 Defense Budget* (Brookings, 1987), p. 44.

expected it to be. Given that low WGM to which my empirical researches have led, I am today more comfortable assuming the somewhat lower 1.7 than I am assuming 1.85 (though, given the data's variability, there is no compelling statistical reason to prefer one over the other). This is one reason I use 1.7 as the base case and treat 1.85 in the sensitivity analyses (appendix D) rather than the other way around. Another reason is that at 1.85, there is no observable difference in the front's movement between CFE I and CFE II; it is thus a less revealing choice for a *comparative* study such as this, where the absolute outcome—and hence, the absolute inputs—are of secondary importance in any case.

Some may think it is "inconsistent" to entertain 1.7 once one has published 1.85—that it is "inconsistent" to change one's judgment as more historical data become available. I do not. Rigid adherence to a particular number despite the evidence is not "scientific consistency"; it is unscientific obstinacy. To be "consistent" in an intellectually respectable sense is to be consistently open and responsive to the evidence available. As that changes, numerical judgments change. Science is always provisional on the data available at the time. No physicist would be called "inconsistent" for refining his measurements when new data appear; he would be foolish not to. While our levels of precision are not comparable, it is nonetheless incumbent on social scientists to do likewise. It is in that spirit that I display the 1.7 runs. My claim for this number is weak. It is not proffered as a universal constant or a rule of thumb applicable to all wars. It is deemed merely to be plausible for this balance at this time.

Since considerable uncertainty must surround any such estimate, in the sensitivity analyses of appendix D, every scenario treated in the text is rerun at each of four other ρ-values, and additionally on the assumption that ρ is not a constant, but, rather, varies in the course of battle as a function of the changing force ratio.

Those who wish to begin the assessment with a different base case are welcome to do so.

The Threshold Attrition Rates α_{aT} and α_{dT}

When a body of *daily* movement and *daily* attrition rate data becomes available, these parameters may prove to be estimable by statistical means. For now, we must use a surrogate. The natural surrogate for the attrition levels attackers are *willing* to suffer on a sustained basis is the level they have suffered historically. In the entire 189-battle data base, the highest average daily tank attrition rate that was sustained for a week or more was 6 percent. And there is only one case, Pogorelove (8 days) where it is that high.

To be conservative, the WTO is assumed to be this ferocious. There is no reason to assume that NATO would be less willing to endure attrition to defend its territory than the WTO would be to conquer it. Hence, NATO is assigned the same value; $\alpha_{dT} = 0.06$.

W_{max}

Ninety-five percent of the opposed advance rates on the 189 battle data base fall below 21 kilometers a day.[6] Hence, as a maximum value for use in the model, $W_{max} = 20$ is reasonable.

Close Air Support Variables

The conservatism of my assumptions concerning armored fighting vehicles killed per close air sortie on each side (NATO $K_d = 0.5$; WTO $K_a = 0.25$) and attrition rates per sortie on each side (NATO α_{da} = WTO $\alpha_{aa} = 0.05$) are defended in Joshua M. Epstein, *Strategy and Force Planning: The Case of the Persian Gulf* (Brookings, 1987), p. 129, notes *q* and *w*. The same values are used and discussed in Barry R. Posen, "Measuring the European Conventional Balance: Coping with Complexity in Threat Assessment," *International Security*, vol. 9 (Winter 1984–85), p. 72. See also Posen, "Correspondence: Reassessing Net Assessment," *International Security*, vol. 13 (Spring 1989), pp. 148–49). In this base case, the WTO sortie rate ($S_a = 2$) is set lower than NATO's ($S_a = 3$) due to the WTO's smaller and relatively inefficient ground support and battlefield maintenance infrastructures.[7]

6. McQuie, *A Set of Templates*, No. 7b. In only three battles is this value exceeded.

7. These sortie rate values are twice as high as those assumed in my Persian Gulf analysis because the sortie generation infrastructure permanently in place in Europe is much larger than the infrastructure either would have in a Persian Gulf superpower war. No such change is imperative in the other variables since target densities (air-to-ground and ground-to-air) for division-level engagements proper should not vary between the two cases. On the relative inefficiency of the Soviet ground support environment, see Joshua M. Epstein, *Measuring Military Power: The Soviet Air Threat to Europe* (Princeton University Press, 1984), chaps. 2 and 3.

Remaining Constants

The front is assumed to be stationary before the war breaks out ($W(1)$ = 0). There are assumed to be 99,314 WUV points per ADE[8] and 1200 armored fighting vehicles per ADE.[9] The attacker's opening prosecution rate must, mathematically, be set at a value below α_{aT}; for the base case, it is set at $\alpha_{aT}/2 = 0.03$.

---

8. U.S. Army Concepts Analysis Agency, *Weapons Effectiveness Indices/Weighted Unit Values III (WEI/WUVIII)*, CAA-SR-79-12 (Bethesda, Md., November 1979), p. 13-11.

9. Posen, "Measuring the European Conventional Balance," p. 73.

MOBILIZATION SCHEDULES AND
WEAPONS SCORINGS

The essential aim of this book is to compare simulated combat outcomes (mutual attrition and movement of the front) for a fixed set of test, or control, scenarios over a range of conventional force reduction regimes. These reduction schemes are basically stated in terms of specific weapon categories—such as tanks, artillery, and armored vehicles.

As discussed in chapter 2, note 3, one can use a so-called heterogeneous model of combat in which the disparate weapon types affected by arms control are individually represented. Or one can use a simpler homogeneous model, such as the adaptive dynamic model (see appendix A), which takes as its input a single aggregate index such as an overall weighted unit value (WUV) or, equivalently, an armored division equivalent (ADE) score for the forces in question.

The latter, aggregate, method is adopted here. It requires that all weapons and weapon reductions be converted into the standardized scores employed in the dynamic model. This conversion is the function of appendix C.

Table C-1 estimates the current mobilization capacity of the WTO, scored in a modified and updated version of the U.S. Army's WUV units. The notes to table C-1 provide a complete explanation of these schedules, which are fed into the dynamic model as reinforcements in the various scenarios. The notes explain which units are counted, when they arrive, what weapons they possess, how their weapons are scored (in WUVs), and how equipment in storage, repair, and training units is treated.

This last issue is crucial in assessing arms reductions, since cuts can in part be made in these "extra" holdings rather than in the immediate holdings of combat units, a distinction affecting dynamic outcomes. The allocation of weapons—and of reductions—between active and extra weaponry is described in the notes to table C-1. Based on the accounting in table C-1, the overall weapon inventories—the bean counts—for the WTO are given in table C-2. This is, in fact, an extract from table C-1, which is crucial in translating the raw weapon cuts of arms control schemes into the engaged WUV scores of interest.

Tables C-3 and C-4 are the corresponding tables for NATO.

Table C-5 gives the details of the multisector feint attack.

Table C-6 recalculates the WTO's mobilization and deployment schedules in WUVs after the WTO's unilateral cuts.

Table C-7 (an extract from C-6) gives the corresponding weapon counts.

Tables C-8 and C-9 give the analogous WTO calculations assuming implementation of CFE I.

Tables C-10 and C-11 give NATO after CFE I.

Tables C-12 and C-13 (WTO) and C-14 and C-15 (NATO) provide the analogous computations for CFE II.

These tables are summarized in the following key.

Scenario	Units, TO&E, arrival, and WUVs	Derived weapon totals
WTO current case	C-1	C-2
NATO current case	C-3	C-4
WTO feint attack	C-5	. . .
WTO after unilateral cuts	C-6	C-7
WTO after CFE I	C-8	C-9
NATO after CFE I	C-10	C-11
WTO after CFE II	C-12	C-13
NATO after CFE II	C-14	C-15

Abbreviations and Acronyms Used in Appendix C

ACR	Armored cavalry regiment	Hun	Hungary
ADE	Armored division equivalent	IFV	Infantry fighting vehicle
		Inf	Infantry
A/I	Armored infantry	Len	Leningrad military district
AIR	Air assault	Lt Arm	Light armored
Airbn	Airborne	Mech	Mechanized
Anti-Arm	Antiarmor	Mech/Inf	Mechanized infantry
APC	Armored personnel carrier	Mosc	Moscow military district
		Mou	Mountain
ARM	Armored	MR	Motorized rifle
Art Bg	Artillery brigade	NG	National Guard
Art Rt	Artillery regiment	NGF	Northern group of forces
Arty	Artillery	Pol	Poland
ARV	Armored reconnaissance vehicle	POMCUS	Prepositioned overseas materiel configured to unit sets
ATTU	Atlantic-to-the-Urals		
Balt	Baltic military district	Reg	Regiment
Btlns	Battalions	Res	Reserve
Bul	Bulgaria	Rom	Romania
Byel	Byelorussian military district	SGF	Southern group of forces
		Sil	Silesian military district
Carp	Carpathian military district	Terr Army	Territorial army
		SH	Schleswig-Holstein
CAV	Cavalry	TK	Tank
CGF	Central group of forces	TO&E	Table of organization and equipment
CONUS	Continental United States		
CW	Category weight	Ural	Ural military district
Czech	Czechoslovakia	UKMF	United Kingdom Contingent, Allied Command Europe Mobile Force
DV	Division		
East	Eastern military district		
FAR	French rapid action force		
FRG	Federal Republic of Germany	Vol	Volga military district
		War	Warsaw military district
GDR	German Democratic Republic	WEI	Weapon effectiveness index
Group-Brig	Group brigade	WUV	Weighted unit value
GSFG	Group of Soviet Forces Germany		

TABLE C-1. WTO Units, Central Front Arrival Times, and WUV Scores, Current Balance

Time; State; Military District	Unit Title; Readiness Category	TANKS TO&E T-55/T-34	T-64	T-72	T-80	TANKS EFFECTIVENESS T-55/T-34	T-64	T-72	T-80	WEI	WUV (WEI CW 100)	ARTILLERY TO&E M-38 D-30 Others	MRL	152mm	M74	ARTILLERY EFFECTIVENESS M-38 D-30 Others	MRL	152mm	M74	WEI	WUV (WEI CW 92)
	M+1 to M+5																				
	USSR																				
GSFG	16 Tk Dv (1)			134	188	1.06	1.23	1.24	1.31	413	41,265		24	18	54	.77	.90	.89	.96	89	8,230
GSFG	21 MR Dv (1)			214	40	1.06	1.23	1.24	1.31	318	31,836	54	36	18	36	.77	.90	.89	.96	125	11,460
GSFG	94 MR Dv (1)			214	40	1.06	1.23	1.24	1.31	318	31,836	54	36	18	36	.77	.90	.89	.96	125	11,460
GSFG	207 MR Dv (1)			214	40	1.06	1.23	1.24	1.31	318	31,836	54	36	18	36	.77	.90	.89	.96	125	11,460
GSFG	Art Bg (1)					1.06	1.23	1.24	1.31				30	31	31	.77	.90	.89	.96	84	7,760
GSFG	Art Bg (1)					1.06	1.23	1.24	1.31				30	31	31	.77	.90	.89	.96	84	7,760
GSFG	Other Bts (1)					1.06	1.23	1.24	1.31							.77	.90	.89	.96		
GSFG	7 Tk Dv (1)			134	188	1.06	1.23	1.24	1.31	413	41,265		24	18	54	.77	.90	.89	.96	89	8,230
GSFG	10 Tk Dv (1)			134	188	1.06	1.23	1.24	1.31	413	41,265		24	18	54	.77	.90	.89	.96	89	8,230
GSFG	72 Tk Dv (1)			134	188	1.06	1.23	1.24	1.31	413	41,265		24	18	54	.77	.90	.89	.96	89	8,230
GSFG	47 Tk Dv (1)			134	188	1.06	1.23	1.24	1.31	413	41,265		24	18	54	.77	.90	.89	.96	89	8,230
GSFG	304 Art Dv (1)					1.06	1.23	1.24	1.31			20				.77	.90	.89	.96	15	1,417
GSFG	Other Bts (1)					1.06	1.23	1.24	1.31							.77	.90	.89	.96		
GSFG	25 Tk Dv (1)			134	188	1.06	1.23	1.24	1.31	413	41,265		24	18	54	.77	.90	.89	.96	89	8,230
GSFG	32 Tk Dv (1)			134	188	1.06	1.23	1.24	1.31	413	41,265		24	18	54	.77	.90	.89	.96	89	8,230
GSFG	90 Tk Dv (1)			134	188	1.06	1.23	1.24	1.31	413	41,265		24	18	54	.77	.90	.89	.96	89	8,230
GSFG	35 MR Dv (1)			214	40	1.06	1.23	1.24	1.31	318	31,836	54	36	18	36	.77	.90	.89	.96	125	11,460
GSFG	71 Art Bg (1)					1.06	1.23	1.24	1.31			20				.77	.90	.89	.96	15	1,417
GSFG	Other Bts (1)					1.06	1.23	1.24	1.31							.77	.90	.89	.96		
GSFG	79 Tk Dv (1)			134	188	1.06	1.23	1.24	1.31	413	41,265		24	18	54	.77	.90	.89	.96	89	8,230
GSFG	27 MR Dv (1)			214	40	1.06	1.23	1.24	1.31	318	31,836	54	36	18	36	.77	.90	.89	.96	125	11,460
GSFG	39 MR Dv (1)			214	40	1.06	1.23	1.24	1.31	318	31,836	54	36	18	36	.77	.90	.89	.96	125	11,460
GSFG	57 MR Dv (1)			214	40	1.06	1.23	1.24	1.31	318	31,836	54	36	18	36	.77	.90	.89	.96	125	11,460
GSFG	43 Art Bg (1)					1.06	1.23	1.24	1.31			20				.77	.90	.89	.96	15	1,417
GSFG	Other Bts (1)					1.06	1.23	1.24	1.31							.77	.90	.89	.96		
GSFG	9 Tk Dv (1)			134	188	1.06	1.23	1.24	1.31	413	41,265		24	18	54	.77	.90	.89	.96	89	8,230
GSFG	11 Tk Dv (1)			134	188	1.06	1.23	1.24	1.31	413	41,265		24	18	54	.77	.90	.89	.96	89	8,230
GSFG	20 MR Dv (1)			214	40	1.06	1.23	1.24	1.31	318	31,836	54	36	18	36	.77	.90	.89	.96	125	11,460
GSFG	43 Art Dv (1)					1.06	1.23	1.24	1.31				144	144	144	.77	.90	.89	.96	396	36,432
GSFG	35 Assault(1)					1.06	1.23	1.24	1.31			10				.77	.90	.89	.96	8	708
GSFG	Spetsnaz (1)			45	10	1.06	1.23	1.24	1.31	69	6,903					.77	.90	.89	.96		
GSFG	MR Bg (1)					1.06	1.23	1.24	1.31			11				.77	.90	.89	.96	8	765
GSFG	Other Bts (1)					1.06	1.23	1.24	1.31							.77	.90	.89	.96		
CGF	15 Tk Dv (1)			134	188	1.06	1.23	1.24	1.31	413	41,265		24	18	54	.77	.90	.89	.96	89	8,230
CGF	18 MR Dv (1)			214	40	1.06	1.23	1.24	1.31	318	31,836	54	36	18	36	.77	.90	.89	.96	125	11,460
CGF	48 MR Dv (1)			214	40	1.06	1.23	1.24	1.31	318	31,836	54	36	18	36	.77	.90	.89	.96	125	11,460

CGF	Art Bg (1)				1.06	1.23	1.24	1.31				30	31	31	.77	.90	.89	.96	84	7,760
CGF	Other Bts (1)				1.06	1.23	1.24	1.31							.77	.90	.89	.96		
						1.23	1.24	1.31												
M+5																				
USSR																				
NGF	20 Tk Dv (1)		134	188	1.06	1.23	1.24	1.31	413	41,265		24	18	54	.77	.90	.89	.96	89	8,230
NGF	6 MR Dv (1)		214	40	1.06	1.23	1.24	1.31	318	31,836	54	36	18	36	.77	.90	.89	.96	125	11,460
GDR																				
III	7 Tk Dv (1)	232	94		.98	1.12	1.13	1.19	334	33,358	66	18	6		.76	.89	.96	.96	72	6,657
III	11 MR Dv (1)	218			.98	1.12	1.13	1.19	214	21,364	54	18		18	.77	.89	.96	.96	75	6,889
III	4 MR Dv (1)	218			.98	1.12	1.13	1.19	214	21,364	54	18		18	.77	.89	.96	.96	75	6,889
III	Art Rt (1)				1.06	1.12	1.13	1.19				14	14	14	.77	.90	.89	.96	39	3,575
III	9 Tk Dv (1)	232	94		.98	1.12	1.13	1.19	334	33,358	66	18	6		.76	.89	.96	.96	72	6,657
III	8 MR Dv (1)	218			.98	1.12	1.13	1.19	214	21,364	54	18		18	.77	.89	.96	.96	75	6,889
III	1 MR Dv (1)	218			.98	1.12	1.13	1.19	214	21,364	54	18		18	.77	.89	.96	.96	75	6,889
III	Art Rt (1)				1.06	1.12	1.13	1.19				14	14	14	.77	.90	.89	.96	39	3,575
Czech																				
West	1 Tk Dv (1)	287	40		.98	1.12	1.12	1.19	326	32,606	18	24	18	18	.77	.89	.71	.96	65	6,006
West	2 MR Dv (1)	215			.98	1.12	1.13	1.19	211	21,070	36	36	18	18	.77	.89	.71	.96	90	8,263
West	22 Assault(1)				1.06	1.12	1.13	1.19							.77	.90	.89	.96		
West	Other Bts (1)				1.06	1.12	1.13	1.19							.77	.90	.89	.96		
Pol																				
War	6 Assault(1)				1.06	1.12	1.13	1.19			30				.77	.90	.89	.96	23	2,125
M+10																				
Pol																				
Pom	16 Tk Dv (1)	162	121		.98	1.12	1.13	1.19	295	29,549	36	12		6	.77	.90	.71	.96	44	4,074
Pom	20 Tk Dv (1)	162	121		.98	1.12	1.13	1.19	295	29,549	36	12		6	.77	.90	.71	.96	44	4,074
Pom	12 MR Dv (1)	202	40		.98	1.12	1.13	1.19	243	24,316	36	12	12	18	.77	.90	.71	.96	64	5,917
Pom	8 MR Dv (1)	202	40		.98	1.12	1.13	1.19	243	24,316	36	12	12	18	.77	.90	.71	.96	64	5,917
Pom	Art Rt (1)				1.06	1.12	1.13	1.19				14	14	14	.77	.90	.89	.96	39	3,575
Sil	5 Tk Dv (1)	162	121		.98	1.12	1.13	1.19	295	29,549	36	12		6	.77	.90	.71	.96	44	4,074
Sil	10 Tk Dv (1)	162	121		.98	1.12	1.13	1.19	295	29,549	36	12		6	.77	.90	.71	.96	44	4,074
Sil	11 Tk Dv (1)	162	121		.98	1.12	1.13	1.19	295	29,549	36	12		6	.77	.90	.71	.96	44	4,074
Sil	Art Rt (1)				1.06	1.12	1.13	1.19				14	14	14	.77	.90	.89	.96	39	3,575
War	Art Rt (1)				1.06	1.12	1.13	1.19				14	14	14	.77	.90	.89	.96	39	3,575
USSR																				
Byel	120 MR Dv (1)		214	40	1.06	1.12	1.13	1.19	289	28,942	54	36	18	36	.77	.90	.89	.96	125	11,460
Byel	8 Tk Dv (1)		134	188	1.06	1.12	1.13	1.19	375	37,514		24	18	54	.77	.90	.89	.96	89	8,230
Carp	15 MR Dv (1)		214	40	1.06	1.12	1.13	1.19	289	28,942	54	36	18	36	.77	.90	.89	.96	125	11,460
Carp	23 Tk Dv (1)		134	188	1.06	1.12	1.13	1.19	375	37,514		24	18	54	.77	.90	.89	.96	89	8,230
Balt	7 Airbn (1)				1.06	1.12	1.13	1.19			30				.77	.90	.89	.96	23	2,125
SGF	93 MR Dv (1)		214	40	1.06	1.12	1.13	1.19	289	28,942	54	36	18	36	.77	.90	.89	.96	125	11,460
SGF	13 MR Dv (1)		214	40	1.06	1.12	1.13	1.19	289	28,942	54	36	18	36	.77	.90	.89	.96	125	11,460
SGF	2 Tk Dv (1)		134	188	1.06	1.12	1.13	1.19	375	37,514		24	18	54	.77	.90	.89	.96	89	8,230
SGF	13 Tk Dv (1)		134	188	1.06	1.12	1.13	1.19	375	37,514		24	18	54	.77	.90	.89	.96	89	8,230

TABLE C-1. *continued*

Time; State; Military District	Unit Title; Readiness Category	TANKS TO&E				TANKS EFFECTIVENESS				WEI	WUV: (WEI-CW 100)	ARTILLERY TO&E				ARTILLERY EFFECTIVENESS				WEI	WUV: (WEI-CW 92)
		T-55/T-34	T-64	T-72	T-80	T-55/T-34	T-64	T-72	T-80			M-38 D-30 Others	MRL	152mm	M74	M-38 D-30 Others	MRL	152mm	M74		
M+15 **USSR**																					
Mosc	MR Dv (1)			214	40	1.06	1.12	1.13	1.19	289	28,942	54	36	18	36	.77	.90	.89	.96	125	11,460
Mosc	2 MR Dv (1)			214	40	1.06	1.12	1.13	1.19	289	28,942	54	36	18	36	.77	.90	.89	.96	125	11,460
Mosc	106 Airbn (1)					1.06	1.12	1.13	1.19			30				.77	.90	.89	.96	23	2,125
Mosc	Art Dv (1)					1.06	1.12	1.13	1.19				144	144	144	.77	.90	.89	.96	396	36,432
M+20 **USSR**																					
Byel	MR Dv (2)	40	40	174		1.06	1.12	1.13	1.19	284	28,382	72	36	18	18	.77	.90	.89	.96	121	11,145
Carp	70 MR Dv (2)	40	40	174		1.06	1.12	1.13	1.19	284	28,382	72	36	18	18	.77	.90	.89	.96	121	11,145
Balt	1 MR Dv (2)	40	40	174		1.06	1.12	1.13	1.19	284	28,382	72	36	18	18	.77	.90	.89	.96	121	11,145
M+25 **USSR**																					
Byel	8 Tk Dv (2)		134	188		1.06	1.12	1.13	1.19	363	36,252	18	24	18	36	.77	.90	.89	.96	86	7,916
Carp	128 MR Dv (2)	40	40	174		1.06	1.12	1.13	1.19	284	28,382	72	36	18	18	.77	.90	.89	.96	121	11,145
Balt	1 Tk Dv (2)		134	188		1.06	1.12	1.13	1.19	363	36,252	18	24	18	36	.77	.90	.89	.96	86	7,916
M+30 **USSR**																					
Byel	29 Tk Dv (2)		134	188		1.06	1.12	1.13	1.19	363	36,252	18	24	18	36	.77	.90	.89	.96	86	7,916
Byel	3 Tk Dv (2)		134	188		1.06	1.12	1.13	1.19	363	36,252	18	24	18	36	.77	.90	.89	.96	86	7,916
Byel	27 Tk Dv (2)		134	188		1.06	1.12	1.13	1.19	363	36,252	18	24	18	36	.77	.90	.89	.96	86	7,916
Carp	61 MR Dv (2)	40	40	174		1.06	1.12	1.13	1.19	284	28,382	72	36	18	18	.77	.90	.89	.96	121	11,145
Carp	24 MR Dv (2)	40	40	174		1.06	1.12	1.13	1.19	284	28,382	72	36	18	18	.77	.90	.89	.96	121	11,145
Carp	13 Tk Dv (2)		134	188		1.06	1.12	1.13	1.19	363	36,252	18	24	18	36	.77	.90	.89	.96	86	7,916
Balt	40 Tk Dv (2)		134	188		1.06	1.12	1.13	1.19	363	36,252	18	24	18	36	.77	.90	.89	.96	86	7,916
Balt	24 Tk Dv (2)		134	188		1.06	1.12	1.13	1.19	363	36,252	18	24	18	36	.77	.90	.89	.96	86	7,916
Pol																					
Sil	4 MR Dv (2)	204				.98	1.12	1.13	1.19	200	19,992	66	12			.77	.90	.89	.96	62	5,669
Pom	7 Assualt (2)					1.06	1.12	1.13	1.19							.77	.90	.89	.96		

M+35																			
USSR																			
Byel	47 Tk Dv (2)	134	188	1.06	1.12	1.13	1.19	363	36,252	18	24	18	36	.77	90	.89	.96	86	7,916
Byel	34 Tk Dv (2)	134	188	1.06	1.12	1.13	1.19	363	36,252	18	24	18	36	.77	90	.89	.96	86	7,916
Byel	Art A Dv (2)			1.06	1.12	1.13	1.19				144	144	144	.77	90	.89	.96	396	36,432
Byel	Art B Dv (2)			1.06	1.12	1.13	1.19				30	31	31	.77	90	.89	.96	84	7,760
Carp	117 Tk Dv (2)	134	188	1.06	1.12	1.13	1.19	363	36,252	18	24	18	36	.77	90	.89	.96	86	7,916
Carp	Art A Dv (2)			1.06	1.12	1.13	1.19				144	144	144	.77	90	.89	.96	396	36,432
Carp	Art B Dv (2)			1.06	1.12	1.13	1.19				30	31	31	.77	90	.89	.96	84	7,760
Carp	Art A Dv (2)			1.06	1.12	1.13	1.19				30	31	31	.77	90	.89	.96	84	7,760
Balt	Art A Dv (2)			1.06	1.12	1.13	1.19				144	144	144	.77	90	.89	.96	396	36,432
Balt	Art A Dv (2)			1.06	1.12	1.13	1.19				144	144	144	.77	90	.89	.96	396	36,432
M+40																			
Czech																			
West	4 Tk Dv (2)	327		.93	1.12	1.12	1.19	302	30,248	18	24	18	18	.71	82	.89	.96	60	5,561
West	9 Tk Dv (2)	327		.93	1.12	1.12	1.19	302	30,248	18	24	18	18	.71	82	.89	.96	60	5,561
West	3 MR Dv (2)	215		.98	1.12	1.12	1.19	211	21,070	54	30	12		.77	89	.77	.96	78	7,132
USSR																			
Mosc	15 Tk Dv (2)	134	188	1.06	1.12	1.13	1.19	363	36,252	18	24	18	36	.77	90	.89	.96	86	7,916
Mosc	4 Tk Dv (2)	134	188	1.06	1.12	1.13	1.19	363	36,252	18	24	18	36	.77	90	.89	.96	86	7,916
M+45																			
USSR																			
Balt	3 MR Dv (3)	254		.98	1.12	1.13	1.19	249	24,892	90	36	18		.70	80	.80	.96	106	9,770
M+50																			
USSR																			
Len	64 MR Dv (3)	254		.98	1.12	1.13	1.19	249	24,892	90	36	18		.70	80	.80	.96	106	9,770

TABLE C-1. continued

Time; State; Military District	Unit Title; Readiness Category	TANKS TO&E				TANKS EFFECTIVENESS						ARTILLERY TO&E				ARTILLERY EFFECTIVENESS					
		T-55/T-34	T-64	T-72	T-80	T-55/T-34	T-64	T-72	T-80	WEI	WUV: (WEI-CW 100)	M-38 D-30 Others	MRL	152mm	M74	M-38 D-30 Others	MRL	152mm	M74	WEI	WUV: (WEI-CW 92)
M+55 USSR																					
Carp	66 MR Dv (3)	254				.98	1.12	1.13	1.19	249	24,892	90	36	18		.70	.80	.80	.96	106	9,770
Len	111 MR Dv (3)	254				.98	1.12	1.13	1.19	249	24,892	90	36	18		.70	.80	.80	.96	106	9,770
M+60 USSR																					
Byel	50 MR Dv (3)	254				.98	1.12	1.13	1.19	249	24,892	90	36	18		.70	.80	.80	.96	106	9,770
Len	77 MR Dv (3)	254				.98	1.12	1.13	1.19	249	24,892	90	36	18		.70	.80	.80	.96	106	9,770
Balt	88 MR Dv (3)	254				.98	1.12	1.13	1.19	249	24,892	90	36	18		.70	.80	.80	.96	106	9,770
Czech East	13 Tk Dv (3)	327				.93	1.12	1.12	1.19	302	30,248	18	24	18	18	.71	.82	.66	.89	60	5,561
East	14 Tk Dv (3)	327				.93	1.12	1.12	1.19	302	30,248	18	24	18	18	.71	.82	.66	.89	60	5,561
M+65 USSR																					
Carp	17 MR Dv (3)	254				.98	1.12	1.13	1.19	249	24,892	90	36	18		.70	.80	.80	.96	106	9,770
Balt	26 MR Dv (3)	254				.98	1.12	1.13	1.19	249	24,892	90	36	18		.70	.80	.80	.96	106	9,770
Len	69 MR Dv (3)	254				.98	1.12	1.13	1.19	249	24,892	90	36	18		.70	.80	.80	.96	106	9,770
M+70 USSR																					
Carp	97 MR Dv (3)	254				.98	1.12	1.13	1.19	249	24,892	90	36	18		.70	.80	.80	.96	106	9,770
Balt	44 MR Dv (3)	254				.98	1.12	1.13	1.19	249	24,892	90	36	18		.70	.80	.80	.96	106	9,770
Len	45 MR Dv (3)	254				.98	1.12	1.13	1.19	249	24,892	90	36	18		.70	.80	.80	.96	106	9,770
M+75 USSR																					
Len	45 MR Dv (3)	254				.98	1.12	1.13	1.19	249	24,892	90	36	18		.70	.80	.80	.96	106	9,770
Balt	107 MR Dv (3)	254				.98	1.12	1.13	1.19	249	24,892	90	36	18		.70	.80	.80	.96	106	9,770

M+80																	
USSR																	
Mos 13 MR Dv (3)	254	.98	1.12	1.13	1.19	249	24,892	90	36	18		.70	.80	.80	.96	106	9,770
Vol 43 MR Dv (3)	254	.98	1.12	1.13	1.19	249	24,892	90	36	18		.70	.80	.80	.96	106	9,770
Vol Art A Dv (3)		1.06	1.12	1.13	1.19				144	144	144	.77	.90	.89	.96	396	36,432
Czech																	
East 15 MR Dv (3)	215	.98	1.12	1.13	1.19	211	21,070	54	30	12		.77	.89	.77	.96	78	7,132
Pol																	
War 1 MR Dv (3)	174	.91	1.12	1.13	1.19	158	15,834	54	12	12		.77	.89	.71	.96	61	5,592
M+85																	
USSR																	
Mos 32 MR Dv (3)	254	.98	1.12	1.13	1.19	249	24,892	90	36	18		.70	.80	.80	.96	106	9,770
Vol 96 MR Dv (3)	254	.98	1.12	1.13	1.19	249	24,892	90	36	18		.70	.80	.80	.96	106	9,770
Ural 77 MR Dv (3)	254	.98	1.12	1.13	1.19	249	24,892	90	36	18		.70	.80	.80	.96	106	9,770
Czech																	
East 19 MR Dv (3)	215	.98	1.12	1.13	1.19	211	21,070	54	30	12		.77	.89	.77	.96	78	7,132
Pol																	
War 3 MR Dv (3)	174	.91	1.12	1.13	1.19	158	15,834	54	12	12		.77	.89	.71	.96	61	5,592
M+90																	
USSR																	
Vol 21 MR Dv (3)	254	.98	1.12	1.13	1.19	249	24,892	90	36	18		.70	.80	.80	.96	106	9,770
Ural MR Dv (3)	254	.98	1.12	1.13	1.19	249	24,892	90	36	18		.70	.80	.80	.96	106	9,770
Czech																	
East 20 MR Dv (3)	215	.98	1.12	1.13	1.19	211	21,070	54	30	12		.77	.89	.77	.96	78	7,132
Pol																	
War 9 MR Dv (3)	174	.91	1.12	1.13	1.19	158	15,834	54	12	12		.77	.89	.71	.96	61	5,592

TABLE C-1. continued

Time; State; Military District	Unit Title; Readiness Category	TANKS TO&E T-55/T-34	T-64	T-72	T-80	TANKS EFF. T-55/T-34	T-64	T-72	T-80	WEI	WUV (WEI-CW 100)	ARTILLERY TO&E M-38 D-30 Others	MRL	152mm	M74	ARTILLERY EFF. M-38 D-30 Others	MRL	152mm	M74	WEI	WUV (WEI-CW 92)
	ATTU Units Not Allocated to Central Front																				
	USSR																				
NW	MR Dv (1)	40	40	174		1.06	1.12	1.13	1.19	284	28,382	72	36	18	18	.77	.90	.89	.96	121	11,145
NW	MR Dv (1)	40	40	174		1.06	1.12	1.13	1.19	284	28,382	72	36	18	18	.77	.90	.89	.96	121	11,145
NW	MR Dv (1)	40	40	174		1.06	1.12	1.13	1.19	284	28,382	72	36	18	18	.77	.90	.89	.96	121	11,145
NW	MR Dv (1)	40	40	174		1.06	1.12	1.13	1.19	284	28,382	72	36	18	18	.77	.90	.89	.96	121	11,145
NW	MR Dv (1)	40	40	174		1.06	1.12	1.13	1.19	284	28,382	72	36	18	18	.77	.90	.89	.96	121	11,145
NW	MR Dv (1)	40	40	174		1.06	1.12	1.13	1.19	284	28,382	72	36	18	18	.77	.90	.89	.96	121	11,145
NW	MR Dv (1)	40	40	174		1.06	1.12	1.13	1.19	284	28,382	72	36	18	18	.77	.90	.89	.96	121	11,145
NW	MR Dv (1)	40	40	174		1.06	1.12	1.13	1.19	284	28,382	72	36	18	18	.77	.90	.89	.96	121	11,145
NW	MR Dv (1)	40	40	174		1.06	1.12	1.13	1.19	284	28,382	72	36	18	18	.77	.90	.89	.96	121	11,145
SW	MR Dv (1)	40	40	174		1.06	1.12	1.13	1.19	284	28,382	72	36	18	18	.77	.90	.89	.96	121	11,145
SW	Art A Dv (1)												144	144	144		.90	.89	.96	396	36,432
SW	MR Dv (1)	40	40	174		1.06	1.12	1.13	1.19	284	28,382	72	36	18	18	.77	.90	.89	.96	121	11,145
SW	MR Dv (1)	40	40	174		1.06	1.12	1.13	1.19	284	28,382	72	36	18	18	.77	.90	.89	.96	121	11,145
SW	MR Dv (1)	40	40	174		1.06	1.12	1.13	1.19	284	28,382	72	36	18	18	.77	.90	.89	.96	121	11,145
SW	MR Dv (1)	40	40	174		1.06	1.12	1.13	1.19	284	28,382	72	36	18	18	.77	.90	.89	.96	121	11,145
SW	MR Dv (1)	40	40	174		1.06	1.12	1.13	1.19	284	28,382	72	36	18	18	.77	.90	.89	.96	121	11,145
SW	MR Dv (1)	40	40	174		1.06	1.12	1.13	1.19	284	28,382	72	36	18	18	.77	.90	.89	.96	121	11,145
SW	MR Dv (1)	40	40	174		1.06	1.12	1.13	1.19	284	28,382	72	36	18	18	.77	.90	.89	.96	121	11,145
SW	MR Dv (1)	40	40	174		1.06	1.12	1.13	1.19	284	28,382	72	36	18	18	.77	.90	.89	.96	121	11,145
SW	MR Dv (1)	40	40	174		1.06	1.12	1.13	1.19	284	28,382	72	36	18	18	.77	.90	.89	.96	121	11,145
SW	MR Dv (1)	40	40	174		1.06	1.12	1.13	1.19	284	28,382	72	36	18	18	.77	.90	.89	.96	121	11,145
SW	MR Dv (1)	40	40	174		1.06	1.12	1.13	1.19	284	28,382	72	36	18	18	.77	.90	.89	.96	121	11,145
SW	MR Dv (1)	40	40	174		1.06	1.12	1.13	1.19	284	28,382	72	36	18	18	.77	.90	.89	.96	121	11,145
SW	MR Dv (1)	40	40	174		1.06	1.12	1.13	1.19	284	28,382	72	36	18	18	.77	.90	.89	.96	121	11,145
SW	MR Dv (1)	40	40	174		1.06	1.12	1.13	1.19	284	28,382	72	36	18	18	.77	.90	.89	.96	121	11,145
SW	MR Dv (1)	40	40	174		1.06	1.12	1.13	1.19	284	28,382	72	36	18	18	.77	.90	.89	.96	121	11,145
SW	MR Dv (1)	40	40	174		1.06	1.12	1.13	1.19	284	28,382	72	36	18	18	.77	.90	.89	.96	121	11,145
SW	MR Dv (1)	40	40	174		1.06	1.12	1.13	1.19	284	28,382	72	36	18	18	.77	.90	.89	.96	121	11,145
SW	Tk Dv (1)		134	188		1.06	1.12	1.13	1.19	363	36,252	18	24	18	36	.77	.90	.89	.96	86	7,916
SW	Tk Dv (1)		134	188		1.06	1.12	1.13	1.19	363	36,252	18	24	18	36	.77	.90	.89	.96	86	7,916
SW	Tk Dv (1)		134	188		1.06	1.12	1.13	1.19	363	36,252	18	24	18	36	.77	.90	.89	.96	86	7,916
SW	Tk Dv (1)		134	188		1.06	1.12	1.13	1.19	363	36,252	18	24	18	36	.77	.90	.89	.96	86	7,916
SW	Tk Dv (1)		134	188		1.06	1.12	1.13	1.19	363	36,252	18	24	18	36	.77	.90	.89	.96	86	7,916

SW	Tk Dv (1)		134	188	1.06	1.12	1.13	1.19	363	36,252	18	24	18	36		.90	.89	.96	86	7,916
SW	Tk Dv (1)		134	188	1.06	1.12	1.13	1.19	363	36,252	18	24	18	36		.90	.89	.96	86	7,916
SW	Tk Dv (1)		134	188	1.06	1.12	1.13	1.19	363	36,252	18	24	18	36		.90	.89	.96	86	7,916
SW	Tk Dv (1)		134	188	1.06	1.12	1.13	1.19	363	36,252	18	24	18	36		.90	.89	.96	86	7,916
SW	Tk Dv (1)		134	188	1.06	1.12	1.13	1.19	363	36,252	18	24	18	36		.90	.89	.96	86	7,916
SW	Art A Dv (1)				1.06				363	36,252		144	144	144					396	36,432
Hun	MR Dv (1)	215			.98	1.12	1.13	1.19	211	21,070	54	30	12		.77	.89	.77	.96	78	7,132
Hun	MR Dv (1)	215			.98	1.12	1.13	1.19	211	21,070	54	30	12		.77	.89	.77	.96	78	7,132
Hun	MR Dv (1)	215			.98	1.12	1.13	1.19	211	21,070	54	30	12		.77	.89	.77	.96	78	7,132
Hun	MR Dv (1)	215			.98	1.12	1.13	1.19	211	21,070	54	30	12		.77	.89	.77	.96	78	7,132
Hun	MR Dv (1)	215			.98	1.12	1.13	1.19	211	21,070	54	30	12		.77	.89	.77	.96	78	7,132
Hun	MR Dv (1)	215			.98	1.12	1.13	1.19	211	21,070	54	30	12		.77	.89	.77	.96	78	7,132
Hun	MR Dv (1)	215			.98	1.12	1.13	1.19	211	21,070	54	30	12		.77	.89	.77	.96	78	7,132
Rom	MR Dv (1)	215			.98	1.12	1.13	1.19	211	21,070	54	30	12		.77	.89	.77	.96	78	7,132
Rom	MR Dv (1)	215			.98	1.12	1.13	1.19	211	21,070	54	30	12		.77	.89	.77	.96	78	7,132
Rom	MR Dv (1)	215			.98	1.12	1.13	1.19	211	21,070	54	30	12		.77	.89	.77	.96	78	7,132
Rom	MR Dv (1)	215			.98	1.12	1.13	1.19	211	21,070	54	30	12		.77	.89	.77	.96	78	7,132
Rom	MR Dv (1)	215			.98	1.12	1.13	1.19	211	21,070	54	30	12		.77	.89	.77	.96	78	7,132
Rom	MR Dv (1)	215			.98	1.12	1.13	1.19	211	21,070	54	30	12		.77	.89	.77	.96	78	7,132
Rom	MR Dv (1)	215			.98	1.12	1.12	1.19	211	21,070	54	30	12		.77	.89	.77	.96	78	7,132
Rom	MR Dv (1)	215			.98	1.12	1.12	1.19	211	21,070	54	30	12		.77	.89	.77	.96	78	7,132
Rom	MR Dv (1)	215			.98	1.12	1.12	1.19	211	21,070	54	30	12		.77	.89	.77	.96	78	7,132
Rom	MR Dv (1)	215			.98	1.12	1.12	1.19	211	21,070	54	30	12		.77	.89	.77	.96	78	7,132
Rom	MR Dv (1)	215			.98	1.12	1.13	1.19	211	21,070	54	30	12		.77	.89	.77	.96	78	7,132
Bul	MR Dv (1)	327			.93	1.12	1.13	1.19	302	30,248	18	24	18	18		.82	.66	.89	60	5,561
Bul	MR Dv (1)	327			.93	1.12	1.13	1.19	302	30,248	18	24	18	18		.82	.66	.89	60	5,561
Bul	MR Dv (1)	327			.93	1.12	1.13	1.19	302	30,248	18	24	18	18		.82	.66	.89	60	5,561
Bul	MR Dv (1)	327			.93	1.12	1.13	1.19	302	30,248	18	24	18	18		.82	.66	.89	60	5,561
Bul	MR Dv (1)	327			.93	1.12	1.13	1.19	302	30,248	18	24	18	18		.82	.66	.89	60	5,561
S	MR Dv (1)	40	40	174	1.06	1.12	1.13	1.19	284	28,382	72	36	18	18	.77	.90	.89	.96	121	11,145
S	MR Dv (1)	40	40	174	1.06	1.12	1.13	1.19	284	28,382	72	36	18	18	.77	.90	.89	.96	121	11,145
S	MR Dv (1)	40	40	174	1.06	1.12	1.13	1.19	284	28,382	72	36	18	18	.77	.90	.89	.96	121	11,145
S	MR Dv (1)	40	40	174	1.06	1.12	1.13	1.19	284	28,382	72	36	18	18	.77	.90	.89	.96	121	11,145
S	MR Dv (1)	40	40	174	1.06	1.12	1.13	1.19	284	28,382	72	36	18	18	.77	.90	.89	.96	121	11,145
S	MR Dv (1)	40	40	174	1.06	1.12	1.13	1.19	284	28,382	72	36	18	18	.77	.90	.89	.96	121	11,145
S	Tk Dv (1)	40	40	174	1.06	1.12	1.13	1.19	363	36,252	18	24	18	36	.77	.90	.89	.96	86	7,916
S	Art A Dv (1)		134	188	1.06			1.19				144	144	144					396	36,432

TABLE C-1. *continued*

Time: M+1 to M+5 State: USSR

Time / State / MD	Unit Title; Readiness Category	Mort TO&E 82MM	120MM	Others	Mort Eff Others	82MM	120MM	WEI	WUV (WEI-CW 48)	AntiArm TO&E T-21 Others	T12	RPG7	ATGM	AntiArm Eff T-21 Others	T12	RPG7	ATGM	WEI	WUV (WEI-CW 55)	IFV TO&E BMP	EFF	WEI	WUV (WEI-CW 69)
GSFG	16 Tk Dv (1)	4	18		.82	.90	1.07	23	1,097			346	46			.35	.72	154	8,482	147	.89	131	9,027
GSFG	21 MR Dv (1)	12	54		.82	.90	1.07	69	3,292	12	18	529	36	.45	.67	.35	.72	229	12,569	117	.89	104	7,185
GSFG	94 MR Dv (1)	12	54		.82	.90	1.07	69	3,292	12	18	529	36	.45	.67	.35	.72	229	12,569	117	.89	104	7,185
GSFG	207 MR Dv (1)	12	54		.82	.90	1.07	69	3,292	12	18	529	36	.45	.67	.35	.72	229	12,569	117	.89	104	7,185
GSFG	Art Bg (1)																						
GSFG	Art Bg (1)																						
GSFG	Other Bts (1)											40	10			.35	.57	20	1,084	10	.85	9	587
GSFG	7 Tk Dv (1)	4	18		.82	.90	1.07	23	1,097			346	46			.35	.72	154	8,482	147	.89	131	9,027
GSFG	10 Tk Dv (1)	4	18		.82	.90	1.07	23	1,097			346	46			.35	.72	154	8,482	147	.89	131	9,027
GSFG	72 Tk Dv (1)	4	18		.82	.90	1.07	23	1,097			346	46			.35	.72	154	8,482	147	.89	131	9,027
GSFG	47 Tk Dv (1)	4	18		.82	.90	1.07	23	1,097			346	46			.35	.72	154	8,482	147	.89	131	9,027
GSFG	304 Art Bg (1)		15		.82		1.07	16	770	10	10	130	10	.69	.75	.35	.57	66	3,608	40	.85	34	2,346
GSFG	Other Bts (1)											40	10			.35	.57	20	1,084	10	.85	9	587
GSFG	25 Tk Dv (1)	4	18		.82	.90	1.07	23	1,097			346	46			.35	.72	154	8,482	147	.89	131	9,027
GSFG	32 Tk Dv (1)	4	18		.82	.90	1.07	23	1,097			346	46			.35	.72	154	8,482	147	.89	131	9,027
GSFG	90 Tk Dv (1)	4	18		.82	.90	1.07	23	1,097			346	46			.35	.72	154	8,482	147	.89	131	9,027
GSFG	35 MR Dv (1)	12	54		.82	.90	1.07	69	3,292	12	18	529	36	.45	.67	.35	.72	229	12,569	117	.89	104	7,185
GSFG	71 Art Bg (1)		15		.82		1.07	16	770	10	10	130	10	.69	.75	.35	.57	66	3,608	40	.85	34	2,346
GSFG	Other Bts (1)											40	10			.35	.57	20	1,084	10	.85	9	587
GSFG	79 Tk Dv (1)	4	18		.82	.90	1.07	23	1,097			346	46			.35	.72	154	8,482	147	.89	131	9,027
GSFG	27 MR Dv (1)	12	54		.82	.90	1.07	69	3,292	12	18	529	36	.45	.67	.35	.72	229	12,569	117	.89	104	7,185
GSFG	39 MR Dv (1)	12	54		.82	.90	1.07	69	3,292	12	18	529	36	.45	.67	.35	.72	229	12,569	117	.89	104	7,185
GSFG	57 MR Dv (1)	12	54		.82	.90	1.07	69	3,292	12	18	529	36	.45	.67	.35	.72	229	12,569	117	.89	104	7,185
GSFG	43 Art Bg (1)		15		.82		1.07	16	770	10	10	130	10	.69	.75	.35	.57	66	3,608	40	.85	34	2,346
GSFG	Other Bts (1)											40	10			.35	.57	20	1,084	10	.85	9	587
GSFG	9 Tk Dv (1)	4	18		.82	.90	1.07	23	1,097			346	46			.35	.72	154	8,482	147	.89	131	9,027
GSFG	11 Tk Dv (1)	4	18		.82	.90	1.07	23	1,097			346	46			.35	.72	154	8,482	147	.89	131	9,027
GSFG	20 MR Dv (1)	12	54		.82	.90	1.07	69	3,292	12	18	529	36	.45	.67	.35	.72	229	12,569	117	.89	104	7,185
GSFG	43 Art Dv (1)									36		36	27	.69		.35	.72	48	2,653	40	.89	34	2,346
GSFG	35 Assault (1)		6		.82		1.07	6	308	4	10	140	13	.69	.75	.35	.57	67	3,667	6	.85	5	352
GSFG	Spetsnaz (1)											25	5			.35	.57	12	638	23	.89	21	1,437
GSFG	MR Bg (1)		15		.82		1.07	16	770	2	4	106	7	.45	.75	.35	.72	46	2,514	6	.85	5	638
GSFG	Other Bts (1)											25	5			.35	.57	12	638	6	.85	5	352
CGF	15 Tk Dv (1)	4	18		.82	.90	1.07	23	1,097			346	46			.35	.72	154	8,482	147	.89	131	9,027
CGF	18 MR Dv (1)	12	54		.82	.90	1.07	69	3,292	12	18	529	36	.45	.67	.35	.72	229	12,569	117	.89	104	7,185
CGF	48 MR Dv (1)	12	54		.82	.90	1.07	69	3,292	12	18	529	36	.45	.67	.35	.72	229	12,569	117	.89	104	7,185
CGF	Art Bg (1)																						
CGF	Other Bts (1)											25	5			.35	.57	12	638	6	.85	5	352

M+5																							
USSR																							
NGF	20 Tk Dv (1)		4	18	.82	.90	1.07	23	1,097			346	46			.35	.72	154	8,482	147	.89	131	9,027
NGF	6 MR Dv (1)		12	54	.82	.90	1.07	69	3,292	12	18	529	36	.45	.67	.35	.72	229	12,569	117	.89	104	7,185
GDR																							
III	7 Tk Dv (1)			18	.82	.90	1.07	19	924		9	167	9	.33	.45	.28	.75	58	3,166	51	.89	45	3,132
III	11 MR Dv (1)			54	.82	.90	1.07	58	2,773	18	27	324	54	.67	.45	.28	.74	155	8,504	115	.89	102	7,062
III	4 MR Dv (1)			54	.82	.90	1.07	58	2,773	18	27	324	54	.67	.45	.28	.74	155	8,504	115	.89	102	7,062
III	Art Rt (1)				.82	.90	1.07			3	3		3	.45	.67	.35	.72	5	257		.89		
III	9 Tk Dv (1)			18	.82	.90	1.07	19	924		9	167	9	.33	.45	.28	.75	58	3,166	51	.89	45	3,132
III	8 MR Dv (1)			54	.82	.90	1.07	58	2,773	18	27	324	54	.67	.45	.28	.74	155	8,504	115	.89	102	7,062
III	1 MR Dv (1)			54	.82	.90	1.07	58	2,773	18	27	324	54	.67	.45	.28	.74	155	8,504	115	.89	102	7,062
III	Art Rt (1)				.82	.90	1.07			3		3	3	.45	.67	.35	.72	5	257		.89		
Czech																							
West	1 Tk Dv (1)				.82	.90	1.07			120		234	15	.33	.69	.28	.74	116	6,392	126	.89	112	7,738
West	2 MR Dv (1)				.82	.90	1.07			12		379	45	.33	.69	.28	.74	143	7,886	117	.89	104	7,185
West	22 Assault(1)				.82	.90	1.07					25	5	.69	.75	.35	.57	12	638	6	.85	5	352
West	Other Bts (1)				.82	.90	1.07					100	20	.69	.75	.35	.57	46	2,552	35	.85	30	2,053
Pol																							
War	6 Assault(1)			18	.82	.90	1.07	19	924	12	31	415	42	.69	.75	.35	.57	201	11,040	120	.85	102	7,038
M+10																							
Pol																							
Pom	16 Tk Dv (1)	9		9	.82	.90	1.07	17	816	9		135	9	.41	.69	.28	.63	47	2,594	101	.89	90	6,202
Pom	20 Tk Dv (1)	9		9	.82	.90	1.07	17	816	9		135	9	.41	.69	.28	.63	47	2,594	101	.89	90	6,202
Pom	12 MR Dv (1)	27		27	.82	.90	1.07	51	2,449	18	18	313	36	.45	.69	.28	.66	132	7,256	101	.89	90	6,202
Pom	8 MR Dv (1)	27		27	.82	.90	1.07	51	2,449	18	18	313	36	.45	.69	.28	.66	132	7,256	101	.89	90	6,202
Pom	Art Rt (1)				.82	.90	1.07			3		3	3	.45	.67	.35	.72	5	257		.89		
Sil	5 Tk Dv (1)	9		9	.82	.90	1.07	17	816	9		135	9	.41	.69	.28	.63	47	2,594	101	.89	90	6,202
Sil	10 Tk Dv (1)	9		9	.82	.90	1.07	17	816	9		135	9	.41	.69	.28	.63	47	2,594	101	.89	90	6,202
Sil	11 Tk Dv (1)	9		9	.82	.90	1.07	17	816	9		135	9	.41	.69	.28	.63	47	2,594	101	.89	90	6,202
Sil	Art Rt (1)				.82	.90	1.07			3		3	3	.45	.67	.35	.72	5	257		.89		
War	Art Rt (1)				.82	.90	1.07			3		3	3	.45	.67	.35	.72	5	257		.89		
USSR																							
Byel	120 MR Dv (1)		12	54	.82	.90	1.07	69	3,292	12	18	529	36	.45	.67	.35	.72	229	12,569	117	.89	104	7,185
Byel	8 Tk Dv (1)		4	18	.82	.90	1.07	23	1,097			346	46			.35	.72	154	8,482	147	.89	131	9,027
Carp	15 MR Dv (1)		12	54	.82	.90	1.07	69	3,292	12	18	529	36	.45	.67	.35	.72	229	12,569	117	.89	104	7,185
Carp	23 Tk Dv (1)		4	18	.82	.90	1.07	23	1,097			346	46			.35	.72	154	8,482	147	.89	131	9,027
Balt	7 Airbn (1)			18	.82	.90	1.07	19	924	12	31	415	42	.69	.75	.35	.57	201	11,040	120	.85	102	7,038
SGF	93 MR Dv (1)		12	54	.82	.90	1.07	69	3,292	12	18	529	36	.45	.67	.35	.72	229	12,569	117	.89	104	7,185
SGF	13 MR Dv (1)		12	54	.82	.90	1.07	69	3,292	12	18	529	36	.45	.67	.35	.72	229	12,569	117	.89	104	7,185
SGF	2 Tk Dv (1)		4	18	.82	.90	1.07	23	1,097			346	46			.35	.72	154	8,482	147	.89	131	9,027
SGF	13 Tk Dv (1)		4	18	.82	.90	1.07	23	1,097			346	46			.35	.72	154	8,482	147	.89	131	9,027

TABLE C-1. *continued*

Time; State; Military District	Unit Title; Readiness Category	MORTARS TO&E Others	82MM	120MM	MORTARS EFFECTIVENESS Others	82MM	120MM	WEI	WUV (WEI-CW 48)	ANTIARMOR TO&E T-21 Others	T12	RPG7	ATGM	ANTIARMOR EFFECTIVENESS T-21 Others	T12	RPG7	ATGM	WEI	WUV (WEI-CW 55)	IFV TO&E BMP	EFF.	WEI	WUV (WEI-CW 69)
M+15 USSR																							
Mosc	MR Dv (1)		12	54	.82	.90	1.07	69	3,292	12	18	529	36	.45	.67	.35	.72	229	12,569	117	.89	104	7,185
Mosc	2 MR Dv (1)		12	54	.82	.90	1.07	69	3,292	12	18	529	36	.45	.67	.35	.72	229	12,569	117	.89	104	7,185
Mosc	106 Airbn (1)			18	.82	.90	1.07	19	924	12		415	42	.69	.75	.35	.57	201	11,040	120	.85	102	7,038
Mosc	Art Dv (1)									36	31	36	27	.45	.67	.35	.72	48	2,653		.89		
M+20 USSR																							
Byel	MR Dv (2)		12	54	.82	.90	1.07	69	3,292	12	12	476	24	.45	.67	.35	.72	197	10,853	124	.89	110	7,615
Carp	70 MR Dv (2)		12	54	.82	.90	1.07	69	3,292	12	12	476	24	.45	.67	.35	.72	197	10,853	124	.89	110	7,615
Balt	1 MR Dv (2)		12	54	.82	.90	1.07	69	3,292	12	12	476	24	.45	.67	.35	.72	197	10,853	124	.89	110	7,615
M+25 USSR																							
Byel	8 Tk Dv (2)		4	18	.82	.90	1.07	23	1,097	12	12	166	24	.45	.67	.35	.72	58	3,196	117	.89	104	7,185
Carp	128 MR Dv (2)		12	54	.82	.90	1.07	69	3,292			476				.35	.72	197	10,853	124	.89	110	7,615
Balt	1 Tk Dv (2)		4	18	.82	.90	1.07	23	1,097			166				.35	.72	58	3,196	117	.89	104	7,185
M+30 USSR																							
Byel	29 Tk Dv (2)		4	18	.82	.90	1.07	23	1,097			166				.35	.72	58	3,196	117	.89	104	7,185
Byel	3 Tk Dv (2)		4	18	.82	.90	1.07	23	1,097			166				.35	.72	58	3,196	117	.89	104	7,185
Byel	27 Tk Dv (2)		4	18	.82	.90	1.07	23	1,097			166				.35	.72	58	3,196	117	.89	104	7,185
Carp	61 MR Dv (2)		12	54	.82	.90	1.07	69	3,292	12	12	476	24	.45	.67	.35	.72	197	10,853	124	.89	110	7,615
Carp	24 MR Dv (2)		12	54	.82	.90	1.07	69	3,292	12	12	476	24	.45	.67	.35	.72	197	10,853	124	.89	110	7,615
Carp	13 Tk Dv (2)		4	18	.82	.90	1.07	23	1,097			166				.35	.72	58	3,196	117	.89	104	7,185
Balt	40 Tk Dv (2)		4	18	.82	.90	1.07	23	1,097			166				.35	.72	58	3,196	117	.89	104	7,185
Balt	24 Tk Dv (2)		4	18	.82	.90	1.07	23	1,097			166				.35	.72	58	3,196	117	.89	104	7,185
Pol																							
Sil	4 MR Dv (2)	27		27	.82	.90	1.07	51	2,449	18	18	313	18	.45	.69	.28	.66	120	6,602		.89		
Pom	7 Assualt (2)			6	.82	.90	1.07	6	308	4	10	140	13	.69	.75	.35	.57	67	3,667	40	.85	34	2,346

M+35																						
USSR																						
Byel	47 Tk Dv (2)	4	18	.82	.90	1.07	23	1,097			166				.35	.72	58	3,196	117	.89	104	7,185
Byel	34 Tk Dv (2)	4	18	.82	.90	1.07	23	1,097			166				.35	.72	58	3,196	117	.89	104	7,185
Byel	Art A Dv (2)			.82	.90	1.07			36		36	27	.45	.67	.35	.72	48	2,653		.89		
Byel	Art B Dv (2)			.82	.90	1.07							.45	.67	.35	.72		6		.89		
Carp	117 Tk Dv (2)	4	18	.82	.90	1.07	23	1,097			166				.35	.72	58	3,196	117	.89	104	7,185
Carp	Art A Dv (2)			.82	.90	1.07			36		36	27	.45	.67	.35	.72	48	2,653		.89		
Carp	Art B Dv (2)			.82	.90	1.07							.45	.67	.35	.72		6		.89		
Carp	Art B Dv (2)			.82	.90	1.07							.45	.67	.35	.72		6		.89		
Balt	Art A Dv (2)			.82	.90	1.07			36		36	27	.45	.67	.35	.72	48	2,653		.89		
Balt	Art A Dv (2)			.82	.90	1.07			36		36	27	.45	.67	.35	.72	48	2,653		.89		
M+40																						
Czech																						
West	4 Tk Dv (2)			.82	.90	1.07			120		234	15	.26	.60	.22	.64	92	5,075	126	.82	104	7,165
West	9 Tk Dv (2)			.82	.90	1.07			120		234	15	.26	.60	.22	.64	92	5,075	126	.82	104	7,165
West	3 MR Dv (2)			.82	.90	1.07			18		372	27	.33	.69	.28	.73	130	7,140		.89		
USSR																						
Mosc	15 Tk Dv (2)	4	18	.82	.90	1.07	23	1,097			166				.35	.72	58	3,196	117	.89	104	7,185
Mosc	4 Tk Dv (2)	4	18	.82	.90	1.07	23	1,097			166				.35	.72	58	3,196	117	.89	104	7,185
M+45																						
USSR																						
Balt	3 MR Dv (3)	12	54	.71	.79	.95	61	2,925	12	12	476	24	.39	.58	.31	.63	173	9,533	124	.77	96	6,625
M+50																						
USSR																						
Len	64 MR Dv (3)	12	54	.71	.79	.95	61	2,925	12	12	476	24	.39	.58	.31	.63	173	9,533	124	.77	96	6,625

TABLE C-1. continued

Time; State; Military District	Unit Title; Readiness Category	MORTARS								ANTIARMOR										INFANTRY FIGHTING VEHICLES			
		TO&E			EFFECTIVENESS					TO&E				EFFECTIVENESS						TO&E			
		Others	82MM	120MM	Others	82MM	120MM	WEI	WUV: (WEI· CW 48)	T-21 Others	T-12	RPG7	ATGM	T-21 Others	T12	RPG7	ATGM	WEI	WUV: (WEI· CW 55)	BMP	EFF.	WEI	WUV: (WEI· CW 69)
M+55 USSR																							
Carp	66 MR Dv (3)		12	54	.71	.79	.95	61	2,925	12	12	476	24	.39	.58	.31	.63	173	9,533	124	.77	96	6,625
Len	111 MR Dv (3)		12	54	.71	.79	.95	61	2,925	12	12	476	24	.39	.58	.31	.63	173	9,533	124	.77	96	6,625
M+60 USSR																							
Byel	50 MR Dv (3)		12	54	.71	.79	.95	61	2,925	12	12	476	24	.39	.58	.31	.63	173	9,533	124	.77	96	6,625
Len	77 MR Dv (3)		12	54	.71	.79	.95	61	2,925	12	12	476	24	.39	.58	.31	.63	173	9,533	124	.77	96	6,625
Balt	88 MR Dv (3)		12	54	.71	.79	.95	61	2,925	12	12	476	24	.39	.58	.31	.63	173	9,533	124	.77	96	6,625
Czech East	13 Tk Dv (3)				.82	.90	1.07			120		234	15	.26	.60	.22	.64	92	5,075	126	.82	104	7,165
East	14 Tk Dv (3)				.82	.90	1.07			120		234	15	.26	.60	.22	.64	92	5,075	126	.82	104	7,165
M+65 USSR																							
Carp	17 MR Dv (3)		12	54	.71	.79	.95	61	2,925	12	12	476	24	.39	.58	.31	.63	173	9,533	124	.77	96	6,625
Balt	26 MR Dv (3)		12	54	.71	.79	.95	61	2,925	12	12	476	24	.39	.58	.31	.63	173	9,533	124	.77	96	6,625
Len	69 MR Dv (3)		12	54	.71	.79	.95	61	2,925	12	12	476	24	.39	.58	.31	.63	173	9,533	124	.77	96	6,625
M+70 USSR																							
Carp	97 MR Dv (3)		12	54	.71	.79	.95	61	2,925	12	12	476	24	.39	.58	.31	.63	173	9,533	124	.77	96	6,625
Balt	44 MR Dv (3)		12	54	.71	.79	.95	61	2,925	12	12	476	24	.39	.58	.31	.63	173	9,533	124	.77	96	6,625
Len	45 MR Dv (3)		12	54	.71	.79	.95	61	2,925	12	12	476	24	.39	.58	.31	.63	173	9,533	124	.77	96	6,625
M+75 USSR																							
Len	45 MR Dv (3)		12	54	.71	.79	.95	61	2,925	12	12	476	24	.39	.58	.31	.63	173	9,533	124	.77	96	6,625
Balt	107 MR Dv (3)		12	54	.71	.79	.95	61	2,925	12	12	476	24	.39	.58	.31	.63	173	9,533	124	.77	96	6,625

	Unit																					
USSR																						
Mos	13 MR Dv (3)	12	54	.71	.79	.95	61	2,925	12	12	476	24	.39	.58	.31	.63	173	9,533	124	.77	96	6,625
Vol	43 MR Dv (3)	12	54	.71	.79	.95	61	2,925	12	12	476	24	.39	.58	.31	.63	173	9,533	124	.77	96	6,625
Vol	Art A Dv (3)			.82	.90	1.07			36	36	36	27	.45	.67	.35	.72	48	2,653		.89		
Czech	15 MR Dv (3)		27	.82	.90	1.07	51	2,449	18	18	372	27	.33	.69	.28	.73	130	7,140		.89		
East																						
Pol	1 MR Dv (3)		27	.82	.90	1.07	51	2,449	18	36	313	18	.45	.69	.28	.66	132	7,285		.89		
War			27																			
M+85																						
USSR																						
Mos	32 MR Dv (3)	12	54	.71	.79	.95	61	2,925	12	12	476	24	.39	.58	.31	.63	173	9,533	124	.77	96	6,625
Vol	96 MR Dv (3)	12	54	.71	.79	.95	61	2,925	12	12	476	24	.39	.58	.31	.63	173	9,533	124	.77	96	6,625
Ural	77 MR Dv (3)	12	54	.71	.79	.95	61	2,925	12	12	476	24	.39	.58	.31	.63	173	9,533	124	.77	96	6,625
Czech	19 MR Dv (3)		27	.82	.90	1.07	51	2,449	18	18	372	27	.33	.69	.28	.73	130	7,140		.89		
East																						
Pol	3 MR Dv (3)		27	.82	.90	1.07	51	2,449	18	36	313	18	.45	.69	.28	.66	132	7,285		.89		
War			27																			
M+90																						
USSR																						
Vol	21 MR Dv (3)	12	54	.71	.79	.95	61	2,925	12	12	476	24	.39	.58	.31	.63	173	9,533	124	.77	96	6,625
Ural	MR Dv (3)	12	54	.71	.79	.95	61	2,925	12	12	476	24	.39	.58	.31	.63	173	9,533	124	.77	96	6,625
Czech	20 MR Dv (3)		27	.82	.90	1.07	51	2,449	18	18	372	27	.33	.69	.28	.73	130	7,140		.89		
East																						
Pol	9 MR Dv (3)		27	.82	.90	1.07	51	2,449	18	36	313	18	.45	.69	.28	.66	132	7,285		.89		
War			27																			

TABLE C-1. continued

Time; State; Military District	Unit Title; Readiness Category	MORTARS TO&E Others	82MM	120MM	MORTARS EFF Others	82MM	120MM	WEI	WUV (WEI-CW 48)	ANTIARMOR TO&E T-21 Others	T12	RPG7	ATGM	ANTIARMOR EFF T-21 Others	T12	RPG7	ATGM	WEI	WUV (WEI-CW 55)	IFV TO&E BMP	EFF.	WEI	WUV (WEI-CW 69)
ATTU Units Not Allocated to Central Front																							
USSR																							
NW	MR Dv (1)		12	54	.82	.90	1.07	69	3,292	12	12	476	24	.45	.67	.35	.72	197	10,853	124	.89	110	7,615
NW	MR Dv (1)		12	54	.82	.90	1.07	69	3,292	12	12	476	24	.45	.67	.35	.72	197	10,853	124	.89	110	7,615
NW	MR Dv (1)		12	54	.82	.90	1.07	69	3,292	12	12	476	24	.45	.67	.35	.72	197	10,853	124	.89	110	7,615
NW	MR Dv (1)		12	54	.82	.90	1.07	69	3,292	12	12	476	24	.45	.67	.35	.72	197	10,853	124	.89	110	7,615
NW	MR Dv (1)		12	54	.82	.90	1.07	69	3,292	12	12	476	24	.45	.67	.35	.72	197	10,853	124	.89	110	7,615
NW	MR Dv (1)		12	54	.82	.90	1.07	69	3,292	12	12	476	24	.45	.67	.35	.72	197	10,853	124	.89	110	7,615
NW	MR Dv (1)		12	54	.82	.90	1.07	69	3,292	12	12	476	24	.45	.67	.35	.72	197	10,853	124	.89	110	7,615
NW	MR Dv (1)		12	54	.82	.90	1.07	69	3,292	12	12	476	24	.45	.67	.35	.72	197	10,853	124	.89	110	7,615
SW	MR Dv (1)		12	54	.82	.90	1.07	69	3,292	12	12	476	24	.45	.67	.35	.72	197	10,853	124	.89	110	7,615
SW	Art A Dv (1)		12	54	.82	.90	1.07	69	3,292	36	12	36	27	.45	.67	.35	.72	48	2,653	124	.89	110	7,615
SW	MR Dv (1)		12	54	.82	.90	1.07	69	3,292	12	12	476	24	.45	.67	.35	.72	197	10,853	124	.89	110	7,615
SW	MR Dv (1)		12	54	.82	.90	1.07	69	3,292	12	12	476	24	.45	.67	.35	.72	197	10,853	124	.89	110	7,615
SW	MR Dv (1)		12	54	.82	.90	1.07	69	3,292	12	12	476	24	.45	.67	.35	.72	197	10,853	124	.89	110	7,615
SW	MR Dv (1)		12	54	.82	.90	1.07	69	3,292	12	12	476	24	.45	.67	.35	.72	197	10,853	124	.89	110	7,615
SW	MR Dv (1)		12	54	.82	.90	1.07	69	3,292	12	12	476	24	.45	.67	.35	.72	197	10,853	124	.89	110	7,615
SW	MR Dv (1)		12	54	.82	.90	1.07	69	3,292	12	12	476	24	.45	.67	.35	.72	197	10,853	124	.89	110	7,615
SW	MR Dv (1)		12	54	.82	.90	1.07	69	3,292	12	12	476	24	.45	.67	.35	.72	197	10,853	124	.89	110	7,615
SW	MR Dv (1)		12	54	.82	.90	1.07	69	3,292	12	12	476	24	.45	.67	.35	.72	197	10,853	124	.89	110	7,615
SW	MR Dv (1)		12	54	.82	.90	1.07	69	3,292	12	12	476	24	.45	.67	.35	.72	197	10,853	124	.89	110	7,615
SW	MR Dv (1)		12	54	.82	.90	1.07	69	3,292	12	12	476	24	.45	.67	.35	.72	197	10,853	124	.89	110	7,615
SW	MR Dv (1)		12	54	.82	.90	1.07	69	3,292	12	12	476	24	.45	.67	.35	.72	197	10,853	124	.89	110	7,615
SW	MR Dv (1)		12	54	.82	.90	1.07	69	3,292	12	12	476	24	.45	.67	.35	.72	197	10,853	124	.89	110	7,615
SW	MR Dv (1)		12	54	.82	.90	1.07	69	3,292	12	12	476	24	.45	.67	.35	.72	197	10,853	124	.89	110	7,615
SW	Tk Dv (1)		4	18	.82	.90	1.07	23	1,097			166				.35		58	3,196	117	.89	104	7,185
SW	Tk Dv (1)		4	18	.82	.90	1.07	23	1,097			166				.35		58	3,196	117	.89	104	7,185
SW	Tk Dv (1)		4	18	.82	.90	1.07	23	1,097			166				.35		58	3,196	117	.89	104	7,185
SW	Tk Dv (1)		4	18	.82	.90	1.07	23	1,097			166				.35		58	3,196	117	.89	104	7,185
SW	Tk Dv (1)		4	18	.82	.90	1.07	23	1,097			166				.35		58	3,196	117	.89	104	7,185

SW	Tk Dv (1)	4	18	.82	.90	1.07	23	1,097			166				.35	.72	58	3,196	117	.89	104	7,185
SW	Tk Dv (1)	4	18	.82	.90	1.07	23	1,097			166				.35	.72	58	3,196	117	.89	104	7,185
SW	Tk Dv (1)	4	18	.82	.90	1.07	23	1,097			166				.35	.72	58	3,196	117	.89	104	7,185
SW	Tk Dv (1)	4	18	.82	.90	1.07	23	1,097			166				.35	.72	58	3,196	117	.89	104	7,185
SW	Art A Dv (1)			.82	.90	1.07			36		36	27	.45	.67	.35	.72	48	2,653		.89		
Hun	MR Dv (1)			.82	.90	1.07			18		372	27	.33	.69	.28	.73	130	7,140		.89		
Hun	MR Dv (1)			.82	.90	1.07			18		372	27	.33	.69	.28	.73	130	7,140		.89		
Hun	MR Dv (1)			.82	.90	1.07			18		372	27	.33	.69	.28	.73	130	7,140		.89		
Hun	MR Dv (1)			.82	.90	1.07			18		372	27	.33	.69	.28	.73	130	7,140		.89		
Hun	MR Dv (1)			.82	.90	1.07			18		372	27	.33	.69	.28	.73	130	7,140		.89		
Hun	MR Dv (1)			.82	.90	1.07			18		372	27	.33	.69	.28	.73	130	7,140		.89		
Hun	MR Dv (1)			.82	.90	1.07			18		372	27	.33	.69	.28	.73	130	7,140		.89		
Rom	MR Dv (1)			.82	.90	1.07			18		372	27	.33	.69	.28	.73	130	7,140		.89		
Rom	MR Dv (1)			.82	.90	1.07			18		372	27	.33	.69	.28	.73	130	7,140		.89		
Rom	MR Dv (1)			.82	.90	1.07			18		372	27	.33	.69	.28	.73	130	7,140		.89		
Rom	MR Dv (1)			.82	.90	1.07			18		372	27	.33	.69	.28	.73	130	7,140		.89		
Rom	MR Dv (1)			.82	.90	1.07			18		372	27	.33	.69	.28	.73	130	7,140		.89		
Rom	MR Dv (1)			.82	.90	1.07			18		372	27	.33	.69	.28	.73	130	7,140		.89		
Rom	MR Dv (1)			.82	.90	1.07			18		372	27	.33	.69	.28	.73	130	7,140		.89		
Rom	MR Dv (1)			.82	.90	1.07			18		372	27	.33	.69	.28	.73	130	7,140		.89		
Rom	MR Dv (1)			.82	.90	1.07			18		372	27	.33	.69	.28	.73	130	7,140		.89		
Rom	MR Dv (1)			.82	.90	1.07			18		372	27	.33	.69	.28	.73	130	7,140		.89		
Bul	MR Dv (1)			.82	.90	1.07			18		372	27	.33	.69	.28	.73	130	7,140		.89		
Bul	MR Dv (1)			.82	.90	1.07			18		372	27	.33	.69	.28	.73	130	7,140		.89		
Bul	MR Dv (1)			.82	.90	1.07			18		372	27	.33	.69	.28	.73	130	7,140		.89		
Bul	MR Dv (1)			.82	.90	1.07			120		234	15	.26	.60	.22	.64	92	5,075	126	.82	104	7,165
Bul	MR Dv (1)			.82	.90	1.07			120		234	15	.26	.60	.22	.64	92	5,075	126	.82	104	7,165
Bul	MR Dv (1)			.82	.90	1.07			120		234	15	.26	.60	.22	.64	92	5,075	126	.82	104	7,165
Bul	MR Dv (1)			.82	.90	1.07			120		234	15	.26	.60	.22	.64	92	5,075	126	.82	104	7,165
Bul	MR Dv (1)			.82	.90	1.07			120		234	15	.26	.60	.22	.64	92	5,075	126	.82	104	7,165
S	MR Dv (1)	12	54	.82	.90	1.07	69	3,292	12	12	476	24	.45	.67	.35	.72	197	10,853	124	.89	110	7,615
S	MR Dv (1)	12	54	.82	.90	1.07	69	3,292	12	12	476	24	.45	.67	.35	.72	197	10,853	124	.89	110	7,615
S	MR Dv (1)	12	54	.82	.90	1.07	69	3,292	12	12	476	24	.45	.67	.35	.72	197	10,853	124	.89	110	7,615
S	MR Dv (1)	12	54	.82	.90	1.07	69	3,292	12	12	476	24	.45	.67	.35	.72	197	10,853	124	.89	110	7,615
S	MR Dv (1)	12	54	.82	.90	1.07	69	3,292	12	12	476	24	.45	.67	.35	.72	197	10,853	124	.89	110	7,615
S	MR Dv (1)	12	54	.82	.90	1.07	69	3,292	12	12	476	24	.45	.67	.35	.72	197	10,853	124	.89	110	7,615
S	MR Dv (1)	12	54	.82	.90	1.07	69	3,292	12	12	476	24	.45	.67	.35	.72	197	10,853	124	.89	110	7,615
S	Tk Dv (1)	4	18	.82	.90	1.07	23	1,097			166				.35	.72	58	3,196	117	.89	104	7,185
S	Art A Dv (1)			.82	.90	1.07			36		36	27	.45	.67	.35	.72	48	2,653		.89		

TABLE C-1. *continued*

Time; State; Military District: USSR — *M + 1 to M + 5*

Time; State; Mil. Dist.	Unit Title; Readiness Category	Recon TO&E OT65 0th	Recon TO&E BRDM	Recon TO&E BMP	Recon TO&E AT5	Recon EFF OT65 0th	Recon EFF BRDM	Recon EFF BMP	Recon EFF AT5	Recon WEI	Recon WUV (WEI·CW 62)	APC TO&E ARV	APC TO&E APC	APC EFF ARV	APC EFF APC	APC WEI	APC WUV (WEI·CW 36)	SA TO&E	SA WUV (WEI·CW 3.3)	UNIT WUV Division Total
GSFG	16 Tk Dv (1)			12	9		.91	1.03	1.04	22	1,347	29	16	.85	.98	40	1,452	1,176	3,881	74,782
GSFG	21 MR Dv (1)		36	20			.91	1.03	1.04	53	3,308	29	223	.85	.98	243	8,755	2,537	8,372	86,777
GSFG	94 MR Dv (1)		36	20			.91	1.03	1.04	53	3,308	29	223	.85	.98	243	8,755	2,537	8,372	86,777
GSFG	207 MR Dv (1)		36	20			.91	1.03	1.04	53	3,308	29	223	.85	.98	243	8,755	2,537	8,372	86,777
GSFG	Art Bg (1)																	20	66	7,832
GSFG	Art Bg (1)																	20	66	7,832
GSFG	Other Bts (1)						.85	1.03	1.04			5		.85		4	153	144	475	2,298
GSFG	7 Tk Dv (1)			12	9		.91	1.03	1.04	22	1,347	29	16	.85	.98	40	1,452	1,176	3,881	74,782
GSFG	10 Tk Dv (1)			12	9		.91	1.03	1.04	22	1,347	29	16	.85	.98	40	1,452	1,176	3,881	74,782
GSFG	72 Tk Dv (1)			12	9		.91	1.03	1.04	22	1,347	29	16	.85	.98	40	1,452	1,176	3,881	74,782
GSFG	47 Tk Dv (1)			12	9		.91	1.03	1.04	22	1,347	29	16	.85	.98	40	1,452	1,176	3,881	74,782
GSFG	304 Art Bg (1)						.85	1.03	1.04			15		.85		13	459	898	2,963	11,564
GSFG	Other Bts (1)						.85	1.03	1.04			5		.85		4	153	144	475	2,298
GSFG	25 Tk Dv (1)			12	9		.91	1.03	1.04	22	1,347	29	16	.85	.98	40	1,452	1,176	3,881	74,782
GSFG	32 Tk Dv (1)			12	9		.91	1.03	1.04	22	1,347	29	16	.85	.98	40	1,452	1,176	3,881	74,782
GSFG	90 Tk Dv (1)			12	9		.91	1.03	1.04	22	1,347	29	16	.85	.98	40	1,452	1,176	3,881	74,782
GSFG	35 MR Dv (1)		36	20			.91	1.03	1.04	53	3,308	29	223	.85	.98	243	8,755	2,537	8,372	86,777
GSFG	71 Art Bg (1)						.85	1.03	1.04			15		.85		13	459	898	2,963	11,564
GSFG	Other Bts (1)						.85	1.03	1.04			5		.85		4	153	144	475	2,298
GSFG	79 Tk Dv (1)			12	9		.91	1.03	1.04	22	1,347	29	16	.85	.98	40	1,452	1,176	3,881	74,782
GSFG	27 MR Dv (1)		36	20			.91	1.03	1.04	53	3,308	29	223	.85	.98	243	8,755	2,537	8,372	86,777
GSFG	39 MR Dv (1)		36	20			.91	1.03	1.04	53	3,308	29	223	.85	.98	243	8,755	2,537	8,372	86,777
GSFG	57 MR Dv (1)		36	20			.91	1.03	1.04	53	3,308	29	223	.85	.98	243	8,755	2,537	8,372	86,777
GSFG	43 Art Bg (1)						.85	1.03	1.04			15		.85		13	459	898	2,963	11,564
GSFG	Other Bts (1)						.85	1.03	1.04			5		.85		4	153	144	475	2,298
GSFG	9 Tk Dv (1)			12	9		.91	1.03	1.04	22	1,347	29	16	.85	.98	40	1,452	1,176	3,881	74,782
GSFG	11 Tk Dv (1)			12	9		.91	1.03	1.04	22	1,347	29	16	.85	.98	40	1,452	1,176	3,881	74,782
GSFG	20 MR Dv (1)		36	20			.91	1.03	1.04	53	3,308	29	223	.85	.98	243	8,755	2,537	8,372	86,777
GSFG	43 Art Dv (1)		27				.85	1.03	1.04	25	1,523							254	838	41,447
GSFG	35 Assault (1)						.91	1.03	1.04			3		.85		3	92	851	2,808	9,930
GSFG	Spetsnaz (1)						.91	1.03	1.04			3		.85		3	92	67	221	1,303
GSFG	MR Bg (1)		7	4			.91	1.03	1.04	11	662	6	45	.85	.98	49	1,751	515	1,700	16,501
GSFG	Other Bts (1)						.85	1.03	1.04			3		.85		3	92	67	221	1,303
CGF	15 Tk Dv (1)			12	9		.91	1.03	1.04	22	1,347	29	16	.85	.98	40	1,452	1,176	3,881	74,782
CGF	18 MR Dv (1)		36	20			.91	1.03	1.04	53	3,308	29	223	.85	.98	243	8,755	2,537	8,372	86,777
CGF	48 MR Dv (1)		36	20			.91	1.03	1.04	53	3,308	29	223	.85	.98	243	8,755	2,537	8,372	86,777
CGF	Art Bg (1)																	20	66	7,832
CGF	Other Bts (1)						.85	1.03	1.04			3		.85		3	92	67	221	1,303

Dense order-of-battle table (no printed column headers). Values transcribed in the original left-to-right column order; the final (rightmost) column holds the largest figures (personnel-type totals). Blank cells indicate no entry.

Unit																			
M+5																			
USSR																			
NGF — 20 Tk Dv (1)			12	9		.91	1.03	1.04	22	1,347	29	16	.85	.98	40	1,452	1,176	3,881	74,782
NGF — 6 MR Dv (1)		36	20			.91	1.03	1.04	53	3,308	29	223	.85	.98	243	8,755	2,537	8,372	86,777
GDR																			
III — 7 Tk Dv (1)			15		.77	.91	1.03	1.04	15	958	87	96	.85	.95	165	5,945	945	3,119	57,259
III — 11 MR Dv (1)			18		.77	.91	1.03	1.04	19	1,149	126	230	.85	.95	326	11,722	2,482	8,191	67,654
III — 4 MR Dv (1)			18		.77	.91	1.03	1.04	19	1,149	126	230	.85	.95	326	11,722	2,482	8,191	67,654
III — Art Rt (1)		3				.91	1.03	1.04	3	169			.85	.98			29	96	4,097
III — 9 Tk Dv (1)			15		.77	.91	1.03	1.04	15	958	87	96	.85	.95	165	5,945	945	3,119	57,259
III — 8 MR Dv (1)			18		.77	.91	1.03	1.04	19	1,149	126	230	.85	.95	326	11,722	2,482	8,191	67,654
III — 1 MR Dv (1)			18		.77	.91	1.03	1.04	19	1,149	126	230	.85	.95	326	11,722	2,482	8,191	67,654
III — Art Rt (1)		3				.91	1.03	1.04	3	169			.85	.98			29	96	4,097
Czech																			
West — 1 Tk Dv (1)	38		12		.77	.91	1.03	1.04	42	2,580	24	108	.85	.97	105	3,771	1,486	4,904	63,997
West — 2 MR Dv (1)	78				.77	.91	1.03	1.04	60	3,724		302	.85	.97	313	11,280	9,868	32,564	91,973
West — 22 Assault(1)						.85	1.03	1.04			3		.85	.98	3	92	67	221	1,303
West — Other Bts (1)		3				.85	1.03	1.04			15		.85	.98	13	459	416	1,373	6,437
Pol																			
War — 6 Assault(1)						.85	1.03	1.04			8		.85	.98	7	245	2,563	8,458	29,830
M+10																			
Pol																			
Pom — 16 Tk Dv (1)	36		13		.77	.91	1.03	1.04	41	2,549	10	45	.85	.97	52	1,877	1,024	3,379	51,041
Pom — 20 Tk Dv (1)	36		13		.77	.91	1.03	1.04	41	2,549	10	45	.85	.97	52	1,877	1,024	3,379	51,041
Pom — 12 MR Dv (1)	57		13		.77	.91	1.03	1.04	57	3,551	23	182	.85	.97	196	7,059	2,778	9,167	65,919
Pom — 8 MR Dv (1)	57		13		.77	.91	1.03	1.04	57	3,551	23	182	.85	.97	196	7,059	2,778	9,167	65,919
Pom — Art Rt (1)						.85	1.03	1.04	3	169			.85	.98			29	96	4,097
Sil — 5 Tk Dv (1)	36		13		.77	.91	1.03	1.04	41	2,549	10	45	.85	.97	52	1,877	1,024	3,379	51,041
Sil — 10 Tk Dv (1)	36		13		.77	.91	1.03	1.04	41	2,549	10	45	.85	.97	52	1,877	1,024	3,379	51,041
Sil — 11 Tk Dv (1)	36		13		.77	.91	1.03	1.04	41	2,549	10	45	.85	.97	52	1,877	1,024	3,379	51,041
Sil — Art Rt (1)		3				.91	1.03	1.04	3	169			.85	.98			29	96	4,097
War — Art Rt (1)		3				.91	1.03	1.04	3	169			.85	.98			29	96	4,097
USSR																			
Byel — 120 MR Dv (1)		36	20			.91	1.03	1.04	53	3,308	29	223	.85	.98	243	8,755	2,537	8,372	83,883
Byel — 8 Tk Dv (1)			12	9		.91	1.03	1.04	22	1,347	29	16	.85	.98	40	1,452	1,176	3,881	71,030
Carp — 15 MR Dv (1)		36	20			.91	1.03	1.04	53	3,308	29	223	.85	.98	243	8,755	2,537	8,372	83,883
Carp — 23 Tk Dv (1)			12	9		.91	1.03	1.04	22	1,347	29	16	.85	.98	40	1,452	1,176	3,881	71,030
Balt — 7 Airbn (1)						.85	1.03	1.04			8		.85	.98	7	245	2,563	8,458	29,830
SGF — 93 MR Dv (1)		36	20			.91	1.03	1.04	53	3,308	29	223	.85	.98	243	8,755	2,537	8,372	83,883
SGF — 13 MR Dv (1)		36	20			.91	1.03	1.04	53	3,308	29	223	.85	.98	243	8,755	2,537	8,372	83,883
SGF — 2 Tk Dv (1)			12	9		.91	1.03	1.04	22	1,347	29	16	.85	.98	40	1,452	1,176	3,881	71,030
SGF — 13 Tk Dv (1)			12	9		.91	1.03	1.04	22	1,347	29	16	.85	.98	40	1,452	1,176	3,881	71,030

TABLE C-1. continued

Time; State; Military District	Unit Title; Readiness Category	ARMORED RECONNAISSANCE VEHICLES										ARMORED PERSONNEL CARRIERS						SMALL ARMS		UNIT WUV: Division Total
		TO&E				EFFECTIVENESS				WEI	WUV: (WEI-CW 62)	TO&E		EFFECT.		WEI	WUV: (WEI-CW 36)	TO&E	WUV: (WEI-CW 3.3)	
		OT65 Oth	BRDM	BMP	AT5	OT65 Oth	BRDM	BMP	AT5			ARV	APC	ARV	APC					
M+15 USSR																				
Mosc	MR Dv (1)		36	20			.91	1.03	1.04	53	3,308	29	223	.85	.98	243	8,755	2,537	8,372	83,883
Mosc	2 MR Dv (1)		36	20			.91	1.03	1.04	53	3,308	29	223	.85	.98	243	8,755	2,537	8,372	83,883
Mosc	106 Airbn (1)						.85	1.03	1.04			8			.98	7	245	2,563	8,458	29,830
Mosc	Art Dv (1)		27				.91	1.03	1.04	25	1,523			.85	.98			254	838	41,447
M+20 USSR																				
Byel	MR Dv (2)		27	20	18		.91	1.03	1.04	64	3,961	29	232	.85	.95	245	8,822	2,649	8,742	82,811
Carp	70 MR Dv (2)		27	20	18		.91	1.03	1.04	64	3,961	29	232	.85	.95	245	8,822	2,649	8,742	82,811
Balt	1 MR Dv (2)		27	20	18		.91	1.03	1.04	64	3,961	29	232	.85	.95	245	8,822	2,649	8,742	82,811
M+25 USSR																				
Byel	8 Tk Dv (2)			12	9		.91	1.03	1.04	22	1,347	29	26	.85	.98	50	1,805	1,098	3,623	62,420
Carp	128 MR Dv (2)		27	20	18		.91	1.03	1.04	64	3,961	29	232	.85	.95	245	8,822	2,649	8,742	82,811
Balt	1 Tk Dv (2)			12	9		.91	1.03	1.04	22	1,347	29	26	.85	.98	50	1,805	1,098	3,623	62,420
M+30 USSR																				
Byel	29 Tk Dv (2)			12	9		.91	1.03	1.04	22	1,347	29	26	.85	.98	50	1,805	1,098	3,623	62,420
Byel	3 Tk Dv (2)			12	9		.91	1.03	1.04	22	1,347	29	26	.85	.98	50	1,805	1,098	3,623	62,420
Byel	27 Tk Dv (2)			12	9		.91	1.03	1.04	22	1,347	29	26	.85	.98	50	1,805	1,098	3,623	62,420
Carp	61 MR Dv (2)		27	20	18		.91	1.03	1.04	64	3,961	29	232	.85	.95	245	8,822	2,649	8,742	82,811
Carp	24 MR Dv (2)		27	20	18		.91	1.03	1.04	64	3,961	29	232	.85	.95	245	8,822	2,649	8,742	82,811
Carp	13 Tk Dv (2)			12	9		.91	1.03	1.04	22	1,347	29	26	.85	.98	50	1,805	1,098	3,623	62,420
Balt	40 Tk Dv (2)			12	9		.91	1.03	1.04	22	1,347	29	26	.85	.98	50	1,805	1,098	3,623	62,420
Balt	24 Tk Dv (2)			12	9		.91	1.03	1.04	22	1,347	29	26	.85	.98	50	1,805	1,098	3,623	62,420
Pol																				
Sil	4 MR Dv (2)	43		13			.91	1.03	1.04	47	2,883		335	.85	.97	325	11,698	2,482	8,191	57,484
Pom	7 Assualt (2)					.77	.85	1.03	1.04					.85	.98			855	2,822	9,143

M+35																				
USSR																				
Byel	47 Tk Dv (2)			12	9		.91	1.03	1.04	22	1,347	29	26	.85	.98	50	1,805	1,098	3,623	62,420
Byel	34 Tk Dv (2)			12	9		.91	1.03	1.04	22	1,347	29	26	.85	.98	50	1,805	1,098	3,623	62,420
Byel	Art A Dv (2)		27				.91	1.03	1.04	25	1,523			.85	.98			254	838	41,447
Byel	Art B Dv (2)						.91	1.03	1.04					.85	.98			20	66	7,832
Carp	117 Tk Dv (2)			12	9		.91	1.03	1.04	22	1,347	29	26	.85	.98	50	1,805	1,098	3,623	62,420
Carp	Art A Dv (2)		27				.91	1.03	1.04	25	1,523			.85	.98			254	838	41,447
Carp	Art B Dv (2)						.91	1.03	1.04					.85	.98			20	66	7,832
Carp	Art B Dv (2)						.91	1.03	1.04					.85	.98			20	66	7,832
Balt	Art A Dv (2)		27				.91	1.03	1.04	25	1,523			.85	.98			254	838	41,447
Balt	Art A Dv (2)		27				.91	1.03	1.04	25	1,523			.85	.98			254	838	41,447
M+40																				
Czech																				
West	4 Tk Dv (2)	38		12		.71	.84	.95	.96	39	2,389		108	.85	.90	97	3,492	1,379	4,551	58,482
West	9 Tk Dv (2)	38		12		.71	.84	.95	.96	39	2,389		108	.85	.90	97	3,492	1,379	4,551	58,482
West	3 MR Dv (2)	87				.77	.91	1.03	1.04	67	4,153		316	.85	.97	307	11,035	2,446	8,072	58,601
USSR																				
Mosc	15 Tk Dv (2)			12	9		.91	1.03	1.04	22	1,347	29	26	.85	.98	50	1,805	1,098	3,623	62,420
Mosc	4 Tk Dv (2)			12	9		.91	1.03	1.04	22	1,347	29	26	.85	.98	50	1,805	1,098	3,623	62,420
M+45																				
USSR																				
Balt	3 MR Dv (3)		27	20	18		.80	.91	.92	56	3,486	29	232	.75	.84	216	7,763	2,309	7,620	72,614
M+50																				
USSR																				
Len	64 MR Dv (3)		27	20	18		.80	.91	.92	56	3,486	29	232	.75	.84	216	7,763	2,309	7,620	72,614

TABLE C-1. *continued*

Time; State; Military District	Unit Title; Readiness Category	ARV TO&E OT65 Oth	BRDM	BMP	AT5	ARV EFFECTIVENESS OT65 Oth	BRDM	BMP	AT5	WEI	WUV: (WEI-CW 62)	APC TO&E ARV	APC	APC EFFECT. ARV	APC	WEI	WUV: (WEI-CW 36)	SMALL ARMS TO&E	WUV: (WEI-CW 3.3)	UNIT WUV: Division Total
M+55 USSR																				
Carp	66 MR Dv (3)		27	20	18		.80	.91	.92	56	3,486	29	232	.75	.84	216	7,763	2,309	7,620	72,614
Len	111 MR Dv (3)		27	20	18		.80	.91	.92	56	3,486	29	232	.75	.84	216	7,763	2,309	7,620	72,614
M+60 USSR																				
Byel	50 MR Dv (3)		27	20	18		.80	.91	.92	56	3,486	29	232	.75	.84	216	7,763	2,309	7,620	72,614
Len	77 MR Dv (3)		27	20	18		.80	.91	.92	56	3,486	29	232	.75	.84	216	7,763	2,309	7,620	72,614
Balt	88 MR Dv (3)		27	20	18		.80	.91	.92	56	3,486	29	232	.75	.84	216	7,763	2,309	7,620	72,614
Czech																				
East	13 Tk Dv (3)	38		12		.71	.84	.95	.96	39	2,389		108	.85	.90	97	3,492	1,379	4,551	58,482
East	14 Tk Dv (3)	38		12		.71	.84	.95	.96	39	2,389		108	.85	.90	97	3,492	1,379	4,551	58,482
M+65 USSR																				
Carp	17 MR Dv (3)		27	20	18		.80	.91	.92	56	3,486	29	232	.75	.84	216	7,763	2,309	7,620	72,614
Balt	26 MR Dv (3)		27	20	18		.80	.91	.92	56	3,486	29	232	.75	.84	216	7,763	2,309	7,620	72,614
Len	69 MR Dv (3)		27	20	18		.80	.91	.92	56	3,486	29	232	.75	.84	216	7,763	2,309	7,620	72,614
M+70 USSR																				
Carp	97 MR Dv (3)		27	20	18		.80	.91	.92	56	3,486	29	232	.75	.84	216	7,763	2,309	7,620	72,614
Balt	44 MR Dv (3)		27	20	18		.80	.91	.92	56	3,486	29	232	.75	.84	216	7,763	2,309	7,620	72,614
Len	45 MR Dv (3)		27	20	18		.80	.91	.92	56	3,486	29	232	.75	.84	216	7,763	2,309	7,620	72,614
M+75 USSR																				
Len	45 MR Dv (3)		27	20	18		.80	.91	.92	56	3,486	29	232	.75	.84	216	7,763	2,309	7,620	72,614
Balt	107 MR Dv (3)		27	20	18		.80	.91	.92	56	3,486	29	232	.75	.84	216	7,763	2,309	7,620	72,614

The following table is printed sideways (landscape) on the page. Row labels and their aligned data values have been reconstructed. The 19 numeric columns are unlabelled in the source.

Region	Unit																			
M+80																				
USSR																				
Mos	13 MR Dv (3)		27	20	18		.80	.91	.92	56	3,486	29	232	.75	.84	216	7,763	2,309	7,620	72,614
Vol	43 MR Dv (3)		27	20	18		.80	.91	.92	56	3,486	29	232	.75	.84	216	7,763	2,309	7,620	72,614
Vol	Art A Dv (3)		27				.91	1.03	1.04	25	1,523			.85	.98			254	838	41,447
Czech																				
East																				
Pol	15 MR Dv (3)	87				.77	.91	1.03	1.04	67	4,153		316	.85	.97	307	11,035	2,446	8,072	58,601
War	1 MR Dv (3)	43	13			.77	.90	1.03	1.04	45	2,778		202	.85	.97	196	7,054	2,479	8,181	49,173
M+85																				
USSR																				
Mos	32 MR Dv (3)		27	20	18		.80	.91	.92	56	3,486	29	232	.75	.84	216	7,763	2,309	7,620	72,614
Vol	96 MR Dv (3)		27	20	18		.80	.91	.92	56	3,486	29	232	.75	.84	216	7,763	2,309	7,620	72,614
Ural	77 MR Dv (3)		27	20	18		.80	.91	.92	56	3,486	29	232	.75	.84	216	7,763	2,309	7,620	72,614
Czech																				
East																				
Pol	19 MR Dv (3)	87				.77	.91	1.03	1.04	67	4,153		316	.85	.97	307	11,035	2,446	8,072	58,601
War	3 MR Dv (3)	43	13			.77	.90	1.03	1.04	45	2,778		202	.85	.97	196	7,054	2,479	8,181	49,173
M+90																				
USSR																				
Vol	21 MR Dv (3)		27	20	18		.80	.91	.92	56	3,486	29	232	.75	.84	216	7,763	2,309	7,620	72,614
Ural	MR Dv (3)		27	20	18		.80	.91	.92	56	3,486	29	232	.75	.84	216	7,763	2,309	7,620	72,614
Czech																				
East																				
Pol	20 MR Dv (3)	87				.77	.91	1.03	1.04	67	4,153		316	.85	.97	307	11,035	2,446	8,072	58,601
War	9 MR Dv (3)	43	13			.77	.90	1.03	1.04	45	2,778		202	.85	.97	196	7,054	2,479	8,181	49,173

TABLE C-1. continued

ATTU Units Not Allocated to Central Front
USSR

Time; State; Military District	Unit Title; Readiness Category	ARV: TO&E OT65 Oth	BRDM	BMP	AT5	EFFECT. OT65 Oth	BRDM	BMP	AT5	WEI	WUV (WEI-CW 62)	APC TO&E ARV	APC	EFFECT ARV	APC	WEI	WUV (WEI-CW 36)	Small Arms TO&E	WUV (WEI-CW 3.3)	Unit WUV: Division Total
NW	MR Dv (1)		27	20	18		.91	1.03	1.04	64	3,961	29	232	.85	.95	245	8,822	2,649	8,742	82,811
NW	MR Dv (1)		27	20	18		.91	1.03	1.04	64	3,961	29	232	.85	.95	245	8,822	2,649	8,742	82,811
NW	MR Dv (1)		27	20	18		.91	1.03	1.04	64	3,961	29	232	.85	.95	245	8,822	2,649	8,742	82,811
NW	MR Dv (1)		27	20	18		.91	1.03	1.04	64	3,961	29	232	.85	.95	245	8,822	2,649	8,742	82,811
NW	MR Dv (1)		27	20	18		.91	1.03	1.04	64	3,961	29	232	.85	.95	245	8,822	2,649	8,742	82,811
NW	MR Dv (1)		27	20	18		.91	1.03	1.04	64	3,961	29	232	.85	.95	245	8,822	2,649	8,742	82,811
NW	MR Dv (1)		27	20	18		.91	1.03	1.04	64	3,961	29	232	.85	.95	245	8,822	2,649	8,742	82,811
NW	MR Dv (1)		27	20	18		.91	1.03	1.04	64	3,961	29	232	.85	.95	245	8,822	2,649	8,742	82,811
SW	MR Dv (1)		27	20	18		.91	1.03	1.04	64	3,961	29	232	.85	.95	245	8,822	2,649	8,742	82,811
SW	Art A Dv (1)		27	20			.91	1.03	1.04	25	1,523	29	232	.85	.98	245	8,822	254	838	41,447
SW	MR Dv (1)		27	20	18		.91	1.03	1.04	64	3,961	29	232	.85	.95	245	8,822	2,649	8,742	82,811
SW	MR Dv (1)		27	20	18		.91	1.03	1.04	64	3,961	29	232	.85	.95	245	8,822	2,649	8,742	82,811
SW	MR Dv (1)		27	20	18		.91	1.03	1.04	64	3,961	29	232	.85	.95	245	8,822	2,649	8,742	82,811
SW	MR Dv (1)		27	20	18		.91	1.03	1.04	64	3,961	29	232	.85	.95	245	8,822	2,649	8,742	82,811
SW	MR Dv (1)		27	20	18		.91	1.03	1.04	64	3,961	29	232	.85	.95	245	8,822	2,649	8,742	82,811
SW	MR Dv (1)		27	20	18		.91	1.03	1.04	64	3,961	29	232	.85	.95	245	8,822	2,649	8,742	82,811
SW	MR Dv (1)		27	20	18		.91	1.03	1.04	64	3,961	29	232	.85	.95	245	8,822	2,649	8,742	82,811
SW	MR Dv (1)		27	20	18		.91	1.03	1.04	64	3,961	29	232	.85	.95	245	8,822	2,649	8,742	82,811
SW	MR Dv (1)		27	20	18		.91	1.03	1.04	64	3,961	29	232	.85	.95	245	8,822	2,649	8,742	82,811
SW	MR Dv (1)		27	20	18		.91	1.03	1.04	64	3,961	29	232	.85	.95	245	8,822	2,649	8,742	82,811
SW	MR Dv (1)		27	20	18		.91	1.03	1.04	64	3,961	29	232	.85	.95	245	8,822	2,649	8,742	82,811
SW	MR Dv (1)		27	20	18		.91	1.03	1.04	64	3,961	29	232	.85	.95	245	8,822	2,649	8,742	82,811
SW	MR Dv (1)		27	20	18		.91	1.03	1.04	64	3,961	29	232	.85	.95	245	8,822	2,649	8,742	82,811
SW	MR Dv (1)		27	20	18		.91	1.03	1.04	64	3,961	29	232	.85	.95	245	8,822	2,649	8,742	82,811
SW	MR Dv (1)		27	20	18		.91	1.03	1.04	64	3,961	29	232	.85	.95	245	8,822	2,649	8,742	82,811
SW	MR Dv (1)		27	20	18		.91	1.03	1.04	64	3,961	29	232	.85	.95	245	8,822	2,649	8,742	82,811
SW	Tk Dv (1)			12	9		.91	1.03	1.04	22	1,347	29	26	.85	.98	50	1,805	1,098	3,623	62,420
SW	Tk Dv (1)			12	9		.91	1.03	1.04	22	1,347	29	26	.85	.98	50	1,805	1,098	3,623	62,420
SW	Tk Dv (1)			12	9		.91	1.03	1.04	22	1,347	29	26	.85	.98	50	1,805	1,098	3,623	62,420
SW	Tk Dv (1)			12	9		.91	1.03	1.04	22	1,347	29	26	.85	.98	50	1,805	1,098	3,623	62,420
SW	Tk Dv (1)			12	9		.91	1.03	1.04	22	1,347	29	26	.85	.98	50	1,805	1,098	3,623	62,420
SW	Tk Dv (1)			12	9		.91	1.03	1.04	22	1,347	29	26	.85	.98	50	1,805	1,098	3,623	62,420

SW	Tk Dv (1)			12	9		.91	1.03	1.04	22	1,347	29	26	85	98	50	1,805	1,098	3,623	62,420
SW	Tk Dv (1)			12	9		.91	1.03	1.04	22	1,347	29	26	85	98	50	1,805	1,098	3,623	62,420
SW	Tk Dv (1)			12	9		.91	1.03	1.04	22	1,347	29	26	85	98	50	1,805	1,098	3,623	62,420
SW	Tk Dv (1)			12	9		.91	1.03	1.04	22	1,347	29		85	98	50	1,805	1,098	3,623	62,420
SW	Art A Dv (1)		27				.91	1.03	1.04	25	1,523			85	98			254	838	41,447
Hun	MR Dv (1)	87				.77	.91	1.03	1.04	67	4,153		316	85	97	307	11,035	2,446	8,072	58,601
Hun	MR Dv (1)	87				.77	.91	1.03	1.04	67	4,153		316	85	97	307	11,035	2,446	8,072	58,601
Hun	MR Dv (1)	87				.77	.91	1.03	1.04	67	4,153		316	85	97	307	11,035	2,446	8,072	58,601
Hun	MR Dv (1)	87				.77	.91	1.03	1.04	67	4,153		316	85	97	307	11,035	2,446	8,072	58,601
Hun	MR Dv (1)	87				.77	.91	1.03	1.04	67	4,153		316	85	97	307	11,035	2,446	8,072	58,601
Hun	MR Dv (1)	87				.77	.91	1.03	1.04	67	4,153		316	85	97	307	11,035	2,446	8,072	58,601
Rom	MR Dv (1)	87				.77	.91	1.03	1.04	67	4,153		316	85	97	307	11,035	2,446	8,072	58,601
Rom	MR Dv (1)	87				.77	.91	1.03	1.04	67	4,153		316	85	97	307	11,035	2,446	8,072	58,601
Rom	MR Dv (1)	87				.77	.91	1.03	1.04	67	4,153		316	85	97	307	11,035	2,446	8,072	58,601
Rom	MR Dv (1)	87				.77	.91	1.03	1.04	67	4,153		316	85	97	307	11,035	2,446	8,072	58,601
Rom	MR Dv (1)	87				.77	.91	1.03	1.04	67	4,153		316	85	97	307	11,035	2,446	8,072	58,601
Rom	MR Dv (1)	87				.77	.91	1.03	1.04	67	4,153		316	85	97	307	11,035	2,446	8,072	58,601
Rom	MR Dv (1)	87				.77	.91	1.03	1.04	67	4,153		316	85	97	307	11,035	2,446	8,072	58,601
Bul	MR Dv (1)	38				.77	.84	.95	.96	39	2,389		108	85	90	97	3,492	1,379	4,551	58,482
Bul	MR Dv (1)	38				.77	.84	.95	.96	39	2,389		108	85	90	97	3,492	1,379	4,551	58,482
Bul	MR Dv (1)	38				.77	.84	.95	.96	39	2,389		108	85	90	97	3,492	1,379	4,551	58,482
Bul	MR Dv (1)	38				.77	.84	.95	.96	39	2,389		108	85	90	97	3,492	1,379	4,551	58,482
Bul	MR Dv (1)	38				.77	.84	.95	.96	39	2,389		108	85	90	97	3,492	1,379	4,551	58,482
S	MR Dv (1)		27	20	18		.91	1.03	1.04	64	3,961	29	232	85	95	245	8,822	2,649	8,742	82,811
S	MR Dv (1)		27	20	18		.91	1.03	1.04	64	3,961	29	232	85	95	245	8,822	2,649	8,742	82,811
S	MR Dv (1)		27	20	18		.91	1.03	1.04	64	3,961	29	232	85	95	245	8,822	2,649	8,742	82,811
S	MR Dv (1)		27	20	18		.91	1.03	1.04	64	3,961	29	232	85	95	245	8,822	2,649	8,742	82,811
S	MR Dv (1)		27	20	18		.91	1.03	1.04	64	3,961	29	232	85	95	245	8,822	2,649	8,742	82,811
S	MR Dv (1)		27	20	18		.91	1.03	1.04	64	3,961	29	232	85	95	245	8,822	2,649	8,742	82,811
S	Tk Dv (1)		27	12	9		.91	1.03	1.04	22	1,347	29	26	85	98	50	1,805	1,098	3,623	62,420
S	Art A Dv (1)		27				.91	1.03	1.04	25	1,523	29		85	98			254	838	41,447

133

Notes to Table C-1

To arrive at the WTO's current mobilization capacity in WUVs, this table addresses four questions. What units are to be counted? When could they arrive? What weapons are associated with each unit? And what are their WUV scores?

The first two questions are addressed in the two leftmost columns of the table, which list the units' original locations, names, and estimated times of arrival on the central front. At the bottom of these columns are units that are located in the Atlantic-to-the-Urals region but are not considered relevant to the central front.

Warsaw Pact units were taken from three sources: International Institute for Strategic Studies, *The Military Balance 1987–1988* (London, 1987); Mark L. Urban, *Soviet Land Power* (London: Ian Allen, 1985); and David C. Isby, *Weapons and Tactics of the Soviet Army* (London: Jane's Publishing, 1988). While these sources are in broad agreement at the division level, Isby's numbers are used on the margin because they are the most detailed and consistent. In addition Isby's division count falls midway between, for example, John M. Collins and Bernard C. Victory, *U.S./Soviet Military Balance, Statistical Trends, 1980–1987* (As of January 1, 1988, CSR 88-425-S) (Congressional Research Service, 1988), representing the low end; and International Institute for Strategic Studies, *The Military Balance 1988–1989* (London, 1988) and the recently released *The Military Balance 1989–1990* (London, 1989). Isby is not the most recent source, but because of definitional problems, the most recent number is not always the most accurate.

For example, based largely on definitional changes, the numbers reported by IISS change significantly from year to year, and often differ sharply from other sources. For disputes over IISS data, see Anthony H. Cordesman, "Fatal Flaws in Presenting the NATO/Warsaw Pact Balance," *Armed Forces Journal International*, vol. 125 (July 1988), pp. 60–68, and the letter to IISS members (London: IISS, 1989) in response to Cordesman's article. For a comparison of NATO and WTO official estimates see NATO Press Service, *Conventional Forces in Europe: The Facts* (Brussels, 1988); and the declaration on "Correlation of the Armed Forces and Basic Types of Armaments of the Warsaw Treaty Organization in Europe and Adjacent Water Areas," made by the Committee of the Ministers of Defence of the Warsaw Treaty Member States of January 30, 1989, in Sofia, Bulgaria, published by the Conference on Disarmament, February 17, 1989. See also Steven J. Zaloga, "Big Differences between NATO, Warsaw Pact Conventional Force Tallies," *Armed Forces Journal International*, vol. 126 (March 1989), pp. 32–36. For a general comparison of various bean counts showing the large discrepancies among them see table 4-1 in John D. Steinbruner, ed., *Restructuring American Foreign Policy* (Brookings, 1989). For a comprehensive effort to reconcile current differences over data, see Institute for Defense and Disarmament Studies, *Cutting Conventional Forces, 1* (Brookline, Mass., July 1989).

Not all WTO forces in the Atlantic-to-the-Urals (ATTU) region are assumed to be allocated in the central front. The Soviets are assumed to maintain some ATTU forces opposite Turkey and Iran and some oriented toward Norway, for instance. In the more uncertain cases such as the Soviet central reserve, it is assumed, conservatively, that all forces are allocated to the central front. The allocative assumptions used here are consistent with Pentagon Central Front analysis conducted over the last ten years (at least), and are more conservative than those published in Department of Defense, *Soviet Military Power: Prospects for Change, 1989* (1989) or any other edition of *Soviet Military Power*. In detail, the following assumptions were made. With the exception of the Southern group of Soviet forces in Hungary and Soviet forces in the Leningrad Military District, all forces in the western and northwestern theaters of military operations (TVDs) are assumed to be allocated to the central front. For these two exceptions, roughly 50 percent of their forces are allocated to the Central Front. Soviet forces in the southern and southwestern TVDs are withheld, as are forces in the Far Eastern TVD (outside the ATTU).

Turning to the second question, that of arrival times, the estimate is a function of three factors: the state of readiness of the individual units (category I, II, or III), their original distance from the front, and the Soviets' presumed willingness to use, on the central front, units that have not attained full readiness. These factors can be estimated from several sources: Office of the Assistant Secretary of Defense for Program Analysis and Evaluation, *NATO Center Region Military Balance Study, 1978–1984*, (Department of Defense, July 1979); Barry R. Posen, "Measuring the European Conventional Balance: Coping with Complexity in Threat Assessment," *International Security*, vol. 9 (Winter 1984–85); and Michael Sadykiewicz, *Soviet-Warsaw Pact Western Theater of Military Operations: Organization and Missions*, N-2596-AF (Santa Monica, Calif.: Rand Corp., August, 1987).

These sources disagree, particularly about the timing of the category IIs' entry into the theater. For example, Posen estimates the category IIs' arrival on the central front at approximately M+40. Kugler estimates M+10 to M+15 for arrival; see *Alliance and Defense Capabilities in Europe*, Hearings before the Senate Committee on Armed Services, 100 Cong. 1 sess. (Government Printing Office, 1988), p. 226. Kugler's estimates are technically feasible, but there is a trade-off between speed of arrival and combat effectiveness. The Soviets might dispatch their category II units very early, hoping to exploit NATO's mobilization lag. But the WEI/WUV scores of such early-deploying category II (or III) units should be accordingly reduced to reflect incomplete equipage, lack of training, and logistical difficulties. The base case assumes the Soviets would not send units until fully ready but assumes conservatively that they could be readied quite quickly. This produces the mid-range estimate that category IIs flow into the theater at M+25.

Arrival times also depend on the time needed for rail transport and road march from railheads. For the Carpathian, Byelorussian, and Baltic Military Districts, 5 days are estimated. For the Central Reserve, 10 days. Thus, although Category III's begin to enter the theater at M+55, reinforcements peak at M+70. The Czech and Polish category II's and III's precede the Soviets' mobilizing forces (with the exception of the central reserve) throughout the mobilization schedule.

The third question is, what weapons are associated with each unit? First, if one selects any unit, say the Soviet 16th Tank (TK) Division, and reads left to right, the following categories of weapons are possible: tanks, artillery, mortars, antiarmor, infantry fighting vehicles, armored reconnaissance vehicles, armored personnel carriers, and small arms. These categories are further broken down by type (for example, T-55, T-64, T-72, and T-80 tanks).

Every unit has a so-called table of organization and equipment (TO&E) giving the specified number of weapons of each type at full unit readiness. For instance, the Soviet 16th TK Division TO&E calls for 134 T-72 and 188 T-80 tanks. If one examines the table further, one will discover that this unit's TO&E also calls for 24 multiple rocket launchers (MRL), 18 120mm mortars, and so on.

The TO&Es for Soviet divisions were taken from U.S. Army Concepts Analysis Agency, *Weapon Effectiveness Indices/Weighted Unit Values (WEI/WUV) III*, CAA-85-79-12 (Department of Defense, November, 1979; declassified, December 31, 1986); David C. Isby, *Ten Million Bayonets: Inside the Armies of the Soviet Union* (London: Arms and Armour Press, 1988); and Overton Day, *Soviet Divisional Organizational*

Guide, DDB-1100-333-82, (Defense Intelligence Agency, July 1982). Although the WEI/WUV manual gives projections for 1986, these do not differ significantly from current TO&E assessments. See Phillip A. Karber, "The Military Impact of the Gorbachev Reductions," *Armed Forces Journal International*, vol. 126 (January 1989), p. 63. Isby, *Ten Million Bayonets*, was used to update TO&Es for Soviet tank and artillery division types. The DIA study was used to supplement details on other types of divisions, with the exception of low-readiness divisions; when a conflict appeared between Isby's book and another source, Isby's was favored because it is the more detailed.

Any information on low-readiness divisions is bound to be somewhat suspect (it seems doubtful that the Soviets keep especially precise inventories of the central reserve divisions). The changes in the TO&Es of low-readiness divisions are partially a function of the equipment replacement rate of category I divisions, but, due to breakdowns and uneven maintenance, there is no guarantee that low-readiness divisions will actually have second-generation equipment readily available, or that the equipment's effectiveness will not depreciate. Given the strained logistics and confusion created by an actual war, a mobilized category III motorized rifle division might appear in many different configurations and possibly with very low levels of actual effectiveness regardless of the models of equipment used. Given the uncertainty surrounding this question, the WEI/WUV manual's projections for mobilized category II and III divisions' TO&Es were used, although they seem optimistic for the WTO.

Having counted weapons in units, there remains the question of scoring. Obviously, not all weapons are created equal. In arriving at the overall WUV scores, two multipliers are assigned to the raw weapon counts. First, each weapon (for example, T-55 tank) is assigned a normalized weapon effectiveness index (WEI) score. A numeraire, or reference, weapon is selected and assigned the value 1.0. Then, based on a comparison with that numeraire's performance in the areas of firepower, protection, and mobility, every other tank is assigned a normalized WEI. Now, if pistol n is 50 percent better than the reference pistol, its normalized WEI would be 1.5, the same as a tank that is better than the reference tank by 50 percent. Obviously, however, one would not bet on the pistol (WEI = 1.5) in combat with the tank (WEI = 1.5). Different weapon categories obviously deserve different weights in armored war; and in the rightmost tank column in the table, the tank category weight (CW) of 100 is applied. The artillery CW is found to be 92; the mortar CW is 48, and so on (see table entries).

The overall WUV score for each unit, therefore, is computed by assigning normalized

WEI scores to each weapon, multiplying by the appropriate category weight, and summing over the entire TO&E of the unit. For a sample calculation, see *Weapon Effectiveness Indices/Weighted Unit Values*, pp. 13-8, 13-9.

For space considerations, and to make the table legible, the number of weapon types was reduced to four within a weapon category. This does not mean the WEIs are the same for T-34 and T-55 tanks. Instead, either a T-34 WEI or a T-55 WEI is used, depending on the predominant weapon type within the division if both T-34s and T-55s are present. When several types of hand-held antitank weapons were present and the numbers of each type were known, the WEI was combined and averaged to reflect the mix of weapons present. Most units do not have this sort of diversity in their TO&Es, however, and the overall effect on the WEI/WUV scores is negligible.

WEI scores are from U.S. Army Concepts Analysis Agency, *Weapon Effectiveness Indices/Weighted Unit Values, III*. Close air support is treated separately in the adaptive dynamic model used in this study. Hence, to avoid double counting, helicopters and air defenses were removed from the WEI/WUV scores. WUVs were taken from p. 13-7 using WUV scores for Europe. Both WTO and NATO are given offensive WUV scores, because defensive advantage is reflected in the casualty-exchange ratio (see appendix B) and because offensive scoring produces a more conservative result for NATO. WEIs were taken from pp. q-72 to q-87. To reflect the impact of reactive armor, the WEIs of Soviet category I T-64, T-72, and T-80 tanks in the GSFG, NGF, and CGF were increased by a factor of 10 percent.

There is one factor that becomes critical in evaluating the WTO's unilateral cuts and in estimating the effect of CFE I and CFE II: spare equipment. The combat simulations involve the WUV scores of mobilized units (that is, their TO&Es), but arms control agreements are stated in terms of total weapon inventories (TO&Es plus spares). In this analysis, the ratio of total weaponry to TO&E weaponry for NATO and the WTO is assumed to be 1.2. Reductions are always implemented so that after the cuts, the ratio of total weapons in a reduction category (for example, tanks) to TO&E weapons in that category remains 1.2. Hence, under CFE, *total* tanks would fall to the agreed ceiling of 20,000. TO&E tanks, accordingly, would number 16,667. The precise ratio might, of course, vary from weapon to weapon or, for a given weapon, from country to country. But, as a summary estimate, the TO&E "expansion factor" of 1.2 is reasonable, and was derived from data given in Institute for Defense and Disarmament Studies, *Cutting Conventional Forces, 1*; and NATO Press Service, *Conventional Forces in Europe: The Facts*.

The weapon totals arrived at by this "expanded TO&E" method are listed in table C-2 for the WTO and table C-4 for NATO.

TABLE C-2. WTO Weapon Totals and ADE Mobilization Schedule Derived from Table C-1, Current Balance

TANKS

WEAPON TYPE AND AREA	TOTAL	Tank: T-34/T-55	Tank: T-64	Tank: T-72	Tank: T-80
ATTU including spares	55,340				
ATTU TO&E	46,117	19,069	4,816	18,346	3,886
Central Front, including spares	33,605				
Central Front TO&E	28,004	11,774	1,982	10,362	3,886

ARTILLERY

WEAPON TYPE AND AREA	TOTAL	Arty: 122 M-38	Arty: MRL	Arty: 152 D-1	Arty: 122 M74	Mortar: 120MM	Antiarmor: T-21	Antiarmor: 100MM
ATTU including spares	42,457							
ATTU TO&E	35,381	8,697	6,756	4,414	5,170	5,589	3,268	1,486
Central Front, including spares	26,286							
Central Front TO&E	21,905	4,881	4,116	2,842	3,640	3,555	1,792	1,078

ARMORED VEHICLES

WEAPON TYPE AND AREA	TOTAL	ARV: OT-65	ARV: BRDM	ARV: BMP-R	ARV: BRDM AT5	APC: ARV	APC: APC	IFV: BMP
ATTU including spares	75,546							
ATTU TO&E	62,955	3,012	2,617	2,402	1,485	4,403	30,724	18,312
Central Front, including spares	43,165							
Central Front TO&E	35,971	1,082	1,618	1,530	774	3,098	15,690	12,179

CENTRAL FRONT MOBILIZATION SCHEDULE, CURRENT BALANCE

Days After M+0	M+1	M+5	M+10	M+15	M+20	M+25	M+30	M+35	M+40
ADE arrival	12.8	13.9	10.6	2.4	2.5	2.1	6.1	3.8	3.0
Total ADEs	12.8	26.7	37.3	39.7	42.2	44.3	50.4	54.2	57.2
WUV Arrival	1,269,417	1,383,136	1,048,816	239,042	248,433	207,651	606,770	376,545	300,405
Total WUV	1,269,417	2,652,553	3,701,369	3,940,411	4,188,844	4,396,495	5,003,264	5,379,809	5,680,214

Days After M+0	M+45	M+50	M+55	M+60	M+65	M+70	M+75	M+80	M+85	M+90
ADE arrival	.7	.7	1.5	3.4	2.2	2.2	1.5	3.0	3.3	2.5
Total ADEs	57.9	58.7	60.1	63.5	65.7	67.9	69.3	72.3	75.6	78.1
WUV Arrival	72,614	72,614	145,228	334,806	217,842	217,842	145,228	294,449	325,616	253,003
Total WUV	5,752,828	5,825,442	5,970,670	6,305,476	6,523,318	6,741,160	6,886,388	7,180,837	7,506,454	7,759,456

Source: Data given in Table C-1.

Table C-3. NATO Units, Central Front Arrival Times, and WUV Scores, Current Balance

STATE; CORPS	DIVISION	BRIGADE	REGIMENT	ORIGINAL LOCATION	CORPS SECTOR	DAY	TANKS TO&E	TANKS EFFECTIVENESS	WEI	(WEI-CW 100)
Netherlands										
I Netherlands	4th Mech	41,42,43			2	M+5	CENT 53; LEO 1 230	CENT 1.00; LEO 1 1.02	288	28,760
I Netherlands	5th Mech	51,52,53			2	M+5	CENT 53; LEO 1 230	CENT 1.00; LEO 1 1.02	288	28,760
I Netherlands	1st Mech	11,12,13		Schaarsbergen, NE	2	M+10	CENT 53; LEO 1 230	CENT 1.00; LEO 1 1.02	288	28,760
Belgium										
I Belgian	16th Mech	4 mech, 17 Arm		Soest, FRG	4	M+1	LEO 1 82; CHIEF 80	LEO 1 1.02; CHIEF 1.18	178	17,804
I Belgian	1st Div	1 mech, 7 mech		Liege, BE	4	M+1	LEO 1 82; CHIEF 40	LEO 1 1.02; CHIEF 1.18	131	13,084
I Belgian		10 mech		Zonhoven, BE	4	M+10	LEO 1 25; CHIEF 12	LEO 1 1.02; CHIEF 1.18	39	3,925
I Belgian		12 mot		Liege, BE	4	M+10	LEO 1 25; CHIEF 12	LEO 1 1.02; CHIEF 1.18	39	3,925
Denmark										
Jutland	Jutland	1, 2, 3 mech inf		Rendsburg, FRG	1	M+15	CENT 88; LEO 1 120; CHIEF	CENT 1.00; LEO 1 1.02; CHIEF 1.18	210	21,040
United Kingdom										
I British	1 Arm	7, 12, 22		Verden, FRG	3	M+1	CENT; LEO 1; CHIEF 148	CENT 1.00; LEO 1 1.02; CHIEF/C 1.18	175	17,464
I British	4 Arm	11, 20, 30 Arm		Herford, FRG	3	M+1	CHIEF 148	CENT 1.00; LEO 1 1.02; CHIEF 1.18	175	17,464
I British	2 Inf	15, 24, 49 inf		York, UK	3	M+1	CHIEF 148	CENT 1.00; LEO 1 1.02; CHIEF 1.18	175	17,464
I British	Art Div		4 reg	York, UK	3	M+1				
British		5 Air		Aldershot, UK	3	M+5	CHIEF 44	CENT 1.00; LEO 1 1.02; CHIEF 1.18	52	5,239
I British	3 Arm	4 Arm, 6 Arm, 19 inf		Soest, FRG	3	M+10	CHIEF 148	CENT 1.00; LEO 1 1.02; CHIEF 1.18	175	17,464
UKMF		1 Inf		Tidworth, UK	1	M+10	CHIEF 44	CENT 1.00; LEO 1 1.02; CHIEF 1.18	52	5,192
UKMF		Other Btlns		Tidworth, UK	3	M+10	CHIEF 44	CENT 1.00; LEO 1 1.02; CHIEF 1.18	52	5,192
Canada										
C. F. Europe		4 Mech		Lahr, FRG	Res	M+5	CENT 0; LEO 1 65; CHIEF/CM-48 90	CENT 1.00; LEO 1 .90; CHIEF/C 1.18	59	5,850
Mobile Command		5e Groupe-Brig		Valcar, CA	Res	M+10	CENT 0; LEO 1 0; CHIEF/CM-48 90; M-48 20	1.02	18	1,800
Mobile Command		5e Groupe-Brig		Calgary, CA	Res	M+25	CENT 0; LEO 1 0; CHIEF/CM-48 90; M-48 30	1.02	27	2,700

France

	Unit	Location	Rdy	Mob	B2 AMX	CENT	LEO 1	CHIEF/CB2	AMX	CENT	LEO 1	CHIEF/C		
FAR	4th Air	Nancy, FR	Res	M+5	75				.85	1.00	1.02	1:18	64	6,375
FAR	9th lt Arm	Nimes, FR	Res	M+5	125				.85	1.00	1.02	1:18	106	10,625
FAR	11th lt Arm	Toulouse, FR	Res	M+5	125				.85	1.00	1.02	1:18	106	10,625
II	3rd Arm	Freiburg, FRG	Res	M+10	125				.85	1.00	1.02	1:18	106	10,625
II	5th Arm	Landau, FRG	Res	M+10	54				.85	1.00	1.02	1:18	46	4,590
II	1st Arm	Trier, FRG	Res	M+10	75				.85	1.00	1.02	1:18	64	6,375
FAR	27th Mou	Grenoble, FR	Res	M+15	75				.85	1.00	1.02	1:18	64	6,375
II	15th Inf	Limoges, FR	Res	M+15	125				.85	1.00	1.02	1:18	106	10,625
I	12th lt Arm	Saumur, FR	Res	M+15	54				.85	1.00	1.02	1:18	46	4,590
I	14th lt Arm	Montpellier, FR	Res	M+15	125				.85	1.00	1.02	1:18	106	10,625
III	2nd Arm	Versailles, FR	Res	M+15	125				.85	1.00	1.02	1:18	106	10,625
III	8th Inf	Amiens, FR	Res	M+15					.85	1.00	1.02	1:18	46	4,590
III	10th Arm	Chalons, FR	Res	M+15					.85	1.00	1.02	1:18	106	10,625
I	7th Arm	Besancon, FR	Res	M+20					.85	1.00	1.02	1:18	106	10,625

West Germany

Command	Unit	Sub-units	Location	Rdy	Mob	M-48	LEO 1	LEO 1	LEO 2	M-48	LEO 1	LEO 1	LEO 2		
I Korps	1st Arm	1, 2 Arm, 3 Inf	Hanover, FRG	3	M+1		100		150	.99	1.02	1.02	1.22	285	28,500
I Korps	3rd Arm	7 A/l, 8 Arm, 9 Arm	Buxtehude, FRG	2	M+1		100		200	.99	1.02	1.02	1.22	346	34,600
I Korps	6th A/l	16,17 A/l, 18 Arm	Neumunster, FRG	1	M+1		100		150	.99	1.02	1.02	1.22	285	28,500
I Korps	7th Arm	19,20 Arm, 21 A/l	Westphalia, FRG	3	M+1		100		200	.99	1.02	1.02	1.22	346	34,600
II Korps	4th A/l	10,11 A/l, 12 Arm	Regensburg, FRG	8	M+1		100		150	.99	1.02	1.02	1.22	285	28,500
II Korps	1st Mountain	22 A/l, 23 mou, 24 Arm	Garmisch, FRG	8	M+1		100		100	.99	1.02	1.02	1.22	224	22,400
III Korps	2nd A/l	4,5 A/l, 6 Arm	Regensburg, FRG	5	M+1		100		150	.99	1.02	1.02	1.22	285	28,500
III Korps	12th Arm	34 Arm, 35 A/l, 36 Arm	Garmisch, FRG	6	M+1		100		200	.99	1.02	1.02	1.22	346	34,600
I Korps	11th A/l	31,32 A/l, 33 Arm	Oldenburg, FRG	2	M+5		100		150	.99	1.02	1.02	1.22	285	28,500
II Korps	10th Arm	28,29 Arm, 30 A/l	Sigmaringen, FRG	8	M+5		100		200	.99	1.02	1.02	1.22	346	34,600
II Korps	1st Air	25,26,27 airborne	Bruchsal, FRG	8	M+5		0			.99	1.02	1.02	1.22		
III Korps	5th Arm	14,15 Arm, 13 A/l	Sigmaringen, FRG	5	M+5		0		200	.99	1.02	1.02	1.22	346	34,600
Terr Army SH		51 Home Defence	Kiel, FRG	1	M+5	96	0			.99	1.02	1.02	1.22	346	34,600
Terr Army South		56 Home Defence	Munich, FRG	8	M+5	96	0			.99	1.02	1.02	1.22	95	9,504
Terr Army North		52 Home Defence	Hanover, FRG	3	M+10	96	0			.99	1.02	1.02	1.22	95	9,504
Terr Army North		62 Home Defence	Hanover, FRG	Res	M+10	96	0			.99	1.02	1.02	1.22	95	9,504
Terr Army North		53 Home Defence	Dusseldorf, FRG	4	M+10	96	0			.99	1.02	1.02	1.22	95	9,504
Terr Army North		63 Home Defence	Dusseldorf, FRG	Res	M+10	96	0			.99	1.02	1.02	1.22	95	9,504
Terr Army South		52 Home Defence	Mainz, FRG	5	M+10	96	0			.99	1.02	1.02	1.22	95	9,504
Terr Army South		62 Home Defence	Trier, FRG	Res	M+10	96	0			.99	1.02	1.02	1.22	95	9,504
Terr Army South		55 Home Defence	Stuttgart, FRG	8	M+10	96	0			.99	1.02	1.02	1.22	95	9,504
Terr Army SH		61 Home Defence	Kiel, FRG	Res	M+15	96	0			.99	1.02	1.02	1.22	95	9,504
Terr Army South		66 Home Defence	Munich, FRG	Res	M+15	96	0			.99	1.02	1.02	1.22	95	9,504
Terr Army South		65 Home Defence	Stuttgart, FRG	Res	M+20	96	0			.99	1.02	1.02	1.22	95	9,504

Table C-3. *continued*

STATE; CORPS	DIVISION	BRIGADE	REGIMENT	ORIGINAL LOCATION	CORPS SECTOR	DAY	TANKS TO&E M-48	TO&E M-60A1	TO&E M-60A2	TO&E M-1	EFFECTIVENESS M-48	EFF M-60A1	EFF M-60A2	EFF M-1	WEI	(WEI-CW 100)
United States																
VII US	1st Arm	1,2,3	+ Art	Frankfurt, FRG	7	M+1		0	58	232	.99	1.00	1.11	1.31	368	36,830
VII US		Art	17,72,210	Stuttgart, FRG	7	M+1		0	0		.99	1.00	1.11	1.31		
V US	3rd Arm	1,2,3	+ Art	Frankfurt, FRG	6	M+1		0	58	232	.99	1.00	1.11	1.31	368	36,830
V US		Art: 41,42			6	M+1		0	0		.99	1.00	1.11	1.31		
V US	1st Inf	3	11 ACR	Fulda, FRG	6	M+1		0	20	75	.99	1.00	1.11	1.31	120	12,045
VII /III	2nd Arm	3		Goppingen, FRG	7	M+1		0	10	100	.99	1.00	1.11	1.31	142	14,210
III US	3rd Inf			Garstedt, FRG	2	M+1		0	20	75	.99	1.00	1.11	1.31	120	12,045
VII US		1,2,3	+ Art	Wurzburg, FRG	7	M+5		0	36	270	.99	1.00	1.11	1.31	394	39,366
VII US	8th Inf (mech)	1,2,3	2 ACR	Nuremberg, FRG	7	M+5		0	65	65	.99	1.00	1.11	1.31	157	15,730
V US		1,2,3	+ Art	Bad Kreuznach,FRG	Res	M+5		0	58	232	.99	1.00	1.11	1.31	368	36,830
CONUS POMCUS																
US	1st Inf	1,2		Ft. Riley KS	7	M+10		0	20	200	.99	1.00	1.11	1.31	284	28,420
III US			3 ACR	Ft. Bliss TX	7	M+10		0	65	65	.99	1.00	1.11	1.31	157	15,730
III US		Art : 212		Stuttgart, FRG	Res	M+10		0	0		.99	1.00	1.11	1.31		
I US	7th Inf	1,2,3		Ft. Ord, CA	Res	M+15		0	56	14	.99	1.00	1.11	1.31	81	8,050
I US	25th Inf	1,2,3		Schofield, HI	2	M+15		0	56	14	.99	1.00	1.11	1.31	81	8,050
III US	2nd Arm	1,2		Ft. Hood, TX	Res	M+15		0	40	150	.99	1.00	1.11	1.31	241	24,090
III US	1st Cav	1,2,155		Ft. Hood, TX	2	M+15		0	58	232	.99	1.00	1.11	1.31	368	36,830
III US	4th Inf (mech)	1,2,3		Ft. Carson, CO	2	M+15		0	58	232	.99	1.00	1.11	1.31	368	36,830

Reserve and National Guard

Command	Division	Units	Cadre	Location	Mob	Avail	%	%	%	%	Ratio	Ratio	Ratio	Ratio	Personnel	Strength
III US		Art: 75,214		Ft. Knox, KY	Res	M+20		0	0	75	.99	1.00	1.11	1.31	120	12,045
CONUS Res	26th Inf	194 Arm		Ft. Knox, KY	Res	M+25		0	20	75	.99	1.00	1.11	1.31	120	12,045
CONUS Res		197 mech Inf		MA-CT-SC-RI	Res	M+32		100	20	50	.99	1.00	1.11	1.31	228	22,766
NG		1,3,43		PA	Res	M+39		0	56	75	.99	1.00	1.11	1.31	120	12,045
CONUS Res	28th Inf	157 mech Inf		PA-VA-WV	Res	M+46		100	20	50	.99	1.00	1.11	1.31	228	22,766
CONUS Res		2,55,56		IN-IL-PA	Res	M+46		20	56		.99	1.00	1.11	1.31		
NG		Art: 428,424,479		MA-NY-ME	Res	M+53	15	45	20		.99	1.00	1.11	1.31	57	5,705
NG		29 Inf		NC	Res	M+53	10	20	25		.99	1.00	1.11	1.31	96	9,575
NG		30 Inf (mech)		MA-NY-ME	Res	M+53	15	60	20	10	.99	1.00	1.11	1.31	57	5,705
NG		33 Inf	107 ACR	OH-WV	Res	M+53		45	60	10	.99	1.00	1.11	1.31	127	12,660
NG	35th Mech Inf	32 Inf (mech)		NC	Res	M+60	10	150	25	25	.99	1.00	1.11	1.31	96	9,575
NG		67,69,149	116 ACR	CO-KS-KY	Res	M+60	32	60	75	25	.99	1.00	1.11	1.31	298	29,768
NG	29th lt Inf	2,55,56		OH-WV	Res	M+60	50	0	60		.99	1.00	1.11	1.31	127	12,660
NG	38th Mech Inf	2,46,76		MD-VA	Res	M+67	32	150	0		.99	1.00	1.11	1.31	50	4,950
NG		41 Inf		IN-MI-OH	Res	M+67	15	20	75		.99	1.00	1.11	1.31	298	29,768
NG		81 Inf (mech)		OR	Res	M+67	10	45	20		.99	1.00	1.11	1.31	57	5,705
NG		45 Inf		WA	Res	M+74	15	60	25	10	.99	1.00	1.11	1.31	96	9,575
NG		218 Inf (mech)	163 ACR	WI-RI-NC	Res	M+74	10	20	60	10	.99	1.00	1.11	1.31	127	12,660
NG		Art: 45,57,103		OK	Res	M+74	15	45	20		.99	1.00	1.11	1.31	57	5,705
NG		53 Inf		SC	Res	M+74	20	0	25		.99	1.00	1.11	1.31	96	9,575
NG		30 Arm		IN-IL-PA	Res	M+81	15	60	0		.99	1.00	1.11	1.31		
NG		73 Inf		TN	Res	M+81		20	60		.99	1.00	1.11	1.31	127	12,660
NG		Art: 113,115,118		FL	Res	M+81		45	20		.99	1.00	1.11	1.31	57	5,705
NG		Art: 135,138,142	278 ACR	TN	Res	M+81		20	20		.99	1.00	1.11	1.31	87	8,700
NG		31 Arm		OH	Res	M+88		0	20		.99	1.00	1.11	1.31	57	5,705
NG	42nd Inf	1,2		IN-IL-PA	Res	M+88	20	45	0		.99	1.00	1.11	1.31		
NG		Art: 196,197,209		IN-IL-PA	Res	M+88	65	65	40	30	.99	1.00	1.11	1.31	87	8,700
NG		Art: 147,151,169		AL	Res	M+88		0	0		.99	1.00	1.11	1.31	213	21,305
NG		Art: 227,163,631		NY	Res	M+88		0	0		.99	1.00	1.11	1.31		
NG	49th Arm	1,2,3		TX-NM	Res	M+95	75	150	75	25	.99	1.00	1.11	1.31	340	34,025
NG	50th Arm	1,2,86		NJ	Res	M+102	75	150	75	25	.99	1.00	1.11	1.31	340	34,025

Table C-3. *continued*

STATE; CORPS	DIVISION	TO&E			EFFECTIVENESS				WEI	(WEI-CW 100)
ATTU Units Not Allocated to Central Front										
United Kingdom	Inf	20		30		1.00	1.02	1.18	55	5,540
	Inf	20		30		1.00	1.02	1.18	55	5,540
	Inf	20		30		1.00	1.02	1.18	55	5,540
	Inf	20	0	30		1.00	1.02	1.18	55	5,540
	Inf	20	0	30		1.00	1.02	1.18	55	5,540
	Inf	20	0	30		1.00	1.02	1.18	55	5,540
	Inf	20	0	30		1.00	1.02	1.18	55	5,540
	Inf	20	0	30		1.00	1.02	1.18	55	5,540
	Inf	20	0	30		1.00	1.02	1.18	55	5,540
France	Arm	65	0		.85	1.00	1.02	1.18	55	5,525
	Arm	65	0		.85	1.00	1.02	1.18	55	5,525
Netherlands	Inf	25	0			1.00	1.02		25	2,500
Turkey	Mech/Inf	150	0		.88	1.00	1.11	1.31	132	13,200
	Mech/Inf	150	0		.88	1.00	1.11	1.31	132	13,200
	Mech/Inf	150	0		.88	1.00	1.11	1.31	132	13,200
	Mech/Inf	150	0		.88	1.00	1.11	1.31	132	13,200
	Mech/Inf	150	0		.88	1.00	1.11	1.31	132	13,200
	Mech/Inf	150	0		.88	1.00	1.11	1.31	132	13,200
	Mech/Inf	150	0		.88	1.00	1.11	1.31	132	13,200
	Mech/Inf	150	0		.88	1.00	1.11	1.31	132	13,200
	Mech/Inf	150	0		.88	1.00	1.11	1.31	132	13,200
	Mech/Inf	150	0		.88	1.00	1.11	1.31	132	13,200
	Mech/Inf	150	0		.88	1.00	1.11	1.31	132	13,200
	Mech/Inf	150	0		.88	1.00	1.11	1.31	132	13,200
	Mech/Inf	150	0		.88	1.00	1.11	1.31	132	13,200
	Mech/Inf	150	0		.88	1.00	1.11	1.31	132	13,200
	Mech/Inf	150	0		.88	1.00	1.11	1.31	132	13,200
	Mech/Inf	150	0		.88	1.00	1.11	1.31	132	13,200
	Mech/Inf	150	0		.88	1.00	1.11	1.31	132	13,200
	Mech/Inf	150	0		.88	1.00	1.11	1.31	132	13,200
	Mech/Inf	150	0		.88	1.00	1.11	1.31	132	13,200
	Mech/Inf	150	0		.88	1.00	1.11	1.31	132	13,200
	Mech/Inf	150	0		.88	1.00	1.11	1.31	132	13,200

Greece	Mech/Inf	125	0	0	.88	1.00	1.11	1.31	110	11,000
	Mech/Inf	125	0	0	.88	1.00	1.11	1.31	110	11,000
	Mech/Inf	125	0	0	.88	1.00	1.11	1.31	110	11,000
	Mech/Inf	125	0	0	.88	1.00	1.11	1.31	110	11,000
	Mech/Inf	125	0	0	.88	1.00	1.11	1.31	110	11,000
	Mech/Inf	125	0	0	.88	1.00	1.11	1.31	110	11,000
	Mech/Inf	125	0	0	.88	1.00	1.11	1.31	110	11,000
	Mech/Inf	125	0	0	.88	1.00	1.11	1.31	110	11,000
	Mech/Inf	125	0	0	.88	1.00	1.11	1.31	110	11,000
	Mech/Inf	125	0	0	.88	1.00	1.11	1.31	110	11,000
Italy	Mech/Inf	65	120	0	.88	1.00	1.11	1.31	177	17,720
	Mech/Inf	65	120	0	.88	1.00	1.11	1.31	177	17,720
	Mech/Inf	65	120	0	.88	1.00	1.11	1.31	177	17,720
	Mech/Inf	65	120	0	.88	1.00	1.11	1.31	177	17,720
	Mech/Inf	65	120	0	.88	1.00	1.11	1.31	177	17,720
	Mech/Inf	65	120	0	.88	1.00	1.11	1.31	177	17,720
	Mech/Inf	65	120	0	.88	1.00	1.11	1.31	177	17,720
	Mech/Inf	65	120	0	.88	1.00	1.11	1.31	177	17,720
Spain	Mech/Inf	100	0	0	.88	1.00	1.11	1.31	88	8,800
	Mech/Inf	100	0	0	.88	1.00	1.11	1.31	88	8,800
	Mech/Inf	100	0	0	.88	1.00	1.11	1.31	88	8,800
	Mech/Inf	100	0	0	.88	1.00	1.11	1.31	88	8,800
	Mech/Inf	100	0	0	.88	1.00	1.11	1.31	88	8,800
	Mech/Inf	100	0	0	.88	1.00	1.11	1.31	88	8,800
	Mech/Inf	100	0	0	.88	1.00	1.11	1.31	88	8,800
Portugal	Mech/Inf	11	0	0	.88	1.00	1.11	1.31	10	968
	Mech/Inf	11	0	0	.88	1.00	1.11	1.31	10	968
	Mech/Inf	11	0	0	.88	1.00	1.11	1.31	10	968
	Mech/Inf	11	0	0	.88	1.00	1.11	1.31	10	968
	Mech/Inf	11	0	0	.88	1.00	1.11	1.31	10	968
	Mech/Inf	11	0	0	.88	1.00	1.11	1.31	10	968
Norway	Mech/Inf	42	80	0	.99	1.00	1.11	1.31	122	12,158

Table C-3. *continued*

STATE; CORPS	DIVISION	BRIGADE; OR REGIMENT	ARTILLERY TO&E M-108/105MM	155HOW	M110	ARTILLERY EFFECTIVENESS M-108/105MM	155HOW	M110	WEI	WEI-CW 92	MORTARS TO&E 60/51MM	81MM	120MM	M-106/M-107/M-125	MORTARS EFFECTIVENESS 60/51MM	81MM	120MM	M-106/M-107/M-125	WEI	WEI-CW 48
Netherlands																				
I Netherlands	4th Mech	41,42,43		90		.78	.83		75	6,872			54	18			.87	1.00	65	3,119
I Netherlands	5th Mech	51,52,53		90		.78	.83		75	6,872			54	18			.87	1.00	65	3,119
I Netherlands	1st Mech	11,12,13		90		.78	.83		75	6,872			54	18			.87	1.00	65	3,119
Belgium																				
I Belgian	16th Mech	4 mech, 17 Arm	36	18		.78	.88		44	4,041	66	42		16	.78	.80		.89	99	4,758
I Belgian	1st Div	1 mech, 7 mech	36	18		.78	.88		44	4,041	66	42		16	.78	.80		.89	99	4,758
I Belgian		10 mech	14	7		.78	.88		18	1,616	33	21		8	.78	.80		.89	50	2,379
I Belgian		12 mot	14	7		.78	.88		18	1,616	33	21		8	.78	.80		.89	50	2,379
Denmark																				
Jutland	Jutland	1, 2, 3 mech inf	151	72		.78	.88		181	16,679	66	66		8	.78	.80		.89	163	7,815
United Kingdom																				
I British	1 Arm	7, 12, 22	24	12	3	.86	.88	1.00	34	3,146	80	8		24	.74	.80		.96	89	4,293
I British	4 Arm	11, 20, 30 Arm	24	12	3	.86	.88	1.00	34	3,146	80	8		24	.75	.80		.96	89	4,293
I British	2 Inf	15, 24, 49 inf	24	12	3	.86	.88	1.00	34	3,146	80	8		24	.75	.80		.96	89	4,293
I British	Art Div	4 reg	35	20	12	.86	.88	1.00	60	5,492										
British		5 Air	8			.86			7	633	26	3		8	.75	.80		.96	30	1,420
I British	3 Arm	4 Arm, 6 Arm, 19 inf	24	12	3	.86	.88	1.00	34	3,146	80	8		24	.75	.80		.96	89	4,293
UKMF		1 Inf	8			.86			7	633	26	3		8	.75	.80		.96	30	1,420
UKMF		Other Btns	8			.86			7	633	26	3		8	.75	.80		.96	30	1,420
Canada																				
C. F. Europe		4 Mech	190	30		.86	.88	1.00	190	17,462	32	16			.77	.96		.96	40	1,920
Mobile Command		5e Groupe-Brig	10			.86			9	810	32	16			.77	.96		.96	40	1,920
Mobile Command		5e Groupe-Brig	10			.86			9	810	32	16			.77	.96		.96	40	1,920

France

Corps	Formation	105MM	155HOW	M110	105MM	155HOW	M110	60MM	81MM	120MM		60MM	81MM	120MM		
FAR	4th Air		24		.86	.75	1.00	12	12	18	1,656	.77	.80	.87	35	1,656
FAR	9th lt Arm		24		.86	.75	1.00		24	18	1,656	.77	.80	.87	35	1,673
FAR	11th Air		24		.86	.75	1.00	12	12	16	1,656	.77	.80	.87	33	1,572
II	3rd Arm		24		.86	.75	1.00	12	12	16	1,656	.77	.80	.87	33	1,572
II	5th Arm		24		.86	.75	1.00	12	12	16	1,656	.77	.80	.87	33	1,572
I	1st Arm		24		.86	.75	1.00	12	12	16	1,656	.77	.80	.87	33	1,572
FAR	27th Mou		24		.86	.75	1.00	12	12	18	1,656	.77	.80	.87	35	1,656
II	15th Inf		24		.86	.75	1.00	12	12	18	1,656	.77	.80	.87	35	1,656
I	12th lt Arm		24		.86	.75	1.00	12	12	18	1,656	.77	.80	.87	33	1,656
I	14th lt Arm		24		.86	.75	1.00	12	12	16	1,656	.77	.80	.87	33	1,572
III	2nd Arm		24		.86	.75	1.00	12	12	18	1,656	.77	.80	.87	33	1,656
III	8th Inf		24		.86	.75	1.00	12	12	16	1,656	.77	.80	.87	33	1,572
III	10th Arm															
I	7th Arm															

West Germany

Corps	Division	Composition	Var	155HOW	M110	Var	155HOW	MLRS	60MM	81MM	120MM		60MM	81MM	120MM		
I Korps	1st Arm	1, 2 Arm, 3 Inf		54	16	.74	.83	1.00			24	5,595	.77	.92	.92	22	1,060
I Korps	3rd Arm	7 A/l,8 Arm,9 Arm		54	16	.74	.83	1.00			24	5,595	.77	.92	.92	22	1,060
I Korps	6th A/l	16,17 A/l,18 Arm		54	16	.74	.83	1.00			24	5,595	.77	.92	.92	22	1,060
I Korps	7th Arm	19,20 Arm,21 A/l		54	16	.74	.83	1.00			24	5,595	.77	.92	.92	22	1,060
II Korps	4th A/l	10,11 A/l,12 Arm		54	16	.74	.83	1.00			24	5,595	.77	.92	.92	22	1,060
II Korps	1st Mountain	22 A/l,23 mou,24 Arm		54	16	.74	.83	1.00			24	5,595	.77	.92	.92	22	1,060
III Korps	2nd A/l	34 Arm,35 A/l,36 Arm		54	16	.74	.83	1.00			24	5,595	.77	.92	.92	22	1,060
III Korps	12th Arm	31,32 A/l,33 Arm		54	16	.74	.83	1.00			24	5,595	.77	.92	.92	22	1,060
I Korps	11th A/l	28,29 Arm,30 A/l		54	16	.74	.83	1.00			24	5,595	.77	.92	.92	22	1,060
III Korps	10th Arm	25,26,27 airborne		54	16	.74	.83	1.00			50	5,595	.77	.92	.92	46	2,208
I Korps	1st Air	14,15 Arm,13 A/l		54		.74	.83	1.00			24	5,595	.77	.92	.92	22	1,060
II Korps	5th Arm																
Terr Army SH	51 Home Defence		18	18		.74	.83	1.00			18	2,600	.77	.92	.92	17	795
Terr Army South	56 Home Defence		18	18		.74	.83	1.00			18	2,600	.77	.92	.92	17	795
Terr Army North	52 Home Defence		18	18		.74	.83	1.00			18	2,600	.77	.92	.92	17	795
Terr Army North	62 Home Defence		18	18		.74	.83	1.00			18	2,600	.77	.92	.92	17	795
Terr Army North	53 Home Defence		18	18		.74	.83	1.00			18	2,600	.77	.92	.92	17	795
Terr Army North	63 Home Defence		18	18		.74	.83	1.00			18	2,600	.77	.92	.92	17	795
Terr Army North	52 Home Defence		18	18		.74	.83	1.00			18	2,600	.77	.92	.92	17	795
Terr Army South	62 Home Defence		18	18		.74	.83	1.00			18	2,600	.77	.92	.92	17	795
Terr Army South	55 Home Defence		18	18		.74	.83	1.00			18	2,600	.77	.92	.92	17	795
Terr Army SH	61 Home Defence		18	18		.74	.83	1.00			18	2,600	.77	.92	.92	17	795
Terr Army South	66 Home Defence		18	18		.74	.83	1.00			18	2,600	.77	.92	.92	17	795
Terr Army South	65 Home Defence		18	18		.74	.83	1.00			18	2,600	.77	.92	.92	17	795

Table C-3. *continued*

STATE; CORPS	DIVISION	BRIGADE	REGIMENT	ARTILLERY TO&E Var	M110	155HOW	GSRS	EFFECTIVENESS Var	M110	155HOW	GSRS	WEI	(WEI-CW 92)	MORTARS TO&E 81MM	60MM	M-30	EFFECTIVENESS 81MM	60MM	M-30	WEI	(WEI-CW 48)
United States																					
VII US	1st Arm	1,2,3	+ Art		36	72	9	.74	.98	1.02	1.16	84	7,717			66	.97	.81	1.00	66	3,168
VII US		Art	17,72,210			100		.74	.98	1.02	1.16	137	12,630								
V US	3rd Arm	1,2,3	+ Art		36	72	9	.74	.98	1.02	1.16	84	7,717			66	.97	.81	1.00	66	3,168
V US		Art: 41,42				50		.74	.98	1.02	1.16	86	7,938								
V US			11 ACR			25	3	.74	.98	1.02	1.16	29	2,666		15	20	.97	.81	1.00	20	960
VII /III	1st Inf	3			6	15	9	.74	.98	1.02	1.16	32	2,909	5		15	.97	.81	1.00	32	1,536
III US	2nd Arm	3				25	3	.74	.98	1.02	1.16	29	2,666			20	.97	.81	1.00	20	960
VII US	3rd Inf	1,2,3	+ Art		18	48	9	.74	.98	1.02	1.16	77	7,088	18	45	50	.97	.81	1.00	104	4,988
VII US			2 ACR		16	24		.74	.98	1.02	1.16	40	3,695			20	.97	.81	1.00	20	960
V US	8th Inf (mech)	1,2,3	+ Art			72	9	.74	.98	1.02	1.16	84	7,717	10	30	66	.97	.81	1.00	66	3,168
CONUS POMCUS																					
III US	1st Inf	1,2	3 ACR		10	30	9	.74	.98	1.02	1.16	51	4,677			30	.97	.81	1.00	64	3,072
III US		Art : 212			16	24		.74	.98	1.02	1.16	40	3,695								
III US						54	9	.74	.98	1.02	1.16	55	5,067			20	.97	.81	1.00	20	960
I US	7th Inf	1,2,3			18	48	9	.74	.98	1.02	1.16	77	7,088	18	45	50	.97	.81	1.00	104	4,988
I US	25th Inf	1,2,3			18	48	6	.74	.98	1.02	1.16	77	7,088	18	45	50	.97	.81	1.00	104	4,988
III US	2nd Arm	1,2				50	9	.74	.98	1.02	1.16	58	5,332			40	.97	.81	1.00	40	1,920
III US	1st Cav	1,2,155				72	9	.74	.98	1.02	1.16	84	7,717			66	.97	.81	1.00	66	3,168
III US	4th Inf (mech)	1,2,3				72	9	.74	.98	1.02	1.16	84	7,717			66	.97	.81	1.00	66	3,168

Reserve and National Guard

Component	Division	ACR	Arty/Units					.74	.98	1.02	1.16						.97	.81	1.00		
III US			Art: 75,214		36	50		.74	.98	1.02	1.16	86	7,938	38	45	20	.97	.81	1.00	20	960
CONUS Res			194 Arm			25		.74	.98	1.02	1.16	29	2,666			20	.97	.81	1.00	103	4,959
CONUS Res			197 mech Inf			25		.74	.98	1.02	1.16	29	2,666			30	.97	.81	1.00		
NG	26th Inf		1,3,43	18	18	30		.74	.98	1.02	1.16	72	6,624	38	45	30	.97	.81	1.00	103	4,959
CONUS Res			157 mech Inf			25		.74	.98	1.02	1.16	29	2,666				.97	.81	1.00		
NG	28th Inf		2,55,56	18	18	30		.74	.98	1.02	1.16	72	6,624	38	45		.97	.81	1.00		
CONUS Res			Art: 428,424,479		36	100		.74	.98	1.02	1.16	137	12,630			10	.97	.81	1.00	38	1,800
NG			29 Inf	10	10			.74	.98	1.02	1.16	17	1,582	20	10		.97	.81	1.00	22	1,056
NG			30 Inf (mech)	8	8	8		.74	.98	1.02	1.16	22	2,017	16	8		.97	.81	1.00	38	1,800
NG			33 Inf	10	10			.74	.98	1.02	1.16	17	1,582	20	10	10	.97	.81	1.00	19	931
NG		107 ACR		16		24		.74	.98	1.02	1.16	36	3,341	16			.97	.81	1.00	22	1,056
NG	35th Mech Inf		32 Inf (mech)	8	8	8		.74	.98	1.02	1.16	22	2,017	20	8		.97	.81	1.00	55	2,640
NG			67,69,149	24	24	24		.74	.98	1.02	1.16	66	6,050	16	20	10	.97	.81	1.00	19	931
NG		116 ACR		16		24	12	.74	.98	1.02	1.16	36	3,341	40			.97	.81	1.00	124	5,940
NG	29th lt Inf		2,55,56	18	18	24		.74	.98	1.02	1.16	45	4,129	20	45		.97	.81	1.00	55	2,640
NG	38th Mech Inf		2,46,76	24	24			.74	.98	1.02	1.16	66	6,050	90	20		.97	.81	1.00	38	1,800
NG			41 Inf	10	10			.74	.98	1.02	1.16	17	1,582	40	10	10	.97	.81	1.00	22	1,056
NG			81 Inf (mech)	8	8	8		.74	.98	1.02	1.16	22	2,017	20	8		.97	.81	1.00	19	931
NG		163 ACR		16		24		.74	.98	1.02	1.16	36	3,341	16			.97	.81	1.00	38	1,800
NG			45 Inf	10	10			.74	.98	1.02	1.16	17	1,582	20	10	10	.97	.81	1.00	22	1,056
NG			218 Inf (mech)	8	8	8		.74	.98	1.02	1.16	22	2,017	16	8		.97	.81	1.00		
NG			Art: 45,57,103		36	100		.74	.98	1.02	1.16	137	12,630			20	.97	.81	1.00	38	1,800
NG		278 ACR		16		24		.74	.98	1.02	1.16	36	3,341	20			.97	.81	1.00	22	1,056
NG			53 Inf	10	10			.74	.98	1.02	1.16	17	1,582	20	10	10	.97	.81	1.00	19	931
NG			30 Arm	8	8	8		.74	.98	1.02	1.16	22	2,017	16	8		.97	.81	1.00	38	1,800
NG			73 Inf	10	10			.74	.98	1.02	1.16	17	1,582	20	10	10	.97	.81	1.00	22	1,056
NG			Art: 113,115,118		36	100		.74	.98	1.02	1.16	137	12,630				.97	.81	1.00	38	1,800
NG			Art: 135,138,142		36	100		.74	.98	1.02	1.16	137	12,630				.97	.81	1.00		
NG	42nd Inf		31 Arm	8	8	8		.74	.98	1.02	1.16	22	2,017	16	8	20	.97	.81	1.00		
NG			1,2	50	20	20		.74	.98	1.02	1.16	77	7,084	70	20		.97	.81	1.00	22	1,056
NG			Art: 196,197,209		36	100		.74	.98	1.02	1.16	137	12,630				.97	.81	1.00	104	4,997
NG			Art: 147,151,169		36	100		.74	.98	1.02	1.16	137	12,630				.97	.81	1.00		
NG			Art: 227,163,631		36	100		.74	.98	1.02	1.16	137	12,630				.97	.81	1.00		
NG	49th Arm		1,2,3	50	24	24		.74	.98	1.02	1.16	85	7,820	60	20		.97	.81	1.00	74	3,571
NG	50th Arm		1,2,86	50	24	24		.74	.98	1.02	1.16	85	7,820	60	20		.97	.81	1.00	74	3,571

Table C-3. continued

STATE; CORPS	DIVISION	ARTILLERY TO&E	ARTILLERY EFFECTIVENESS				ARTILLERY WEI	ARTILLERY WEI-CW 92	MORTARS TO&E	MORTARS EFFECTIVENESS				MORTARS WEI	MORTARS WEI-CW 48
ATTU Units Not Allocated to Central Front															
United Kingdom	Inf	24	.86	.88		1.00	21	1,899	26	.75	.80		.96	20	936
	Inf	24	.86	.88		1.00	21	1,899	26	.75	.80		.96	20	936
	Inf	24	.86	.88		1.00	21	1,899	26	.75	.80		.96	20	936
	Inf	24	.86	.88		1.00	21	1,899	26	.75	.80		.96	20	936
	Inf	24	.86	.88		1.00	21	1,899	26	.75	.80		.96	20	936
	Inf	24	.86	.88		1.00	21	1,899	26	.75	.80		.96	20	936
	Inf	24	.86	.88		1.00	21	1,899	26	.75	.80		.96	20	936
	Inf	24	.86	.88		1.00	21	1,899	26	.75	.80		.96	20	936
	Inf	24	.86	.88		1.00	21	1,899	26	.75	.80		.96	20	936
France	Arm	30	.86	.75		1.00	48	4,444	12	.77	.80		.87	54	2,575
	Arm	30	.86	.75		1.00	48	4,444	12	.77	.80		.87	54	2,575
Netherlands	Inf	20	.78	.83			16	1,435	20		.87	1.00			
Turkey	Mech/Inf	80	.74	.98	1.02	1.16	59	5,446	40	.80	.81	.97	1.00	68	3,245
	Mech/Inf	80	.74	.98	1.02	1.16	59	5,446	40	.80	.81	.97	1.00	68	3,245
	Mech/Inf	80	.74	.98	1.02	1.16	59	5,446	40	.80	.81	.97	1.00	68	3,245
	Mech/Inf	80	.74	.98	1.02	1.16	59	5,446	40	.80	.81	.97	1.00	68	3,245
	Mech/Inf	80	.74	.98	1.02	1.16	59	5,446	40	.80	.81	.97	1.00	68	3,245
	Mech/Inf	80	.74	.98	1.02	1.16	59	5,446	40	.80	.81	.97	1.00	68	3,245
	Mech/Inf	80	.74	.98	1.02	1.16	59	5,446	40	.80	.81	.97	1.00	68	3,245
	Mech/Inf	80	.74	.98	1.02	1.16	59	5,446	40	.80	.81	.97	1.00	68	3,245
	Mech/Inf	80	.74	.98	1.02	1.16	59	5,446	40	.80	.81	.97	1.00	68	3,245
	Mech/Inf	80	.74	.98	1.02	1.16	59	5,446	40	.80	.81	.97	1.00	68	3,245
	Mech/Inf	80	.74	.98	1.02	1.16	59	5,446	40	.80	.81	.97	1.00	68	3,245
	Mech/Inf	80	.74	.98	1.02	1.16	59	5,446	40	.80	.81	.97	1.00	68	3,245
	Mech/Inf	80	.74	.98	1.02	1.16	59	5,446	40	.80	.81	.97	1.00	68	3,245
	Mech/Inf	80	.74	.98	1.02	1.16	59	5,446	40	.80	.81	.97	1.00	68	3,245
	Mech/Inf	80	.74	.98	1.02	1.16	59	5,446	40	.80	.81	.97	1.00	68	3,245
	Mech/Inf	80	.74	.98	1.02	1.16	59	5,446	40	.80	.81	.97	1.00	68	3,245
	Mech/Inf	80	.74	.98	1.02	1.16	59	5,446	40	.80	.81	.97	1.00	68	3,245

Greece	Mech/Inf	125				.74	.98	1.02	1.16	93	8,510	50	25	25		.80	.81	.97	1.00	85	4,056
	Mech/Inf	125				.74	.98	1.02	1.16	93	8,510	50	25	25		.80	.81	.97	1.00	85	4,056
	Mech/Inf	125				.74	.98	1.02	1.16	93	8,510	50	25	25		.80	.81	.97	1.00	85	4,056
	Mech/Inf	125				.74	.98	1.02	1.16	93	8,510	50	25	25		.80	.81	.97	1.00	85	4,056
	Mech/Inf	125				.74	.98	1.02	1.16	93	8,510	50	25	25		.80	.81	.97	1.00	85	4,056
	Mech/Inf	125				.74	.98	1.02	1.16	93	8,510	50	25	25		.80	.81	.97	1.00	85	4,056
	Mech/Inf	125				.74	.98	1.02	1.16	93	8,510	50	25	25		.80	.81	.97	1.00	85	4,056
	Mech/Inf	125				.74	.98	1.02	1.16	93	8,510	50	25	25		.80	.81	.97	1.00	85	4,056
	Mech/Inf	125				.74	.98	1.02	1.16	93	8,510	50	25	25		.80	.81	.97	1.00	85	4,056
	Mech/Inf	125				.74	.98	1.02	1.16	93	8,510	50	25	25		.80	.81	.97	1.00	85	4,056
	Mech/Inf	125				.74	.98	1.02	1.16	93	8,510	50	25	25		.80	.81	.97	1.00	85	4,056
Italy	Mech/Inf	100	100	50	15	.74	.98	1.02	1.16	223	20,516	40	20	20	50	.80	.81	.97	1.00	118	5,645
	Mech/Inf	100	100	50	15	.74	.98	1.02	1.16	223	20,516	40	20	20	50	.80	.81	.97	1.00	118	5,645
	Mech/Inf	100	100	50	15	.74	.98	1.02	1.16	223	20,516	40	20	20	50	.80	.81	.97	1.00	118	5,645
	Mech/Inf	100	100	50	15	.74	.98	1.02	1.16	223	20,516	40	20	20	50	.80	.81	.97	1.00	118	5,645
	Mech/Inf	100	100	50	15	.74	.98	1.02	1.16	223	20,516	40	20	20	50	.80	.81	.97	1.00	118	5,645
	Mech/Inf	100	100	50	15	.74	.98	1.02	1.16	223	20,516	40	20	20	50	.80	.81	.97	1.00	118	5,645
	Mech/Inf	100	100	50	15	.74	.98	1.02	1.16	223	20,516	40	20	20	50	.80	.81	.97	1.00	118	5,645
Spain	Mech/Inf	50	50	15	15	.74	.98	1.02	1.16	119	10,920	40	10	10	40	.80	.81	.97	1.00	105	5,021
	Mech/Inf	50	50	15	15	.74	.98	1.02	1.16	119	10,920	40	10	10	40	.80	.81	.97	1.00	105	5,021
	Mech/Inf	50	50	15	15	.74	.98	1.02	1.16	119	10,920	40	10	10	40	.80	.81	.97	1.00	105	5,021
	Mech/Inf	50	50	15	15	.74	.98	1.02	1.16	119	10,920	40	10	10	40	.80	.81	.97	1.00	105	5,021
	Mech/Inf	50	50	15	15	.74	.98	1.02	1.16	119	10,920	40	10	10	40	.80	.81	.97	1.00	105	5,021
	Mech/Inf	50	50	15	15	.74	.98	1.02	1.16	119	10,920	40	10	10	40	.80	.81	.97	1.00	105	5,021
	Mech/Inf	50	50	15	15	.74	.98	1.02	1.16	119	10,920	40	10	10	40	.80	.81	.97	1.00	105	5,021
Portugal	Mech/Inf	10	10	10	10	.74	.98	1.02	1.16	39	3,588	5	5	5	2	.80	.81	.97	1.00	15	715
	Mech/Inf	10	10	10	10	.74	.98	1.02	1.16	39	3,588	5	5	5	2	.80	.81	.97	1.00	15	715
	Mech/Inf	10	10	10	10	.74	.98	1.02	1.16	39	3,588	5	5	5	2	.80	.81	.97	1.00	15	715
	Mech/Inf	10	10	10	10	.74	.98	1.02	1.16	39	3,588	5	5	5	2	.80	.81	.97	1.00	15	715
	Mech/Inf	10	10	10	10	.74	.98	1.02	1.16	39	3,588	5	5	5	2	.80	.81	.97	1.00	15	715
	Mech/Inf	10	10	10	10	.74	.98	1.02	1.16	39	3,588	5	5	5	2	.80	.81	.97	1.00	15	715
Norway	Mech/Inf	120	155			.74	.98	1.02	1.16	302	27,802	25	25	25	25	.80	.81	.97	1.00	90	4,296

Table C-3. continued

STATE; CORPS	DIVISION	BRIGADE; OR REGIMENT	ANTIARMOR TO&E	ANTIARMOR EFFECTIVENESS	WEI	(WEI-CW 55)	ARMORED RECON TO&E	ARMORED RECON EFFECTIVENESS	WEI	(WEI-CW 62)
Netherlands										
I Netherlands	4th Mech	41,42,43	GUSTA 210; MAW 90; TOW 60	LAW .25; GUSTA .33; MAW .69; TOW .79	179	9,834	APC 63	APC .85; ARV .99; CFV M2 1.19	104	6,419
I Netherlands	5th Mech	51,52,53	GUSTA 210; MAW 90; TOW 60	LAW .25; GUSTA .33; MAW .69; TOW .79	179	9,834	APC 63	APC .85; ARV .99; CFV M2 1.19	104	6,419
I Netherlands	1st Mech	11,12,13	GUSTA 210; MAW 90; TOW 60	LAW .25; GUSTA .33; MAW .69; TOW .79	179	9,834	APC 63	APC .85; ARV .99; CFV M2 1.19	104	6,419
Belgium										
I Belgian	16th Mech	4 mech, 17 Arm	LAW 600; GUSTA 406; MAW 24; TOW 152	LAW .20; GUSTA .34; MAW .68; TOW .72	384	21,109	CVR 227; SCORPN 98; AMX	CVR .84; SCORPN .97; AMX 1.19	286	17,716
I Belgian	1st Div	1 mech, 7 mech	LAW 600; GUSTA 406; MAW 24; TOW 152	LAW .20; GUSTA .34; MAW .68; TOW .72	384	21,109	CVR 227; SCORPN 98	CVR .84; SCORPN .97	286	17,716
I Belgian		10 mech	LAW 240; GUSTA 162; MAW 10; TOW 46	LAW .20; GUSTA .34; MAW .68; TOW .72	143	7,842	CVR 91; SCORPN 81	CVR .84; SCORPN .97	155	9,612
I Belgian		12 mot	LAW 240; GUSTA 162; MAW 10; TOW 46	LAW .20; GUSTA .34; MAW .68; TOW .72	143	7,842	CVR 91; SCORPN 81	CVR .84; SCORPN .97	155	9,612
Denmark										
Jutland	Jutland	1, 2, 3 mech inf	LAW 50; GUSTA 100; MAW; TOW 70	LAW .20; GUSTA .34; MILAN .68; TOW .72	94	5,192	CVR 16; SCORPN 16; AMX 16	CVR .84; SCORPN .97; AMX 1.19	48	2,976
United Kingdom										
I British	1 Arm	7, 12, 22	LAW 478; MILAN 54	LAW .25; MILAN .72	158	8,711	M8 24; CVR 30; SCORPN 32; SCIMTAR 40	M8 .59; CVR .84; SCORPN .97; SCIMTAR .99	110	6,820
I British	4 Arm	11, 20, 30 Arm	LAW 478; MILAN 54	LAW .25; MILAN .72	158	8,711	M8 24; CVR 30; SCORPN 32; SCIMTAR 40	M8 .59; CVR .84; SCORPN .97; SCIMTAR .99	110	6,820
I British	2 Inf	15, 24, 49 inf	LAW 478; MILAN 100	LAW .25; MILAN .72	192	10,533	M8 24; CVR 30; SCORPN 32; SCIMTAR 40	M8 .59; CVR .84; SCORPN .97; SCIMTAR .99	110	6,820
I British	Art Div	4 reg	LAW 167; ATGM 19	LAW .25; ATGM .72	55	3,049	M8 8; CVR 10; SCORPN 11; SCIMTAR 14	M8 .59; CVR .84; SCORPN .97; SCIMTAR .99	38	2,334
British		5 Air	LAW 478; ATGM 54	LAW .25; ATGM .72	158	8,711	M8 24; CVR 30; SCORPN 32; SCIMTAR 40	M8 .59; CVR .84; SCORPN .97; SCIMTAR .99	110	6,820
I British	3 Arm	4 Arm, 6 Arm, 19 inf	LAW 167; ATGM 20	LAW .25; ATGM .72	56	3,088	M8 8; CVR 10; SCORPN 11; SCIMTAR 14	M8 .59; CVR .84; SCORPN .97; SCIMTAR .99	38	2,334
UKMF	1 Inf		LAW 167; ATGM 20	LAW .25; ATGM .72	56	3,088	M8 8; CVR 10; SCORPN 11; SCIMTAR 14	M8 .59; CVR .84; SCORPN .97; SCIMTAR .99	38	2,334
UKMF		Other Btlns								
Canada										
C. F. Europe	4 Mech		ATLC 128; GUSTA 167; ATGM 24; TOW 149	ATLC .20; GUSTA .33; ATGM .64; TOW .79	214	11,758		M8 .59; CVR .84; SCORPN .97; SCIMTAR .99		
Mobile Command	5e Groupe-Brig		ATLC 128; GUSTA 167; ATGM 24	ATLC .20; GUSTA .33; ATGM .64; TOW .79	96	5,284		CVR .84; SCORPN .97; SCIMTAR .99		
Mobile Command	5e Groupe-Brig		ATLC 128; GUSTA 167; ATGM 24	ATLC .20; GUSTA .33; ATGM .64; TOW .79	96	5,284		CVR .84; SCORPN .97; SCIMTAR .99		

France

Command	Unit	ATLC	GUSTA	ATGM	TOW	ATLC	GUSTA	ATGM	TOW			M8	VA	AMX	SCIMTAR	M8	VA	AMX	SCIMTAR		
FAR	4th Air	20	60			.35	.33	.72	.79	50	2,761		12	36		.59	.90	.98	.99	46	2,857
FAR	9th lt Air	90	72			.35	.33	.72	.79	83	4,584		12	20		.59	.90	.98	.99	30	1,885
FAR	11th Air	20	40			.35	.33	.72	.79	36	1,969		12	36		.59	.90	.98	.99	46	2,857
II	3rd Arm	20	40			.35	.33	.72	.79	36	1,969		12	36		.59	.90	.98	.99	46	2,857
II	5th Arm	20	40			.35	.33	.72	.79	36	1,969		12	36		.59	.90	.98	.99	46	2,857
I	1st Arm	20	40			.35	.33	.72	.79	36	1,969		12	36		.59	.90	.98	.99	46	2,857
FAR	27th Mou	20	60			.35	.33	.72	.79	50	2,761		12	36		.59	.90	.98	.99	46	2,857
II	15th Inf	20	60			.35	.33	.72	.79	50	2,761		12	36		.59	.90	.98	.99	46	2,857
I	12th lt Arm	20	60			.35	.33	.72	.79	50	2,761		12	36		.59	.90	.98	.99	46	2,857
I	14th lt Arm	20	40			.35	.33	.72	.79	36	1,969		12	36		.59	.90	.98	.99	46	2,857
III	2nd Arm	20	60			.35	.33	.72	.79	50	2,761		12	36		.59	.90	.98	.99	46	2,857
III	8th Inf	20	40			.35	.33	.72	.79	36	1,969		12	36		.59	.90	.98	.99	46	2,857
III	10th Arm																				
I	7th Arm																				

West Germany

Command	Unit	Composition	LAW	GUSTA	ATGM	LAW	GUSTA	ATGM	TOW			M8	SPZ	ARV	M8	SPZ	ARV	SCIMTAR		
I Korps	1st Arm	1, 2 Arm, 3 Inf	51	48	144	.26	.33	.79	.79	143	7,857			34	.59	.86	.99	.99	34	2,087
I Korps	3rd Arm	7 A/l, 8 Arm, 9 Arm	15	48	144	.26	.33	.79	.79	134	7,343			34	.59	.86	.99	.99	34	2,087
I Korps	6th A/l	16, 17 A/l, 18 Arm	51	48	144	.26	.33	.79	.79	143	7,857			34	.59	.86	.99	.99	34	2,087
I Korps	7th Arm	19, 20 Arm, 21 A/l	15	48	144	.26	.33	.79	.79	134	7,343			34	.59	.86	.99	.99	34	2,087
II Korps	4th A/l	10, 11 A/l, 12 Arm	51	48	144	.26	.33	.79	.79	143	7,857			34	.59	.86	.99	.99	34	2,087
II Korps	1st Mountain	22 A/l, 23 mou, 24 Arm	71	68	144	.26	.33	.79	.79	155	8,506			50	.59	.86	.99	.99	50	3,069
II Korps	2nd A/l	4, 5 A/l, 6 Arm	51	48	144	.26	.33	.79	.79	143	7,857			34	.59	.86	.99	.99	34	2,087
III Korps	12th Arm	34 Arm, 35 A/l, 36 Arm	51	48	144	.26	.33	.79	.79	134	7,343			34	.59	.86	.99	.99	34	2,087
III Korps	11th A/l	31, 32 A/l, 33 Arm	15	48	144	.26	.33	.79	.79	143	7,857			34	.59	.86	.99	.99	34	2,087
I Korps	10th Arm	28, 29 Arm, 30 A/l	71	68	144	.26	.33	.79	.79	134	7,343			34	.59	.86	.99	.99	34	2,087
II Korps	1st Air	25, 26, 27 airborne	15	68	200	.26	.33	.79	.79	199	10,940			34	.59	.86	.99	.99	34	2,087
III Korps	5th Arm	14, 15 Arm, 13 A/l	15	48	144	.26	.33	.79	.79	134	7,343			34	.59	.86	.99	.99	34	2,087
Terr Army SH	51 Home Defence	51	15	48	18	.26	.33	.79	.79	34	1,868			10	.59	.86	.99	.99	10	614
Terr Army South	56 Home Defence	56	15	48	18	.26	.33	.79	.79	34	1,868			10	.59	.86	.99	.99	10	614
Terr Army North	52 Home Defence	52	15	48	18	.26	.33	.79	.79	34	1,868			10	.59	.86	.99	.99	10	614
Terr Army North	62 Home Defence	62	15	48	18	.26	.33	.79	.79	34	1,868			10	.59	.86	.99	.99	10	614
Terr Army North	53 Home Defence	53	15	48	18	.26	.33	.79	.79	34	1,868			10	.59	.86	.99	.99	10	614
Terr Army North	63 Home Defence	63	15	48	18	.26	.33	.79	.79	34	1,868			10	.59	.86	.99	.99	10	614
Terr Army South	52 Home Defence	52	15	48	18	.26	.33	.79	.79	34	1,868			10	.59	.86	.99	.99	10	614
Terr Army South	62 Home Defence	62	15	48	18	.26	.33	.79	.79	34	1,868			10	.59	.86	.99	.99	10	614
Terr Army South	55 Home Defence	55	15	48	18	.26	.33	.79	.79	34	1,868			10	.59	.86	.99	.99	10	614
Terr Army SH	61 Home Defence	61	15	48	18	.26	.33	.79	.79	34	1,868			10	.59	.86	.99	.99	10	614
Terr Army South	66 Home Defence	66	15	48	18	.26	.33	.79	.79	34	1,868			10	.59	.86	.99	.99	10	614
Terr Army South	65 Home Defence	65	15	48	18	.26	.33	.79	.79	34	1,868			10	.59	.86	.99	.99	10	614

Table C-3. *continued*

STATE: CORPS	DIVISION	BRIGADE	REGIMENT	ANTIARMOR TO&E				ANTIARMOR EFFECTIVENESS				WEI	(WEI-CW 55)	ARV TO&E				ARV EFFECTIVENESS				WEI	(WEI-CW 62)
				LAW	DRAG	ATGM	TOW	LAW	DRAG	ATGM	TOW			Oth	SPZ	ARV	CFV M-2	Oth	SPZ	ARV	CFV M-2		
United States																							
VII US	1st Arm	1,2,3	+ Art		180		60	.20	.69	1.00	1.11	191	10,494				100	.59	.86	.99	1.19	119	7,378
VII US		Art	17,72,210																				
V US	3rd Arm	1,2,3	+ Art		180		60	.20	.69	1.00	1.11	191	10,494				100	.59	.86	.99	1.19	119	7,378
V US		Art: 41,42																					
V US			11 ACR		60		20	.20	.69	1.00	1.11	64	3,498				35	.59	.86	.99	1.19	42	2,582
VII /III US	1st Inf	3			100		75	.20	.69	1.00	1.11	152	8,374				15	.59	.86	.99	1.19	18	1,107
III US	2nd Arm	3			60		20	.20	.69	1.00	1.11	64	3,498				35	.59	.86	.99	1.19	42	2,582
VII US	3rd Inf	1,2,3	+ Art		263		173	.20	.69	1.00	1.11	374	20,543				50	.59	.86	.99	1.19	60	3,689
VII US			2 ACR	100	50			.20	.69	1.00	1.11	55	2,998				30	.59	.86	.99	1.19	36	2,213
V US	8th Inf (mech)	1,2,3	+ Art		180		60	.20	.69	1.00	1.11	191	10,494				100	.59	.86	.99	1.19	119	7,378
CONUS POMCUS																							
US	1st Inf	1,2			200		150	.20	.69	1.00	1.11	305	16,748				30	.59	.86	.99	1.19	36	2,213
III US			3 ACR	100	50			.20	.69	1.00	1.11	55	2,998				30	.59	.86	.99	1.19	36	2,213
III US		Art: 212																					
I US	7th Inf	1,2,3			263		173	.20	.69	1.00	1.11	374	20,543				28	.59	.86	.99	1.19	33	2,066
I US	25th Inf	1,2,3			263		173	.20	.69	1.00	1.11	374	20,543				28	.59	.86	.99	1.19	33	2,066
US	2nd Arm	1,2			120		40	.20	.69	1.00	1.11	127	6,996				70	.59	.86	.99	1.19	83	5,165
III US	1st Cav	1,2,155			180		60	.20	.69	1.00	1.11	191	10,494				100	.59	.86	.99	1.19	119	7,378
III US	4th Inf (mech)		1,2,3		180		60	.20	.69	1.00	1.11	191	10,494				100	.59	.86	.99	1.19	119	7,378

Reserve and National Guard

Component	Unit	ACR	Brigades / Art	A	B	C	.20	.69	1.00	1.11				.59	.86	.99	1.19		
III US																			
CONUS Res																			
CONUS Res			Art: 75,214		60	20	.20	.69	1.00	1.11	64	3,498	35	.59	.86	.99	1.19	42	2,582
NG	26th Inf		194 Arm		60	20	.20	.69	1.00	1.11	64	3,498	35	.59	.86	.99	1.19	42	2,582
			197 mech Inf	300	263	173	.20	.69	1.00	1.11	434	23,843	50	.59	.86	.99	1.19	60	3,689
			1,3,43		60	20	.20	.69	1.00	1.11	64	3,498	35	.59	.86	.99	1.19	42	2,582
NG			157 mech Inf	300	263	173	.20	.69	1.00	1.11	434	23,843	50	.59	.86	.99	1.19	60	3,689
CONUS Res	28th Inf		2,55,56		75	30	.20	.69	1.00	1.11	105	5,778	30	.59	.86	.99	1.19	12	756
CONUS Res			Art: 428,424,479		60	8	.20	.69	1.00	1.11	64	3,535		.59	.86	.99	1.19	24	1,513
NG			29 Inf		75	30	.20	.69	1.00	1.11	105	5,778		.59	.86	.99	1.19	12	756
NG			30 Inf (mech)		50	8	.20	.69	1.00	1.11	55	2,998		.59	.86	.99	1.19	36	2,213
NG			33 Inf		60		.20	.69	1.00	1.11	64	3,535		.59	.86	.99	1.19	24	1,513
NG		107 ACR	32 Inf (mech)		180	20	.20	.69	1.00	1.11	186	10,252		.59	.86	.99	1.19	85	5,295
NG	35th Mech Inf		67,69,149		50		.20	.69	1.00	1.11	55	2,998		.59	.86	.99	1.19	36	2,213
NG		116 ACR	2,55,56		263	82	.20	.69	1.00	1.11	332	18,287		.59	.86	.99	1.19	60	3,689
NG	29th lt Inf		2,46,76		180	20	.20	.69	1.00	1.11	186	10,252		.59	.86	.99	1.19	85	5,295
NG	38th Mech Inf		41 Inf		75	30	.20	.69	1.00	1.11	105	5,778		.59	.86	.99	1.19	12	1,513
NG			81 Inf (mech)		60	8	.20	.69	1.00	1.11	64	3,535		.59	.86	.99	1.19	24	2,213
NG			45 Inf		50		.20	.69	1.00	1.11	55	2,998		.59	.86	.99	1.19	36	756
NG		163 ACR	218 Inf (mech)		75	30	.20	.69	1.00	1.11	105	5,778	30	.59	.86	.99	1.19	12	1,513
NG			Art: 45,57,103		60	8	.20	.69	1.00	1.11	64	3,535		.59	.86	.99	1.19	24	2,213
NG			53 Inf		50	30	.20	.69	1.00	1.11	55	2,998	30	.59	.86	.99	1.19	36	756
NG			30 Arm		75	8	.20	.69	1.00	1.11	105	5,778		.59	.86	.99	1.19	12	1,513
NG		278 ACR	73 Inf		60	30	.20	.69	1.00	1.11	64	3,535		.59	.86	.99	1.19	24	
NG			Art: 113,115,118				.20	.69	1.00	1.11				.59	.86	.99	1.19		
NG			Art: 135,138,142				.20	.69	1.00	1.11				.59	.86	.99	1.19		
NG			31 Arm		60	8	.20	.69	1.00	1.11	64	3,535		.59	.86	.99	1.19	24	1,513
NG	42nd Inf		1,2		150	60	.20	.69	1.00	1.11	230	12,656	10	.59	.86	.99	1.19	36	2,251
NG			Art: 196,197,209				.20	.69	1.00	1.11				.59	.86	.99	1.19		
NG			Art: 147,151,169				.20	.69	1.00	1.11				.59	.86	.99	1.19		
NG			Art: 227,163,631				.20	.69	1.00	1.11				.59	.86	.99	1.19		
NG	49th Arm		1,2,3	300	180	20	.20	.69	1.00	1.11	206	11,352	35	.59	.86	.99	1.19	85	5,295
NG	50th Arm		1,2,86	300	180	20	.20	.69	1.00	1.11	206	11,352	35	.59	.86	.99	1.19	85	5,295

Table C-3. continued

STATE; CORPS	DIVISION	ANTIARMOR TO&E	ANTIARMOR EFFECTIVENESS				ANTIARMOR WEI	ANTIARMOR (WEI-CW 55)	ARV TO&E			ARV EFFECTIVENESS				ARV WEI	ARV (WEI-CW 62)
ATTU Units Not Allocated to Central Front																	
United Kingdom	Inf	100	.25		.72		25	1,375	50	5	5	.59	.84	.97	.99	44	2,697
	Inf	100	.25		.72		25	1,375	50	5	5	.59	.84	.97	.99	44	2,697
	Inf	100	.25		.72		25	1,375	50	5	5	.59	.84	.97	.99	44	2,697
	Inf	100	.25		.72		25	1,375	50	5	5	.59	.84	.97	.99	44	2,697
	Inf	100	.25		.72		25	1,375	50	5	5	.59	.84	.97	.99	44	2,697
	Inf	100	.25		.72		25	1,375	50	5	5	.59	.84	.97	.99	44	2,697
	Inf	100	.25		.72		25	1,375	50	5	5	.59	.84	.97	.99	44	2,697
	Inf	100	.25		.72		25	1,375	50	5	5	.59	.84	.97	.99	44	2,697
	Inf	100	.25		.72		25	1,375	50	5	5	.59	.84	.97	.99	44	2,697
France	Arm	20	.35	.33	.72	.79	7	385				.59	.90	.98	.99		
	Arm	20	.35	.33	.72	.79	7	385				.59	.90	.98	.99		
Netherlands	Inf	75	.25	.33	.69	.79	19	1,031	20				.85	.99	1.19		
Turkey	Mech/Inf	100	4	.20	.69	1.00	1.11	28	1,564	125	5	5	.59	.86	.99	1.19	74	4,573
	Mech/Inf	100	4	.20	.69	1.00	1.11	28	1,564	125	5	5	.59	.86	.99	1.19	74	4,573
	Mech/Inf	100	4	.20	.69	1.00	1.11	28	1,564	125	5	5	.59	.86	.99	1.19	74	4,573
	Mech/Inf	100	4	.20	.69	1.00	1.11	28	1,564	125	5	5	.59	.86	.99	1.19	74	4,573
	Mech/Inf	100	4	.20	.69	1.00	1.11	28	1,564	125	5	5	.59	.86	.99	1.19	74	4,573
	Mech/Inf	100	4	.20	.69	1.00	1.11	28	1,564	125	5	5	.59	.86	.99	1.19	74	4,573
	Mech/Inf	100	4	.20	.69	1.00	1.11	28	1,564	125	5	5	.59	.86	.99	1.19	74	4,573
	Mech/Inf	100	4	.20	.69	1.00	1.11	28	1,564	125	5	5	.59	.86	.99	1.19	74	4,573
	Mech/Inf	100	4	.20	.69	1.00	1.11	28	1,564	125	5	5	.59	.86	.99	1.19	74	4,573
	Mech/Inf	100	4	.20	.69	1.00	1.11	28	1,564	125	5	5	.59	.86	.99	1.19	74	4,573
	Mech/Inf	100	4	.20	.69	1.00	1.11	28	1,564	125	5	5	.59	.86	.99	1.19	74	4,573
	Mech/Inf	100	4	.20	.69	1.00	1.11	28	1,564	125	5	5	.59	.86	.99	1.19	74	4,573
	Mech/Inf	100	4	.20	.69	1.00	1.11	28	1,564	125	5	5	.59	.86	.99	1.19	74	4,573
	Mech/Inf	100	4	.20	.69	1.00	1.11	28	1,564	125	5	5	.59	.86	.99	1.19	74	4,573
	Mech/Inf	100	4	.20	.69	1.00	1.11	28	1,564	125	5	5	.59	.86	.99	1.19	74	4,573
	Mech/Inf	100	4	.20	.69	1.00	1.11	28	1,564	125	5	5	.59	.86	.99	1.19	74	4,573
	Mech/Inf	100	4	.20	.69	1.00	1.11	28	1,564	125	5	5	.59	.86	.99	1.19	74	4,573
	Mech/Inf	100	4	.20	.69	1.00	1.11	28	1,564	125	5	5	.59	.86	.99	1.19	74	4,573
	Mech/Inf	100	4	.20	.69	1.00	1.11	28	1,564	125	5	5	.59	.86	.99	1.19	74	4,573
	Mech/Inf	100	4	.20	.69	1.00	1.11	28	1,564	125	5	5	.59	.86	.99	1.19	74	4,573

Country	Type	(1)	(2)	(3)	(4)	(5)	(6)	(7)	(8)	(9)	(10)	(11)	(12)	(13)	(14)	(15)	(16)	(17)	(18)	(19)	(20)
Greece	Mech/Inf	160	4	4		.20	.69	1.00	1.11	40	2,224	65				.59	.86	.99	1.19	38	2,378
	Mech/Inf	160	4	4		.20	.69	1.00	1.11	40	2,224	65				.59	.86	.99	1.19	38	2,378
	Mech/Inf	160	4	4		.20	.69	1.00	1.11	40	2,224	65				.59	.86	.99	1.19	38	2,378
	Mech/Inf	160	4	4		.20	.69	1.00	1.11	40	2,224	65				.59	.86	.99	1.19	38	2,378
	Mech/Inf	160	4	4		.20	.69	1.00	1.11	40	2,224	65				.59	.86	.99	1.19	38	2,378
	Mech/Inf	160	4	4		.20	.69	1.00	1.11	40	2,224	65				.59	.86	.99	1.19	38	2,378
	Mech/Inf	160	4	4		.20	.69	1.00	1.11	40	2,224	65				.59	.86	.99	1.19	38	2,378
	Mech/Inf	160	4	4		.20	.69	1.00	1.11	40	2,224	65				.59	.86	.99	1.19	38	2,378
	Mech/Inf	160	4	4		.20	.69	1.00	1.11	40	2,224	65				.59	.86	.99	1.19	38	2,378
	Mech/Inf	160	4	4		.20	.69	1.00	1.11	40	2,224	65				.59	.86	.99	1.19	38	2,378
	Mech/Inf	160	4	4		.20	.69	1.00	1.11	40	2,224	65				.59	.86	.99	1.19	38	2,378
Italy	Mech/Inf	100	25	125	25	.20	.69	1.00	1.11	190	10,450	50	50	25	25	.59	.86	.99	1.19	127	7,874
	Mech/Inf	100	25	125	25	.20	.69	1.00	1.11	190	10,450	50	50	25	25	.59	.86	.99	1.19	127	7,874
	Mech/Inf	100	25	125	25	.20	.69	1.00	1.11	190	10,450	50	50	25	25	.59	.86	.99	1.19	127	7,874
	Mech/Inf	100	25	125	25	.20	.69	1.00	1.11	190	10,450	50	50	25	25	.59	.86	.99	1.19	127	7,874
	Mech/Inf	100	25	125	25	.20	.69	1.00	1.11	190	10,450	50	50	25	25	.59	.86	.99	1.19	127	7,874
	Mech/Inf	100	25	125	25	.20	.69	1.00	1.11	190	10,450	50	50	25	25	.59	.86	.99	1.19	127	7,874
	Mech/Inf	100	25	125	25	.20	.69	1.00	1.11	190	10,450	50	50	25	25	.59	.86	.99	1.19	127	7,874
Spain	Mech/Inf	75	25	50	25	.20	.69	1.00	1.11	82	4,524	25	25	50		.59	.86	.99	1.19	86	5,317
	Mech/Inf	75	25	50	25	.20	.69	1.00	1.11	82	4,524	25	25	50		.59	.86	.99	1.19	86	5,317
	Mech/Inf	75	25	50	25	.20	.69	1.00	1.11	82	4,524	25	25	50		.59	.86	.99	1.19	86	5,317
	Mech/Inf	75	25	50	25	.20	.69	1.00	1.11	82	4,524	25	25	50		.59	.86	.99	1.19	86	5,317
	Mech/Inf	75	25	50	25	.20	.69	1.00	1.11	82	4,524	25	25	50		.59	.86	.99	1.19	86	5,317
	Mech/Inf	75	25	50	25	.20	.69	1.00	1.11	82	4,524	25	25	50		.59	.86	.99	1.19	86	5,317
	Mech/Inf	75	25	50	25	.20	.69	1.00	1.11	82	4,524	25	25	50		.59	.86	.99	1.19	86	5,317
Portugal	Mech/Inf	20	10	15	15	.20	.69	1.00	1.11	43	2,340		10	10		.59	.86	.99	1.19	19	1,147
	Mech/Inf	20	10	15	15	.20	.69	1.00	1.11	43	2,340		10	10		.59	.86	.99	1.19	19	1,147
	Mech/Inf	20	10	15	15	.20	.69	1.00	1.11	43	2,340		10	10		.59	.86	.99	1.19	19	1,147
	Mech/Inf	20	10	15	15	.20	.69	1.00	1.11	43	2,340		10	10		.59	.86	.99	1.19	19	1,147
	Mech/Inf	20	10	15	15	.20	.69	1.00	1.11	43	2,340		10	10		.59	.86	.99	1.19	19	1,147
	Mech/Inf	20	10	15	15	.20	.69	1.00	1.11	43	2,340		10	10		.59	.86	.99	1.19	19	1,147
Norway	Mech/Inf	200	100	100	150	.20	.69	1.00	1.11	376	20,653			25	25	.59	.86	.99	1.19	55	3,379

Table C-3. continued

STATE; CORPS	DIVISION	BRIGADE; OR REGIMENT	IFV TO&E	IFV WEI	IFV (WEI-CW 69)	APC TO&E	APC EFFECT	APC WEI	APC (WEI-CW36)	SA WEI	SA (WEI-CW 3.3)	UNIT WUV: Division Total
Netherlands						AMX / M113A1 / APC	AMX / M113A1 / APC					
I Netherlands	4th Mech	41,42,43	MARDER	MARDER .86		30 / 49 / 506	.87 / .95 / .98	569	20,467	2,246	7,412	82,883
I Netherlands	5th Mech	51,52,53		.86		30 / 49 / 506	.87 / .95 / .98	569	20,467	2,246	7,412	82,883
I Netherlands	1st Mech	11,12,13		.86		30 / 49 / 506	.87 / .95 / .98	569	20,467	2,246	7,412	82,883
Belgium						AMX / ARV / APC	AMX / ARV / APC					
I Belgian	16th Mech	4 mech, 17 Arm	MARDER	MARDER .86		227 / 41 / 77	.87 / .89 / .90	303	10,918	2,653	8,755	85,100
I Belgian	1st Div	1 mech, 7 mech		.86		227 / 41 / 77	.87 / .89 / .90	303	10,918	2,453	8,095	79,720
I Belgian		10 mech		.86		91 / 16 / 31	.87 / .89 / .90	121	4,367	981	3,238	32,979
I Belgian		12 mot		.86		91 / 16 / 31	.87 / .89 / .90	121	4,367	981	3,238	32,979
Denmark						AMX / ARV / APC	AMX / ARV / APC					
Jutland	Jutland	1, 2, 3 mech inf	MARDER	MARDER .86		390	.90	351	12,636	2,653	8,755	75,094
United Kingdom						AMX / ARV / APC	AMX / ARV / APC					
I British	1 Arm	7, 12, 22	MARDER	MARDER .86		344 / 33	.89 / .89	336	12,079	2,963	9,778	62,291
I British	4 Arm	11, 20, 30 Arm		.86		344 / 33	.89 / .89	336	12,079	2,963	9,778	62,291
I British	2 Inf	15, 24, 49 inf		.86		344 / 33	.89 / .89	336	12,079	2,963	9,778	64,113
I British	Art Div	4 reg		.86								5,492
British		5 Air		.86		110 / 11	.89 / .89	108	3,877	1,185	3,911	20,463
I British	3 Arm	4 Arm, 6 Arm, 19 inf		.86		344 / 33	.89 / .89	336	12,079	2,963	9,778	62,291
UKMF		1 Inf		.86		110 / 11	.89 / .89	108	3,877	1,185	3,911	20,455
UKMF		Other Bttns		.86		110 / 11	.89 / .89	108	3,877	1,185	3,911	20,455
Canada						AMX / ARV / APC	AMX / ARV / APC					
C. F. Europe	4 Mech		MARDER	MARDER .86		228	.87 / .89 / 1.00	228	8,208	1,384	4,567	49,765
Mobile Command	5e Groupe-Brig			.86		50	1.00	50	1,800	554	1,827	13,440
Mobile Command	5e Groupe-Brig			.86		50	1.00	50	1,800	554	1,827	14,340

Formation	Division	Brigades	MARDER	MARDER (.86)	AMX	ARV	AMX (.87)	ARV (.90)	APC (1.00)					
France														
FAR	4th Air				130	72	.87	.90	1.00	178	6,404	330	1,089	1,089
FAR	9th lt Arm					100	.87	.90	1.00	90	3,240	1,300	4,290	25,999
FAR	11th Air				300	300	.87	.90	1.00	531	19,116	1,500	4,950	17,328
II	3rd Arm				300	300	.87	.90	1.00	531	19,116	1,500	4,950	42,745
II	5th Arm				300	300	.87	.90	1.00	531	19,116	1,500	4,950	42,745
I	1st Arm				300	300	.87	.90	1.00	531	19,116	1,500	4,950	42,745
FAR	27th Mou				130	72	.87	.90	1.00	178	6,404	1,300	4,290	24,214
II	15th Inf				130	72	.87	.90	1.00	178	6,404	1,300	4,290	25,999
I	12th lt Arm				130	72	.87	.90	1.00	178	6,404	1,300	4,290	25,999
I	14th lt Arm				300	300	.87	.90	1.00	531	19,116	1,500	4,950	42,745
III	2nd Arm				130	72	.87	.90	1.00	178	6,404	1,300	4,290	24,214
III	8th Inf				300	300	.87	.90	1.00	531	19,116	1,500	4,950	42,745
III	10th Arm				300	300	.87	.90	1.00	531	19,116	1,500	4,950	42,745
I	7th Arm				300	300	.87	.90	1.00	531	19,116	1,500	4,950	42,745
West Germany			MARDER	MARDER			AMX	ARV	M113A1	M113A1				
I Korps	1st Arm	1, 2 Arm, 3 Inf	166	.86	143	9,850	.87	.90	1.00	30	1,080	3,500	11,550	67,580
I Korps	3rd Arm	7 A/I, 8 Arm, 9 Arm	110	.86	95	6,527	.87	.90	1.00	50	1,800	3,500	11,550	70,562
I Korps	6th A/I	16, 17 A/I, 18 Arm	166	.86	143	9,850	.87	.90	1.00	30	1,080	3,500	11,550	67,580
I Korps	7th Arm	19, 20 Arm, 21 A/I	110	.86	95	6,527	.87	.90	1.00	50	1,800	3,500	11,550	70,562
II Korps	4th A/I	10, 11 A/I, 12 Arm	166	.86	143	9,850	.87	.90	1.00	30	1,080	3,800	12,540	67,580
II Korps	1st Mountain	22 A/I, 23 mou, 24 Arm	166	.86	143	9,850	.87	.90	1.00	50	1,800	3,500	11,550	64,101
III Korps	2nd A/I	4, 5 A/I, 6 Arm	110	.86	95	6,527	.87	.90	1.00	30	1,080	3,500	11,550	70,562
III Korps	12th Arm	34 Arm, 35 A/I, 36 Arm	166	.86	143	9,850	.87	.90	1.00	50	1,800	3,500	11,550	67,580
I Korps	11th A/I	31, 32 A/I, 33 Arm	166	.86	143	6,527	.87	.90	1.00	50	1,800	3,500	11,550	70,562
II Korps	10th Arm	28, 29 Arm, 30 A/I	50	.86	43	2,967	.87	.90	1.00			2,000	6,600	28,310
III Korps	1st Air	25, 26, 27 airborne	110	.86	95	6,527	.87	.90	1.00			3,500	11,550	70,562
1st Air	5th Arm	14, 15 Arm, 13 A/I	110	.86	95	712	.87	.90	1.00	50	1,800	1,300	4,290	21,462
Terr Army SH	51 Home Defence		12	.86	10	712	.87	.90	1.00	30	1,080	1,300	4,290	21,462
Terr Army South	56 Home Defence		12	.86	10	712	.87	.90	1.00	30	1,080	1,300	4,290	21,462
Terr Army North	52 Home Defence		12	.86	10	712	.87	.90	1.00	30	1,080	1,300	4,290	21,462
Terr Army North	62 Home Defence		12	.86	10	712	.87	.90	1.00	30	1,080	1,300	4,290	21,462
Terr Army North	53 Home Defence		12	.86	10	712	.87	.90	1.00	30	1,080	1,300	4,290	21,462
Terr Army North	63 Home Defence		12	.86	10	712	.87	.90	1.00	30	1,080	1,300	4,290	21,462
Terr Army North	52 Home Defence		12	.86	10	712	.87	.90	1.00	30	1,080	1,300	4,290	21,462
Terr Army South	62 Home Defence		12	.86	10	712	.87	.90	1.00	30	1,080	1,300	4,290	21,462
Terr Army South	55 Home Defence		12	.86	10	712	.87	.90	1.00	30	1,080	1,300	4,290	21,462
Terr Army South	61 Home Defence		12	.86	10	712	.87	.90	1.00	30	1,080	1,300	4,290	21,462
Terr Army SH	66 Home Defence		12	.86	10	712	.87	.90	1.00	30	1,080	1,300	4,290	21,462
Terr Army South	65 Home Defence		12	.86	10	712	.87	.90	1.00	30	1,080	1,300	4,290	21,462

Table C-3. continued

STATE: CORPS	DIVISION	BRIGADE	REGIMENT	INFANTRY FIGHTING VEHICLES				ARMORED PERSONNEL VEHICLES								SMALL ARMS		UNIT WUV
				TO&E IFV	TO&E IFV	WEI	(WEI-CW 69)	TO&E Oth ARV	TO&E ARV	TO&E M113A1	EFFECT AMX	EFFECT ARV	EFFECT M113A1	WEI	(WEI-CW 36)	WEI	(WEI-CW 3.3)	Division Total
United States																		
VII US	1st Arm	1,2,3	+ Art	270	.90	243	16,767			175	.87	.90	1.00	175	6,300	3,000	9,900	98,554
VII US		Art	17,72,210															12,630
V US	3rd Arm	1,2,3	+ Art	270	.90	243	16,767			175	.87	.90	1.00	175	6,300	3,000	9,900	98,554
V US		Art: 41,42																7,938
VII /III	1st Inf	3	11 ACR	90	.90	81	5,589			50	.87	.90	1.00	50	1,800	1,000	3,300	32,440
III US	2nd Arm	3		30	.90	27	1,863			60	.87	.90	1.00	60	2,160	1,000	3,300	35,458
VII US	3rd Inf	1,2,3	+ Art	90	.90	81	5,589			50	.87	.90	1.00	50	1,800	1,000	3,300	32,440
V US		1,2,3	+ Art	90	.90	81	5,589			175	.87	.90	1.00	175	6,300	3,600	11,880	99,442
VII US			2 ACR						20	115	.87	.90	1.00	133	4,788	1,022	3,373	33,756
V US	8th Inf (mech)	1,2,3	+ Art	270	.90	243	16,767			175	.87	.90	1.00	175	6,300	3,000	9,900	98,554
CONUS POMCUS																		
US	1st Inf	1,2		60	.90	54	3,726			120	.87	.90	1.00	120	4,320	2,000	6,600	69,776
III US			3 ACR						20	115	.87	.90	1.00	133	4,788	1,022	3,373	33,756
III US		Art: 212																5,067
I US	7th Inf	1,2,3		54	.90	49	3,353			51	.87	.90	1.00	51	1,836	3,600	11,880	59,803
I US	25th Inf	1,2,3		54	.90	49	3,353			51	.87	.90	1.00	51	1,836	3,600	11,880	59,803
III US	2nd Arm	1,2		180	.90	162	11,178			100	.87	.90	1.00	100	3,600	2,000	6,600	64,881
III US	1st Cav	1,2,155		270	.90	243	16,767			175	.87	.90	1.00	175	6,300	3,000	9,900	98,554
III US	4th Inf (mech)	1,2,3		270	.90	243	16,767			175	.87	.90	1.00	175	6,300	3,000	9,900	98,554

Reserve and National Guard

Force	Division	Component	ACR														Total
III US		Art: 75,214															7,938
CONUS Res		194 Arm		.90	90									50	1,800	1,000	3,300	26,851
CONUS Res		197 mech Inf		.90	90									50	1,800	1,000	3,300	32,440
NG	26th Inf	1,3,43				81	5,589	60	30	50	.87	.90	1.00	109	3,931	3,000	9,900	81,301
CONUS Res		157 mech Inf		.90	90	81	5,589	60	30	50	.87	.90	1.00	109	3,931	3,000	9,900	26,851
NG	28th Inf	2,55,56				81	5,589	60	30	50	.87	.90	1.00	109	3,931	3,000	9,900	12,630
CONUS Res		Art: 428,424,479		.90	90													22,252
NG		29 Inf		.90	30	27	1,863	25	10	10	.87	.90	1.00	41	1,467	1,000	3,300	26,677
NG		30 Inf (mech)		.70	90	63	4,347	20	20	20	.87	.90	1.00	55	1,994	800	2,640	22,252
NG		33 Inf		.90	30	27	1,863	25	10	10	.87	.90	1.00	41	1,467	1,000	3,300	29,766
NG			107 ACR											118	4,250	1,022	3,373	26,677
NG	35th Mech Inf	32 Inf (mech)		.90	90	63	4,347	55	55	20	.87	.90	1.00	55	1,994	800	2,640	80,780
NG		67,69,149		.70	270	189	13,041	115	55	55	.87	.90	1.00	152	5,485	2,500	8,250	29,766
NG			116 ACR											118	4,250	1,022	3,373	58,459
NG	29th lt Inf	2,55,56		.70	227	90	4,050	20	20	100	.87	.90	1.00	135	4,874	3,800	12,540	80,780
NG	38th Mech Inf	2,46,76		.70	270	189	13,041	55	55	55	.87	.90	1.00	152	5,485	2,500	8,250	22,252
NG		41 Inf		.90	30	27	1,863	25	10	10	.87	.90	1.00	41	1,467	1,000	3,300	26,677
NG		81 Inf (mech)		.70	90	63	4,347	20	20	20	.87	.90	1.00	55	1,994	800	2,640	29,766
NG			163 ACR											118	4,250	1,022	3,373	22,252
NG		45 Inf		.90	30	27	1,863	25	10	10	.87	.90	1.00	41	1,467	1,000	3,300	26,677
NG		218 Inf (mech)		.90	90	63	4,347	20	20	20	.87	.90	1.00	55	1,994	800	2,640	12,630
NG		Art: 45,57,103									.87	.90	1.00					29,766
NG			278 ACR								.87	.90	1.00	118	4,250	1,022	3,373	22,252
NG		53 Inf		.90	30	27	1,863	20	20	10	.87	.90	1.00	41	1,467	1,000	3,300	25,802
NG		30 Arm		.90	90	63	4,347	25	55	20	.87	.90	1.00	55	1,994	800	2,640	22,252
NG		73 Inf		.90	30	27	1,863	25	10	10	.87	.90	1.00	41	1,467	1,000	3,300	12,630
NG		Art: 113,115,118		.90							.87	.90	1.00					12,630
NG		Art: 135,138,142									.87	.90	1.00					25,802
NG		31 Arm		.90	90	63	4,347	20	20	20	.87	.90	1.00	55	1,994	800	2,640	62,881
NG	42nd Inf	1,2		.70	65	59	4,037	40	25	25	.87	.90	1.00	82	2,963	2,300	7,590	12,630
NG		Art: 196,197,209									.87	.90	1.00					12,630
NG		Art: 147,151,169									.87	.90	1.00					12,630
NG		Art: 227,163,631									.87	.90	1.00					
NG	49th Arm	1,2,3		.70	270	189	13,041	55	55	55	.87	.90	1.00	152	5,485	3,000	9,900	90,489
NG	50th Arm	1,2,86		.70	270	189	13,041	55	55	55	.87	.90	1.00	152	5,485	3,000	9,900	90,489

Table C-3. *continued*

| STATE; CORPS | DIVISION | INFANTRY FIGHTING VEHICLES | | | ARMORED PERSONNEL CARRIERS | | | | SMALL ARMS | | UNIT WUV: |
		TO&E	WEI	(WEI-CW 69)	TO&E	EFFECT.	WEI	(WEI-CW 36)	WEI	(WEI-CW 3.3)	Division Total
ATTU Units Not Allocated to Central Front											
United Kingdom	Inf	.86	50	.87	.89	.89	44	1,566	800	2,640	16,653
	Inf	.86	50	.87	.89	.89	44	1,566	800	2,640	16,653
	Inf	.86	50	.87	.89	.89	44	1,566	800	2,640	16,653
	Inf	.86	50	.87	.89	.89	44	1,566	800	2,640	16,653
	Inf	.86	50	.87	.89	.89	44	1,566	800	2,640	16,653
	Inf	.86	50	.87	.89	.89	44	1,566	800	2,640	16,653
	Inf	.86	50	.87	.89	.89	44	1,566	800	2,640	16,653
	Inf	.86	50	.87	.89	.89	44	1,566	800	2,640	16,653
	Inf	.86	50	.87	.89	.89	44	1,566	800	2,640	16,653
	Inf	.86	50	.87	.89	.89	44	1,566	800	2,640	16,653
France	Arm	.86		.87	.90	1.00			700	2,310	15,238
	Arm	.86		.87	.90	1.00			700	2,310	15,238
Netherlands	Inf	.86	75	.87	.95	.98	65	2,349	500	1,650	8,965
Turkey	Mech/Inf	.70		.87	.90	1.00			3,000	9,900	37,928
	Mech/Inf	.70		.87	.90	1.00			3,000	9,900	37,928
	Mech/Inf	.70		.87	.90	1.00			3,000	9,900	37,928
	Mech/Inf	.70		.87	.90	1.00			3,000	9,900	37,928
	Mech/Inf	.70		.87	.90	1.00			3,000	9,900	37,928
	Mech/Inf	.70		.87	.90	1.00			3,000	9,900	37,928
	Mech/Inf	.70		.87	.90	1.00			3,000	9,900	37,928
	Mech/Inf	.70		.87	.90	1.00			3,000	9,900	37,928
	Mech/Inf	.70		.87	.90	1.00			3,000	9,900	37,928
	Mech/Inf	.70		.87	.90	1.00			3,000	9,900	37,928
	Mech/Inf	.70		.87	.90	1.00			3,000	9,900	37,928
	Mech/Inf	.70		.87	.90	1.00			3,000	9,900	37,928
	Mech/Inf	.70		.87	.90	1.00			3,000	9,900	37,928
	Mech/Inf	.70		.87	.90	1.00			3,000	9,900	37,928
	Mech/Inf	.70		.87	.90	1.00			3,000	9,900	37,928
	Mech/Inf	.70		.87	.90	1.00			3,000	9,900	37,928
	Mech/Inf	.70		.87	.90	1.00			3,000	9,900	37,928
	Mech/Inf	.70		.87	.90	1.00			3,000	9,900	37,928
	Mech/Inf	.70		.87	.90	1.00			3,000	9,900	37,928
	Mech/Inf	.70		.87	.90	1.00			3,000	9,900	37,928

Greece	Mech/Inf	8	.70	6	386				.87	.90	1.00			3,000	9,900	38,454
	Mech/Inf	8	.70	6	386				.87	.90	1.00			3,000	9,900	38,454
	Mech/Inf	8	.70	6	386				.87	.90	1.00			3,000	9,900	38,454
	Mech/Inf	8	.70	6	386				.87	.90	1.00			3,000	9,900	38,454
	Mech/Inf	8	.70	6	386				.87	.90	1.00			3,000	9,900	38,454
	Mech/Inf	8	.70	6	386				.87	.90	1.00			3,000	9,900	38,454
	Mech/Inf	8	.70	6	386				.87	.90	1.00			3,000	9,900	38,454
	Mech/Inf	8	.70	6	386				.87	.90	1.00			3,000	9,900	38,454
	Mech/Inf	8	.70	6	386				.87	.90	1.00			3,000	9,900	38,454
	Mech/Inf	8	.70	6	386				.87	.90	1.00			3,000	9,900	38,454
	Mech/Inf	8	.70	6	386				.87	.90	1.00			3,000	9,900	38,454
Italy	Mech/Inf	6	.70	4	290	50	100	250	.87	.90	1.00	384	13,806	3,000	9,900	86,201
	Mech/Inf	6	.70	4	290	50	100	250	.87	.90	1.00	384	13,806	3,000	9,900	86,201
	Mech/Inf	6	.70	4	290	50	100	250	.87	.90	1.00	384	13,806	3,000	9,900	86,201
	Mech/Inf	6	.70	4	290	50	100	250	.87	.90	1.00	384	13,806	3,000	9,900	86,201
	Mech/Inf	6	.70	4	290	50	100	250	.87	.90	1.00	384	13,806	3,000	9,900	86,201
	Mech/Inf	6	.70	4	290	50	100	250	.87	.90	1.00	384	13,806	3,000	9,900	86,201
	Mech/Inf	6	.70	4	290	50	100	250	.87	.90	1.00	384	13,806	3,000	9,900	86,201
Spain	Mech/Inf		.70			25	50	175	.87	.90	1.00	242	8,703	3,000	9,900	53,184
	Mech/Inf		.70			25	50	175	.87	.90	1.00	242	8,703	3,000	9,900	53,184
	Mech/Inf		.70			25	50	175	.87	.90	1.00	242	8,703	3,000	9,900	53,184
	Mech/Inf		.70			25	50	175	.87	.90	1.00	242	8,703	3,000	9,900	53,184
	Mech/Inf		.70			25	50	175	.87	.90	1.00	242	8,703	3,000	9,900	53,184
	Mech/Inf		.70			25	50	175	.87	.90	1.00	242	8,703	3,000	9,900	53,184
	Mech/Inf		.70			25	50	175	.87	.90	1.00	242	8,703	3,000	9,900	53,184
	Mech/Inf		.70			25	50	175	.87	.90	1.00	242	8,703	3,000	9,900	53,184
Portugal	Mech/Inf		.70				5	20	.87	.90	1.00	25	882	3,000	9,900	19,540
	Mech/Inf		.70				5	20	.87	.90	1.00	25	882	3,000	9,900	19,540
	Mech/Inf		.70				5	20	.87	.90	1.00	25	882	3,000	9,900	19,540
	Mech/Inf		.70				5	20	.87	.90	1.00	25	882	3,000	9,900	19,540
	Mech/Inf		.70				5	20	.87	.90	1.00	25	882	3,000	9,900	19,540
	Mech/Inf		.70				5	20	.87	.90	1.00	25	882	3,000	9,900	19,540
Norway	Mech/Inf		.70			25	50	150	.87	.90	1.00	217	7,803	3,000	9,900	85,991

Notes to Table C-3

This table employs the same TO&E-based accounting method used in table C-1. See the notes to table C-1 for a full explanation.

NATO forces are arranged by nationality. This reflects the fact that reductions are made nation by nation rather than on an alliancewide basis.

The WEI/WUV and ADE totals over the course of mobilization were calculated by determining which forces would be available, when they would be deployed, their TO&Es, and their WEI/WUV scores.

The estimate of forces available for use on the central front was made for military units down to the brigade level in every NATO nation that supplies forces to the central front. For non-U.S. NATO forces this was a relatively direct process, the main source being David C. Isby and Charles Kamps, Jr., *Armies of NATO's Central Front* (London: Jane's, 1985). This was checked against Friedrich Weiner, *The Armies of the NATO Nations: Organization-Concept of War, Weapons, and Equipment*, "Truppendienst" Handbooks, vol. 3 (Vienna: Herold Publishers, 1987); and the International Institute for Strategic Studies, *The Military Balance 1987–1988* (London, 1987). There were few discrepancies between Isby and Kamps and Weiner, and they were used in preference to IISS. Finally, David Isby and Colonel Karl Lowe of the National Defense University were consulted for mission and force structure changes since 1985.

For U.S. forces, Isby and Kamps, Weiner, and IISS were used in a similar manner. Additional sources included U.S. Army War College, *Army Reference Data Handbook* (U.S. Department of the Army, 1984); and "The Total Army at a Glance" (enclosure), *Army Magazine*, vol. 38 (May 1988). A list of U.S. forces withheld was created using the assumption that U.S. forces would be withheld for a simultaneous Persian Gulf contingency and a minor Pacific contingency. Sources for withholds included Joshua M. Epstein, *Strategy and Force Planning: The Case of the Persian Gulf* (Brookings, 1987); Thomas L. McNaugher, *Arms and Oil: U.S. Military Strategy and the Persian Gulf* (Brookings, 1985); and Office of the Assistant Secretary of Defense for Program Analysis and Evaluation, *NATO Center Region Military Balance Study, 1978–1984* (Department of Defense, 1979).

Next, mobilization and deployment schedules for military units down to the brigade level were estimated. In some cases (for example, where distance from the front is the determining factor), an estimate can be made with relatively high confidence from

Isby and Kamps, *Armies of NATO's Central Front*; OSD, *NATO Center Region Military Balance Study*; and Hugh Faringdon, *Confrontation: the Strategic Geography of NATO and the Warsaw Pact* (London: Routledge & Kegan Paul, 1986).

Mobilization and deployment of U.S. reserves are more dependent on uncertain variables, such as sealift and airlift capacity. The estimates from the *NATO Center Region Military Balance Study* do not show National Guard units (other than roundout units) appearing in the theater until M + 40. Richard Kugler, while director of the Strategic Concepts Development Center, advanced the same schedule in *Alliance and Defense Capabilities in Europe*, Hearings before the Senate Committee on Armed Services, 100 Cong. 1 sess. (Government Printing Office, 1988), p. 227. Such an estimate may err slightly on the conservative side, but it is respected in this mobilization schedule: the first National Guard division arrives on the central front at M + 39. After this, a National Guard division (plus accompanying separate infantry, mechanized, field artillery, or armored brigades) arrives every seven days until M + 102. The spread is relatively even, but the mobilization and deployment schedule has more independent brigades accompanying the divisions as logistical support from the continental United States increases. NATO receives its peak National Guard reinforcement at M + 67 and tapers off to M + 46 levels at M + 102. While the specific reinforcing numbers for each week cannot be given with high confidence, the overall shape of the National Guard mobilization is credible.

The TO&Es for NATO divisions were taken from the WEI/WUV Manual; Isby and Kamps, *Armies of NATO's Central Front*; IISS, *The Military Balance, 1987–1988*; U.S. Army Concepts Analysis Agency, *Analysis of Force Potential System* (Springfield, Va: NTIC, 1984); and Anthony H. Cordesman, *NATO's Central Region Forces* (London: Jane's, 1988). The WEI/WUV manual TO&E was used as the baseline although it is a projection for 1986. *Analysis of Force Potential System* was used to update the U.S. TO&Es. Isby and Kamps was used to update European divisions, as was Cordesman. When there was disagreement, Isby and Kamps was used because the level of detail is higher. The new version of the French light tank, the AMX, was moved from the ARV category into the tank category of the WEI/WUV scoring system based on discussions with Isby. IISS, *Military Balance, 1987–1988*, was used mainly to extrapolate TO&Es (in this case from aggregate numbers) for non–central front NATO nations such as Turkey and Spain. NATO Press Service, *Conventional Forces in Europe: The Facts* (Brussels, 1988) was also used for this purpose.

Finally, for each unit down to the brigade level, a WUV score was computed using WEI scores from U.S. Army Concepts Analysis Agency, *Weapons Effectiveness Indices/ Weighted Unit Values (WEI/WUV) III.* Close air support is treated separately in the adaptive dynamic model used in this study. To avoid double counting, helicopters and air defense assets were removed from the WEI/WUV scores. The U.S. Army study gives WEI scores for 1979 and 1986 division structures with 1986 weaponry (with or without the then-projected Division 86 structure). When a unit was not included in the WEI/WUV manual, a comparable unit was used based on Isby and Kamps, *Armies of NATO's Central Front*; and IISS, *Military Balance, 1987–1988.*

TABLE C-4. NATO Weapon Totals and ADE Mobilization Schedule Derived from Table C-3, Current Balance

TANKS

WEAPON TYPE AND AREA	TOTAL	Tank: M-48	Tank: M-60A1 CENT LEO 1	Tank: M-60A2/A3	Tank: M-1/M1A1 CHIEF LEO 2
ATTU including spares	21,604				
ATTU TO&E	18,003	8,418	2,612	1,766	5,206
Central Front (without CONUS) including spares	12,456				
Central Front (without CONUS) TO&E	10,380	2,360	1,347	1,766	4,906

ARTILLERY

WEAPON TYPE AND AREA	TOTAL	Arty: 155 HOW 105MM Var	Arty: 155HOW M110A1/A2	Arty: 155 HOW M110E2	Arty: GSRS	Mortar: 120MM	Mortar: M-30
ATTU including spares	17,885						
ATTU TO&E	14,904	5,493	3,160	1,817	437	2,541	1,456
Central Front (without CONUS) including spares	6,860						
Central Front (without CONUS) TO&E	5,717	813	1,840	1,117	102	1,146	699

ARMORED VEHICLES

WEAPON TYPE AND AREA	TOTAL	ARV: M8	ARV: CVR SPZ	ARV: SCORPN AMX	ARV: CFV M2 SCIMTAR	APC: 0th	APC: 0th	APC: AFV, ARV, VAB	APC: M113A1	IFV: MARDER
ATTU including spares	45,659									
ATTU TO&E	38,049	4,520	1,857	2,232	1,470	4,825	4,676	5,848	8,739	3,882
Central Front (without CONUS) including spares	24,972									
Central Front (without CONUS) TO&E	20,810	120	1,147	1,497	1,195		3,476	4,568	5,069	3,738

CENTRAL FRONT MOBILIZATION SCHEDULE, CURRENT BALANCE

Days After M + 0	M + 1	M + 5	M + 10	M + 15	M + 20	M + 25	M + 32	M + 39
ADE arrival	13.0	8.0	6.3	6.3	.7	1.0	.3	.8
Total ADEs	13.0	21.0	27.3	33.6	34.3	35.3	35.7	36.5
WUV Arrival	1,292,279	792,085	626,141	625,414	72,146	101,310	32,440	81,301
Total WUV	1,292,279	2,084,364	2,710,505	3,335,919	3,408,064	3,509,374	3,541,815	3,623,115

Days After M + 0	M + 46	M + 53	M + 60	M + 67	M + 74	M + 81	M + 88	M + 95	M + 102
ADE arrival	1.1	.8	1.4	1.7	1.3	1.1	1.3	1.2	.9
Total ADEs	37.6	38.4	39.8	41.5	42.8	43.9	45.2	46.4	47.3
WUV Arrival	108,152	83,810	137,224	169,006	127,624	112,701	126,573	115,748	90,488.60
Total WUV	3,731,267	3,815,077	3,952,301	4,121,306	4,248,930	4,361,631	4,488,204	4,603,952	4,694,440

Source: Data given in Table C-3.

Table C-5. Details of Multisector Feint Attack, WUV Scores from Current Balance

Force	Days after mobilization	Deployment sector							
		1	2	3	4	5	6	7	8
NATO	M+5	136,079	376,836	307,738	207,303	166,749	261,004	376,642	252,015
	M+10	31,591	82,883	104,209	108,884	18,784	18,784	207,531	53,477
	M+15		62,594		276,119	206,387		80,316	
	M+20				36,073	36,073			
	M+25				50,655	50,655			
	M+32				16,220	16,220			
	M+39				40,651	40,651			
	M+46				54,076	54,076			
	M+53				41,905	41,905			
	M+60				68,612	68,612			
	M+67				84,503	84,503			
	M+74				63,812	63,812			
	M+81				56,351	56,351			
	M+88				63,287	63,287			
	M+95				57,874	57,874			
	M+102				45,244	45,244			
WTO	M+10	370,137	555,205	370,137	925,342	370,137	370,137	370,137	370,137
	M+15				119,521	119,521			
	M+20				124,217	124,217			
	M+25				130,826	130,826			
	M+30				303,385	303,385			
	M+35				188,273	188,273			
	M+40				150,203	150,203			
	M+45				36,307	36,307			
	M+50				36,307	36,307			
	M+55				72,614	72,614			
	M+60				167,403	167,403			
	M+65				108,921	108,921			
	M+70				108,921	108,921			
	M+75				72,614	72,614			
	M+80				147,225	147,225			
	M+85				162,808	162,808			
	M+90				126,502	126,502			

Source: Attack conforms to force level constraints given in tables C-2 and C-4. Given its eight corps sectors, NATO is assumed to allocate one-eighth of its close air support (CAS) aircraft to the defense of corps sector V. The WTO is assumed to allocate one-tenth of its CAS aircraft to the attack, a fraction equal to the initial fraction of WTO ADEs allocated to that sector.

Table C-6. WTO Units, Central Front Arrival Times, and WUV Scores, after Unilateral Cuts

Group headers: **TANKS** (T-55/T-34, T-64, T-72, T-80, WUV WEI-CW 100) · **ARTILLERY** (M-38/D-30/Others, MRL, 152mm, M74, WUV WEI-CW 92) · **MORTAR** (Others, 82MM, 120MM, WUV WEI-CW 48) · **ANTIARMOR** (T-21/Oth, T-12, RPG7, ATGM, WUV WEI-CW 55) · **INFANTRY FIGHTING VEHICLES** (BMP, WUV WEI-CW 69)

Time; State; Military District	Unit Title; Readiness Category	T-55 T-34	T-64	T-72	T-80	WUV (WEI-CW 100)	M-38 D-30 Others	MRL	152mm	M74	WUV (WEI-CW 92)	Others	82MM	120MM	WUV (WEI-CW 48)	T-21 Oth	T-12	RPG7	ATGM	WUV (WEI-CW 55)	BMP	WUV (WEI-CW 69)
M + 1 to M + 5																						
USSR																						
GSFG	16 Tk Dv (1)		70		180	32,263		24	18	54	8,230		4	18	1,097			346	46	8,482	147	9,027
GSFG	21 MR Dv (1)		120		40	20,152		36	18	36	11,460		12	54	3,292	12	18	529	36	12,569	117	7,185
GSFG	94 MR Dv (1)		120		40	20,152		36	18	36	11,460		12	54	3,292	12	18	529	36	12,569	117	7,185
GSFG	207 MR Dv (1)		120		40	20,152		36	18	36	11,460		12	54	3,292	12	18	529	36	12,569	117	7,185
GSFG	Art Bg (1)						54	30	31	31	7,760					10		130	10	3,608	40	2,346
GSFG	Art Bg (1)						54	30	31	31	7,760					10		130	10	3,608	40	2,346
GSFG	Other Bts (1)													15	770	10		40	10	1,084	10	587
GSFG	7 Tk Dv (1)		50		180	29,777		24	18	54	8,230		4	18	1,097			346	46	8,482	147	9,027
GSFG	10 Tk Dv (1)							24	18	54	8,230		4	18	1,097			346	46	8,482	147	9,027
GSFG	72 Tk Dv (1)		50		180	29,777		24	18	54	8,230		4	18	1,097			346	46	8,482	147	9,027
GSFG	47 Tk Dv (1)							24	18	54	8,230		4	18	1,097			346	46	8,482	147	9,027
GSFG	304 Art Bg (1)						20				1,417					10		40	10	1,084	10	587
GSFG	Other Bts (1)													15	770	10		40	10	1,084	10	587
GSFG	25 Tk Dv (1)		50		180	29,777		24	18	54	8,230		4	18	1,097			346	46	8,482	147	9,027
GSFG	32 Tk Dv (1)		80		40	15,180		24	18	54	8,230		4	18	1,097			346	46	8,482	147	9,027
GSFG	90 Tk Dv (1)							24	18	54	8,230		4	18	1,097			346	46	8,482	147	9,027
GSFG	35 MR Dv (1)							36	18	36	11,460		12	54	3,292	12	18	529	36	12,569	117	7,185
GSFG	71 Art Bg (1)						20				1,417					10		130	10	3,608	10	587
GSFG	Other Bts (1)													15	770	10		40	10	1,084	10	587
GSFG	79 Tk Dv (1)		50		180	29,777		24	18	54	8,230		4	18	1,097			346	46	8,482	147	9,027
GSFG	27 MR Dv (1)		80		40	15,180		36	18	36	11,460		12	54	3,292	12	18	529	36	12,569	117	7,185
GSFG	39 MR Dv (1)		80		40	15,180		36	18	36	11,460		12	54	3,292	12	18	529	36	12,569	117	7,185
GSFG	57 MR Dv (1)		80		40	15,180		36	18	36	11,460		12	54	3,292	12	18	529	36	12,569	117	7,185
GSFG	43 Art Bg (1)						20				1,417					10		130	10	3,608	10	587
GSFG	Other Bts (1)													15	770	10		40	10	1,084	10	587
GSFG	9 Tk Dv (1)		50		180	29,777		24	18	54	8,230		4	18	1,097			346	46	8,482	147	9,027
GSFG	11 Tk Dv (1)		50		180	29,777		24	18	54	8,230		4	18	1,097			346	46	8,482	147	9,027
GSFG	20 MR Dv (1)		80		40	15,180		36	18	36	11,460		12	54	3,292	12	18	529	36	12,569	117	7,185
GSFG	43 Art Dv (1)						10	144	144	144	36,432			6	308	36		36	27	2,653	40	2,346
GSFG	35 Assault (1)										708			6	308	36	10	140	13	3,667	40	2,346
GSFG	Spetsnaz (1)						11				765			15	770	2	4	25	7	638	6	352
GSFG	MR Bg (1)																	106	5	2,514	23	1,437
GSFG	Other Bts (1)													15	770			25	5	638	6	352
CGF	15 Tk Dv (1)		80		40	15,180		24	18	54	8,230		4	18	1,097			346	46	8,482	147	9,027
CGF	18 MR Dv (1)		80		40	15,180		36	18	36	11,460		12	54	3,292	12	18	529	36	12,569	117	7,185
CGF	48 MR Dv (1)							36	18	36	11,460		12	54	3,292	12	18	529	36	12,569	117	7,185
CGF	Art Bg (1)						54	30	31	31	7,760											
CGF	Other Bts (1)													15	770			25	5	638	6	352

M+5																					
USSR																					
NGF	20 Tk Dv (1)		50	180	29,777		24	18	54	8,230		4	18	1,097			346	46	8,482	147	9,027
NGF	6 MR Dv (1)		80	40	15,180	54	36	18	36	11,460		12	54	3,292	12	18	529	36	12,569	117	7,185
GDR																					
III	7 Tk Dv (1)	140	90		23,890	54	18	6	12	6,657			18	924		9	167	9	3,166	51	3,132
III	11 MR Dv (1)	135			13,230	54	18		18	6,889			54	2,773	18	27	324	54	8,504	115	7,062
III	4 MR Dv (1)	135			13,230	54	18		18	6,889			54	2,773	18	27	324	54	8,504	115	7,062
III	Art Rt (1)						14	14	14	3,575					3		3	3	257		
III	9 Tk Dv (1)	140	90		23,890	54	18	6	12	6,657			18	924		9	167	9	3,166	51	3,132
III	8 MR Dv (1)	135			13,230	54	18		18	6,889			54	2,773	18	27	324	54	8,504	115	7,062
III	1 MR Dv (1)	135			13,230	54	18		18	6,889			54	2,773	18	27	324	54	8,504	115	7,062
III	Art Rt (1)						14	14	14	3,575					3		3	3	257		
Czech																					
West	1 Tk Dv (1)	247	40		28,686	18	24	18	18	6,006					120		234	15	6,392	126	7,738
West	2 MR Dv (1)	200			19,600	36	36	18	18	8,263					12		379	45	7,886	117	7,185
West	22 Assault (1)																25	5	638	6	352
West	Other Bts (1)																100	20	2,552	35	2,053
Poland																					
War	6 Assault (1)																415	42	9,305	120	7,038
M+10																					
Pol																					
Pom	16 Tk Dv (1)										9			354			135	9	2,391		
Pom	20 Tk Dv (1)	162	121		29,549		12		6	1,524	9			354			135	9	2,391	101	6,202
Pom	12 MR Dv (1)	202	40		24,316		12	12	18	3,367	27			1,063			313	36	6,127	101	6,202
Pom	8 MR Dv (1)	202	40		24,316		12	12	18	3,367	27			1,063			313	36	6,127	101	6,202
Pom	Art Rt (1)						14	14	14	3,575							3	3	177		
Sil	5 Tk Dv (1)	162	121		29,549		12		6	1,524	9			354			135	9	2,391	101	6,202
Sil	10 Tk Dv (1)	162	121		29,549		12		6	1,524	9			354			135	9	2,391	101	6,202
Sil	11 Tk Dv (1)										9			354			135	9	2,391		
Sil	Art Rt (1)						14	14	14	3,575							3	3	183		
War	Art Rt (1)																3	3	183		
USSR																					
Byel	120 MR Dv (1)		214	40	28,942	54	36	18	36	11,460		12	54	3,292	12	18	529	36	12,569	117	7,185
Byel	8 Tk Dv (1)		134	188	37,514		24	18	54	8,230		4	18	1,097			346	46	8,482	147	9,027
Carp	15 MR Dv (1)		214	40	28,942	54	36	18	36	11,460		12	54	3,292	12	18	529	36	12,569	117	7,185
Carp	23 Tk Dv (1)		134	188	37,514		24	18	54	8,230		4	18	1,097			346	46	8,482	147	9,027
Balt	7 Airbn (1)					30				2,125			18	924	12	31	415	42	11,040	120	7,038
SGF	93 MR Dv (1)		80	40	13,800	54	36	18	36	11,460		12	54	3,292	12	18	529	36	12,569	117	7,185
SGF	13 MR Dv (1)		80	40	13,800	54	36	18	36	11,460		12	54	3,292	12	18	529	36	12,569	117	7,185
SGF	2 Tk Dv (1)		50	180	27,070		24	18	54	8,230		4	18	1,097			346	46	8,482	147	9,027
SGF	13 Tk Dv (1)						24	18	54	8,230		4	18	1,097			346	46	8,482	147	9,027

Table C-6. continued

Time; State; Military District	Unit Title; Readiness Category	TANKS T-55/T-34	T-64	T-72	T-80	WUV (WEI-CW 100)	ART M-38 D-30 Others	MRL	152mm	M74	WUV (WEI-CW 92)	MORT Others	82MM	120MM	WUV (WEI-CW 48)	T-21 Oth	T-12	RPG7	ATGM	WUV (WEI-CW 55)	IFV BMP	WUV (WEI-CW 69)
M+15 USSR																						
Mosc	MR Dv (1)	40		214	40	28,942	54	36	18	36	11,460		12	54	3,292	12	18	529	36	12,569	117	7,185
Mosc	2 MR Dv (1)	40		214	40	28,942	54	36	18	36	11,460		12	54	3,292	12	18	529	36	12,569	117	7,185
Mosc	106 Airbn (1)	40					30				2,125			18	924	12	31	415	42	11,040	120	7,038
Mosc	Art Dv (1)							144	144	144	36,432					36		36	27	2,653		
M+20 USSR																						
Byel	MR Dv (2)		40	174		28,382	72	36	18	18	11,145		12	54	3,292		12	476	24	10,556	124	7,615
Carp	70 MR Dv (2)		40	174		28,382	72	36	18	18	11,145		12	54	3,292		12	476	24	10,556	124	7,615
Balt	I MR Dv (2)		40	174		28,382	72	36	18	18	11,145		12	54	3,292		12	476	24	10,556	124	7,615
M+25 USSR																						
Byel	8 Tk Dv (2)		134	188		36,252	18	24	18	36	7,916		4	18	1,097			166	24	3,196	117	7,185
Carp	128 MR Dv (2)	40	40	174		28,382	72	36	18	18	11,145		12	54	3,292	12		476		10,556	124	7,615
Balt	1 Tk Dv (2)		134	188		36,252	18	24	18	36	7,916		4	18	1,097			166		3,196	117	7,185
M+30 USSR																						
Byel	29 Tk Dv (2)		134	188		36,252	18	24	18	36	7,916		4	18	1,097			166		3,196	117	7,185
Byel	3 Tk Dv (2)		134	188		36,252	18	24	18	36	7,916		4	18	1,097			166		3,196	117	7,185
Byel	27 Tk Dv (2)		134	188		36,252	18	24	18	36	7,916		4	18	1,097			166		3,196	117	7,185
Carp	61 MR Dv (2)	40	40	174		28,382	72	36	18	18	11,145		12	54	3,292		12	476	24	10,556	124	7,615
Carp	24 MR Dv (2)	40	40	174		28,382	72	36	18	18	11,145		12	54	3,292		12	476	24	10,556	124	7,615
Carp	13 Tk Dv (2)		134	188		36,252	18	24	18	36	7,916		4	18	1,097			166		3,196	117	7,185
Balt	40 Tk Dv (2)		134	188		36,252	18	24	18	36	7,916		4	18	1,097			166		3,196	117	7,185
Balt	24 Tk Dv (2)		134	188		36,252	18	24	18	36	7,916		4	18	1,097			166		3,196	117	7,185
Pol																						
Sil	4 MR Dv (2)	204				19,992									1,063			313	18	5,474		
Pom	7 Assualt (2)											27						140	13	3,103	40	2,346

168

M+35																					
USSR																					
173	Byel	47 Tk Dv (2)		134	188	36,252	18	24	18	36	7,916	4	18	1,097			166		3,196	117	7,185
178	Byel	34 Tk Dv (2)		134	188	36,252	18	24	18	36	7,916	4	18	1,097			166		3,196	117	7,185
183	Byel	Art A Dv (2)						144	144	144	36,432						36	27	1,762		
188	Byel	Art B Dv (2)						30	31	31	7,760								6		
193	Carp	117 Tk Dv (2)		134	188	36,252	18	24	18	36	7,916	4	18	1,097			166		3,196	117	7,185
198	Carp	Art A Dv (2)						144	144	144	36,432						36	27	1,762		
203	Carp	Art B Dv (2)						30	31	31	7,760								6		
208	Carp	Art B Dv (2)						30	31	31	7,760								6		
213	Balt	Art A Dv (2)						144	144	144	36,432						36	27	1,762		
218	Balt	Art A Dv (2)						144	144	144	36,432						36	27	1,762		
M+40																					
Czech																					
225	West	4 Tk Dv (2)	227			20,998	18	24	18	18	5,561				120		234	15	5,075	126	7,165
230	West	9 Tk Dv (2)	227			20,998	18	24	18	18	5,561				120		234	15	5,075	126	7,165
235	West	3 MR Dv (2)	175			17,150	54	30	12		7,132				18		372	27	7,140		
USSR																					
241	Mosc	15 Tk Dv (2)		134	188	36,252	18	24	18	36	7,916	4	18	1,097			166		3,196	117	7,185
246	Mosc	4 Tk Dv (2)		134	188	36,252	18	24	18	36	7,916	4	18	1,097			166		3,196	117	7,185
M+45																					
USSR																					
253	Balt	3 MR Dv (3)	200			19,600		36	18		3,974	12	54	2,925		12	476	24	9,275	124	6,625
M+50																					
USSR																					
260	Len	64 MR Dv (3)	200			19,600		36	18		3,974	12	54	2,925		12	476	24	9,275	124	6,625

Table C-6. *continued*

Time; State; Military District	Unit Title; Readiness Category	TANKS TO&E				TANKS WUV: (WEI-CW 100)	ARTILLERY TO&E				ARTILLERY WUV: (WEI-CW 92)	MORTAR TO&E			MORTAR WUV: (WEI-CW 48)	T-21 Oth	ANTIARMOR TO&E			ANTIARMOR WUV: (WEI-CW 55)	IFV TO&E	IFV WUV: (WEI-CW 69)
		T-55/T-34	T-64	T-72	T-80		M-38 D-30/Others	MRL	152mm	M74		Others	82MM	120MM			T-12	RPG7	ATGM		BMP	
M+55																						
USSR																						
Carp	66 MR Dv (3)	200				19,600		36	18		3,974		12	54	2,925		12	476	24	9,275	124	6,625
Len	111 MR Dv (3)	200				19,600		36	18		3,974		12	54	2,925		12	476	24	9,275	124	6,625
M+60																						
USSR																						
Byel	50 MR Dv (3)	200				19,600		36	18		3,974	12		54	2,925			476	24	9,275	124	6,625
Len	77 MR Dv (3)	200				19,600		36	18		3,974		12	54	2,925		12	476	24	9,275	124	6,625
Balt	88 MR Dv (3)	200				19,600		36	18		3,974		12	54	2,925		12	476	24	9,275	124	6,625
Czech																						
East	13 Tk Dv (3)	227				20,998	18	24		18	5,561					120		234	15	5,075	126	7,165
East	14 Tk Dv (3)	227				20,998	18	24		18	5,561					120		234	15	5,075	126	7,165
M+65																						
USSR																						
Carp	17 MR Dv (3)	200				19,600		36	18		3,974		12	54	2,925		12	476	24	9,275	124	6,625
Balt	26 MR Dv (3)	200				19,600		36	18		3,974		12	54	2,925		12	476	24	9,275	124	6,625
Len	69 MR Dv (3)	200				19,600		36	18		3,974		12	54	2,925		12	476	24	9,275	124	6,625
M+70																						
USSR																						
Carp	97 MR Dv (3)	200				19,600		36	18		3,974		12	54	2,925		12	476	24	9,275	124	6,625
Balt	44 MR Dv (3)	200				19,600		36	18		3,974		12	54	2,925		12	476	24	9,275	124	6,625
Len	45 MR Dv (3)	200				19,600		36	18		3,974		12	54	2,925		12	476	24	9,275	124	6,625

M+75																			
USSR																			
Len	45 MR Dv (3)	200	19,600		36	18		3,974		12	54	2,925	1	12	476	24	9,297	124	6,625
Balt	107 MR Dv (3)	200	19,600		36	18		3,974		12	54	2,925	12	12	476	24	9,533	124	6,625
M+80																			
USSR																			
Mos	13 MR Dv (3)	200	19,600		36	18		3,974		12	54	2,925	12	12	476	24	9,533	124	6,625
Vol	43 MR Dv (3)	200	19,600		36	18		3,974		12	54	2,925	12	12	476	24	9,533	124	6,625
Vol	Art A Dv (3)				144	144	144	36,432					36		36	27	2,653		
Czech																			
East	15 MR Dv (3)	125	12,250	54	30	12		7,132			27	2,449	18		372	27	7,140		
Pol	1 MR Dv (3)			54	12	12		5,592	27				18	36	313	18	7,285		
War																			
M+85																			
USSR																			
Mos	32 MR Dv (3)	200	19,600		36	18		3,974		12	54	2,925	12	12	476	24	9,533	124	6,625
Vol	96 MR Dv (3)	200	19,600		36	18		3,974		12	54	2,925	12	12	476	24	9,533	124	6,625
Ural	77 MR Dv (3)	200	19,600		36	18		3,974		12	54	2,925	12	12	476	24	9,533	124	6,625
Czech																			
East	19 MR Dv (3)	125	12,250	54	30	12		7,132			27	2,449	18		372	27	7,140		
Pol	3 MR Dv (3)																		
War																			
M+90																			
USSR																			
Vol	21 MR Dv (3)	200	19,600		36	18		3,974		12	54	2,925	12	12	476	24	9,533	124	6,625
Ural	MR Dv (3)	200	19,600		36	18		3,974		12	54	2,925	12	12	476	24	9,533	124	6,625
Czech																			
East	20 MR Dv (3)	125	12,250	54	30	12		7,132					18		313	18	327		
Pol																			
War	9 MR Dv (3)																5,474		

Table C-6. *continued*

ATTU Units Not Allocated to Central Front

USSR

Military District	Unit Title; Readiness Category	T-55 T-34	T-64	T-72	T-80	WUV (WEI-CW 100)	M-38 D-30 Others	MRL	152mm	M74	WUV (WEI-CW 92)	82MM	120MM	WUV (WEI-CW 48)	T-21 Oth	T-12	RPG7	ATGM	WUV (WEI-CW 55)	BMP	WUV (WEI-CW 69)
						TANKS					**ARTILLERY**			**MORTAR**					**ANTIARMOR**		**INFANTRY FIGHTING VEHICLES**
NW	MR Dv (1)		19	174		21,790		36	18	18	6,044	12	50	3,086			476	24	10,113	124	7,615
NW	MR Dv (1)		19	174		21,790		36	18	18	6,044	12	50	3,086			476	24	10,113	124	7,615
NW	MR Dv (1)		19	174		21,790		36	18	18	6,044	12	50	3,086			476	24	10,113	124	7,615
NW	MR Dv (1)		19	174		21,790		36	18	18	6,044	12	50	3,086			476	24	10,113	124	7,615
NW	MR Dv (1)		19	174		21,790		36	18	18	6,044	12	50	3,086			476	24	10,113	124	7,615
NW	MR Dv (1)		19	174		21,790		36	18	18	6,044	12	50	3,086			476	24	10,113	124	7,615
NW	MR Dv (1)		19	174		21,790		36	18	18	6,044	12	50	3,086			476	24	10,113	124	7,615
NW	MR Dv (1)		19	174		21,790		36	18	18	6,044	12	50	3,086			476	24	10,113	124	7,615
SW	MR Dv (1)		19	174		21,790		36	18	18	6,044	12	50	3,086			476	24	10,113	124	7,615
SW	MR Dv (1)		19	174		21,790		36	18	18	6,044	12	50	3,086			476	24	10,113	124	7,615
SW	Art A Dv (1)							144	144	144	36,432						36	27	1,762		
SW	MR Dv (1)		20	174		21,902		36	18	18	6,044	12	50	3,086			476	24	10,113	124	7,615
SW	MR Dv (1)		20	174		21,902		36	18	18	6,044	12	50	3,086			476	24	10,113	124	7,615
SW	MR Dv (1)		20	174		21,902		36	18	18	6,044	12	50	3,086			476	24	10,113	124	7,615
SW	MR Dv (1)		20	174		21,902		36	18	18	6,044	12	50	3,086			476	24	10,113	124	7,615
SW	MR Dv (1)		20	174		21,902		36	18	18	6,044	12	50	3,086			476	24	10,113	124	7,615
SW	MR Dv (1)		20	174		21,902		36	18	18	6,044	12	50	3,086			476	24	10,113	124	7,615
SW	MR Dv (1)		20	174		21,902		36	18	18	6,044	12	50	3,086			476	24	10,113	124	7,615
SW	MR Dv (1)		20	174		21,902		36	18	18	6,044	12	50	3,086			476	24	10,113	124	7,615
SW	MR Dv (1)		20	174		21,902		36	18	18	6,044	12	50	3,086			476	24	10,113	124	7,615
SW	MR Dv (1)		20	174		21,902		36	18	18	6,044	12	50	3,086			476	24	10,113	124	7,615
SW	MR Dv (1)		20	174		21,902		36	18	18	6,044	12	50	3,086			476	24	10,113	124	7,615
SW	MR Dv (1)		20	174		21,902		36	18	18	6,044	12	50	3,086			476	24	10,113	124	7,615
SW	MR Dv (1)		20	174		21,902		36	18	18	6,044	12	50	3,086			476	24	10,113	124	7,615
SW	MR Dv (1)		20	174		21,902		36	18	18	6,044	12	50	3,086			476	24	10,113	124	7,615
SW	MR Dv (1)		20	174		21,902		36	18	18	6,044	12	50	3,086			476	24	10,113	124	7,615
SW	MR Dv (1)		20	174		21,902		36	18	18	6,044	12	50	3,086			476	24	10,113	124	7,615
SW	Tk Dv (1)		75	188		29,644			18	36	4,653	4		173			166		3,196	117	7,185
SW	Tk Dv (1)		75	188		29,644			18	36	4,653	4		173			166		3,196	117	7,185
SW	Tk Dv (1)		75	188		29,644			18	36	4,653	4		173			166		3,196	117	7,185
SW	Tk Dv (1)		75	188		29,644			18	36	4,653	4		173			166		3,196	117	7,185
SW	Tk Dv (1)		75	188		29,644			18	36	4,653	4		173			166		3,196	117	7,185
SW	Tk Dv (1)		75	188		29,644			18	36	4,653	4		173			166		3,196	117	7,185

SW	Tk Dv (1)		75	188	29,644			18	36	4,653	4		173		166		3,196	117	7,185
SW	Tk Dv (1)		75	188	29,644			18	36	4,653	4		173		166		3,196	117	7,185
SW	Tk Dv (1)		75	188	29,644			18	36	4,653	4		173		166		3,196	117	7,185
SW	Tk Dv (1)		75	188	29,644			18	36	4,653	4		173		166		3,196	117	7,185
SW	Art A Dv														36		1,762		
Hun	MR Dv (1)	199			19,502	50	30	12		6,848					372	27	6,813		
Hun	MR Dv (1)	199			19,502	50	30	12		6,848					372	27	6,813		
Hun	MR Dv (1)	199			19,502	50	30	12		6,848					372	27	6,813		
Hun	MR Dv (1)	199			19,502	50	30	12		6,848					372	27	6,813		
Hun	MR Dv (1)	199			19,502	50	30	12		6,848					372	27	6,813		
Rom	MR Dv (1)	199			19,502	50	30	12		6,848					372	27	6,813		
Rom	MR Dv (1)	199			19,502	50	30	12		6,848					372	27	6,813		
Rom	MR Dv (1)	199			19,502	50	30	12		6,848					372	27	6,813		
Rom	MR Dv (1)	199			19,502	50	30	12		6,848					372	27	6,813		
Rom	MR Dv (1)	199			19,502	50	30	12		6,848					372	27	6,813		
Rom	MR Dv (1)	199			19,502	50	30	12		6,848					372	27	6,813		
Rom	MR Dv (1)	199			19,502	50	30	12		6,848					372	27	6,813		
Rom	MR Dv (1)	199			19,502	50	30	12		6,848					372	27	6,813		
Rom	MR Dv (1)	199			19,502	50	30	12		6,848					372	27	6,813		
Rom	MR Dv (1)	200			19,600		24	12		6,848					372	27	6,813		
Rom	MR Dv (1)	200			19,600		24	12		6,848					372	27	6,813		
Rom	MR Dv (1)	200			19,600		24	12		6,848					372	27	6,813		
Bul	MR Dv (1)	300			27,750		24	18		4,381				113	234	15	4,975	126	7,165
Bul	MR Dv (1)	300			27,750		24	18		4,381				113	234	15	4,975	126	7,165
Bul	MR Dv (1)	300			27,750		24	18		4,381				113	234	15	4,975	126	7,165
Bul	MR Dv (1)	300			27,750		24	18		4,381				113	234	15	4,975	126	7,165
Bul	MR Dv (1)	300			27,750		24	18		4,381				113	234	15	4,975	126	7,165
S	MR Dv (1)		20	174	21,902		36	18	18	6,044	12	50	3,086		476	24	10,113	124	7,615
S	MR Dv (1)		20	174	21,902		36	18	18	6,044	12	50	3,086		476	24	10,113	124	7,615
S	MR Dv (1)		15	174	21,342		36	18	18	6,044	12	50	3,086		476	24	10,113	124	7,615
S	MR Dv (1)		15	174	21,342		36	18	18	6,044	12	50	3,086		476	24	10,113	124	7,615
S	MR Dv (1)		15	174	21,342		36	18	18	6,044	12	50	3,086		476	24	10,113	124	7,615
S	MR Dv (1)		15	174	21,342		36	18	18	6,044	12	50	3,086		476	24	10,113	124	7,615
S	Tk Dv (1)		70	188	29,084						4		173		166		3,196	117	7,185
S	Art A Dv (1)						24	36		6,641			173		36	27	1,762		
								144	144	24,509									

Table C-6. continued

Time; State; Military District	Unit Title; Readiness Category	OT65 Oth	BRDM	BMP	AT5	WUV: (WEI-CW 62)	ARV	APC	WUV: (WEI-CW 36)	TO&E	WUV: (WEI-CW 3.3)	UNIT WUV: Division Total
M+1 to M+5												
USSR												
GSFG	16 Tk Dv (1)			12	9	1,347	29	16	1,452	1,176	3,881	65,779
GSFG	21 MR Dv (1)		36	20		3,308	29	223	8,755	2,537	8,372	75,093
GSFG	94 MR Dv (1)		36	20		3,308	29	223	8,755	2,537	8,372	75,093
GSFG	207 MR Dv (1)		36	20		3,308	29	223	8,755	2,537	8,372	75,093
GSFG	Art Bg (1)									20	66	7,832
GSFG	Art Bg (1)									20	66	7,832
GSFG	Other Bts (1)						5		153	144	475	2,298
GSFG	7 Tk Dv (1)			12	9	1,347	29	16	1,452	1,176	3,881	33,516
GSFG	10 Tk Dv (1)			12	9	1,347	29	16	1,452	1,176	3,881	63,293
GSFG	72 Tk Dv (1)			12	9	1,347	29	16	1,452	1,176	3,881	33,516
GSFG	47 Tk Dv (1)			12	9	1,347	29	16	1,452	1,176	3,881	63,293
GSFG	304 Art Bg (1)						15		459	898	2,963	11,564
GSFG	Other Bts (1)						5		153	144	475	2,298
GSFG	25 Tk Dv (1)			12	9	1,347	29	16	1,452	1,176	3,881	33,516
GSFG	32 Tk Dv (1)			12	9	1,347	29	16	1,452	1,176	3,881	33,516
GSFG	90 Tk Dv (1)			12	9	1,347	29	16	1,452	1,176	3,881	63,293
GSFG	35 MR Dv (1)		36	20		3,308	29	223	8,755	2,537	8,372	70,121
GSFG	71 Art Bg (1)						15		459	898	2,963	11,564
GSFG	Other Bts (1)						5		153	144	475	2,298
GSFG	79 Tk Dv (1)			12	9	1,347	29	16	1,452	1,176	3,881	63,293
GSFG	27 MR Dv (1)		36	20		3,308	29	223	8,755	2,537	8,372	70,121
GSFG	39 MR Dv (1)		36	20		3,308	29	223	8,755	2,537	8,372	70,121
GSFG	57 MR Dv (1)		36	20		3,308	29	223	8,755	2,537	8,372	70,121
GSFG	43 Art Bg (1)						15		459	898	2,963	11,564
GSFG	Other Bts (1)						5		153	144	475	2,298
GSFG	9 Tk Dv (1)			12	9	1,347	29	16	1,452	1,176	3,881	63,293
GSFG	11 Tk Dv (1)			12	9	1,347	29	16	1,452	1,176	3,881	63,293
GSFG	20 MR Dv (1)		36	20		3,308	29	223	8,755	2,537	8,372	70,121
GSFG	43 Art Dv (1)		27			1,523				254	838	41,447
GSFG	35 Assault (1)						3		92	851	2,808	9,930
GSFG	Spetsnaz (1)		7				3		92	67	221	1,303
GSFG	MR Bg (1)			4		662	6	45	1,751	515	1,700	9,598
GSFG	Other Bts (1)						3		92	67	221	1,303
CGF	15 Tk Dv (1)			12	9	1,347	29	16	1,452	1,176	3,881	33,516
CGF	18 MR Dv (1)		36	20		3,308	29	223	8,755	2,537	8,372	70,121
CGF	48 MR Dv (1)		36	20		3,308	29	223	8,755	2,537	8,372	70,121
CGF	Art Bg (1)									20	66	7,832
CGF	Other Bts (1)						3		92	67	221	1,303

USSR												
	NGF	20 Tk Dv (1)		36	12		1,347	29	16	1,452	1,176	3,881	63,293
	NGF	6 MR Dv (1)			20	9	3,308	29	223	8,755	2,537	8,372	70,121
GDR													
	III	7 Tk Dv (1)		3	15		958	87	96	5,945	945	3,119	47,791
	III	11 MR Dv (1)			18		1,149	126	230	11,722	2,482	8,191	59,520
	III	4 MR Dv (1)			18		1,149	126	230	11,722	2,482	8,191	59,520
	III	Art Rt (1)					169				29	96	4,097
	III	9 Tk Dv (1)		3	15		958	87	96	5,945	945	3,119	47,791
	III	8 MR Dv (1)			18		1,149	126	230	11,722	2,482	8,191	59,520
	III	1 MR Dv (1)			18		1,149	126	230	11,722	2,482	8,191	59,520
	III	Art Rt (1)					169				29	96	4,097
Czech													
	West	1 Tk Dv (1)	38		12		2,580	24	108	3,771	1,486	4,904	60,077
	West	2 MR Dv (1)	78				3,724		302	11,280	9,868	32,564	90,503
	West	22 Assault(1)						3		92	67	221	1,303
	West	Other Bts (1)						15		459	416	1,373	6,437
Poland													
	War	6 Assault(1)						8		245	2,563	8,458	25,046

Pol													
	Pom	16 Tk Dv (1)	36					10	45		1,024	3,379	6,124
	Pom	20 Tk Dv (1)			13		2,549	23	182	1,877	1,024	3,379	47,825
	Pom	12 MR Dv (1)	57		13		3,551	23	182	7,059	2,778	9,167	60,853
	Pom	8 MR Dv (1)	57		13		3,551			7,059	2,778	9,167	60,853
	Pom	Art Rt (1)					169				29	96	4,017
	Sil	5 Tk Dv (1)	36		13		2,549	10	45	1,877	1,024	3,379	47,825
	Sil	10 Tk Dv (1)	36		13		2,549	10	45	1,877	1,024	3,379	47,825
	Sil	11 Tk Dv (1)									1,024	3,379	6,124
	Sil	Art Rt (1)				9	169				29	96	4,023
	War	Art Rt (1)				9	169				29	96	448
USSR													
	Byel	120 MR Dv (1)		36	20		3,308	29	223	8,755	2,537	8,372	83,883
	Byel	8 Tk Dv (1)			12		1,347	29	16	1,452	1,176	3,881	71,030
	Carp	15 MR Dv (1)		36	20		3,308	29	223	8,755	2,537	8,372	83,883
	Carp	23 Tk Dv (1)			12		1,347	29	16	1,452	1,176	3,881	71,030
	Balt	7 Airbn (1)						8		245	2,563	8,458	29,830
	SGF	93 MR Dv (1)		36	20		3,308	29	223	8,755	2,537	8,372	68,741
	SGF	13 MR Dv (1)		36	20		3,308	29	223	8,755	2,537	8,372	68,741
	SGF	2 Tk Dv (1)			12	9	1,347	29	16	1,452	1,176	3,881	60,586
	SGF	13 Tk Dv (1)			12	9	1,347	29	16	1,452	1,176	3,881	33,516

Table C-6. *continued*

Time; State; Military District	Unit Title; Readiness Category	ARMORED RECONNAISSANCE VEHICLES TO&E					ARMORED PERSONNEL CARRIERS TO&E			SMALL ARMS		UNIT WUV: Division Total
		OT65 Oth	BRDM	BMP	AT5	WUV: (WEI-CW 62)	ARV	APC	WUV: (WEI-CW 36)	TO&E	WUV: (WEI-CW 3.3)	
M+15												
USSR												
Mosc	MR Dv (1)		36	20		3,308	29	223	8,755	2,537	8,372	83,883
Mosc	2 MR Dv (1)		36	20		3,308	29	223	8,755	2,537	8,372	83,883
Mosc	106 Airbn (1)						8		245	2,563	8,458	29,830
Mosc	Art Dv (1)		27			1,523				254	838	41,447
M+20												
USSR												
Byel	MR Dv (2)		27	20	18	3,961	29	232	8,822	2,649	8,742	82,514
Carp	70 MR Dv (2)		27	20	18	3,961	29	232	8,822	2,649	8,742	82,514
Balt	1 MR Dv (2)		27	20	18	3,961	29	232	8,822	2,649	8,742	82,514
M+25												
USSR												
Byel	8 Tk Dv (2)			12	9	1,347	29	26	1,805	1,098	3,623	62,420
Carp	128 MR Dv (2)		27	20	18	3,961	29	232	8,822	2,649	8,742	82,514
Balt	1 Tk Dv (2)			12	9	1,347	29	26	1,805	1,098	3,623	62,420
M+30												
USSR												
Byel	29 Tk Dv (2)			12	9	1,347	29	26	1,805	1,098	3,623	62,420
Byel	3 Tk Dv (2)			12	9	1,347	29	26	1,805	1,098	3,623	62,420
Byel	27 Tk Dv (2)			12	9	1,347	29	26	1,805	1,098	3,623	62,420
Carp	61 MR Dv (2)		27	20	18	3,961	29	232	8,822	2,649	8,742	82,514
Carp	24 MR Dv (2)		27	26	18	3,961	29	232	8,822	2,649	8,742	82,514
Carp	13 Tk Dv (2)			12	9	1,347	29	26	1,805	1,098	3,623	62,420
Balt	40 Tk Dv (2)			12	9	1,347	29	26	1,805	1,098	3,623	62,420
Balt	24 Tk Dv (2)			12	9	1,347	29	26	1,805	1,098	3,623	62,420
Pol												
Sil	4 MR Dv (2)	43		13		2,883		335	11,698	2,482	8,191	49,300
Pom	7 Assualt (2)									855	2,822	8,270

M+35												
USSR												
Byel	47 Tk Dv (2)			12	9	1,347	29	26	1,805	1,098	3,623	62,420
Byel	34 Tk Dv (2)			12	9	1,347	29	26	1,805	1,098	3,623	62,420
Byel	Art A Dv (2)		27			1,523				254	838	40,556
Byel	Art B Dv (2)					1,523				20	66	7,832
Carp	117 Tk Dv (2)		27	12	9	1,347	29	26	1,805	1,098	3,623	62,420
Carp	Art A Dv (2)					1,523				254	838	40,556
Carp	Art B Dv (2)									20	66	7,832
Balt	Art A Dv (2)		27			1,523				254	838	40,556
Balt	Art A Dv (2)		27			1,523				254	838	40,556
M+40												
Czech	4 Tk Dv (2)	38				2,389		108	3,492	1,379	4,551	49,232
West	9 Tk Dv (2)	38				2,389		108	3,492	1,379	4,551	49,232
West	3 MR Dv (2)	87				4,153		316	11,035	2,446	8,072	54,681
USSR												
Mosc	15 Tk Dv (2)			12	9	1,347	29	26	1,805	1,098	3,623	62,420
Mosc	4 Tk Dv (2)			12	9	1,347	29	26	1,805	1,098	3,623	62,420
M+45												
USSR												
Balt	3 MR Dv (3)		27	20	18	3,486	29	232	7,763	2,309	7,620	61,268
M+50												
USSR												
Len	64 MR Dv (3)		27	20	18	3,486	29	232	7,763	2,309	7,620	61,268

Table C-6. *continued*

Time; State; Military District	Unit Title; Readiness Category	ARMORED RECONNAISSANCE VEHICLES					ARMORED PERSONNEL CARRIERS			SMALL ARMS		UNIT WUV: Division Total
		TO&E				WUV: (WEI-CW 62)	TO&E		WUV: (WEI-CW 36)	TO&E	WUV: (WEI-CW 3.3)	
		OT65 Oth	BRDM	BMP	AT5		ARV	APC				
M + 55												
USSR												
Carp	66 MR Dv (3)		27	20	18	3,486	29	232	7,763	2,309	7,620	61,268
Len	111 MR Dv (3)		27	20	18	3,486	29	232	7,763	2,309	7,620	61,268
M + 60												
USSR												
Byel	50 MR Dv (3)		27	20	18	3,486	29	232	7,763	2,309	7,620	61,268
Len	77 MR Dv (3)		27	20	18	3,486	29	232	7,763	2,309	7,620	61,268
Balt	88 MR Dv (3)		27	20	18	3,486	29	232	7,763	2,309	7,620	61,268
Czech												
East	13 Tk Dv (3)	38		12		2,389		108	3,492	1,379	4,551	49,232
East	14 Tk Dv (3)	38		12		2,389		108	3,492	1,379	4,551	49,232
M + 65												
USSR												
Carp	17 MR Dv (3)		27	20	18	3,486	29	232	7,763	2,309	7,620	61,268
Balt	26 MR Dv (3)		27	20	18	3,486	29	232	7,763	2,309	7,620	61,268
Len	69 MR Dv (3)		27	20	18	3,486	29	232	7,763	2,309	7,620	61,268
M + 70												
USSR												
Carp	97 MR Dv (3)		27	20	18	3,486	29	232	7,763	2,309	7,620	61,268
Balt	44 MR Dv (3)		27	20	18	3,486	29	232	7,763	2,309	7,620	61,268
Len	45 MR Dv (3)		27	20	18	3,486	29	232	7,763	2,309	7,620	61,268
M + 75												
USSR												
Len	45 MR Dv (3)		27	20	18	3,486	29	232	7,763	2,309	7,620	61,289
Balt	107 MR Dv (3)		27	20	18	3,486	29	232	7,763	2,309	7,620	61,526

Time	Location	Unit										
M+80													
	USSR												
	Mos	13 MR Dv (3)	27		20	18	3,486	29	232	7,763	2,309	7,620	61,526
	Vol	43 MR Dv (3)	27		20	18	3,486	29	232	7,763	2,309	7,620	61,526
	Vol	Art A Dv (3)	27				1,523				254	838	41,447
	Czech												
	East	15 MR Dv (3)		87			4,153		266	9,289	2,446	8,072	48,035
	Pol												
	War	1 MR Dv (3)	13	28			2,062				2,479	8,181	25,569
M+85													
	USSR												
	Mos	32 MR Dv (3)	27		20	18	3,486	29	232	7,763	2,309	7,620	61,526
	Vol	96 MR Dv (3)	27		20	18	3,486	29	232	7,763	2,309	7,620	61,526
	Ural	77 MR Dv (3)	27		20	18	3,486	29	232	7,763	2,309	7,620	61,526
	Czech												
	East	19 MR Dv (3)		87			4,153		266	9,289	2,446	8,072	48,035
	Pol												
	War	3 MR Dv (3)											
M+90													
	USSR												
	Vol	21 MR Dv (3)	27		20	18	3,486	29	232	7,763	2,309	7,620	61,526
	Ural	MR Dv (3)	27		20	18	3,486	29	232	7,763	2,309	7,620	61,526
	Czech												
	East	20 MR Dv (3)									2,446	8,072	27,780
	Pol												
	War	9 MR Dv (3)											5,474

Table C-6. *continued*

Time; State; Military District	Unit Title; Readiness Category	OT65 0th	ARMORED RECONNAISSANCE VEHICLES TO&E BRDM	BMP	AT5	WUV: (WEI-CW 62)	ARMORED PERSONNEL CARRIERS TO&E ARV	APC	WUV: (WEI-CW 36)	SMALL ARMS TO&E	WUV: (WEI-CW 3.3)	UNIT WUV: Division Total
ATTU Units Not Allocated to Central Front												
USSR												
NW	MR Dv (1)		27	20	18	3,961	29	232	8,822	2,649	8,742	70,174
NW	MR Dv (1)		27	20	18	3,961	29	232	8,822	2,649	8,742	70,174
NW	MR Dv (1)		27	20	18	3,961	29	232	8,822	2,649	8,742	70,174
NW	MR Dv (1)		27	20	18	3,961	29	232	8,822	2,649	8,742	70,174
NW	MR Dv (1)		27	20	18	3,961	29	232	8,822	2,649	8,742	70,174
NW	MR Dv (1)		27	20	18	3,961	29	232	8,822	2,649	8,742	70,174
NW	MR Dv (1)		27	20	18	3,961	29	232	8,822	2,649	8,742	70,174
NW	MR Dv (1)		27	20	18	3,961	29	232	8,822	2,649	8,742	70,174
SW	MR Dv (1)		27	20	18	3,961	29	232	8,822	2,649	8,742	70,174
SW	Art A Dv (1)		27	20	18	1,523				254	838	40,556
SW	MR Dv (1)		27	20	18	3,961	29	232	8,822	2,649	8,742	70,286
SW	MR Dv (1)		27	20	18	3,961	29	232	8,822	2,649	8,742	70,286
SW	MR Dv (1)		27	20	18	3,961	29	232	8,822	2,649	8,742	70,286
SW	MR Dv (1)		27	20	18	3,961	29	232	8,822	2,649	8,742	70,286
SW	MR Dv (1)		27	20	18	3,961	29	232	8,822	2,649	8,742	70,286
SW	MR Dv (1)		27	20	18	3,961	29	232	8,822	2,649	8,742	70,286
SW	MR Dv (1)		27	20	18	3,961	29	232	8,822	2,649	8,742	70,286
SW	MR Dv (1)		27	20	18	3,961	29	232	8,822	2,649	8,742	70,286
SW	MR Dv (1)		27	20	18	3,961	29	232	8,822	2,649	8,742	70,286
SW	MR Dv (1)		27	20	18	3,961	29	232	8,822	2,649	8,742	70,286
SW	MR Dv (1)		27	20	18	3,961	29	232	8,822	2,649	8,742	70,286
SW	MR Dv (1)		27	20	18	3,961	29	232	8,822	2,649	8,742	70,286
SW	MR Dv (1)		27	20	18	3,961	29	232	8,822	2,649	8,742	70,286
SW	MR Dv (1)		27	20	18	3,961	29	232	8,822	2,649	8,742	70,286
SW	MR Dv (1)		27	20	18	3,961	29	232	8,822	2,649	8,742	70,286
SW	MR Dv (1)		27	20	18	3,961	29	232	8,822	2,649	8,742	70,286
SW	MR Dv (1)		27	20	18	3,961	29	232	8,822	2,649	8,742	70,286
SW	Tk Dv (1)			12	9	1,347	29	26	1,805	1,098	3,623	51,625
SW	Tk Dv (1)			12	9	1,347	29	26	1,805	1,098	3,623	51,625
SW	Tk Dv (1)			12	9	1,347	29	26	1,805	1,098	3,623	51,625
SW	Tk Dv (1)			12	9	1,347	29	26	1,805	1,098	3,623	51,625
SW	Tk Dv (1)			12	9	1,347	29	26	1,805	1,098	3,623	51,625
SW	Tk Dv (1)			12	9	1,347	29	26	1,805	1,098	3,623	51,625

SW	Tk Dv (1)			12	9	1,347	29	26	1,805	1,098	3,623	51,625
SW	Tk Dv (1)			12	9	1,347	29	26	1,805	1,098	3,623	51,625
SW	Tk Dv (1)			12	9	1,347	29	26	1,805	1,098	3,623	51,625
SW	Tk Dv (1)			12	9	1,347	29	26	1,805	1,098	3,623	51,625
SW	Art A Dv (1)		27			1,523				254	838	4,124
Hun	MR Dv (1)	87				4,153		324	11,314	2,446	8,072	56,703
Hun	MR Dv (1)	87				4,153		314	10,965	2,446	8,072	56,353
Hun	MR Dv (1)	87				4,153		314	10,965	2,446	8,072	56,353
Hun	MR Dv (1)	87				4,153		314	10,965	2,446	8,072	56,353
Hun	MR Dv (1)	87				4,153		314	10,965	2,446	8,072	56,353
Hun	MR Dv (1)	87				4,153		314	10,965	2,446	8,072	56,353
Rom	MR Dv (1)	87				4,153		314	10,965	2,446	8,072	56,353
Rom	MR Dv (1)	87				4,153		314	10,965	2,446	8,072	56,353
Rom	MR Dv (1)	87				4,153		314	10,965	2,446	8,072	56,353
Rom	MR Dv (1)	87				4,153		314	10,965	2,446	8,072	56,353
Rom	MR Dv (1)	87				4,153		314	10,965	2,446	8,072	56,451
Rom	MR Dv (1)	87				4,153		314	10,965	2,446	8,072	56,451
Rom	MR Dv (1)	87				4,153		314	10,965	2,446	8,072	56,451
Bul	MR Dv (1)	38				2,389		108	3,492	1,379	4,551	54,703
Bul	MR Dv (1)	38				2,389		108	3,492	1,379	4,551	54,703
Bul	MR Dv (1)	38				2,389		108	3,492	1,379	4,551	54,703
Bul	MR Dv (1)	38				2,389		108	3,492	1,379	4,551	54,703
Bul	MR Dv (1)	38				2,389		108	3,492	1,379	4,551	54,703
S	MR Dv (1)		27	20	18	3,961	29	232	8,822	2,649	8,742	70,286
S	MR Dv (1)		27	20	18	3,961	29	232	8,822	2,649	8,742	70,286
S	MR Dv (1)		27	20	18	3,961	29	232	8,822	2,649	8,742	69,726
S	MR Dv (1)		27	20	18	3,961	29	232	8,822	2,649	8,742	69,726
S	MR Dv (1)		27	20	18	3,961	29	232	8,822	2,649	8,742	69,726
S	MR Dv (1)		27	20	18	3,961	29	232	8,822	2,649	8,742	69,726
S	MR Dv (1)		27	20	18	3,961	29	232	8,822	2,649	8,742	69,726
S	Tk Dv (1)			12	9	1,347		26	1,805	1,098	3,623	53,053
S	Art A Dv (1)		27			1,523				254	838	28,633

Notes to Table C-6

When the unilateral reductions were first announced, Gorbachev stated that six tank divisions would be "disbanded." The Soviets also announced that their divisions in Eastern Europe would be "defensively restructured." On February 23, 1989, statements were made to the effect that, although divisions were losing tanks, armored vehicles, and other assets, "restructuring" also meant that the average division would receive a 50 percent increase in antiarmor and air defense weapons. It became clear through a careful reading of the Soviet press that many of the assets of the six tank divisions were going to be redistributed to the remaining divisions. This was further confirmed by the fact-finding excursion of a House committee delegation (see sources below). Several ambiguities regarding the reduction of the six announced tank divisions have recently appeared. While there is conflicting information at this time, this analysis assumes the worst case: only tanks are withdrawn from the six tank divisions; other assets are kept intact. The WEI/WUV totals and mobilization curves are recalculated accordingly. A motorized rifle brigade and several other small units were withdrawn.

Gorbachev also pledged to reduce Soviet tanks in Eastern Europe by 5,300. Assuming preservation of the prereduction ratio of total tanks (including spares) to TO&E tanks— that is, applying the 1.2 expansion factor from table C.1—this translates into a withdrawal of 4,417 tanks from active TO&Es and 883 tanks from non-TO&E spares. All non-Soviet WTO reductions were executed similarly, always assuming that the worst weapons would be cut first.

Statements have been made on how these cuts are to be allocated between motorized rifle divisions and tank divisions. There are uncertainties as to whether the current division structure will continue (one plausible change would be to replace every two tank divisions with one "defensive" division and a stronger motorized rifle division). Given these uncertainties, the reductions were distributed pro rata: each Soviet tank division was assumed to lose about 70 tanks, each motorized rifle division about 90. Almost all of the reductions were taken in T-72s, the least effective tank available, with about 100 T-80s included.

Any announced Soviet reductions not specifically taken from Eastern Europe were assumed to be taken from within the ATTU. The artillery reduction was taken from mortar systems of 100mm with equal percentages from the Soviet central reserve, southern TVD, and southwestern TVD.

Sources are as follows: "M.S. Gorbachev's United Nations Address," *Pravada*, December 8, 1988, in Foreign Broadcast Information Service (FBIS) Daily Report: Soviet Union, December 8, 1988, p. 17; "Six Tank Divisions to Go from Warsaw Pact Nations," *Jane's Defence Weekly*, December 17, 1988; "GDR's Honecker Announces Unilateral Troop Cut," Tass, January 24, 1989, in FBIS *Daily Report: Soviet Union*, January 26, 1989, p. 1; "Hungarian Military Cutback, Conversions Noted," *Izvestia*, January 17, 1989, p. 1, in FBIS *Daily Report: Soviet Union*, January 19, 1989, p. 35; "*Izvestia* Corrects Hungarian Cutback Figure," *Izvestia*, January 24, 1989, p. 4, in FBIS *Daily Report: Soviet Union*, January 27, 1989, p. 39; "General Says Military Reductions Planned," Associated Press, January 24, 1989, PM cycle; "Moiseyev Evaluates Military on Army-Navy Day," *Krasnaya Zvezda*, February 23, 1989, p. 2, in FBIS *Daily Report: Soviet Union*, February 23, 1989, p. 101–04; "Yazov Cited on Impact of Arms Cuts at Home, Abroad," FBIS *Daily Report: Soviet Union*, February 28, 1989, pp. 1–3; "East Germany to Cut Its Armed Forces by 10,000," *New York Times*, January 24, 1989, p. A9; Jackson Diehl, "Two More Soviet Allies Announce Arms Cuts," *Washington Post*, January 28, 1989, p. A17; David C. Isby, *Weapons and Tactics of the Soviet Army* (New York: Jane's, 1988); James Smith, "Restructuring of Tank and Motor Rifle Divisions in GSFG", *Jane's Soviet Intelligence Review*, vol. 1 (April 1989), pp. 154–55; *Status of the Soviet Union's Unilateral Force Reductions and Restructuring of its Forces*, Hearings before the House Committee on Armed Services, 100 Cong. 1 sess. (GPO, 1989); Phillip A. Karber, "The Military Impact of the Gorbachev Reductions," *Armed Forces Journal International*, vol. 126 (January 1989), pp. 54–64; and Henry Dodds, "Perestroika in the Polish Army", *Jane's Soviet Intelligence Review*, vol. 1 (July 1989), pp. 290–92.

TABLE C-7. WTO Weapon Totals and ADE Mobilization Schedule Derived from Table C-6, after Unilateral Cuts

TANKS

WEAPON TYPE AND AREA	TOTAL	Tank: T-34/T-55	Tank: T-64	Tank: T-72	Tank: T-80
ATTU including spares	41,946				
ATTU TO&E	34,955				
Central Front, including spares	24,026	13,943	3,447	14,889	2,676
Central Front TO&E	20,022	8,549	1,982	6,905	2,676

ARTILLERY

WEAPON TYPE AND AREA	TOTAL	Arty: 122 M-38	Arty: MRL	Arty: 152 D-1	Arty: 122 M74	Mortar: 120MM	Antiarmor: T-21	Antiarmor: 100MM
ATTU including spares	31,929							
ATTU TO&E	26,607							
Central Front, including spares	22,099	3,445	6,154	4,232	5,000	5,051	1,814	911
Central Front TO&E	18,416	2,445	4,042	2,804	3,614	3,351	1,249	911

ARMORED VEHICLES

WEAPON TYPE AND AREA	TOTAL	ARV: OT-65	ARV: BRDM	ARV: BMP-R	ARV: BRDM AT5	APC: ARV	APC: APC	IFV: BMP
ATTU including spares	75,546							
ATTU TO&E	62,955							
Central Front, including spares	43,165	3,012	2,617	2,402	1,485	4,403	30,724	18,312
Central Front TO&E	35,971	1,082	1,618	1,530	774	3,098	15,690	12,179

CENTRAL FRONT MOBILIZATION SCHEDULE, BALANCE AFTER UNILATERAL CUTS

Days After M+0	M+1	M+5	M+10	M+15	M+20	M+25	M+30	M+35	M+40
ADE arrival	9.8	11.5	8.6	2.4	2.5	2.1	6.0	3.8	2.8
Total ADEs	9.8	21.3	30.0	32.4	34.9	37.0	43.0	46.7	49.5
WUV Arrival	974,241	1,145,904	857,159	239,042	247,542	207,354	597,119	372,981	277,985
Total WUV	974,241	2,120,145	2,977,304	3,216,346	3,463,888	3,671,242	4,268,361	4,641,341	4,919,327

Days After M+0	M+45	M+50	M+55	M+60	M+65	M+70	M+75	M+80	M+85	M+90
ADE arrival	.6	.6	1.2	2.8	1.9	1.9	1.2	2.4	2.3	1.6
Total ADEs	50.1	50.8	52.0	54.8	56.7	58.5	59.8	62.2	64.5	66.1
WUV Arrival	61,268	61,268	122,535	282,266	183,803	183,803	122,815	238,103	232,613	156,306
Total WUV	4,980,594	5,041,862	5,164,397	5,446,663	5,630,466	5,814,269	5,937,084	6,175,187	6,407,801	6,564,106

Source: Data given in Table C-6.

Table C-8. WTO Units, Central Front Arrival Times, and WUV Scores, after CFE

M + 1 to M + 5

USSR

Time; State; Military District	Unit Title; Readiness Category	TANKS					ARTILLERY					MORTAR				ANTIARMOR					INFANTRY FIGHTING VEHICLES	
		T-55 T-34	T-64	T-72	T-80	WUV (WEI-CW 100)	M-38 D-30 Others	MRL	152mm	M74	WUV (WEI-CW 92)	Others	82MM	120MM	WUV (WEI-CW 48)	T-21 Oth	T-12	RPG7	ATGM	WUV (WEI-CW 55)	BMP	WUV (WEI-CW 69)
GSFG	16 Tk Dv (1)			49	180	29,653		24	18	54	8,230		4		173			346	46	8,482	109	6,680
GSFG	21 MR Dv (1)			84	40	15,677		36	18	36	7,634		12		518			529	36	11,609	87	5,317
GSFG	94 MR Dv (1)			84	40	15,677		36	18	36	7,634		12		518			529	36	11,609	87	5,317
GSFG	207 MR Dv (1)			84	40	15,677		36	18	36	7,634		12		518			529	36	11,609	87	5,317
GSFG	Art Bg (1)							30	31	31	7,760											
GSFG	Art Bg (1)							30	31	31	7,760											
GSFG	Other Bts (1)																	40	10	1,084	7	434
GSFG	7 Tk Dv (1)			35	180	27,913		24	18	54	8,230		4		173			346	46	8,482	109	6,680
GSFG	10 Tk Dv (1)							24	18	54	8,230		4		173			346	46	8,482	109	6,680
GSFG	72 Tk Dv (1)							24	18	54	8,230		4		173			346	46	8,482	109	6,680
GSFG	47 Tk Dv (1)			35	180	27,913		24	18	54	8,230		4		173			346	46	8,482	109	6,680
GSFG	304 Art Bg (1)						1				71							130	10	2,816	30	1,736
GSFG	Other Bts (1)																	40	10	1,084	7	434
GSFG	25 Tk Dv (1)			35	180	27,913		24	18	54	8,230		4		173			346	46	8,482	109	6,680
GSFG	32 Tk Dv (1)			56	40	12,197		24	18	54	8,230		4		173			346	46	8,482	109	6,680
GSFG	90 Tk Dv (1)						1	24	18	54	8,230		4		173			346	46	8,482	109	6,680
GSFG	35 MR Dv (1)						1	36	18	36	7,705		12		518			529	36	11,609	87	5,317
GSFG	71 Art Bg (1)						1				71							130	10	2,816	30	1,736
GSFG	Other Bts (1)																	40	10	1,084	7	434
GSFG	79 Tk Dv (1)			35	180	27,913		24	18	54	8,230		4		173			346	46	8,482	109	6,680
GSFG	27 MR Dv (1)			56	40	12,197		36	18	36	7,705		12		518			529	36	11,609	87	5,317
GSFG	39 MR Dv (1)			56	40	12,197		36	18	36	7,705		12		518			529	36	11,609	87	5,317
GSFG	57 MR Dv (1)			56	40	12,197		36	18	36	7,705		12		518			529	36	11,609	87	5,317
GSFG	43 Art Bg (1)						1				71							130	10	2,816	30	1,736
GSFG	Other Bts (1)																	40	10	1,084	7	434
GSFG	9 Tk Dv (1)			35	180	27,913		24	18	54	8,230		4		173			346	46	8,482	109	6,680
GSFG	11 Tk Dv (1)			35	180	27,913		24	18	54	8,230		4		173			346	46	8,482	109	6,680
GSFG	20 MR Dv (1)			56	40	12,197		36	18	36	7,705		12		518			529	36	11,609	87	5,317
GSFG	43 Art Dv (1)						1	144	144	144	36,432							36	27	1,762	30	1,736
GSFG	35 Assault(1)						1				71							140	13	3,103	4	260
GSFG	Spetsnaz (1)						1				71							25	5	638	17	1,063
GSFG	MR Bg (1)																	106	7	2,322	4	260
GSFG	Other Bts (1)																	25	5	638		
CGF	15 Tk Dv (1)						1	24	18	54	8,230		4		173			346	46	8,482	109	6,680
CGF	18 MR Dv (1)			56	40	12,197		36	18	36	7,705		12		518			529	36	11,609	87	5,317
CGF	48 MR Dv (1)			56	40	12,197		36	18	36	7,705		12		518			529	36	11,609	87	5,317
CGF	Art Bg (1)							30	31	31	7,760											
CGF	Other Bts (1)																	25	5	638	4	260

Unit	1	2	3	4	5	6	7	8	9	10	11	12	13	14	15	16	17	18	19
M+5																			
USSR																			
NGF 20 Tk Dv (1)		35	180	27,913	1	24	18	54	8,230			4	173		346	46	8,482	109	6,680
NGF 6 MR Dv (1)		56	40	12,197		36	18	36	7,705			12	518		529	36	11,609	87	5,317
GDR																			
III 7 Tk Dv (1)	76	90		17,579	54	18	6	12	6,657		18		924		167	9	3,166	51	3,132
III 11 MR Dv (1)	73			7,144	54	18		18	6,889		54		2,773	9	324	54	8,504	115	7,062
III 4 MR Dv (1)	73			7,144	54	14		18	6,889		54		2,773	27	324	54	8,504	115	7,062
III Art Rt (1)								14	3,575					27	3	3	257		
III 9 Tk Dv (1)	76	90		17,579	54	18	14	12	6,657		18		924		167	9	3,166	51	3,132
III 8 MR Dv (1)	73			7,144	54	18	6	18	6,889		54		2,773	9	324	54	8,504	115	7,062
III 1 MR Dv (1)	73			7,144	54	18		18	6,889		54		2,773	27	324	54	8,504	115	7,062
III Art Rt (1)						14		14	3,575					27	3	3	257		
Czech																			
West 1 Tk Dv (1)	133	40		17,551		24	14	18	6,006						234	15	6,392	126	7,738
West 2 MR Dv (1)	108			10,584		36		18	8,263						379	45	7,886	117	7,185
West 22 Assault(1)					18						18				25	5	638	6	352
West Other Bts (1)					36						36				100	20	2,552	35	2,053
Pol																			
War 6 Assault(1)												120			415	42	9,305	120	7,038
M+10																			
Pol																			
Pom 16 MR Dv (1)	87	121		22,246	54	12	12	6	1,524	9			354		135	9	2,391	101	6,202
Pom 20 Tk Dv (1)	109	40		15,210		12	12	18	3,367	9			354		135	9	2,391	101	6,202
Pom 12 MR Dv (1)	109	40		15,210		12	14	18	3,367	27			1,063		313	36	6,127	101	6,202
Pom 8 MR Dv (1)						14		14	3,575	27			1,063		313	36	6,127		
Pom Art Rt (1)															3	3	177		
Sil 5 Tk Dv (1)	87	121		22,246	54	12	14	6	1,524	9			354		135	9	2,391	101	6,202
Sil 10 Tk Dv (1)	87	121		22,246		12		6	1,524	9			354		135	9	2,391	101	6,202
Sil 11 Tk Dv (1)										9			354		135	9	2,391		
Sil Art Rt (1)															3	3	183		
War Art Rt (1)						14		14	3,575						3	3	183		
USSR																			
Byel 120 MR Dv (1)		150	40	21,687		36	18	36	11,460		12		3,189		529	36	11,609	87	5,317
Byel 8 Tk Dv (1)		94	188	32,971		24	18	54	8,230		4		173		346	46	8,482	109	6,680
Carp 15 MR Dv (1)		150	40	21,687		36	18	36	11,460		12		518		529	36	11,609	87	5,317
Carp 23 Tk Dv (1)		94	188	32,971		24	18	54	8,230		4		173		346	46	8,482	109	6,680
Balt 7 Airbn (1)			40		30	42			2,125						415	42	9,305	89	5,208
SGF 93 MR Dv (1)		56	40	11,088	1	36	18	36	7,705		12		518		529	36	11,609	87	5,317
SGF 13 MR Dv (1)		56		11,088	1	36	18	36	7,705		12		518		529	36	11,609	87	5,317
SGF 2 Tk Dv (1)		21		23,793		24	18	54	8,230		4		173		346	46	8,482	109	6,680
SGF 13 Tk Dv (1)			180			24	18	54	8,230		4		173		346	46	8,482	109	6,680

Table C-8. *continued*

Time; State; Military District	Unit Title; Readiness Category	TANKS TO&E T-55/T-34	T-64	T-72	T-80	TANKS WUV (WEI-CW 100)	ARTILLERY TO&E M-38 D-30 Others	MRL	152mm	M74	ARTILLERY WUV (WEI-CW 92)	MORTAR Others	TO&E 82MM	120MM	MORTAR WUV (WEI-CW 48)	ANTIARMOR T-21 Oth	T-12	TO&E RPG7	ATGM	ANTIARMOR WUV (WEI-CW 55)	IFV TO&E BMP	IFV WUV (WEI-CW 69)
M+15																						
USSR																						
Mosc	MR Dv (1)			150	40	21,687	54	36	18	36	11,460		12		518			529	36	11,609	87	5,317
Mosc	2 MR Dv (1)			150	40	21,687	54	36	18	36	11,460		12		518			529	36	11,609	87	5,317
Mosc	106 Airbn (1)						30				2,125							415	42	9,305	89	5,208
Mosc	Art Dv (1)							144	144	144	36,432							36	27	1,762		
M+20																						
USSR																						
Byel	MR Dv (2)			110		12,430	72	36	18	18	11,145		12		518			476	24	10,113	92	5,635
Carp	70 MR Dv (2)			110		12,430	72	36	18	18	11,145		12		518			476	24	10,113	92	5,635
Balt	I MR Dv (2)			110		12,430	72	36	18	18	11,145		12		518			476	24	10,113	92	5,635
M+25																						
USSR																						
Byel	8 Tk Dv (2)			119		13,447	18	24	18	36	7,916		4		173			166		3,196	87	5,317
Carp	128 MR Dv (2)			119		12,430	72	36	18	18	11,145		12		518			476	24	10,113	92	5,635
Balt	1 Tk Dv (2)			119		13,447	18	24	18	36	7,916		4		173			166		3,196	87	5,317
M+30																						
USSR																						
Byel	29 Tk Dv (2)			119		13,447	18	24	18	36	7,916		4		173			166		3,196	87	5,317
Byel	3 Tk Dv (2)			119		13,447	18	24	18	36	7,916		4		173			166		3,196	87	5,317
Byel	27 Tk Dv (2)			119		13,447	18	24	18	36	7,916		4		173			166		3,196	87	5,317
Carp	61 MR Dv (2)			110		12,430	72	36	18	18	11,145		12		518			476	24	10,113	92	5,635
Carp	24 MR Dv (2)			110		12,430	72	36	18	18	11,145		12		518			476	24	10,113	92	5,635
Carp	13 Tk Dv (2)			119		13,447	18	24	18	36	7,916		4		173			166		3,196	87	5,317
Balt	40 Tk Dv (2)			119		13,447	18	24	18	36	7,916		4		173			166		3,196	87	5,317
Balt	24 Tk Dv (2)			119		13,447	18	24	18	36	7,916		4		173			166		3,196	87	5,317
Pol																						
Sil	4 MR Dv (2)	110				10,780						27			1,063			313	18	5,474	40	2,346
Pom	7 Assualt (2)																	140	13	3,103		

M+35																
USSR																
Byel	47 Tk Dv (2)	119	13,447	18	24	18	36	7,916	4	173		166		3,196	87	5,343
Byel	34 Tk Dv (2)	119	13,447	18	24	18	36	7,916	4	173		166		3,196	87	5,343
Byel	Art A Dv (2)				144	144	144	36,432				36	27	1,762		
Byel	Art B Dv (2)				30	31	31	7,760								
Carp	117 Tk Dv (2)	119	13,447	18	24	18	36	7,916	4	173		166		3,196	87	5,343
Carp	Art A Dv (2)				144	144	144	36,432				36	27	1,762		
Carp	Art B Dv (2)				30	31	31	7,760								
Carp	Art B Dv (2)				30	31	31	7,760								
Balt	Art A Dv (2)				144	144	144	36,432				36	27	1,762		
Balt	Art A Dv (2)				144	144	144	36,432				36	27	1,762		
M+40																
Czech																
West	4 Tk Dv (2)	123	11,378	18	24	18	18	5,561			120	234	15	5,075	126	7,165
West	9 Tk Dv (2)	123	11,378	18	24	18	18	5,561			120	234	15	5,075	126	7,165
West	3 MR Dv (2)	95	9,310	54	30	12		7,132			18	372	27	7,140		
USSR																
Mosc	15 Tk Dv (2)	119	13,447	18	24	18	36	7,916	4	173		166		3,196	87	5,343
Mosc	4 Tk Dv (2)	119	13,447	18	24	18	36	7,916	4	173		166		3,196	87	5,343
M+45																
USSR																
Balt	3 MR Dv (3)				36	18		3,974	12	456		476	24	8,890	92	4,915
M+50																
USSR																
Len	64 MR Dv (3)				36	18		3,974	12	456		476	24	8,890	92	4,915

Table C-8. *continued*

Time; State; Military District	Unit Title; Readiness Category	TANKS TO&E					ARTILLERY TO&E					MORTAR TO&E				ANTIARMOR TO&E					INFANTRY FIGHTING VEHICLES	
		T-55 T-34	T-64	T-72	T-80	WUV: (WEI- CW 100)	M-38 D-30 Others	MRL	152mm	M74	WUV: (WEI- CW 92)	Others	82MM	120MM	WUV: (WEI- CW 48)	T-21 Oth	T-12	RPG7	ATGM	WUV: (WEI- CW 55)	BMP	WUV: (WEI- CW 69)
M+55 USSR																						
Carp	66 MR Dv (3)							36	18		3,974		12		456			476	24	8,890	92	4,915
Len	111 MR Dv (3)							36	18		3,974		12		456			476	24	8,890	92	4,915
M+60 USSR																						
Byel	50 MR Dv (3)							36	18		3,974		12		456			476	24	8,890	92	4,915
Len	77 MR Dv (3)							36	18		3,974		12		456			476	24	8,890	92	4,915
Balt	88 MR Dv (3)							36	18		3,974		12		456			476	24	8,890	92	4,915
Czech																						
East	13 Tk Dv (3)	123				11,378	18	24	18	18	5,561					120		234	15	5,075	126	7,165
East	14 Tk Dv (3)	123				11,378	18	24	18	18	5,561					120		234	15	5,075	126	7,165
M+65 USSR																						
Carp	17 MR Dv (3)							36	18		3,974		12		456			476	24	8,890	92	4,915
Balt	26 MR Dv (3)							36	18		3,974		12		456			476	24	8,890	92	4,915
Len	69 MR Dv (3)							36	18		3,974		12		456			476	24	8,890	92	4,915
M+70 USSR																						
Carp	97 MR Dv (3)							36	18		3,974		12		456			476	24	8,890	92	4,915
Balt	44 MR Dv (3)							36	18		3,974		12		456			476	24	8,890	92	4,915
Len	45 MR Dv (3)							36	18		3,974		12		456			476	24	8,890	92	4,915

M+75														
USSR														
Len	45 MR Dv (3)				36	18	3,974	12	456		476	24	8,890	92	4,915
Balt	107 MR Dv (3)				36	18	3,974	12	456	36	476	24	8,890	92	4,915
M+80														
USSR														
Mos	13 MR Dv (3)				36	18	3,974	12	456		476	24	8,890	92	4,915
Vol	43 MR Dv (3)				36	18	3,974	12	456		476	24	8,890	92	4,915
Vol	Art A Dv (3)				144	144	36,432				36	27	1,762		
Czech														
East	15 MR Dv (3)	46	4,508	54	30	12	7,132			18	372	27	7,140		
Pol														
War	1 MR Dv (3)			54	12	12	5,592	27	2,449	18	313	18	7,285		
M+85														
USSR														
Mos	32 MR Dv (3)				36	18	3,974	12	456		476	24	8,890	92	4,915
Vol	96 MR Dv (3)				36	18	3,974	12	456		476	24	8,890	92	4,915
Ural	77 MR Dv (3)				36	18	3,974	12	456		476	24	8,890	92	4,915
Czech														
East	19 MR Dv (3)	46	4,508	54	30	12	7,132			18	372	27	7,140		
Pol														
War	3 MR Dv (3)														
M+90														
USSR														
Vol	21 MR Dv (3)				36	18	3,974	12	456		476	24	8,890	92	4,915
Ural	MR Dv (3)				36	18	3,974	12	456		476	24	8,890	92	4,915
Czech														
East	20 MR Dv (3)	46	4,508	54	30	12	7,132			18			327		
Pol														
War	9 MR Dv (3)										313	18	5,474		

Table C-8. *continued*

ATTU Units Not Allocated to Central Front

USSR

Time; State; Military District	Unit Title; Readiness Category	TANKS TO&E T-55 / T-34	T-64	T-72	T-80	TANKS WUV: WEI-CW 100	ARTILLERY TO&E M-38 D-30 Others	MRL	152mm	M74	ARTILLERY WUV: WEI-CW 92	MORTAR Others	MORTAR TO&E 82MM	120MM	MORTAR WUV: WEI-CW 48	ANTIARMOR T-21 Oth	T-12	ANTIARMOR TO&E RPG7	ATGM	ANTIARMOR WUV: WEI-CW 55	IFV TO&E BMP	IFV WUV: WEI-CW 69
NW	MR Dv (1)			105		11,865		36	18	18	6,044		12		518			476	24	10,113	92	5,650
NW	MR Dv (1)			105		11,865		36	18	18	6,044		12		518			476	24	10,113	92	5,650
NW	MR Dv (1)			105		11,865		36	18	18	6,044		12		518			476	24	10,113	92	5,650
NW	MR Dv (1)			105		11,865		36	18	18	6,044		12		518			476	24	10,113	92	5,650
NW	MR Dv (1)			105		11,865		36	18	18	6,044		12		518			476	24	10,113	92	5,650
NW	MR Dv (1)			105		11,865		36	18	18	6,044		12		518			476	24	10,113	92	5,650
NW	MR Dv (1)			105		11,865		36	18	18	6,044		12		518			476	24	10,113	92	5,650
NW	MR Dv (1)			105		11,865		36	18	18	6,044		12		518			476	24	10,113	92	5,650
SW	MR Dv (1)			105		11,865		36	18	18	6,044		12		518			476	24	10,113	92	5,650
SW	Art A Dv (1)							144	144	144	36,432							36	27	1,762		
SW	MR Dv (1)			105		11,865		36	18	18	6,044		12		518			476	24	10,113	92	5,650
SW	MR Dv (1)			105		11,865		36	18	18	6,044		12		518			476	24	10,113	92	5,650
SW	MR Dv (1)			105		11,865		36	18	18	6,044		12		518			476	24	10,113	92	5,650
SW	MR Dv (1)			105		11,865		36	18	18	6,044		12		518			476	24	10,113	92	5,650
SW	MR Dv (1)			105		11,865		36	18	18	6,044		12		518			476	24	10,113	92	5,650
SW	MR Dv (1)			105		11,865		36	18	18	6,044		12		518			476	24	10,113	92	5,650
SW	MR Dv (1)			105		11,865		36	18	18	6,044		12		518			476	24	10,113	92	5,650
SW	MR Dv (1)			105		11,865		36	18	18	6,044		12		518			476	24	10,113	92	5,650
SW	MR Dv (1)			105		11,865		36	18	18	6,044		12		518			476	24	10,113	92	5,650
SW	MR Dv (1)			105		11,865		36	18	18	6,044		12		518			476	24	10,113	92	5,650
SW	MR Dv (1)			105		11,865		36	18	18	6,044		12		518			476	24	10,113	92	5,650
SW	MR Dv (1)			105		11,865		36	18	18	6,044		12		518			476	24	10,113	92	5,650
SW	MR Dv (1)			105		11,865		36	18	18	6,044		12		518			476	24	10,113	92	5,650
SW	MR Dv (1)			105		11,865		36	18	18	6,044		12		518			476	24	10,113	92	5,650
SW	MR Dv (1)			105		11,865		36	18	18	6,044		12		518			476	24	10,113	92	5,650
SW	MR Dv (1)			105		11,865		36	18	18	6,044		12		518			476	24	10,113	92	5,650
SW	Tk Dv (1)			119		13,447			18	36	4,653		4		173			166		3,196	87	5,343
SW	Tk Dv (1)			119		13,447			18	36	4,653		4		173			166		3,196	87	5,343
SW	Tk Dv (1)			119		13,447			18	36	4,653		4		173			166		3,196	87	5,343
SW	Tk Dv (1)			119		13,447			18	36	4,653		4		173			166		3,196	87	5,343
SW	Tk Dv (1)			119		13,447			18	36	4,653		4		173			166		3,196	87	5,343

SW	Tk Dv (1)		119	13,447			18	36	4,653	4	173		166	27	3,196	87	5,343
SW	Tk Dv (1)		119	13,447			18	36	4,653	4	173		166	27	3,196	87	5,343
SW	Tk Dv (1)		119	13,447			18	36	4,653	4	173		166	27	3,196	87	5,343
SW	Tk Dv (1)		119	13,447			18	36	4,653	4	173		166	27	3,196	87	5,343
SW	Art A Dv (1)												36		1,762		
Hun	MR Dv (1)	85		8,330	50	30	12	18	6,848				372	27	6,813		
Hun	MR Dv (1)	85		8,330	50	30	12	18	6,848				372	27	6,813		
Hun	MR Dv (1)	85		8,330	50	30	12	18	6,848				372	27	6,813		
Hun	MR Dv (1)	85		8,330	50	30	12	18	6,848				372	27	6,813		
Hun	MR Dv (1)	85		8,330	50	30	12	18	6,848				372	27	6,813		
Hun	MR Dv (1)	85		8,330	50	30	12	18	6,848				372	27	6,813		
Hun	MR Dv (1)	85		8,330	50	30	12	18	6,848				372	27	6,813		
Rom	MR Dv (1)	85		8,330	50	30	12	18	6,848				372	27	6,813		
Rom	MR Dv (1)	85		8,330	50	30	12	18	6,848				372	27	6,813		
Rom	MR Dv (1)	85		8,330	50	30	12	18	6,848				372	27	6,813		
Rom	MR Dv (1)	85		8,330	50	30	12	18	6,848				372	27	6,813		
Rom	MR Dv (1)	85		8,330	50	30	12	18	6,848				372	27	6,813		
Rom	MR Dv (1)	85		8,330	50	30	12	18	6,848				372	27	6,813		
Rom	MR Dv (1)	85		8,330	50	30	12	18	6,848				372	27	6,813		
Rom	MR Dv (1)	85		8,330	50	30	12	18	6,848				372	27	6,813		
Bul	MR Dv (1)	130		12,025		24	18	18	4,381			113	234	15	4,975		
Bul	MR Dv (1)	130		12,025		24	18	18	4,381			113	234	15	4,975		
Bul	MR Dv (1)	130		12,025		24	18	18	4,381			113	234	15	4,975		
Bul	MR Dv (1)	130		12,025		24	18	18	4,381			113	234	15	4,975		
Bul	MR Dv (1)	117		10,823		24	18	18	4,381			113	234	15	4,975		
S	MR Dv (1)		105	11,865		36	18	18	6,044	12	518		476	24	10,113	126	7,165
S	MR Dv (1)		105	11,865		36	18	18	6,044	12	518		476	24	10,113	126	7,165
S	MR Dv (1)		105	11,865		36	18	18	6,044	12	518		476	24	10,113	126	7,165
S	MR Dv (1)		105	11,865		36	18	18	6,044	12	518		476	24	10,113	126	7,165
S	MR Dv (1)		105	11,865		36	18	18	6,044	12	518		476	24	10,113	126	7,165
S	MR Dv (1)		105	11,865		36	18	18	6,044	12	518		476	24	10,113	90	5,527
S	Tk Dv (1)		110	12,430		24	18	36	6,641	4	173		166	27	3,196	90	5,527
S	Art A Dv (1)						144	144	24,509				36		1,762	75	4,606

Table C-8. continued

Time; State; Military District	Unit Title; Readiness Category	ARMORED RECONNAISSANCE VEHICLES TO&E OT65 Oth	BRDM	BMP	AT5	WUV: (WEI-CW 62)	ARMORED PERSONNEL CARRIERS TO&E ARV	APC	WUV: (WEI-CW 36)	SMALL ARMS TO&E	WUV: (WEI-CW 3.3)	UNIT WUV: Division Total
M + 1 to M + 5												
USSR												
GSFG	16 Tk Dv (1)			12	9	1,347				1,176	3,881	58,446
GSFG	21 MR Dv (1)			20		1,277				2,537	8,372	50,405
GSFG	94 MR Dv (1)			20		1,277				2,537	8,372	50,405
GSFG	207 MR Dv (1)			20		1,277				2,537	8,372	50,405
GSFG	Art Bg (1)									20	66	7,826
GSFG	Art Bg (1)									20	66	7,826
GSFG	Other Bts (1)									144	475	1,993
GSFG	7 Tk Dv (1)			12	9	1,347				1,176	3,881	28,793
GSFG	10 Tk Dv (1)			12	9	1,347				1,176	3,881	56,705
GSFG	72 Tk Dv (1)			12	9	1,347				1,176	3,881	28,793
GSFG	47 Tk Dv (1)			12	9	1,347				1,176	3,881	56,705
GSFG	304 Art Bg (1)									898	2,963	7,586
GSFG	Other Bts (1)									144	475	1,993
GSFG	25 Tk Dv (1)			12	9	1,347				1,176	3,881	28,793
GSFG	32 Tk Dv (1)			12	9	1,347				1,176	3,881	28,793
GSFG	90 Tk Dv (1)			12	9	1,347				1,176	3,881	56,705
GSFG	35 MR Dv (1)			20		1,277				2,537	8,372	46,995
GSFG	71 Art Bg (1)									898	2,963	7,586
GSFG	Other Bts (1)									144	475	1,993
GSFG	79 Tk Dv (1)			12	9	1,347				1,176	3,881	56,705
GSFG	27 MR Dv (1)			20		1,277				2,537	8,372	46,995
GSFG	39 MR Dv (1)			20		1,277				2,537	8,372	46,995
GSFG	57 MR Dv (1)			20		1,277				2,537	8,372	46,995
GSFG	43 Art Bg (1)									898	2,963	7,586
GSFG	Other Bts (1)									144	475	1,993
GSFG	9 Tk Dv (1)			12	9	1,347				1,176	3,881	56,705
GSFG	11 Tk Dv (1)			12	9	1,347				1,176	3,881	56,705
GSFG	20 MR Dv (1)			20		1,277				2,537	8,372	46,995
GSFG	43 Art Dv (1)									254	838	39,032
GSFG	35 Assault(1)									851	2,808	7,718
GSFG	Spetsnaz (1)			4		255				67	221	1,120
GSFG	MR Bg (1)									515	1,700	5,411
GSFG	Other Bts (1)									67	221	1,120
CGF	15 Tk Dv (1)			12	9	1,347				1,176	3,881	28,793
CGF	18 MR Dv (1)			20		1,277				2,537	8,372	46,995
CGF	48 MR Dv (1)			20		1,277				2,537	8,372	46,995
CGF	Art Bg (1)									20	66	7,826
CGF	Other Bts (1)									67	221	1,120

Front	Unit										
M+5											
USSR											
NGF	20 Tk Dv (1)			12	9	1,347			1,176	3,881	56,705
NGF	6 MR Dv (1)			20		1,277			2,537	8,372	46,995
GDR											
III	7 Tk Dv (1)			15		958	24	821	945	3,119	36,355
III	11 MR Dv (1)			18		1,149	58	1,967	2,482	8,191	43,679
III	4 MR Dv (1)			18		1,149	58	1,967	2,482	8,191	43,679
III	Art Rt (1)		3			169			29	96	4,097
III	9 Tk Dv (1)			15		958	24	821	945	3,119	36,355
III	8 MR Dv (1)			18		1,149	58	1,967	2,482	8,191	43,679
III	1 MR Dv (1)			18		1,149	58	1,967	2,482	8,191	43,679
III	Art Rt (1)		3			169			29	96	4,097
Czech											
West	1 Tk Dv (1)	38		12		2,580	27	943	1,486	4,904	46,114
West	2 MR Dv (1)	78				3,724	76	2,636	9,868	32,564	72,843
West	22 Assault(1)								67	221	1,211
West	Other Bts (1)								416	1,373	5,978
Pol											
War	6 Assault(1)								2,563	8,458	24,801
M+10											
Pol											
Pom	16 Tk Dv (1)	36		13		2,549	11	9	1,024	3,379	6,133
Pom	20 Tk Dv (1)	57		13		3,551	46	393	1,024	3,379	39,038
Pom	12 MR Dv (1)	57		13		3,551	46	1,589	2,778	9,167	46,277
Pom	8 MR Dv (1)							1,589	2,778	9,167	46,277
Pom	Art Rt (1)		3			169			96	96	4,017
Sil	5 Tk Dv (1)	36		13		2,549	11	393	1,024	3,379	39,038
Sil	10 Tk Dv (1)	36		13		2,549	11	393	1,024	3,379	39,038
Sil	11 Tk Dv (1)								1,024	3,379	6,124
Sil	Art Rt (1)		3			169			29	96	4,023
War	Art Rt (1)		3			169			29	96	448
USSR											
Byel	120 MR Dv (1)			20		1,277			2,537	8,372	62,911
Byel	8 Tk Dv (1)			12	9	1,347			1,176	3,881	61,764
Carp	15 MR Dv (1)			20		1,277			2,537	8,372	60,240
Carp	23 Tk Dv (1)			12	9	1,347			1,176	3,881	61,764
Balt	7 Airbn (1)								2,563	8,458	25,097
SGF	93 MR Dv (1)			20		1,277			2,537	8,372	45,886
SGF	13 MR Dv (1)			20		1,277			2,537	8,372	45,886
SGF	2 Tk Dv (1)			12	9	1,347			1,176	3,881	52,586
SGF	13 Tk Dv (1)			12	9	1,347			1,176	3,881	28,793

Table C-8. *continued*

Time; State; Military District	Unit Title; Readiness Category	ARMORED RECONNAISSANCE VEHICLES TO&E OT65 Oth	BRDM	BMP	AT5	WUV: (WEI-CW 62)	ARMORED PERSONNEL CARRIERS TO&E ARV	APC	WUV: (WEI-CW 36)	SMALL ARMS TO&E	WUV: (WEI-CW 3.3)	UNIT WUV: Division Total
M+15												
USSR												
Mosc	MR Dv (1)			20		1,277				2,537	8,372	60,240
Mosc	2 MR Dv (1)			20		1,277				2,537	8,372	60,240
Mosc	106 Airbn (1)									2,563	8,458	25,097
Mosc	Art Dv (1)									254	838	39,032
M+20												
USSR												
Byel	MR Dv (2)			20	18	2,438				2,649	8,742	51,021
Carp	70 MR Dv (2)			20	18	2,438				2,649	8,742	51,021
Balt	1 MR Dv (2)			20	18	2,438				2,649	8,742	51,021
M+25												
USSR												
Byel	8 Tk Dv (2)			12	9	1,347				1,098	3,623	35,018
Carp	128 MR Dv (2)			20	18	2,438				2,649	8,742	51,021
Balt	1 Tk Dv (2)			12	9	1,347				1,098	3,623	35,018
M+30												
USSR												
Byel	29 Tk Dv (2)			12	9	1,347				1,098	3,623	35,018
Byel	3 Tk Dv (2)			12	9	1,347				1,098	3,623	35,018
Byel	27 Tk Dv (2)			12	9	1,347				1,098	3,623	35,018
Carp	61 MR Dv (2)			20	18	2,438				2,649	8,742	51,021
Carp	24 MR Dv (2)			20	18	2,438				2,649	8,742	51,021
Carp	13 Tk Dv (2)			12	9	1,347				1,098	3,623	35,018
Balt	40 Tk Dv (2)			12	9	1,347				1,098	3,623	35,018
Balt	24 Tk Dv (2)			12	9	1,347				1,098	3,623	35,018
Pol												
Sil	4 MR Dv (2)	43		13		2,883				2,482	8,191	31,323
Pom	7 Assualt (2)							84	2,933	855	2,822	8,270

M+35									
USSR									
Byel	47 Tk Dv (2)		12	9	1,347			1,098	3,623
Byel	34 Tk Dv (2)		12	9	1,347			1,098	3,623
Byel	Art A Dv (2)							254	838
Byel	Art B Dv (2)							20	66
Carp	117 Tk Dv (2)		12	9	1,347			1,098	3,623
Carp	Art A Dv (2)							254	838
Carp	Art B Dv (2)							20	66
Balt	Art A Dv (2)							254	838
Balt	Art A Dv (2)							254	838
M+40									
Czech									
West	4 Tk Dv (2)	38			2,389	27	873	1,379	4,551
West	9 Tk Dv (2)	38			2,389	27	873	1,379	4,551
West	3 MR Dv (2)	87			4,153	79	2,759	2,446	8,072
USSR									
Mosc	15 Tk Dv (2)		12	9	1,347			1,098	3,623
Mosc	4 Tk Dv (2)		12	9	1,347			1,098	3,623
M+45									
USSR									
Balt	3 MR Dv (3)		20	18	2,145			2,309	7,620
M+50									
USSR									
Len	64 MR Dv (3)		20	18	2,145			2,309	7,620

47 Tk Dv (2)	35,044
34 Tk Dv (2)	35,044
Art A Dv (2)	39,032
Art B Dv (2)	7,826
117 Tk Dv (2)	35,044
Art A Dv (2)	39,032
Art B Dv (2)	7,826
Art A Dv (2)	39,032
Art A Dv (2)	39,032
4 Tk Dv (2)	36,993
9 Tk Dv (2)	36,993
3 MR Dv (2)	38,565
15 Tk Dv (2)	35,044
4 Tk Dv (2)	35,044
3 MR Dv (3)	28,001
64 MR Dv (3)	28,001

Table C-8. *continued*

Time; State; Military District	Unit Title; Readiness Category	ARMORED RECONNAISSANCE VEHICLES TO&E					ARMORED PERSONNEL CARRIERS TO&E			SMALL ARMS		UNIT
		OT65 Oth	BRDM	BMP	AT5	WUV: (WEI- CW 62)	ARV	APC	WUV: (WEI- CW 36)	TO&E	WUV: (WEI- CW 3.3)	WUV: Division Total
M+55 USSR												
Carp	66 MR Dv (3)			20	18	2,145				2,309	7,620	28,001
Len	111 MR Dv (3)			20	18	2,145				2,309	7,620	28,001
M+60 USSR												
Byel	50 MR Dv (3)			20	18	2,145				2,309	7,620	28,001
Len	77 MR Dv (3)			20	18	2,145				2,309	7,620	28,001
Bait	88 MR Dv (3)			20	18	2,145				2,309	7,620	28,001
Czech												
East	13 Tk Dv (3)	38		12		2,389		27	873	1,379	4,551	36,993
East	14 Tk Dv (3)	38		12		2,389		27	873	1,379	4,551	36,993
M+65 USSR												
Carp	17 MR Dv (3)			20	18	2,145				2,309	7,620	28,001
Bait	26 MR Dv (3)			20	18	2,145				2,309	7,620	28,001
Len	69 MR Dv (3)			20	18	2,145				2,309	7,620	28,001
M+70 USSR												
Carp	97 MR Dv (3)			20	18	2,145				2,309	7,620	28,001
Bait	44 MR Dv (3)			20	18	2,145				2,309	7,620	28,001
Len	45 MR Dv (3)			20	18	2,145				2,309	7,620	28,001

M+75											
USSR											
Len	45 MR Dv (3)			20	18	2,145			2,309	7,620	28,001
Balt	107 MR Dv (3)			20	18	2,145			2,309	7,620	28,001
M+80											
USSR											
Mos	13 MR Dv (3)			20	18	2,145			2,309	7,620	28,001
Vol	43 MR Dv (3)			20	18	2,145			2,309	7,620	28,001
Vol	Art A Dv (3)								254	838	39,032
Czech											
East	15 MR Dv (3)	87				4,153	67	2,340	2,446	8,072	33,344
Pol											
War	1 MR Dv (3)	28	13			2,062			2,479	8,181	25,569
M+85											
USSR											
Mos	32 MR Dv (3)			20	18	2,145			2,309	7,620	28,001
Vol	96 MR Dv (3)			20	18	2,145			2,309	7,620	28,001
Ural	77 MR Dv (3)			20	18	2,145			2,309	7,620	28,001
Czech											
East	19 MR Dv (3)	87				4,153	67	2,340	2,446	8,072	33,344
Pol											
War	3 MR Dv (3)										
M+90											
USSR											
Vol	21 MR Dv (3)			20	18	2,145			2,309	7,620	28,001
Ural	MR Dv (3)			20	18	2,145			2,309	7,620	28,001
Czech											
East	20 MR Dv (3)								2,446	8,072	20,038
Pol											
War	9 MR Dv (3)										5,474

Table C-8. *continued*

ATTU Units Not Allocated to Central Front

USSR

Time; State; Military District	Unit Title; Readiness Category	ARMORED RECONNAISSANCE VEHICLES					ARMORED PERSONNEL CARRIERS			SMALL ARMS		UNIT WUV: Division Total
		TO&E				WUV: (WEI-CW 62)	TO&E		WUV: (WEI-CW 36)	TO&E	WUV: (WEI-CW 3.3)	
		OT65 Oth	BRDM	BMP	AT5		ARV	APC				
NW	MR Dv (1)			20	18	2,438				2,649	8,742	45,370
NW	MR Dv (1)			20	18	2,438				2,649	8,742	45,370
NW	MR Dv (1)			20	18	2,438				2,649	8,742	45,370
NW	MR Dv (1)			20	18	2,438				2,649	8,742	45,370
NW	MR Dv (1)			20	18	2,438				2,649	8,742	45,370
NW	MR Dv (1)			20	18	2,438				2,649	8,742	45,370
NW	MR Dv (1)			20	18	2,438				2,649	8,742	45,370
NW	MR Dv (1)			20	18	2,438				2,649	8,742	45,370
SW	MR Dv (1)			20	18	2,438				2,649	8,742	45,370
SW	Art A Dv (1)									254	838	39,032
SW	MR Dv (1)			20	18	2,438				2,649	8,742	45,370
SW	MR Dv (1)			20	18	2,438				2,649	8,742	45,370
SW	MR Dv (1)			20	18	2,438				2,649	8,742	45,370
SW	MR Dv (1)			20	18	2,438				2,649	8,742	45,370
SW	MR Dv (1)			20	18	2,438				2,649	8,742	45,370
SW	MR Dv (1)			20	18	2,438				2,649	8,742	45,370
SW	MR Dv (1)			20	18	2,438				2,649	8,742	45,370
SW	MR Dv (1)			20	18	2,438				2,649	8,742	45,370
SW	MR Dv (1)			20	18	2,438				2,649	8,742	45,370
SW	MR Dv (1)			20	18	2,438				2,649	8,742	45,370
SW	MR Dv (1)			20	18	2,438				2,649	8,742	45,370
SW	MR Dv (1)			20	18	2,438				2,649	8,742	45,370
SW	MR Dv (1)			20	18	2,438				2,649	8,742	45,370
SW	MR Dv (1)			20	18	2,438				2,649	8,742	45,370
SW	MR Dv (1)			20	18	2,438				2,649	8,742	45,370
SW	Tk Dv (1)			12	9	1,347				1,098	3,623	31,781
SW	Tk Dv (1)			12	9	1,347				1,098	3,623	31,781
SW	Tk Dv (1)			12	9	1,347				1,098	3,623	31,781
SW	Tk Dv (1)			12	9	1,347				1,098	3,623	31,781
SW	Tk Dv (1)			12	9	1,347				1,098	3,623	31,781
SW	Tk Dv (1)			12	9	1,347				1,098	3,623	31,781

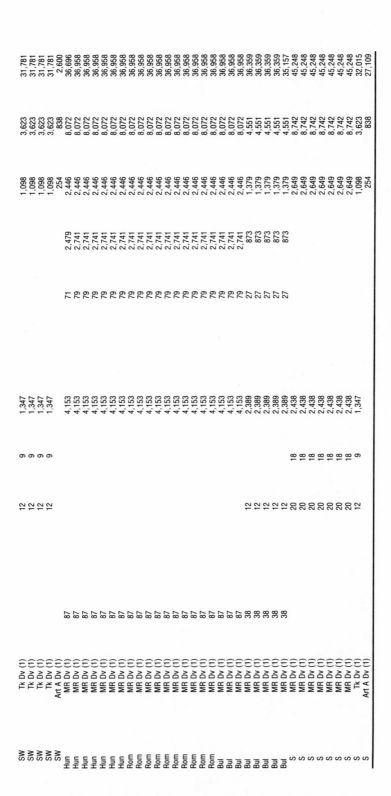

SW	Tk Dv (1)		12	9	1,347			1,098	3,623	31,781
SW	Tk Dv (1)		12	9	1,347			1,098	3,623	31,781
SW	Tk Dv (1)		12	9	1,347			1,098	3,623	31,781
SW	Tk Dv (1)		12	9	1,347			1,098	3,623	31,781
SW	Art A Dv (1)							254	838	2,600
Hun	MR Dv (1)	87			4,153	71	2,479	2,446	8,072	36,696
Hun	MR Dv (1)	87			4,153	79	2,741	2,446	8,072	36,958
Hun	MR Dv (1)	87			4,153	79	2,741	2,446	8,072	36,958
Hun	MR Dv (1)	87			4,153	79	2,741	2,446	8,072	36,958
Hun	MR Dv (1)	87			4,153	79	2,741	2,446	8,072	36,958
Hun	MR Dv (1)	87			4,153	79	2,741	2,446	8,072	36,958
Rom	MR Dv (1)	87			4,153	79	2,741	2,446	8,072	36,958
Rom	MR Dv (1)	87			4,153	79	2,741	2,446	8,072	36,958
Rom	MR Dv (1)	87			4,153	79	2,741	2,446	8,072	36,958
Rom	MR Dv (1)	87			4,153	79	2,741	2,446	8,072	36,958
Rom	MR Dv (1)	87			4,153	79	2,741	2,446	8,072	36,958
Rom	MR Dv (1)	87			4,153	79	2,741	2,446	8,072	36,958
Rom	MR Dv (1)	87			4,153	79	2,741	2,446	8,072	36,958
Rom	MR Dv (1)	87			4,153	79	2,741	2,446	8,072	36,958
Rom	MR Dv (1)	87			4,153	79	2,741	2,446	8,072	36,958
Rom	MR Dv (1)	87			4,153	79	2,741	2,446	8,072	36,958
Rom	MR Dv (1)	87			4,153	79	2,741	2,446	8,072	36,958
Rom	MR Dv (1)	87			4,153	79	2,741	2,446	8,072	36,958
Rom	MR Dv (1)	87			4,153	79	2,741	2,446	8,072	36,958
Rom	MR Dv (1)	87			4,153	79	2,741	2,446	8,072	36,958
Bul	MR Dv (1)	38	12	18	2,389	27	873	1,379	4,551	36,359
Bul	MR Dv (1)	38	12	18	2,389	27	873	1,379	4,551	36,359
Bul	MR Dv (1)	38	12	18	2,389	27	873	1,379	4,551	36,359
Bul	MR Dv (1)	38	12	18	2,389	27	873	1,379	4,551	36,359
Bul	MR Dv (1)	38	12	18	2,389	27	873	1,379	4,551	35,157
S	MR Dv (1)		20		2,438			2,649	8,742	45,248
S	MR Dv (1)		20		2,438			2,649	8,742	45,248
S	MR Dv (1)		20		2,438			2,649	8,742	45,248
S	MR Dv (1)		20		2,438			2,649	8,742	45,248
S	MR Dv (1)		20		2,438			2,649	8,742	45,248
S	MR Dv (1)		20		2,438			2,649	8,742	45,248
S	Tk Dv (1)		12	9	1,347			1,098	3,623	32,015
S	Art A Dv (1)							254	838	27,109

Notes to Table C-8

See the notes to table C-1 for methodology and sources. This reduction was done in three stages, with Soviet force levels after the Gorbachev reductions as the starting point. The first two CFE sublimits affect the Soviet Union only.

The first sublimit—on forces outside national territory—forces the Soviets to accept reductions of 20 in tanks (an effect of the unilateral Gorbachev cuts), 2,312 in artillery, and 2,877 in armored vehicles. All of these reductions come from Soviet forces in Eastern Europe. All reduction numbers are given in "unit assigned," not expanded, TO&Es.

The second sublimit—on Soviet forces in any one country—forces the Soviets to accept reductions of 17,791 in tanks, 6,639 in artillery, and 33,842 in armored vehicles. The Soviets were assumed to take the cut where it will reduce the WEI/WUV score the least and, ceteris paribus, to cut the latest-arriving units first. This meant that non-Western TVD forces (Soviet units that are in the ATTU but are not designated to fight on the central front), due to their older equipment, were more heavily cut. Indeed, non-Western TVD forces took these cuts at a rate of more than 2 to 1. No forces in Eastern Europe were reduced by this sublimit.

The third and final limit—on alliancewide weapon levels—forces the WTO as a whole to accept reductions of 4,966 in tanks, 0 in artillery, and 8,662 in armored vehicles. Because only the Soviets are affected by the first two sublimits, it is assumed that the non-Soviet WTO nations take all these cuts. In executing them they are assumed to observe the principle of cutting the worst weapons first.

Table C-9. WTO Weapon Totals and ADE Mobilization Schedule Derived from Table C-8, after CFE

WEAPONS AND CFE CONDITONS	TOTAL	Tank: T-34/T-55	Tank: T-64	Tank: T-72	Tank: T-80	WEAPON NAME
TANKS						
OUTSIDE OF NATIONAL TERRITORY						
CFE Sublimit: "Outside of National Territory"	4,500					
Soviet Tanks including spares, "Outside of National Territory"	4,524					
Soviet Tank TO&E "Outside of National Territory" before reduction	3,770					
Reductions in Soviet Tank TO&E "Outside of National Territory"	−20					
Soviet Tank TO&E "Outside of National Territory" after reduction	3,750					
ANY ONE COUNTRY						
CFE Sublimit: "Any One Country"	14,000					
Soviet Tanks including spares, "Any One Country"	35,350					
Soviet Tank TO&E "Any One Country" before reduction	29,458					
Reductions in Soviet Tank TO&E "Any One Country"	−17,791					
Soviet Tank TO&E "Any One Country" after reduction	11,667					
ALLIANCEWIDE						
CFE Final limit: "Alliancewide"	20,000					
WTO Tanks including spares, "Alliancewide"	25,959					
WTO Tank TO&E "Alliancewide" before reduction	21,633					
Reductions in WTO Tank TO&E "Alliancewide"	−4,966					
WTO Tank TO&E "Alliancewide" after reduction	16,667					
ATTU, including spares	20,000	4,337		9,654	2,676	
ATTU TO&E	16,667					
Central Front Total including spares	13,535	3,819		4,784	2,676	
Central Front TO&E	11,279					

ARTILLERY

		Arty: 122 M-38	Arty: MRL	Arty: 152 D-1	Arty: 122 M74	Mortar: 120MM	Antiarmor: T-21	Antiarmor: 100MM
OUTSIDE OF NATIONAL TERRITORY								
CFE Sublimit: "Outside of National Territory"	4,000							
Soviet Artillery including spares, "Outside of National Territory"	6,774							
Soviet Artillery TO&E "Outside of National Territory" before reduction	5,645							
Reductions in Soviet Artillery TO&E "Outside of National Territory"	−2,312							
Soviet Artillery TO&E "Outside of National Territory" after reduction	3,333							
ANY ONE COUNTRY								
CFE Sublimit: "Any One Country"	17,000							
Soviet Artillery including spares, "Any One Country"	24,967							
Soviet Artillery TO&E "Any One Country" before reduction	20,806							
Reductions in Soviet Artillery TO&E "Any One Country"	−6,639							
Soviet Artillery TO&E "Any One Country" after reduction	14,167							
ALLIANCEWIDE								
CFE Final limit: "Alliancewide"	24,000							
WTO Artillery including spares, "Alliancewide"	23,882							
WTO Artillery TO&E "Alliancewide" before reduction	19,901							
Reductions in WTO Artillery TO&E "Alliancewide"	0							
WTO Artillery TO&E "Alliancewide" after reduction	19,901							
ATTU including spares	23,882							
ATTU TO&E	19,901	2,677	6,154	4,232	5,000	330	1,345	163
Central Front including spares	16,092							
Central Front TO&E	13,410	1,677	4,042	2,804	3,614	330	780	163

Table C-9. Continued

WEAPONS AND CFE CONDITONS	TOTAL
ARMORED VEHICLES	
OUTSIDE OF NATIONAL TERRITORY	
CFE Sublimit: "Outside of National Territory"	7,500
Soviet Armored Vehicles including spares, "Outside of National Territory"	10,952
Soviet Armored Vehicle TO&E "Outside of National Territory" before reduction	9,127
Reductions in Soviet Armored Vehicle TO&E "Outside of National Territory"	-2,877
Soviet Armored Vehicle TO&E "Outside of National Territory" after reduction	6,250
ANY ONE COUNTRY	
CFE Sublimit: "Any One Country"	18,000
Soviet Armored Vehicles including spares, "Any One Country"	58,610
Soviet Armored Vehicle TO&E's "Any One Country" before reduction	48,842
Reductions in Soviet Armored Vehicle TO&E "Any One Country"	-33,842
Soviet Armored Vehicles TO&E "Any One Country" after reduction	15,000
ALLIANCEWIDE	
CFE Final limit: "Alliancewide"	28,000
WTO Armored Vehicles including spares, "Alliancewide"	38,393
WTO Armored Vehicle TO&E "Alliancewide" before reduction	31,995
Reductions in WTO Armored Vehicle TO&E "Alliancewide"	-8,662
WTO Armored Vehicle TO&E "Alliancewide" after reduction	23,333

WEAPON NAME

	Total	ARV: OT-65	ARV: BRDM	ARV: BMP-R	ARV: BRDM AT5	APC: ARV	APC: APC	IFV: BMP
ATTU including spares	28,000							
ATTU TO&E	23,333	2,752	28	2,376	1,485		2,609	14,083
Central Front including spares	16,121							
Central Front TO&E	13,434	822	28	1,504	774		912	9,395

CENTRAL FRONT MOBILIZATION SCHEDULE AFTER CFE

Days After M+0	M+1	M+5	M+10	M+15	M+20	M+25	M+30	M+35	M+40
ADE arrival	7.6	8.9	6.8	1.9	1.5	1.2	3.5	2.9	1.8
Total ADE's	7.6	16.5	23.3	25.2	26.7	28.0	31.5	34.4	36.2
WUV Arrival	754,958	887,862	675,340	184,610	153,064	121,057	351,743	284,739	182,638
Total WUV	754,958	1,642,820	2,318,160	2,502,770	2,655,834	2,776,891	3,128,634	3,413,373	3,596,011

	M+45	M+50	M+55	M+60	M+65	M+70	M+75	M+80	M+85	M+90
ADE arrival	.3	.3	.6	1.6	.8	.8	.6	.1	1.2	.8
Total ADE	36.5	36.8	37.3	38.9	39.8	40.6	41.2	42.7	43.9	44.7
WUV Arrival	28,001	28,001	56,002	157,989	84,003	84,003	56,002	153,948	117,348	81,514
Total WUV	3,624,012	3,652,013	3,708,016	3,866,004	3,950,008	4,034,011	4,090,013	4,243,961	4,361,309	4,442,823

Source: Data given in Table C-8.

Table C-10. NATO Units, Central Front Arrival Times, and WUV Scores, after CFE

STATE; CORPS	DIVISION	BRIGADE	REGIMENT	ORIGINAL LOCATION	CORPS SECTOR	DAY	TANKS TO&E	TANKS WEI	TANKS (WEI-CW 100)	ARTILLERY TO&E	ARTILLERY WEI	ARTILLERY (WEI-CW 92)
Netherlands							CENT / LEO 1			M-108 / 155HOW		
I Netherlands	4th Mech	41,42,43			2	M+5	33 / 230	268	26,760	90	75	6,872
I Netherlands	5th Mech	51,52,53			2	M+5	33 / 230	268	26,760	90	75	6,872
I Netherlands	1st Mech	11,12,13		Schaarsbergen,FRG	2	M+10	33 / 230	268	26,760	90	75	6,872
Belgium							CENT / LEO 1			M-108 / 155HOW		
I Belgian	16th Mech	4 mech, 17 Arm		Soest, FRG	4	M+1	74 / 80	170	16,988	36 / 18	44	4,041
I Belgian	1st Div	1 mech, 7 mech		Liege, BE	4	M+1	74 / 40	123	12,268	36 / 18	44	4,041
I Belgian		10 mech		Zonhoven, BE	4	M+10	20 / 12	35	3,456	14 / 7	18	1,616
I Belgian		12 mot		Liege, BE	4	M+10	20 / 12	35	3,456	14 / 7	18	1,616
Denmark							CENT / LEO 1			M-108 / 155HOW		
Jutland	Jutland	1, 2, 3 mech inf		Rendsburg, DE	1	M+15	73 / 120	195	19,540	151 / 72	181	16,679
United Kingdom							CENT / LEO 1			105MM / 155HOW / M110		
I British	1 Arm	7, 12, 22		Verden, FRG	3	M+1	0 / CHIEF 140	165	16,520	24 / 12 / 3	34	3,146
I British	4 Arm	11, 20, 30 Arm		Herford, FRG	3	M+1	0 / 140	165	16,520	24 / 12 / 3	34	3,146
I British	2 Inf	15, 24, 49 inf		York, UK	3	M+1	0 / 140	165	16,520	24 / 12 / 3	34	3,146
I British	Art Div		4 reg	York, UK	3	M+1	0 / 0			35 / 20 / 12	60	5,492
British		5 Air		Aldershot, UK	3	M+5	0 / 0	47	4,720	8	7	633
I British	3 Arm	4 Arm, 6 Arm, 19 inf		Soest, FRG	3	M+10	0 / 140	165	16,520	24 / 12 / 3	34	3,146
UKMF		1 Inf		Tidworth, UK	1	M+10	0 / 40	47	4,720	8	7	633
UKMF		Other Bttns		Tidworth, UK	3	M+10	0 / 35	41	4,130	8	7	633
Canada							CENT / LEO 1 / M-48			105MM / 155HOW / M110		
C. F. Europe	4 Mech			Lahr, FRG	Reserve	M+5	0 / 60 / 20	54	5,400	190 / 30	190	17,462
Mobile Command		5e Groupe-Brig		Valcar, CA	Reserve	M+10	0 / 0 / 30	18	1,800	10	9	810
Mobile Command		5e Groupe-Brig		Calgary, CA	Reserve	M+25	0 / 0	27	2,700	10	9	810

Command	Formation	Units	Location	Status	Readiness	B2 AMX / M-48	CENT / LEO 1	LEO 1	CHIEF / LEO 2		Personnel	105MM / Var	155HOW	M110 / MLRS		
France													155HOW	MLRS		
FAR	4th Air		Nancy, FR	Reserve	M+5	0	0	0		62	6,205		24		18	1,656
FAR	9th lt Arm		Nimes, FR	Reserve	M+5	73	0	0		98	9,775		24		18	1,656
FAR	11th Air		Toulouse, FR	Reserve	M+5		0	0					24		18	1,656
II	3rd Arm		Freiburg, FRG	Reserve	M+10	115	0	0		98	9,775		24		18	1,656
II	5th Arm		Landau, FRG	Reserve	M+10	115	0	0		98	9,775		24		18	1,656
I	1st Arm		Trier, FRG	Reserve	M+10	115	0	0		98	9,775		24		18	1,656
FAR	27th Mou		Grenoble, FR	Reserve	M+15	115	0	0		43	4,250		24		18	1,656
II	15th Inf		Limoges, FR	Reserve	M+15	50	0	0		60	5,950		24		18	1,656
I	12th lt Arm		Saumur, FR	Reserve	M+15	70	0	0		64	6,375		24		18	1,656
I	14th lt Arm		Montpellier, FR	Reserve	M+15	75	0	0		98	9,775		24		18	1,656
II	2nd Arm		Versailles, FR	Reserve	M+15	115	0	0		43	4,250		24		18	1,656
III	8th Inf		Amiens, FR	Reserve	M+15	50	0	0		98	9,775		24		18	1,656
III	10th Arm		Chalons, FR	Reserve	M+15	115	0	0		98	9,775		24		18	1,656
I	7th Arm		Besancon, FR	Reserve	M+20	115	0	0					24		18	1,656
West Germany						M-48	LEO 1	LEO 1	LEO 2			Var				
I Korps	1st Arm	1, 2 Arm, 3 Inf	Hanover, FRG	3	M+1		100	0	150	285	28,500		54	16	61	5,595
I Korps	3rd Arm	7 A/I, 8 Arm, 9 Arm	Buxtehude, FRG	2	M+1		100	0	200	346	34,600		54	16	61	5,595
I Korps	6th A/I	16, 17 A/I, 18 Arm	Neumunster, FRG	1	M+1		100	0	150	285	28,500		54	16	61	5,595
II Korps	7th Arm	19, 20 Arm, 21 A/I	Westphalia, FRG	3	M+1		100	0	200	346	34,600		54	16	61	5,595
II Korps	4th A/I	10, 11 A/I, 12 Arm	Regensburg, FRG	8	M+1		100	0	200	285	28,500		54	16	61	5,595
II Korps	1st Mountain	22 A/I, 23 mou, 24 Arm	Garmisch, FRG	8	M+1		100	0	100	224	22,400		54	16	61	5,595
III Korps	2nd A/I	4, 5 A/I, 6 Arm	Regensburg, FRG	5	M+1		100	0	150	285	28,500		54	16	61	5,595
III Korps	12th Arm	34 Arm, 35 A/I, 36 Arm	Garmisch, FRG	6	M+1		100	0	200	346	34,600		54	16	61	5,595
III Korps	11th A/I	31, 32 A/I, 33 Arm	Oldenburg, FRG	2	M+5		100	0	150	285	28,500		54	16	61	5,595
I Korps	10th Arm	28, 29 Arm, 30 A/I	Sigmaringen, FRG	8	M+5		100	0	200	346	34,600				61	5,595
II Korps	1st Air	25, 26, 27 airborne	Bruchsal, FRG	8	M+5		0	0							61	5,595
III Korps	5th Arm	14, 15 Arm, 13 A/I	Sigmaringen, FRG	5	M+5		100	0	200	346	34,600				61	5,595
Terr Army SH	51 Home Defence		Kiel, FRG	1	M+5		0	0		71	7,128	18	18		28	2,600
Terr Army South	56 Home Defence		Munich, FRG	8	M+5	72	0	0		71	7,128	18	18		28	2,600
Terr Army North	52 Home Defence		Hanover, FRG	3	M+10	72	0	0		71	7,128	18	18		28	2,600
Terr Army North	62 Home Defence		Hanover, FRG	Reserve	M+10	72	0	0		71	7,128	18	18		28	2,600
Terr Army North	53 Home Defence		Dusseldorf, FRG	4	M+10	72	0	0		71	7,128	18	18		28	2,600
Terr Army North	63 Home Defence		Dusseldorf, FRG	Reserve	M+10	72	0	0		71	7,128	18	18		28	2,600
Terr Army South	52 Home Defence		Mainz, FRG	5	M+10	72	0	0		71	7,128	18	18		28	2,600
Terr Army South	62 Home Defence		Trier, FRG	Reserve	M+10	72	0	0		71	7,128	18	18		28	2,600
Terr Army South	55 Home Defence		Stuttgart, FRG	8	M+10	72	0	0		71	7,128	18	18		28	2,600
Terr Army SH	61 Home Defence		Kiel, FRG	Reserve	M+15	72	0	0		71	7,128	18	18		28	2,600
Terr Army South	66 Home Defence		Munich, FRG	Reserve	M+15	72	0	0		71	7,128	18	18		28	2,600
Terr Army South	65 Home Defence		Stuttgart, FRG	Reserve	M+20	72	0	0		71	7,128	18	18		28	2,600

Table C-10. *continued*

STATE: CORPS	DIVISION	BRIGADE	REGIMENT	ORIGINAL LOCATION	CORPS SECTOR	DAY	TANKS TO&E						ARTILLERY TO&E				
							M-48	M-60A1	M-60A2	M-1	WEI	WEI-CW 100	Var M110	155HOW	GSRS	WEI	WEI-CW 92
United States																	
VII US	1st Arm	1,2,3	+ Art	Frankfurt, FRG	7	M+1		0	70	232	382	38,162		72	9	84	7,717
VII US		Art	17,72,210	Stuttgart, FRG	7	M+1		0	0				36	100		137	12,630
V US	3rd Arm	1,2,3	+ Art	Frankfurt, FRG	6	M+1		0	70	232	382	38,162		72	9	84	7,717
V US		Art: 41,42			6	M+1		0	0				36	50		86	7,938
V US	1st Inf	3	11 ACR	Fulda, FRG	6	M+1		0	40	75	143	14,265	6	25	3	29	2,666
VII /III US	2nd Arm	3		Goppingen, FRG	7	M+1		0	20	100	153	15,320		15	9	32	2,909
III US	3rd Inf	1,2,3	+ Art	Garlstedt, FRG	2	M+1		0	30	75	132	13,155		25	3	29	2,666
VII US			2 ACR	Wurzburg, FRG	7	M+5		0	40	270	398	39,810	18	48	9	77	7,088
VII US	8th Inf (mech)	1,2,3	+ Art	Nuremberg, FRG	7	M+5		0	70	65	163	16,285	16	24		40	3,695
V US			+ Art	Bad Kreuznach, FRG	Reserve	M+5		0	70	232	382	38,162		72	9	84	7,717
CONUS POMCUS																	
US	1st Inf	1,2		Ft. Riley KS	7	M+10		0	20	200	284	28,420	10	30	9	51	4,677
III US			3 ACR	Ft. Bliss TX	7	M+10		0	0	65	85	8,515	16	24		40	3,695
III US		Art: 212		Stuttgart, FRG	7	M+10		0	0					54	9	55	5,067
I US	7th Inf	1,2,3		Ft. Ord, CA	Reserve	M+15		0	0	14	18	1,834	18	48	9	77	7,088
I US	25th Inf	1,2		Schofield, HI	Reserve	M+15		0	0	14	18	1,834	18	48	9	77	7,088
III US	2nd Arm	1,2		Ft. Hood, TX	2	M+15		0	7	150	204	20,427		50	6	58	5,332
III US	1st Cav	1,2,155		Ft. Hood, TX	Reserve	M+15		0	20	232	326	32,612		72	9	84	7,717
III US	4th Inf (mech)	1,2,3		Ft. Carson, CO	2	M+15		0	20	232	326	32,612		72	9	84	7,717

Reserve and National Guard

Comp	Units	Formation	Location	Status	M+													
III US	Art: 75,214		Ft. Knox, KY	Reserve	M+20		0	0	75	120	12,045	36	36		50		86	7,938
CONUS Res	194 Arm		Ft. Knox, KY	Reserve	M+25		0	20	75	120	12,045				25	3	29	2,666
CONUS Res	197 mech Inf	26th Inf	MA-CT-SC-RI	Reserve	M+32		0	20	50	228	22,766	18		18	25	3	29	2,666
NG	1,3,43		PA	Reserve	M+39		100	56	75	120	12,045				30	9	72	6,624
CONUS Res	157 mech Inf	28th Inf	PA	Reserve	M+46		0	20	50	228	22,766	18		18	25	3	29	2,666
NG	2,55,56		PA-VA-WV	Reserve	M+46		100	56				36		36	30	9	72	6,624
CONUS Res	Art: 428,424,479		IN-IL-PA	Reserve	M+53		0	0				10		10	100	9	137	12,630
NG	29 Inf		MA-NY-ME	Reserve	M+53	15	20	25	10	57	5,705	8		8			17	1,582
NG	30 Inf (mech)		NC	Reserve	M+53	10	45	20		96	9,575	8		8	8		22	2,017
NG	33 Inf		MA-NY-ME	Reserve	M+53	15	20	60		57	5,705	10		10			17	1,582
NG		107 ACR	NC	Reserve	M+60		60	60		127	12,660				24		36	3,341
NG	32 Inf (mech)	35th Mech Inf	OH-WV	Reserve	M+60	10	45	25	10	96	9,575	8		8	8		22	2,017
NG	67,69,149		CO-KS-KY	Reserve	M+67	32	150	75	25	298	29,768	24		24	24		66	6,050
NG		116 ACR	OH-WV	Reserve	M+67		60	60		127	12,660	16		16			36	3,341
NG	2,55,56	29th lt Inf	MD-VA	Reserve	M+67	50	0	0		50	4,950	18					45	4,129
NG	2,46,76	38th Mech Inf	IN-MI-OH	Reserve	M+74	32	150	75	25	298	29,768	24		24	24	12	66	6,050
NG	41 Inf		OR	Reserve	M+74	15	20	20	10	57	5,705	10		10			17	1,582
NG	81 Inf (mech)		WA	Reserve	M+74	10	45	25		96	9,575	8		8	8		22	2,017
NG		163 ACR	WI-RI-NC	Reserve	M+74		60	60		127	12,660	8			24		36	3,341
NG	45 Inf		OK	Reserve	M+81	15	20	20	10	57	5,705	10		10	8		17	1,582
NG	218 Inf (mech)		SC	Reserve	M+81	10	45	25		96	9,575	8		8			22	2,017
NG	Art: 45,57,103		IN-IL-PA	Reserve	M+81		0	0							100		137	12,630
NG		278 ACR	TN	Reserve	M+88		60	60		127	12,660	36		36	24		36	3,341
NG	53 Inf		FL	Reserve	M+81	15	20	20		57	5,705	10		10			17	1,582
NG	30 Arm		TN	Reserve	M+81	20	45	20		87	8,700	8		8	8		22	2,017
NG	73 Inf		OH	Reserve	M+81	15	20	20		57	5,705	10		10			17	1,582
NG	Art: 113,115,118		IN-IL-PA	Reserve	M+88		0	0				36		36	100		137	12,630
NG	Art: 135,138,142		IN-IL-PA	Reserve	M+88		0	0				36		36	100		137	12,630
NG	31 Arm		AL	Reserve	M+88	20	45	20		87	8,700	8	8	8	20		22	2,017
NG	1,2	42nd Inf	NY	Reserve	M+88	65	65	40	30	213	21,305	20	50	20	100		77	7,084
NG	Art: 196,197,209			Reserve	M+88		0	0				36		36	100		137	12,630
NG	Art: 147,151,169			Reserve	M+95		0	0				36		36	100		137	12,630
NG	Art: 227,163,631			Reserve	M+95		0	0				36		36	100		137	12,630
NG	1,2,3	49th Arm	TX-NM	Reserve	M+95	75	150	75	25	340	34,025	24	50	24	24		85	7,820
NG	1,2,86	50th Arm	NJ	Reserve	M+102	75	150	75	25	340	34,025	24	50	24	24		85	7,820

Table C-10. *continued*

STATE; CORPS	DIVISION		TANKS TO&E	TANKS WEI	TANKS (WEI-CW 100)	ARTILLERY TO&E	ARTILLERY WEI	ARTILLERY (WEI-CW 92)
ATTU Units Not Allocated to Central Front								
United Kingdom	Inf	11	30	46	4,640	24	21	1,899
	Inf	11	30	46	4,640	24	21	1,899
	Inf	11	30	46	4,640	24	21	1,899
	Inf	12	30	47	4,740	24	21	1,899
	Inf	12	30	47	4,740	24	21	1,899
	Inf	12	30	47	4,740	24	21	1,899
	Inf	12	30	47	4,740	24	21	1,899
	Inf	12	30	47	4,740	24	21	1,899
	Inf	12	30	47	4,740	24	21	1,899
France	Arm	0	40	34	3,400	30	48	4,444
	Arm	0	40	34	3,400	30	48	4,444
Netherlands	Inf	0	25	25	2,500	20	16	1,435
Turkey	Mech/Inf	0	150	132	13,200	80	59	5,446
	Mech/Inf	0	150	132	13,200	80	59	5,446
	Mech/Inf	0	150	132	13,200	80	59	5,446
	Mech/Inf	0	150	132	13,200	80	59	5,446
	Mech/Inf	0	150	132	13,200	80	59	5,446
	Mech/Inf	0	150	132	13,200	80	59	5,446
	Mech/Inf	0	150	132	13,200	80	59	5,446
	Mech/Inf	0	150	132	13,200	80	59	5,446
	Mech/Inf	0	150	132	13,200	80	59	5,446
	Mech/Inf	0	150	132	13,200	80	59	5,446
	Mech/Inf	0	150	132	13,200	80	59	5,446
	Mech/Inf	0	150	132	13,200	80	59	5,446
	Mech/Inf	0	150	132	13,200	80	59	5,446
	Mech/Inf	0	150	132	13,200	80	59	5,446
	Mech/Inf	0	150	132	13,200	80	59	5,446
	Mech/Inf	0	150	132	13,200	80	59	5,446
	Mech/Inf	0	150	132	13,200	80	59	5,446
	Mech/Inf	0	150	132	13,200	80	59	5,446
	Mech/Inf	0	150	132	13,200	80	59	5,446

Greece	Mech/Inf	115	0	0	101	10,120	125				93	8,510
	Mech/Inf	115	0	0	101	10,120	125				93	8,510
	Mech/Inf	115	0	0	101	10,120	125				93	8,510
	Mech/Inf	115	0	0	101	10,120	125				93	8,510
	Mech/Inf	115	0	0	101	10,120	125				93	8,510
	Mech/Inf	115	0	0	101	10,120	125				93	8,510
	Mech/Inf	115	0	0	101	10,120	125				93	8,510
	Mech/Inf	115	0	0	101	10,120	125				93	8,510
	Mech/Inf	115	0	0	101	10,120	125				93	8,510
	Mech/Inf	115	0	0	101	10,120	125				93	8,510
	Mech/Inf	115	0	0	101	10,120	125				93	8,510
Italy	Mech/Inf	50	110	0	154	15,400	100	100	50		223	20,516
	Mech/Inf	50	110	0	154	15,400	100	100	50		223	20,516
	Mech/Inf	50	110	0	154	15,400	100	100	50		223	20,516
	Mech/Inf	50	110	0	154	15,400	100	100	50		223	20,516
	Mech/Inf	50	110	0	154	15,400	100	100	50		223	20,516
	Mech/Inf	50	110	0	154	15,400	100	100	50		223	20,516
	Mech/Inf	50	110	0	154	15,400	100	100	50		223	20,516
	Mech/Inf	50	110	0	154	15,400	100	100	50		223	20,516
Spain	Mech/Inf	90	0	0	79	7,920	50	50	50	15	119	10,920
	Mech/Inf	90	0	0	79	7,920	50	50	50	15	119	10,920
	Mech/Inf	90	0	0	79	7,920	50	50	50	15	119	10,920
	Mech/Inf	90	0	0	79	7,920	50	50	50	15	119	10,920
	Mech/Inf	90	0	0	79	7,920	50	50	50	15	119	10,920
	Mech/Inf	90	0	0	79	7,920	50	50	50	15	119	10,920
	Mech/Inf	90	0	0	79	7,920	50	50	50	15	119	10,920
Portugal	Mech/Inf	12	0	0	11	1,056	10	10	10	10	39	3,588
	Mech/Inf	12	0	0	11	1,056	10	10	10	10	39	3,588
	Mech/Inf	12	0	0	11	1,056	10	10	10	10	39	3,588
	Mech/Inf	12	0	0	11	1,056	10	10	10	10	39	3,588
	Mech/Inf	12	0	0	11	1,056	10	10	10	10	39	3,588
	Mech/Inf	12	0	0	11	1,056	10	10	10	10	39	3,588
Norway	Mech/Inf	35	80	0	115	11,465			120	155	302	27,802

Table C-10. *continued*

STATE; CORPS	DIVISION	BRIGADE; OR REGIMENT	Mortars 60MM/120MM	81MM/M-106	M-107/M-125	Mortars WEI	(WEI CW 48)	Antiarmor LAW/ATLC	GUSTA	MAW/MILAN/ATGM	TOW	Antiarmor WEI	(WEI CW 55)	IFV TO&E	IFV WEI	(WEI CW 69)	ARV M8	APC/CVR	ARV/SCORPN	CFV M2/AMX/SCIMTAR	ARV WEI	(WEI CW 62)
Netherlands																						
I Netherlands	4th Mech	41,42,43	54	18		65	3,119	210	210	90	60	179	9,834	MARDER				63		42	104	6,419
I Netherlands	5th Mech	51,52,53	54	18		65	3,119	210	210	90	60	179	9,834					63		42	104	6,419
I Netherlands	1st Mech	11,12,13	54	18		65	3,119	210	210	90	60	179	9,834					63		42	104	6,419
Belgium																						
I Belgian	16th Mech	4 mech, 17 Arm	66	42	16	99	4,758	600	406	24	152	384	21,109	MARDER				210	98	AMX	271	16,831
I Belgian	1st Div	1 mech, 7 mech	66	42	16	99	4,758	600	406	24	152	384	21,109					210	98		271	16,831
I Belgian		10 mech	33	21	8	50	2,379	240	162	10	46	143	7,842					80	80		145	8,978
I Belgian		12 mot	33	21	8	50	2,379	240	162	10	46	143	7,842					80	80		145	8,978
Denmark																						
Jutland	Jutland	1, 2, 3 mech inf	66	66	66	163	7,815	50	100	100	70	94	5,192	MARDER				16	16	AMX 16	48	2,976
United Kingdom																						
I British	1 Arm	7, 12, 22	80	8	24	89	4,293	478		54		158	8,711	MARDER				24	32	40	106	6,560
I British	4 Arm	11, 20, 30 Arm	80	8	24	89	4,293	478		54		158	8,711					24	32	40	106	6,560
I British	2 Inf	15, 24, 49 inf	80	8	24	89	4,293	478		100		192	10,533					24	32	40	106	6,560
I British	Art Div	4 reg																			
British		5 Air	26	3	8	30	1,420	167	19			55	3,049				8	10	11	14	38	2,334
I British	3 Arm	4 Arm, 6 Arm, 19 inf	80	8	24	89	4,293	167	54			158	8,711					24	32	40	106	6,560
UKMF		1 Inf	26	3	8	30	1,420	167		20		56	3,088				8	10	11	14	38	2,334
UKMF		Other Btlns	26	3	8	30	1,420	167		20		56	3,088				8	10	11	14	38	2,334
Canada																						
C. F. Europe	4 Mech		32	16		40	1,920	128	167	24	149	214	11,758	MARDER								
Mobile Command		5e Groupe-Brig	32	16		40	1,920	128	167	24		96	5,284									
Mobile Command		5e Groupe-Brig	32	16		40	1,920	128	167	24		96	5,284									

France

Formation	Unit	Composition	60MM	81MM	120MM	ATLC		GUSTA/ATLC	ATGM			M8	AMX	SCIMTAR	
FAR	4th Air		12	12	18	35	1,656	20	60	50	2,761	12	36	46	2,857
FAR	9th lt Arm			24	18	35	1,673	90	72	83	4,584	12	20	30	1,885
FAR	11th Air			24	16	33	1,572	20	40	36	1,969	12	36	36	2,857
II	3rd Arm		12	12	16	33	1,572	20	40	36	1,969	12	36	46	2,857
II	5th Arm		12	12	16	33	1,572	20	40	36	1,969	12	36	46	2,857
I	1st Arm		12	12	16	33	1,572	20	40	36	1,969	12	36	46	2,857
FAR	27th Mou		12	12	18	35	1,656	20	60	50	2,761	12	36	46	2,857
II	15th Inf		12	12	18	35	1,656	20	60	50	2,761	12	36	46	2,857
—	12th lt Arm		12	12	18	33	1,572	20	60	50	2,761	12	36	46	2,857
—	14th lt Arm		12	12	16	33	1,572	20	40	36	1,969	12	36	46	2,857
III	2nd Arm		12	12	18	35	1,656	20	60	50	2,761	12	36	46	2,857
III	8th Inf		12	12	18	33	1,572	20	40	36	1,969	12	36	46	2,857
III	10th Arm		12	12	16	33	1,572	20	40	36	1,969	12	36	46	2,857
—	7th Arm		12	12	16	33	1,572	20	40	36	1,969	12	36	46	2,857

West Germany

Formation	Unit	Composition	120MM	ATLC		LAW	GUSTA	ATGM			MARDER			SPZ		ARV	
I Korps	1st Arm	1, 2 Arm, 3 Inf	24	22	1,060	51	48	144	143	7,857	166	143	9,850	13	13	13	798
I Korps	3rd Arm	7 A/I, 8 Arm, 9 Arm	24	22	1,060	15	48	144	134	7,343	110	95	6,527	13	13	13	798
I Korps	6th A/I	16,17 A/I, 18 Arm	24	22	1,060	51	48	144	143	7,857	166	143	9,850	13	13	13	798
I Korps	7th Arm	19,20 Arm, 21 A/I	24	22	1,060	15	48	144	134	7,343	110	95	6,527	13	13	13	798
II Korps	4th A/I	10,11 A/I, 12 Arm	24	22	1,060	51	48	144	143	7,857	166	143	9,850	13	13	13	798
III Korps	1st Mount	22 A/I, 23 mou, 24 Arm	24	22	1,060	71	68	144	155	8,506	166	143	9,850	13	13	13	798
III Korps	2nd A/I	4,5 A/I, 6 Arm	24	22	1,060	51	48	144	143	7,857	166	143	9,850	13	13	13	798
III Korps	12th Arm	34 Arm, 35 A/I, 36 Arm	24	22	1,060	15	48	144	134	7,343	110	95	6,527	13	13	13	798
I Korps	11th A/I	31,32 A/I, 33 Arm	24	22	1,060	51	48	144	143	7,857	166	143	9,850	13	13	13	798
II Korps	10th A/I	28,29 A/I, 30 A/I	24	22	1,060	15	48	144	134	7,343	110	95	6,527				
II Korps	1st Air	25,26,27 airborne	50	46	2,208	71	68	200	199	10,940	50	43	2,967			13	798
III Korps	5th Arm	14,15 Arm, 13 A/I	24	22	1,060	15	48	144	134	7,343	110	95	6,527				
Terr Army SH	51 Home Defence		18	17	795	15	48	18	34	1,868	12	10	712				
Terr Army South	56 Home Defence		18	17	795	15	48	18	34	1,868	12	10	712				
Terr Army North	52 Home Defence		18	17	795	15	48	18	34	1,868	12	10	712				
Terr Army North	62 Home Defence		18	17	795	15	48	18	34	1,868	12	10	712				
Terr Army North	53 Home Defence		18	17	795	15	48	18	34	1,868	12	10	712				
Terr Army North	63 Home Defence		18	17	795	15	48	18	34	1,868	12	10	712				
Terr Army South	52 Home Defence		18	17	795	15	48	18	34	1,868	12	10	712				
Terr Army South	62 Home Defence		18	17	795	15	48	18	34	1,868	12	10	712				
Terr Army South	55 Home Defence		18	17	795	15	48	18	34	1,868	12	10	712				
Terr Army SH	61 Home Defence		18	17	795	15	48	18	34	1,868	12	10	712				
Terr Army South	66 Home Defence		18	17	795	15	48	18	34	1,868	12	10	712				
Terr Army South	65 Home Defence		18	17	795	15	48	18	34	1,868	12	10	712				

Table C-10. *continued*

STATE; CORPS	DIVISION	BRIGADE	REGIMENT	MORTARS					ANTIARMOR					INFANTRY FIGHTING VEHICLE			ARMORED RECON VEHICLE			
				81MM	60MM	TO&E M-30	WEI	(WEI-CW 48)	LAW	TO&E DRAG	ATGM	WEI	(WEI-CW 55)	TO&E IFV	WEI	(WEI-CW 69)	TO&E Oth SPZ ARV	M-2	WEI	(WEI-CW 62)
United States																				
VII US	1st Arm	1,2,3	+ Art			66	66	3,168		180	60	191	10,494	270	243	16,767		100	119	7,378
VII US	Art		17,72,210																	
V US	3rd Arm	1,2,3	+ Art			66	66	3,168		180	60	191	10,494	270	243	16,767		150	179	11,067
V US		Art: 41,42																		
VII/III	1st Inf	3	11 ACR	5	15	20	20	960		60	20	64	3,498	90	81	5,589		35	42	2,582
III US	2nd Arm	3				15	32	1,536		100	75	152	8,374	30	27	1,863		15	18	1,107
VII US	3rd Inf	1,2,3	+ Art	18	45	20	20	960	100	60	20	64	3,498	90	81	5,589		35	42	2,582
VII US			2 ACR			50	104	4,988		263	173	374	20,543					50	60	3,689
VII US			+ Art			20	20	960		50		55	2,998					30	36	2,213
V US	8th Inf (mech)	1,2,3				66	66	3,168		180	60	191	10,494	270	243	16,767		150	179	11,067
CONUS POMCUS																				
US	1st Inf	1,2	3 ACR	10		30	64	3,072	100	200	150	305	16,748	60	54	3,726		30	36	2,213
III US						20	20	960		50		55	2,998					30	36	2,213
III US		Art: 212																		
I US	7th Inf	1,2,3		18	45	50	104	4,988		263	173	374	20,543	54	49	3,353		28	33	2,066
I US	25th Inf	1,2,3		18	45	50	104	4,988		263	173	374	20,543	54	49	3,353		28	33	2,066
III US	2nd Arm	1,2				40	40	1,920		120	40	127	6,996	180	162	11,178		70	83	5,165
III US	1st Cav	1,2,155				66	66	3,168		180	60	191	10,494	270	243	16,767		50	60	3,689
III US	4th Inf (mech)	1,2,3				66	66	3,168		180	60	191	10,494	270	243	16,767		88	105	6,493

214

Reserve and National Guard

Note: This page is a large rotated data table. No column headers are printed; the numeric columns are transcribed as Col 1–Col 6 in their left‑to‑right order, and values are placed against the unit line to which they align.

Component	Division	Subunit / Battalions	Col 1	Col 2	Col 3	Col 4	Col 5	Col 6
III US		Art: 75,214						
CONUS Res								
CONUS Res	26th Inf	194 Arm	960	60	64	3,498	42	2,582
CONUS Res		197 mech Inf	960	60	64	3,498	42	2,582
NG		1,3,43	4,959	263	434	23,843	60	3,689
CONUS Res	28th Inf	157 mech Inf	960	60	64	3,498	42	2,582
NG		2,55,56	4,959	263	434	23,843	60	3,689
CONUS Res		Art: 428,424,479						
NG		29 Inf	1,800	75	105	5,778	12	756
NG		30 Inf (mech)	1,056	60	64	3,535	24	1,513
NG		33 Inf	1,800	75	105	5,778	12	756
NG	107 ACR	32 Inf (mech)	931	50	55	2,998	36	2,213
NG	35th Mech Inf	67,69,149	1,056	60	64	3,535	24	1,513
NG		(35th Mech Inf)	2,640	180	186	10,252	85	5,295
NG	116 ACR		931	50	55	2,998	36	2,213
NG	29th lt Inf	2,55,56	5,940	263	332	18,287	60	3,689
NG	38th Mech Inf	2,46,76	2,640	180	186	10,252	85	5,295
NG		41 Inf (mech)	1,800	75	105	5,778	12	756
NG		81 Inf (mech)	1,056	60	64	3,535	24	1,513
NG	163 ACR	45 Inf	931	50	55	2,998	36	2,213
NG		218 Inf (mech)	1,800	75	105	5,778	12	756
NG		Art: 45,57,103	1,056	60	64	3,535	24	1,513
NG	278 ACR		931	50	55	2,998	36	2,213
NG		53 Inf	1,800	75	105	5,778	12	756
NG		30 Arm	1,056	60	64	5,778	24	1,513
NG		73 Inf	1,800	75	105	3,535	24	1,513
NG		Art: 113,115,118						
NG		Art: 135,138,142						
NG	42nd Inf	31 Arm		150	230	3,535	24	1,513
NG		1,2	4,997	150	230	12,656	36	2,251
NG		Art: 196,197,209						
NG		Art: 147,151,169						
NG		Art: 227,163,631						
NG	49th Arm	1,2,3	3,571	180	206	11,352	85	5,295
NG	50th Arm	1,2,86	3,571	180	206	11,352	85	5,295

Table C-10. *continued*

ATTU Units Not Allocated to Central Front

STATE; CORPS	DIVISION	MORTARS TO&E	MORTARS —	MORTARS WEI	MORTARS (WEI-CW 48)	ANTIARMOR TO&E	ANTIARMOR WEI	ANTIARMOR (WEI-CW 55)	IFV TO&E	IFV WEI	IFV (WEI-CW 69)	ARV TO&E	ARV —	ARV WEI	ARV (WEI-CW 62)
United Kingdom	Inf	26		20	936	100	25	1,375				50	5	44	2,697
	Inf	26		20	936	100	25	1,375				50	5	44	2,697
	Inf	26		20	936	100	25	1,375				50	5	44	2,697
	Inf	26		20	936	100	25	1,375				50	5	44	2,697
	Inf	26		20	936	100	25	1,375				50	5	44	2,697
	Inf	26		20	936	100	25	1,375				50	5	44	2,697
	Inf	26		20	936	100	25	1,375				50	5	44	2,697
	Inf	26		20	936	100	25	1,375				50	5	44	2,697
	Inf	26		20	936	100	25	1,375				50	5	44	2,697
	Inf	26		20	936	100	25	1,375				50	5	44	2,697
France	Arm	12	40	54	2,575	20	7	385							
	Arm	12	40	54	2,575	20	7	385							
Netherlands	Inf	20				75	19	1,031				20			
Turkey	Mech/Inf	40	20	68	3,245	4	28	1,564				125	5	74	4,573
	Mech/Inf	40	20	68	3,245	4	28	1,564				125	5	74	4,573
	Mech/Inf	40	20	68	3,245	4	28	1,564				125	5	74	4,573
	Mech/Inf	40	20	68	3,245	4	28	1,564				125	5	74	4,573
	Mech/Inf	40	20	68	3,245	4	28	1,564				125	5	74	4,573
	Mech/Inf	40	20	68	3,245	4	28	1,564				125	5	74	4,573
	Mech/Inf	40	20	68	3,245	4	28	1,564				125	5	74	4,573
	Mech/Inf	40	20	68	3,245	4	28	1,564				125	5	74	4,573
	Mech/Inf	40	20	68	3,245	4	28	1,564				125	5	74	4,573
	Mech/Inf	40	20	68	3,245	4	28	1,564				125	5	74	4,573
	Mech/Inf	40	20	68	3,245	4	28	1,564				125	5	74	4,573
	Mech/Inf	40	20	68	3,245	4	28	1,564				125	5	74	4,573
	Mech/Inf	40	20	68	3,245	4	28	1,564				125	5	74	4,573
	Mech/Inf	40	20	68	3,245	4	28	1,564				125	5	74	4,573
	Mech/Inf	40	20	68	3,245	4	28	1,564				125	5	74	4,573
	Mech/Inf	40	20	68	3,245	4	28	1,564				125	5	74	4,573
	Mech/Inf	40	20	68	3,245	4	28	1,564				125	5	74	4,573
	Mech/Inf	40	20	68	3,245	4	28	1,564				125	5	74	4,573
	Mech/Inf	40	20	68	3,245	4	28	1,564				125	5	74	4,573

Greece	Mech/Inf	50	25	25		85	4,056	160	4	4	4	40	2,224	5	4	242	65				38	2,378
	Mech/Inf	50	25	25		85	4,056	160	4	4	4	40	2,224	5	4	242	65				38	2,378
	Mech/Inf	50	25	25		85	4,056	160	4	4	4	40	2,224	6	4	290	65				38	2,378
	Mech/Inf	50	25	25		85	4,056	160	4	4	4	40	2,224	5	4	242	65				38	2,378
	Mech/Inf	50	25	25		85	4,056	160	4	4	4	40	2,224	5	4	242	65				38	2,378
	Mech/Inf	50	25	25		85	4,056	160	4	4	4	40	2,224	5	4	242	65				38	2,378
	Mech/Inf	50	25	25		85	4,056	160	4	4	4	40	2,224	6	4	290	65				38	2,378
	Mech/Inf	50	25	25		85	4,056	160	4	4	4	40	2,224	5	4	242	65				38	2,378
	Mech/Inf	50	25	25		85	4,056	160	4	4	4	40	2,224	5	4	290	65				38	2,378
	Mech/Inf	50	25	25		85	4,056	160	4	4	4	40	2,224	6	4	242	65				38	2,378
	Mech/Inf	50	25	25		85	4,056	160	4	4	4	40	2,224	5	4	242	65				38	2,378
	Mech/Inf	50	25	25		85	4,056	160	4	4	4	40	2,224	5	4	242	65				38	2,378
Italy	Mech/Inf	40	20	20	50	118	5,645	100	25	125	25	190	10,450	4	3	193	50			25	127	7,874
	Mech/Inf	40	20	20	50	118	5,645	100	25	125	25	190	10,450	4	3	193	50			25	127	7,874
	Mech/Inf	40	20	20	50	118	5,645	100	25	125	25	190	10,450	4	3	193	50			25	127	7,874
	Mech/Inf	40	20	20	50	118	5,645	100	25	125	25	190	10,450	4	3	193	50			25	127	7,874
	Mech/Inf	40	20	20	50	118	5,645	100	25	125	25	190	10,450	4	3	193	50			25	127	7,874
	Mech/Inf	40	20	20	50	118	5,645	100	25	125	25	190	10,450	4	3	193	50			25	127	7,874
	Mech/Inf	40	20	20	50	118	5,645	100	25	125	25	190	10,450	4	3	193	50			25	127	7,874
	Mech/Inf	40	20	20	50	118	5,645	100	25	125	25	190	10,450	4	3	193	50			25	127	7,874
Spain	Mech/Inf	10	10	50	40	105	5,021	75	25	50		82	4,524				25	50	50	25	86	5,317
	Mech/Inf	10	10	50	40	105	5,021	75	25	50		82	4,524				25	50	50	25	86	5,317
	Mech/Inf	10	10	50	40	105	5,021	75	25	50		82	4,524				25	50	50	25	86	5,317
	Mech/Inf	10	10	50	40	105	5,021	75	25	50		82	4,524				25	50	50	25	86	5,317
	Mech/Inf	10	10	50	40	105	5,021	75	25	50		82	4,524				25	50	50	25	86	5,317
	Mech/Inf	10	10	50	40	105	5,021	75	25	50		82	4,524				25	50	50	25	86	5,317
	Mech/Inf	10	10	50	40	105	5,021	75	25	50		82	4,524				25	50	50	25	86	5,317
	Mech/Inf	10	10	50	40	105	5,021	75	25	50		82	4,524				25	50	50	25	86	5,317
Portugal	Mech/Inf	5	5	5	2	15	715	20	10	15	15	43	2,340					10	10	10	19	1,147
	Mech/Inf	5	5	5	2	15	715	20	10	15	15	43	2,340					10	10	10	19	1,147
	Mech/Inf	5	5	5	2	15	715	20	10	15	15	43	2,340					10	10	10	19	1,147
	Mech/Inf	5	5	5	2	15	715	20	10	15	15	43	2,340					10	10	10	19	1,147
	Mech/Inf	5	5	5	2	15	715	20	10	15	15	43	2,340					10	10	10	19	1,147
	Mech/Inf	5	5	5	2	15	715	20	10	15	15	43	2,340					10	10	10	19	1,147
Norway	Mech/Inf	25	25	25	25	90	4,296	200	100	100	150	376	20,653					25	25	25	55	3,379

Table C-10. *continued*

STATE; CORPS	DIVISION	BRIGADE	REGIMENT	TO&E (M113A1)	TO&E (APC)	TO&E (ARV)	TO&E (AMX)	WEI	WEI-CW 36	WEI (Small Arms)	WEI-CW 3.3	UNIT WUV: Division Total
Netherlands												
I Netherlands	4th Mech	41, 42, 43		10	300		6	309	11,114	2,246	7,412	71,530
I Netherlands	5th Mech	51, 52, 53		10	300		6	309	11,114	2,246	7,412	71,530
I Netherlands	1st Mech	11, 12, 13		10	300		6	309	11,114	2,246	7,412	71,530
Belgium												
I Belgian	16th Mech	4 mech, 17 Arm			50	20	25	85	3,044	2,653	8,755	75,525
I Belgian	1st Div	1 mech, 7 mech			50	20	25	85	3,044	2,453	8,095	70,145
I Belgian		10 mech			10	10	15	31	1,114	981	3,238	28,623
I Belgian		12 mot			10	10	15	31	1,114	981	3,238	28,623
Denmark												
Jutland	Jutland	1, 2, 3 mech inf			220			198	7,128	2,653	8,755	68,086
United Kingdom												
I British	1 Arm	7, 12, 22			33	150		163	5,863	2,963	9,778	54,871
I British	4 Arm	11, 20, 30 Arm			33	150		163	5,863	2,963	9,778	54,871
I British	2 Inf	15, 24, 49 inf			33	150		163	5,863	2,963	9,778	56,693
I British	Art Div		4 reg									5,492
British	5 Air				11	50		54	1,954	1,185	3,911	18,022
I British	3 Arm	4 Arm, 6 Arm, 19 inf			33	150		163	5,863	2,963	9,778	54,871
UKMF	1 Inf				11	50		54	1,954	1,185	3,911	18,061
UKMF	Other Btlns				11	50		54	1,954	1,185	3,911	17,471
Canada												
C. F. Europe		4 Mech			140			140	5,040	1,384	4,567	46,147
Mobile Command		5e Groupe-Brig			50			50	1,800	554	1,827	13,440
Mobile Command		5e Groupe-Brig			50			50	1,800	554	1,827	14,340

	Unit	Divisions	AMX	VAB (ARV)	APC (M113A1)				
France									
FAR	4th Air						330	1,089	1,089
FAR	9th lt Arm		20	72	82	2,959	1,300	4,290	22,384
FAR	11th Air		20	100	107	3,866	1,300	4,290	17,954
II	3rd Arm		50	300	314	11,286	1,500	4,950	34,065
II	5th Arm		50	300	314	11,286	1,500	4,950	34,065
I	1st Arm		50	300	314	11,286	1,500	4,950	34,065
FAR	27th Mou		50	300	314	11,286	1,500	4,950	34,065
II	15th Inf		20	72	82	2,959	1,300	4,290	20,429
I	12th lt Arm		20	72	82	2,959	1,300	4,290	22,129
I	14th lt Arm		50	72	108	3,899	1,300	4,290	23,494
III	2nd Arm		50	300	314	11,286	1,300	4,950	34,065
III	8th Inf		10	72	74	2,646	1,300	4,290	20,116
III	10th Arm		50	300	314	11,286	1,500	4,950	34,065
I	7th Arm			300	270	9,720	1,500	4,950	32,499
West Germany									
I Korps	1st Arm	1, 2 Arm, 3 Inf					3,500	11,550	65,211
I Korps	3rd Arm	7 A/l,8 Arm,9 Arm					3,500	11,550	67,473
I Korps	6th A/l	16,17 A/l,18 Arm					3,500	11,550	65,211
I Korps	7th Arm	19,20 Arm,21 A/l					3,500	11,550	67,473
II Korps	4th A/l	10,11 A/l,12 Arm					3,500	11,550	65,211
II Korps	1st Mountain	22 A/l,23 mou,24 Arm					3,800	12,540	60,750
III Korps	2nd A/l	4,5 A/l,6 Arm					3,500	11,550	65,211
III Korps	12th Arm	34 Arm,35 A/l,36 Arm					3,500	11,550	67,473
I Korps	11th A/l	31,32 A/l,33 Arm					3,500	11,550	65,211
II Korps	10th Arm	28,29 Arm,30 A/l					3,500	11,550	67,473
II Korps	1st Air	25,26,27 airborne					2,000	6,600	28,310
III Korps	5th Arm	14,15 Arm,13 A/l					3,500	11,550	67,473
Terr Army SH	51 Home Defence						1,300	4,290	17,393
Terr Army South	56 Home Defence						1,300	4,290	17,393
Terr Army North	52 Home Defence						1,300	4,290	17,393
Terr Army North	62 Home Defence						1,300	4,290	17,393
Terr Army North	53 Home Defence						1,300	4,290	17,393
Terr Army North	63 Home Defence						1,300	4,290	17,393
Terr Army South	52 Home Defence						1,300	4,290	17,393
Terr Army South	62 Home Defence						1,300	4,290	17,393
Terr Army South	55 Home Defence						1,300	4,290	17,393
Terr Army SH	61 Home Defence						1,300	4,290	17,393
Terr Army South	66 Home Defence						1,300	4,290	17,393
Terr Army South	65 Home Defence						1,300	4,290	17,393

Table C-10. *continued*

STATE; CORPS	DIVISION	BRIGADE	REGIMENT	ARMORED PERSONNEL CARRIER					SMALL ARMS		UNIT WUV: Division Total
				TO&E			WEI	(WEI-CW 36)	WEI	(WEI-CW 3.3)	
				ARV	M113A1	0th					
United States											
VII US	1st Arm	1,2,3	+ Art						3,000	9,900	93,586
VII US		Art	17,72,210								12,630
V US	3rd Arm	1,2,3	+ Art						3,000	9,900	97,275
V US		Art: 41,42									7,938
V US			11 ACR						1,000	3,300	32,860
VII /III	1st Inf	3							1,000	3,300	34,408
III US	2nd Arm	3							1,000	3,300	31,750
VII US	3rd Inf	1,2,3	+ Art						3,600	11,880	93,586
VII US			2 ACR						1,022	3,373	29,523
V US	8th Inf (mech)	1,2,3	+ Art						3,000	9,900	97,275
CONUS POMCUS											
US	1st Inf	1,2							2,000	6,600	65,456
III US			3 ACR						1,022	3,373	21,753
III US		Art : 212									5,067
I US	7th Inf	1,2,3							3,600	11,880	51,751
I US	25th Inf	1,2,3							3,600	11,880	51,751
III US	2nd Arm	1,2							2,000	6,600	57,618
III US	1st Cav	1,2,155							3,000	9,900	84,347
III US	4th Inf (mech)	1,2,3							3,000	9,900	87,151

220

Reserve and National Guard

Component	Division	ACR	Units								Total
III US											7,938
CONUS Res			Art: 75,214	60	30	50	50	1,800	1,000	3,300	26,851
CONUS Res			194 Arm	60	30	50	50	1,800	1,000	3,300	32,440
NG	26th Inf		197 mech Inf	25	10	30	109	3,931	3,000	9,900	81,301
CONUS Res			1,3,43	20	20	50	50	1,800	1,000	3,300	26,851
NG	28th Inf		157 mech Inf	25	10	30	109	3,931	3,000	9,900	81,301
CONUS Res			2,55,56								12,630
CONUS Res			Art: 428,424,479	115	20	10	41	1,467	1,000	3,300	22,252
NG			29 Inf	20	20	20	55	1,994	800	2,640	26,677
NG		107 ACR	30 Inf (mech)	55	55	10	41	1,467	1,000	3,300	22,252
NG			33 Inf	115	20	20	118	4,250	1,022	2,640	29,766
NG		116 ACR	32 Inf (mech)	20	55	55	55	1,994	800	3,373	26,677
NG	35th Mech Inf		67,69,149	55	10	100	152	5,485	2,500	3,373	80,780
NG			2,55,56	25	20	55	118	4,250	1,022	12,540	29,766
NG	29th lt Inf		2,46,76	20	10	10	135	4,874	3,800	8,250	58,459
NG	38th Mech Inf		41 Inf	115	20	20	152	5,485	2,500	3,300	80,780
NG			81 Inf (mech)	25	20	10	41	1,467	1,000	2,640	22,252
NG		163 ACR	45 Inf	20	25	20	55	1,994	800	3,373	26,677
NG			218 Inf (mech)	115	55	20	118	4,250	1,022	3,300	29,766
NG			Art: 45,57,103	25	55	25	41	1,467	1,000	2,640	22,252
NG		278 ACR	53 Inf	20		20	55	1,994	800	3,373	26,677
NG			30 Arm								12,630
NG			73 Inf	25		25	118	4,250	1,022	3,300	29,766
NG			Art: 113,115,118	20		55	41	1,467	1,000	2,640	22,252
NG			Art: 135,138,142	40		55	55	1,994	800	3,373	25,802
NG			31 Arm	55			41	1,467	1,000	3,300	22,252
NG			1,2								12,630
NG			Art: 196,197,209	55			55	1,994	2,300	2,640	25,802
NG	42nd Inf		Art: 147,151,169				82	2,963	800	7,590	62,881
NG			Art: 227,163,631								12,630
NG			1,2,3								12,630
NG			1,2,86								12,630
NG	49th Arm						152	5,485	3,000	9,900	90,489
NG	50th Arm						152	5,485	3,000	9,900	90,489

Table C-10. continued

STATE; CORPS	DIVISION	ARMORED PERSONNEL CARRIER			SMALL ARMS		UNIT WUV
		TO&E	WEI	(WEI-CW 36)	WEI	(WEI-CW 3.3)	Division Total
ATTU Units Not Allocated to Central Front							
United Kingdom	Inf	20	17	626	800	2,640	14,813
	Inf	20	17	626	800	2,640	14,813
	Inf	20	17	626	800	2,640	14,813
	Inf	20	17	626	800	2,640	14,913
	Inf	20	17	626	800	2,640	14,913
	Inf	20	17	626	800	2,640	14,913
	Inf	20	17	626	800	2,640	14,913
	Inf	20	17	626	800	2,640	14,913
	Inf	20		626	800	2,640	14,913
France	Arm				700	2,310	13,113
	Arm				700	2,310	13,113
Netherlands	Inf	20	17	626	500	1,650	7,243
Turkey	Mech/Inf				3,000	9,900	37,928
	Mech/Inf				3,000	9,900	37,928
	Mech/Inf				3,000	9,900	37,928
	Mech/Inf				3,000	9,900	37,928
	Mech/Inf				3,000	9,900	37,928
	Mech/Inf				3,000	9,900	37,928
	Mech/Inf				3,000	9,900	37,928
	Mech/Inf				3,000	9,900	37,928
	Mech/Inf				3,000	9,900	37,928
	Mech/Inf				3,000	9,900	37,928
	Mech/Inf				3,000	9,900	37,928
	Mech/Inf				3,000	9,900	37,928
	Mech/Inf				3,000	9,900	37,928
	Mech/Inf				3,000	9,900	37,928
	Mech/Inf				3,000	9,900	37,928
	Mech/Inf				3,000	9,900	37,928
	Mech/Inf				3,000	9,900	37,928
	Mech/Inf				3,000	9,900	37,928
	Mech/Inf				3,000	9,900	37,928
	Mech/Inf				3,000	9,900	37,928
	Mech/Inf				3,000	9,900	37,928

Greece	Mech/Inf				3,000	9,900	37,429
	Mech/Inf				3,000	9,900	37,429
	Mech/Inf				3,000	9,900	37,478
	Mech/Inf				3,000	9,900	37,429
	Mech/Inf				3,000	9,900	37,429
	Mech/Inf				3,000	9,900	37,478
	Mech/Inf				3,000	9,900	37,429
	Mech/Inf				3,000	9,900	37,429
	Mech/Inf				3,000	9,900	37,478
	Mech/Inf				3,000	9,900	37,429
	Mech/Inf				3,000	9,900	37,429
Italy	Mech/Inf	200	200	7,200	3,000	9,900	77,178
	Mech/Inf	200	200	7,200	3,000	9,900	77,178
	Mech/Inf	200	200	7,200	3,000	9,900	77,178
	Mech/Inf	200	200	7,200	3,000	9,900	77,178
	Mech/Inf	200	200	7,200	3,000	9,900	77,178
	Mech/Inf	200	200	7,200	3,000	9,900	77,178
	Mech/Inf	200	200	7,200	3,000	9,900	77,178
	Mech/Inf	200	200	7,200	3,000	9,900	77,178
Spain	Mech/Inf	100	100	3,600	3,000	9,900	47,201
	Mech/Inf	100	100	3,600	3,000	9,900	47,201
	Mech/Inf	100	100	3,600	3,000	9,900	47,201
	Mech/Inf	100	100	3,600	3,000	9,900	47,201
	Mech/Inf	100	100	3,600	3,000	9,900	47,201
	Mech/Inf	100	100	3,600	3,000	9,900	47,201
	Mech/Inf	100	100	3,600	3,000	9,900	47,201
	Mech/Inf	100	100	3,600	3,000	9,900	47,201
Portugal	Mech/Inf	10	10	360	3,000	9,900	19,106
	Mech/Inf	10	10	360	3,000	9,900	19,106
	Mech/Inf	10	10	360	3,000	9,900	19,106
	Mech/Inf	10	10	360	3,000	9,900	19,106
	Mech/Inf	10	10	360	3,000	9,900	19,106
	Mech/Inf	10	10	360	3,000	9,900	19,106
Norway	Mech/Inf	28	28	1,008	3,000	9,900	78,503

Notes to Table C-10

See the notes to table C-1 for methodology and the notes to table C-3 for sources.

Only the CFE alliancewide limits were imposed because none of the NATO forces is large enough to be affected by the sublimits. NATO forces are arranged by nationality. This reflects the fact that reductions are made nation-by-nation rather than on an alliancewide basis. Each nation is presumed to take a percentage cut equal to the percentage cut imposed on the alliance at large. Each nation is assumed to take the cut where it will reduce the WEI/WUV score the least and, ceteris paribus, to cut the latest-arriving units first.

TABLE C-11. NATO Weapon Totals and ADE Mobilization Schedule Derived from Table C-10, after CFE

TANKS

WEAPONS AND CFE CEILINGS	TOTAL	Tanks: M-48	Tanks: M60A1 CENT LEO 1	Tanks: M-60A2/A3	Tanks: M-1/M1A1 CHIEF LEO 2
ALLIANCEWIDE					
CFE limit: "Alliancewide"	20,000				
NATO Tanks including spares, "Alliancewide"	21,604				
NATO Tank TO&E "Alliancewide" before reduction	18,003				
Reductions in NATO Tank TO&E "Alliancewide"	-1,303				
NATO Tank TO&E "Alliancewide" after reduction	16,700				
ATTU including spares	20,088	7,674	2,374	1,535	5,157
ATTU TO&E	16,740	1,987	1,272	1,535	4,857
Central Front (without CONUS) including spares	11,581				
Central Front (without CONUS) TO&E	9,651				

ARTILLERY

WEAPONS AND CFE CEILINGS	TOTAL	Arty: 155 HOW 105MM Var	Arty: M110A1/A2 155HOW	Arty: 155 HOW M110E2	Arty: GSRS	Mortar: 120MM	Mortar: M-30
ALLIANCEWIDE							
CFE limit: "Alliancewide"	24,000						
NATO Artillery including spares, "Alliancewide"	17,885						
NATO Artillery TO&E "Alliancewide" before reduction	14,904						
Reductions in NATO Artillery TO&E "Alliancewide"	0						
NATO Artillery TO&E "Alliancewide" after reduction	14,904						
ATTU including spares	17,885	5,493	3,160	1,817	437	2,541	1,456
ATTU TO&E	14,904	813	1,840	1,117	102	1,146	699
Central Front (without CONUS) including spares	6,860						
Central Front (without CONUS) TO&E	5,717						

ARMORED VEHICLES

WEAPONS AND CFE CEILINGS	TOTAL
ALLIANCEWIDE	
CFE limit: "Alliancewide"	28,000
NATO Armored Vehicles including spares, "Alliancewide"	45,659
NATO Armored Vehicles TO&E "Alliancewide" before reduction	38,049
Reductions in NATO Armored Vehicles TO&E "Alliancewide"	-14,749
NATO Armored Vehicles TO&E "Alliancewide" after reduction	23,300

WEAPON NAME

	Total	ARV: M8	ARV: CVR SPZ	ARV: SCORPN AMX	ARV: CFV M2 SCIMTAR	APC: Oth	APC: Oth	APC: AFV, ARV, VAB	APC: M113A1	IFV: MARDER
ATTU including spares	27,955	4,520	1,789	1,893	1,470	1,600	758	3,400	4,033	3,833
ATTU TO&E	23,296									
Central Front (without CONUS) including spares	15,328									
Central Front (without CONUS) TO&E	12,773	120	1,071	1,128	1,233		538	3,400	1,545	3,738

CENTRAL FRONT MOBILIZATION SCHEDULE AFTER CFE

Days After M+0	M+1	M+5	M+10	M+15	M+20	M+25	M+32	M+39
ADE arrival	12.2	7.4	5.3	5.4	.6	.9	.3	.8
Total ADEs	12.2	19.6	24.8	30.3	30.8	31.8	32.1	32.9
WUV Arrival	1,212,476	732,278	522,475	538,028	57,830	92,952	32,440	81,301
Total WUV	1,212,476	1,944,754	2,467,229	3,005,257	3,063,087	3,156,039	3,188,479	3,269,780

	M+46	M+53	M+60	M+67	M+74	M+81	M+88	M+95	M+102
ADE arrival	1.1	.8	1.4	1.7	1.3	1.1	1.3	1.2	.9
Total ADEs	34.0	34.9	36.2	37.9	39.2	40.4	41.6	42.8	43.7
WUV Arrival	108,152	83,810	137,224	169,006	127,624	112,701	126,573	115,748	90,489
Total WUV	3,377,932	3,461,742	3,598,965	3,767,971	3,895,595	4,008,296	4,134,868	4,250,616	4,341,105

Source: Data given in Table C-10.

227

Table C-12. WTO Units, Central Front Arrival Times, and WUV Scores, after CFE II

M + 1 to M + 5

USSR

Time; State; Military District	Unit Title; Readiness Category	TANKS TO&E T-55 T-34	T-64	T-72	T-80	WUV (WEI-CW 100)	ARTILLERY M-38 D-30 0th	MRL	152MM	M74	WUV (WEI-CW 92)	MORTAR 82MM	120MM	0th	WUV (WEI-CW 48)	ANTIARMOR T-21 0th	T12	RPG7	ATGM	WUV (WEI-CW 55)	IFV BMP	WUV (WEI-CW 69)
GSFG	16 Tk Dv (1)			35	180	27,913		20	5	54	6,835	4			173			346	46	8,482	64	3,909
GSFG	21 MR Dv (1)			50	40	11,451		24	5	36	5,556	12			518			529	36	11,609	50	3,071
GSFG	94 MR Dv (1)			50	40	11,451		24	5	36	5,556	12			518			529	36	11,609	50	3,071
GSFG	207 MR Dv (1)			50	40	11,451		24	8	36	5,032	12			518			529	36	11,609	50	3,071
GSFG	Art Bg (1)							20	8	31	5,032											
GSFG	Art Bg (1)							20		31	5,032											
GSFG	Other Bts (1)																					
GSFG	7 Tk Dv (1)			22	180	26,297		20	5	54	6,835	4			173			40	10	1,084	60	3,715
GSFG	10 Tk Dv (1)							20	5	54	6,835	4			173			346	46	8,482	60	3,715
GSFG	72 Tk Dv (1)							20	5	54	6,835	4			173			346	46	8,482	60	3,715
GSFG	47 Tk Dv (1)			25	180	26,670		20	5	54	6,835	4			173			346	46	8,482	60	3,715
GSFG	304 Art Bg (1)																	130	10	2,816	16	965
GSFG	Other Bts (1)																	40	10	1,084		
GSFG	25 Tk Dv (1)			25	180	26,670		20	5	54	6,835	4			173			346	46	8,482	60	3,715
GSFG	32 Tk Dv (1)			35	40	9,587		20	5	54	6,835	4			173			346	46	8,482	60	3,715
GSFG	90 Tk Dv (1)							20	5	54	6,835	4			173			346	46	8,482	60	3,715
GSFG	35 MR Dv (1)							24	5	36	5,556	12			518			529	36	11,609	50	3,071
GSFG	71 Art Bg (1)																	130	10	2,816	16	965
GSFG	Other Bts (1)																	40	10	1,084		
GSFG	79 Tk Dv (1)			25	180	26,670		20	5	54	6,835	4			173			346	46	8,482	60	3,715
GSFG	27 MR Dv (1)			35	40	9,587		24	5	36	5,556	12			518			529	36	11,609	60	3,071
GSFG	39 MR Dv (1)			35	40	9,587		24	5	36	5,556	12			518			529	36	11,609	50	3,071
GSFG	57 MR Dv (1)			35	40	9,587		24	5	36	5,556	12			518			529	36	11,609	50	3,071
GSFG	43 Art Bg (1)																	130	10	2,816	16	965
GSFG	Other Bts (1)																	40	10	1,084		
GSFG	9 Tk Dv (1)			25	180	26,670		20	5	54	6,835	4			173			346	46	8,482	60	3,715
GSFG	11 Tk Dv (1)			25	180	26,670		16	5	54	6,490	4			173			346	46	8,482	60	3,715
GSFG	20 MR Dv (1)			35	40	9,587		24	5	36	5,556	12			518			529	36	11,609	50	3,071
GSFG	43 Art Dv (1)							95	36	144	23,535							36	27	1,762		
GSFG	35 Assault (1)																	140	13	3,103	16	965
GSFG	Spetsnaz (1)																	25	5	638		
GSFG	MR Bg (1)																	106	7	2,322		
GSFG	Other Bts (1)																	25	5	638		
CGF	15 Tk Dv (1)			35	40	9,587		16	5	54	6,490	4			173			346	46	8,482	60	3,715
CGF	18 MR Dv (1)			35	40	9,587		24	5	36	5,556	12			518			529	36	11,609	50	3,071
CGF	48 MR Dv (1)							24	5	36	5,556	12			518			529	36	11,609	50	3,071
CGF	Art Bg (1)							20	8	31	5,032											
CGF	Other Bts (1)																	25	5	638		

228

M+5																	
USSR	NGF	20 Tk Dv (1)	25	180	26,670	16	5	54	6,490		4	173	346	46	8,482	60	3,715
	NGF	6 MR Dv (1)	35	40	9,587	24	5	36	5,556		12	518	529	36	11,609	50	3,071
GDR	III	7 Tk Dv (1)	55		6,215	12	2	12	1,977				167	9	2,943	28	1,742
	III	11 MR Dv (1)				12		18	2,562				324	54	7,173	64	3,927
	III	4 MR Dv (1)				12		18	2,562				324	54	7,173	64	3,927
	III	Art Rt (1)				10	4	14	2,351				3	3	177		
	III	9 Tk Dv (1)	55		6,215	12	2	12	1,977				167	9	2,943	28	1,742
	III	8 MR Dv (1)				12		18	2,562				324	54	7,173	64	3,927
	III	1 MR Dv (1)				12		18	2,562				324	54	7,173	64	3,927
	III	Art Rt (1)				10	4	14	2,351				3	3	177		
Czech	West	1 Tk Dv (1)	25		2,800	16	5	18	3,213				234	15	4,214	70	4,303
	West	2 MR Dv (1)				24	5	18	3,862				379	45	7,668	65	3,996
	West	22 Assault(1)											25	5	638	5	
	West	Other Bts (1)											100	20	2,552	19	1,142
Pol	War	6 Assault(1)											415	42	9,305	67	3,914
M+10																	
Pol	Pom	16 Tk Dv (1)	70		7,910	8	3	6	1,186	9		354	135	9	2,391	56	3,449
	Pom	20 Tk Dv (1)	25		2,825	8	3	18	2,441	9		354	135	9	2,391	56	3,449
	Pom	12 MR Dv (1)	25		2,825	8		18	2,441	27		1,063	313	36	6,127	56	3,449
	Pom	8 MR Dv (1)				10		14	2,351	27		1,063	313	36	6,127		
	Pom	Art Rt (1)				8	4	6	1,186				3	3	177		
	Sil	5 Tk Dv (1)	70		7,910	8		6	1,186	9		354	135	9	2,391	56	3,449
	Sil	10 Tk Dv (1)	70		7,910	8		6	1,186	9		354	135	9	2,391	56	3,449
	Sil	11 Tk Dv (1)								9		354	135	9	2,391		
	War	Art Rt (1)				10	4	14	2,351				3	3	177		
USSR	Byel	120 MR Dv (1)	86	40	14,478	24	5	36	5,556		12	581	529	36	11,609	50	3,071
	Byel	8 Tk Dv (1)	55	188	28,587	16	5	54	6,490		4	173	346	46	8,482	60	3,715
	Carp	15 MR Dv (1)	86	40	14,478	24	5	36	5,556		12	518	529	36	11,609	50	3,071
	Carp	23 Tk Dv (1)	55	188	28,587	16	5	54	6,490		4	173	346	46	8,482	60	3,715
	Balt	7 Airbn (1)	35	40	8,715	24	5	36	5,556			518	415	42	9,305	50	2,933
	SGF	93 MR Dv (1)	35	40	8,715	24	5	36	5,556		12	518	529	36	11,609	50	3,071
	SGF	13 MR Dv (1)	15	180	23,115	16	5	54	6,490		12	173	529	36	11,609	50	3,071
	SGF	2 Tk Dv (1)				16	5	54	6,490		4	173	346	46	8,482	60	3,715
	SGF	13 Tk Dv (1)				16	5	54	6,490		4	173	346	46	8,482	60	3,715

Table C-12. continued

Time; State; Military District	Unit Title; Readiness Category	TANKS TO&E T-55/T-34	T-64	T-72	T-80	WUV (WEI-CW 100)	ART M-38 D-30 0th	TO&E MRL	152mm	M74	WUV (WEI-CW 92)	MORT T-21 0th	TO&E 82MM	120MM	WUV (WEI-CW 48)	ANTIARM TO&E T12	RPG7	ATGM	WUV (WEI-CW 55)	IFV TO&E BMP	WUV (WEI-CW 69)
M+15																					
USSR																					
Mosc	MR Dv (1)			86	40	14,478		24	5	36	5,556		12		518		529	36	11,609	50	3,071
Mosc	2 MR Dv (1)			86	40	14,478		24	5	36	5,556		12		518		529	36	11,609	50	3,071
Mosc	106 Airbn (1)																415	42	9,305	50	2,933
Mosc	Art Dv (1)							95	36	144	23,535						36	27	1,762		
M+20																					
USSR																					
Byel	MR Dv (2)			65		7,345		24	5	18	3,966		12		518		476	24	10,113	50	3,071
Carp	70 MR Dv (2)			65		7,345		24	5	18	3,966		12		518		476	24	10,113	50	3,071
Bait	1 MR Dv (2)			65		7,345		24	5	18	3,966		12		518		476	24	10,113	50	3,071
M+25																					
USSR																					
Byel	8 Tk Dv (2)			70		7,910		16	5	36	4,900		4		173		166		3,196	50	3,071
Carp	128 MR Dv (2)			65		7,910		24	5	18	3,966		12		518		476	24	10,113	50	3,071
Bait	1 Tk Dv (2)			70		7,910		16	5	36	4,900		4		173		166		3,196	50	3,071
M+30																					
USSR																					
Byel	29 Tk Dv (2)			70		7,910		16	5	36	4,900		4		173		166		3,196	50	3,071
Byel	3 Tk Dv (2)			70		7,910		16	5	36	4,900		4		173		166		3,196	50	3,071
Byel	27 Tk Dv (2)			70		7,910		16	5	36	4,900		4		173		166		3,196	50	3,071
Carp	61 MR Dv (2)			65		7,345		24	5	18	3,966		12		518		476	24	10,113	50	3,071
Carp	24 MR Dv (2)			65		7,910		24	5	18	3,966		12		518		476	24	10,113	50	3,071
Carp	13 Tk Dv (2)			70		7,910		16	5	36	4,900		4		173		166		3,196	50	3,071
Bait	40 Tk Dv (2)			68		7,721		16	5	36	4,900		4		173		166		3,196	50	3,071
Bait	24 Tk Dv (2)			68		7,721		16	5	36	4,900		4		173		166		3,196	50	3,071
Pol	4 MR Dv (2)						27								1,063		313	18	5,474		
Pom	7 Assault (2)																140	13	3,103		

M+35														
USSR														
Byel	47 Tk Dv (2)	70	7,910	16	5	36	4,900	4	173	166		3,196	50	3,071
Byel	34 Tk Dv (2)	68	7,721	16	5	36	4,900	4	173	166		3,196	50	3,071
Byel	Art A Dv (2)			95	36	144	23,535			36	27	1,762		
Byel	Art B Dv (2)			20	8	31	5,032							
Carp	117 Tk Dv (2)	68	7,721	16	5	36	4,900	4	173	166		3,196	48	2,971
Carp	Art A Dv (2)			95	36	144	23,535			36	27	1,762		
Carp	Art B Dv (2)			20	8	31	5,032							
Carp	Art A Dv (2)			95	36	144	23,535			36	27	1,762		
Balt	Art A Dv (2)			95	36	144	23,535			36	27	1,762		
Balt	Art A Dv (2)			95	36	144	23,535			36	27	1,762		
M+40														
Czech														
West	4 Tk Dv (2)			16	5	18	2,976			234	15	3,359	70	3,984
West	9 Tk Dv (2)			16	5	18	2,976			234	15	3,359	70	3,984
West	3 MR Dv (2)			20	3		1,834			372	27	6,813		
USSR														
Mosc	15 Tk Dv (2)	68	7,721	16	5	36	4,900	4	173	166		3,196	48	2,971
Mosc	4 Tk Dv (2)	68	7,721	16	5	36	4,900	4	173	166		3,196	48	2,971
M+45														
USSR														
Balt	3 MR Dv (3)			24	5		2,117	12	456	476	24	8,890	51	2,725
M+50														
USSR														
Len	64 MR Dv (3)			24	5		2,117	12	456	476	24	8,890	51	2,725

Table C-12. *continued*

Time; State; Military District	Unit Title; Readiness Category	TANKS TO&E T-55 / T-34	T-64	T-72	T-80	TANKS WUV: (WEI- CW 100)	ARTILLERY M-38 D-30 Oth	ARTILLERY TO&E MRL	152mm	M74	ARTILLERY WUV: (WEI- CW 92)	MORTAR Oth	MORTAR TO&E 82MM	120MM	MORTAR WUV: (WEI- CW 48)	ANTIARMOR T-21 Oth	T12	ANTIARMOR TO&E RPG7	ATGM	ANTIARMOR WUV: (WEI- CW 55)	IFV TO&E BMP	IFV WUV: (WEI- CW 69)
M+55																						
USSR																						
Carp	66 MR Dv (3)							24	5		2,117		12		456			476	24	8,890	51	2,725
Len	111 MR Dv (3)							24	5		2,117		12		456			476	24	8,890	51	2,725
M+60																						
USSR																						
Byel	50 MR Dv (3)							24	5		2,117		12		456			476	24	8,890	51	2,725
Len	77 MR Dv (3)							24	5		2,117		12		456			476	24	8,890	51	2,725
Balt	88 MR Dv (3)							24	5		2,117		12		456			476	24	8,890	51	2,725
Czech																						
East	13 Tk Dv (3)							16	5	18	2,976							234	15	3,359	70	3,984
East	14 Tk Dv (3)							16	5	18	2,976							234	15	3,359	70	3,984
M+65																						
USSR																						
Carp	17 MR Dv (3)							24	5		2,117		12		456			476	24	8,890	51	2,725
Balt	26 MR Dv (3)							24	5		2,117		12		456			476	24	8,890	51	2,725
Len	69 MR Dv (3)							24	5		2,117		12		456			476	24	8,890	51	2,725
M+70																						
USSR																						
Carp	97 MR Dv (3)							24	5		2,117		12		456			476	24	8,890	51	2,725
Balt	44 MR Dv (3)							24	5		2,117		12		456			476	24	8,890	51	2,725
Len	45 MR Dv (3)							24	5		2,117		12		456			476	24	8,890	51	2,725

M+75											
USSR											
Len	45 MR Dv (3)	24	5	2,117	12	456	476	24	8,890	51	2,725
Balt	107 MR Dv (3)	24	5	2,117	12	456	476	24	8,890	51	2,725
M+80											
USSR											
Mosc	13 MR Dv (3)	24	5	2,117	12	456	476	24	8,890	51	2,725
Vol	43 MR Dv (3)	24	5	2,117	12	456	476	24	8,890	51	2,725
Vol	Art A Dv (3)	95	36	144 / 23,535			36	27	1,762		
Czech											
East	15 MR Dv (3)	20	3	1,834			372	27	6,813		
Pol											
War	1 MR Dv (3)			27		1,063	313	18	5,474		
M+85											
USSR											
Mosc	32 MR Dv (3)	24	5	2,117	12	456	476	24	8,890	51	2,733
Vol	96 MR Dv (3)	24	5	2,117	12	456	476	24	8,890	51	2,733
Ural	77 MR Dv (3)	24	5	2,117	12	456	476	24	8,890	51	2,733
Czech											
East	19 MR Dv (3)	20	3	1,834			372	27	6,813		
Pol											
War	3 MR Dv (3)	20	3	1,834			313	18			
M+90											
USSR											
Vol	21 MR Dv (3)	24	5	2,117	12	456	476	24	8,890	51	2,733
Ural	MR Dv (3)	24	5	2,117	12	456	476	24	8,890	51	2,733
Czech											
East	20 MR Dv (3)	20	3	1,834			313	18	5,474		
Pol											
War	9 MR Dv (3)										

Table C-12. *continued*

Time; State; Military District	Unit Title; Readiness Category	T-55 T-34	T-64	T-72	T-80	WUV (WEI-CW 100)	M-38 D-30 0th	MRL	152mm	M74	WUV (WEI-CW 92)	0th	82MM	120MM	WUV (WEI-CW 48)	T-21 0th	T12	RPG7	ATGM	WUV (WEI-CW 55)	BMP	WUV (WEI-CW 69)
				TANKS TO&E					**ARTILLERY TO&E**				**MORTAR TO&E**					**ANTIARMOR TO&E**			**INFANTRY FIGHTING VEHICLES TO&E**	
ATTU Units Not Allocated to Central Front																						
USSR																						
NW	MR Dv (1)			60		6,813		24	3	18	3,803		12		518			476	24	10,113	51	3,142
NW	MR Dv (1)			60		6,813		24	3	18	3,803		12		518			476	24	10,113	51	3,142
NW	MR Dv (1)			60		6,813		24	3	18	3,803		12		518			476	24	10,113	51	3,142
NW	MR Dv (1)			60		6,813		24	3	18	3,803		12		518			476	24	10,113	51	3,142
NW	MR Dv (1)			60		6,813		24	3	18	3,803		12		518			476	24	10,113	51	3,142
NW	MR Dv (1)			60		6,813		24	3	18	3,803		12		518			476	24	10,113	51	3,142
NW	MR Dv (1)			60		6,813		24	3	18	3,803		12		518			476	24	10,113	51	3,142
NW	MR Dv (1)			60		6,813		24	3	18	3,803		12		518			476	24	10,113	51	3,142
SW	MR Dv (1)			60		6,813		24	3	18	3,803		12		518			476	24	10,113	51	3,142
SW	MR Dv (1)			60		6,813		24	3	18	3,803		12		518			476	24	10,113	51	3,142
SW	Art A Dv (1)							95		144	20,587							36	27	1,762		
SW	MR Dv (1)			60		6,813		24	3	18	3,803		12		518			476	24	10,113	51	3,142
SW	MR Dv (1)			60		6,813		24	3	18	3,803		12		518			476	24	10,113	51	3,142
SW	MR Dv (1)			60		6,813		24	3	18	3,803		12		518			476	24	10,113	51	3,071
SW	MR Dv (1)			60		6,813		24	3	18	3,803		12		518			476	24	10,113	51	3,071
SW	MR Dv (1)			60		6,813		24	3	18	3,803		12		518			476	24	10,113	51	3,071
SW	MR Dv (1)			60		6,813		24	3	18	3,803		12		518			476	24	10,113	51	3,071
SW	MR Dv (1)			60		6,813		24	3	18	3,803		12		518			476	24	10,113	50	3,071
SW	MR Dv (1)			60		6,813		24	3	18	3,803		12		518			476	24	10,113	50	3,071
SW	MR Dv (1)			60		6,813		24	3	18	3,803		12		518			476	24	10,113	50	3,071
SW	MR Dv (1)			60		6,813		24	3	18	3,803		12		518			476	24	10,113	50	3,071
SW	MR Dv (1)			60		6,813		24	3	18	3,803		12		518			476	24	10,113	50	3,071
SW	MR Dv (1)			60		6,813		24	3	18	3,803		12		518			476	24	10,113	50	3,071
SW	Tk Dv (1)			68		7,721				36	3,180		4		173			166		3,196	48	2,971
SW	Tk Dv (1)			68		7,721				36	3,180		4		173			166		3,196	48	2,971
SW	Tk Dv (1)			68		7,721				36	3,180		4		173			166		3,196	48	2,971
SW	Tk Dv (1)			68		7,721				36	3,180		4		173			166		3,196	48	2,971
SW	Tk Dv (1)			68		7,721				36	3,180		4		173			166		3,196	48	2,971

SW	Tk Dv (1)	68	7,721			36	3,180	4	173	166		3,196	48	2,971
SW	Tk Dv (1)	68	7,721			36	3,180	4	173	166		3,196	48	2,971
SW	Tk Dv (1)	68	7,721			36	3,180	4	173	166		3,196	48	2,971
SW	Tk Dv (1)	68	7,721			36	3,180	4	173	166		3,196	48	2,971
SW	Art A Dv (1)	68	7,721			36	3,180	4	173	36	27	1,762	48	2,971
Hun	MR Dv (1)			20	3		1,834			372	27	6,813		
Hun	MR Dv (1)			20	3		1,834			372	27	6,813		
Hun	MR Dv (1)			20	3		1,834			372	27	6,813		
Hun	MR Dv (1)			20	3		1,834			372	27	6,813		
Hun	MR Dv (1)			20	3		1,834			372	27	6,813		
Hun	MR Dv (1)			20	3		1,834			372	27	6,813		
Rom	MR Dv (1)			20	3		1,834			372	27	6,813		
Rom	MR Dv (1)			20	3		1,834			372	27	6,813		
Rom	MR Dv (1)			20	3		1,834			372	27	6,813		
Rom	MR Dv (1)			20	3		1,621			372	27	6,813		
Rom	MR Dv (1)			20	3		1,621			372	27	6,813		
Rom	MR Dv (1)			20	3		1,621			372	27	6,813		
Rom	MR Dv (1)			20	3		1,621			372	27	6,813		
Bul	MR Dv (1)			16	3	18	2,855	12	518	234	15	3,359	70	3,984
Bul	MR Dv (1)			16	3	18	2,855	12	518	234	15	3,359	70	3,984
Bul	MR Dv (1)			16	3	18	2,855	12	518	234	15	3,359	70	3,984
Bul	MR Dv (1)			16	3	18	2,855	12	518	234	15	3,359	70	3,984
Bul	MR Dv (1)			16	3	18	2,855	12	518	234	15	3,359	70	3,984
S	MR Dv (1)	60	6,813	24	3	18	3,803	12	518	476	24	10,113	50	3,074
S	MR Dv (1)	60	6,813	24	3	18	3,803	12	518	476	24	10,113	50	3,074
S	MR Dv (1)	60	6,813	24	3	18	3,803	12	518	476	24	10,113	50	3,074
S	MR Dv (1)	60	6,813	24	3	18	3,803	12	518	476	24	10,113	50	3,074
S	MR Dv (1)	60	6,813	24	3	18	3,803	12	518	476	24	10,113	50	3,074
S	MR Dv (1)	60	6,813	24	3	18	3,803	12	518	476	24	10,113	50	3,074
S	Tk Dv (1)	63	7,160	14		36	4,584			166		3,196	42	
S	Art A Dv (1)					144	12,718	4	173	36	27	1,762		2,561

Table C-12. continued

M+1 to M+5

USSR

Time; State; Military District	Unit Title; Readiness Category	ARV: OT65 Oth	BRDM	BMP	AT5	WUV: (WEI-CW 62)	ARV	APC	WUV: (WEI-CW 36)	Small Arms TO&E	WUV: (WEI-CW 3.3)	UNIT WUV: Division Total
GSFG	16 Tk Dv (1)			12	9	1,347				1,176	3,881	52,538
GSFG	21 MR Dv (1)			20		1,277				2,537	8,372	41,854
GSFG	94 MR Dv (1)			20		1,277				2,537	8,372	41,854
GSFG	207 MR Dv (1)			20		1,277				2,537	8,372	41,854
GSFG	Art Bg (1)									20	66	5,098
GSFG	Art Bg (1)									20	66	5,098
GSFG	Other Bts (1)									144	475	1,559
GSFG	7 Tk Dv (1)			12	9	1,347				1,176	3,881	24,432
GSFG	10 Tk Dv (1)			12	9	1,347				1,176	3,881	50,728
GSFG	72 Tk Dv (1)			12	9	1,347				1,176	3,881	24,432
GSFG	47 Tk Dv (1)			12	9	1,347				1,176	3,881	51,101
GSFG	304 Art Bg (1)									898	2,963	6,745
GSFG	Other Bts (1)									144	475	1,559
GSFG	25 Tk Dv (1)			12	9	1,347				1,176	3,881	24,432
GSFG	32 Tk Dv (1)			12	9	1,347				1,176	3,881	24,432
GSFG	90 Tk Dv (1)			12	9	1,347				1,176	3,881	51,101
GSFG	35 MR Dv (1)			20		1,277				2,537	8,372	39,990
GSFG	71 Art Bg (1)									898	2,963	6,745
GSFG	Other Bts (1)									144	475	1,559
GSFG	79 Tk Dv (1)			12	9	1,347				1,176	3,881	51,101
GSFG	27 MR Dv (1)			20		1,277				2,537	8,372	39,990
GSFG	39 MR Dv (1)			20		1,277				2,537	8,372	39,990
GSFG	57 MR Dv (1)			20		1,277				2,537	8,372	39,990
GSFG	43 Art Bg (1)									898	2,963	6,745
GSFG	Other Bts (1)									144	475	1,559
GSFG	9 Tk Dv (1)			12	9	1,347				1,176	3,881	51,101
GSFG	11 Tk Dv (1)			12	9	1,347				1,176	3,881	50,757
GSFG	20 MR Dv (1)			20		1,277				2,537	8,372	39,990
GSFG	43 Art Dv (1)									254	838	26,135
GSFG	35 Assault(1)									851	2,808	6,876
GSFG	MR Bg (1)									221	859	859
GSFG	Spetsnaz (1)									515	1,700	4,021
GSFG	Other Bts (1)									67	221	859
CGF	15 Tk Dv (1)			12	9	1,347				1,176	3,881	24,087
CGF	18 MR Dv (1)			20		1,277				2,537	8,372	39,990
CGF	48 MR Dv (1)			20		1,277				2,537	8,372	39,990
CGF	Art Bg (1)									20	66	5,098
CGF	Other Bts (1)									67	221	859

	Unit						
M+5							
USSR							
NGF	20 Tk Dv (1)	12		1,347	1,176	3,881	50,757
NGF	6 MR Dv (1)	20	9	1,277	2,537	8,372	39,990
GDR							
III	7 Tk Dv (1)	15		958	945	3,119	16,953
III	11 MR Dv (1)	18		1,149	2,482	8,191	23,002
III	4 MR Dv (1)	18		1,149	2,482	8,191	23,002
III	Art Rt (1)				29	96	2,623
III	9 Tk Dv (1)	15		958	945	3,119	16,953
III	8 MR Dv (1)	18		1,149	2,482	8,191	23,002
III	1 MR Dv (1)	18		1,149	2,482	8,191	23,002
	Art Rt (1)				29	96	2,623
Czech							
West	1 Tk Dv (1)	12		766	1,486	4,904	20,200
West	2 MR Dv (1)				9,868	32,564	48,090
West	22 Assault(1)				67	221	859
West	Other Bts (1)				416	1,373	5,066
Pol							
War	6 Assault(1)				2,563	8,458	21,677
M+10							
Pol							
Pom	16 Tk Dv (1)	13		830	1,024	3,379	6,124
Pom	20 Tk Dv (1)	13		830	1,024	3,379	19,499
Pom	12 MR Dv (1)	13		830	2,778	9,167	25,903
Pom	8 MR Dv (1)				2,778	9,167	25,903
Pom	Art Rt (1)				29	96	2,623
Sil	5 Tk Dv (1)	13		830	1,024	3,379	19,499
Sil	10 Tk Dv (1)	13		830	1,024	3,379	19,499
Sil	11 Tk Dv (1)				1,024	3,379	6,124
Sil	Art Rt (1)				29	96	2,623
War	Art Rt (1)				29	96	272
USSR							
Byel	120 MR Dv (1)	20		1,277	2,537	8,372	44,881
Byel	8 Tk Dv (1)	12	9	1,347	1,176	3,881	52,674
Carp	15 MR Dv (1)	20		1,277	2,537	8,372	44,881
Carp	23 Tk Dv (1)	12	9	1,347	1,176	3,881	52,674
Balt	7 Airbn (1)				2,563	8,458	20,696
SGF	93 MR Dv (1)	20		1,277	2,537	8,372	39,118
SGF	13 MR Dv (1)	20		1,277	2,537	8,372	39,118
SGF	2 Tk Dv (1)	12	9	1,347	1,176	3,881	47,202
SGF	13 Tk Dv (1)	12	9	1,347	1,176	3,881	24,087

Table C-12. *continued*

Time; State; Military District	Unit Title; Readiness Category	ARMORED RECONNAISSANCE VEHICLES TO&E					ARMORED PERS CARRIERS TO&E			SMALL ARMS		UNIT
		OT65 Oth	BRDM	BMP	AT5	WUV: (WEI-CW 62)	ARV	APC	WUV: (WEI-CW 36)	TO&E	WUV: (WEI-CW 3.3)	WUV: Division Total
M+15												
USSR												
Mosc	MR Dv (1)			20		1,277				2,537	8,372	44,881
Mosc	2 MR Dv (1)			20		1,277				2,537	8,372	44,881
Mosc	106 Airbn (1)									2,563	8,458	20,696
Mosc	Art Dv (1)									254	838	26,135
M+20												
USSR												
Byel	MR Dv (2)			20	18	2,438				2,649	8,742	36,193
Carp	70 MR Dv (2)			20	18	2,438				2,649	8,742	36,193
Balt	I MR Dv (2)			20	18	2,438				2,649	8,742	36,193
M+25												
USSR												
Byel	8 Tk Dv (2)			12	9	1,347				1,098	3,623	24,219
Carp	128 MR Dv (2)			20	18	2,438				2,649	8,742	36,193
Balt	1 Tk Dv (2)			12	9	1,347				1,098	3,623	24,219
M+30												
USSR												
Byel	29 Tk Dv (2)			12	9	1,347				1,098	3,623	24,219
Byel	3 Tk Dv (2)			12	9	1,347				1,098	3,623	24,219
Byel	27 Tk Dv (2)			12	9	1,347				1,098	3,623	24,219
Carp	61 MR Dv (2)			20	18	2,438				2,649	8,742	36,193
Carp	24 MR Dv (2)			20	18	2,438				2,649	8,742	36,193
Carp	13 Tk Dv (2)			12	9	1,347				1,098	3,623	24,219
Balt	40 Tk Dv (2)			12	9	1,347				1,098	3,623	24,031
Balt	24 Tk Dv (2)			12	9	1,347				1,098	3,623	24,031
Pol												
Sil	4 MR Dv (2)			13		830				2,482	8,191	15,557
Pom	7 Assualt (2)									855	2,822	5,924

M+35							
USSR							
Byel	47 Tk Dv (2)	12	9	1,347	1,098	3,623	24,219
Byel	34 Tk Dv (2)	12	9	1,347	1,098	3,623	24,031
Byel	Art A Dv (2)				254	838	26,135
Byel	Art B Dv (2)				20	66	5,098
Carp	117 Tk Dv (2)	12	9	1,347	1,098	3,623	23,931
Carp	Art A Dv (2)				254	838	26,135
Carp	Art B Dv (2)				20	66	5,098
Carp	Art B Dv (2)				20	66	5,098
Balt	Art A Dv (2)				254	838	26,135
Balt	Art A Dv (2)				254	838	26,135
M+40							
Czech							
West	4 Tk Dv (2)	12		710	1,379	4,551	15,580
West	9 Tk Dv (2)	12		710	1,379	4,551	15,580
West	3 MR Dv (2)				2,446	8,072	16,718
USSR							
Mosc	15 Tk Dv (2)	12	9	1,347	1,098	3,623	23,931
Mosc	4 Tk Dv (2)	12	9	1,347	1,098	3,623	23,931
M+45							
USSR							
Balt	3 MR Dv (3)	20	18	2,145	2,309	7,620	23,953
M+50							
USSR							
Len	64 MR Dv (3)	20	18	2,145	2,309	7,620	23,953

Table C-12. *continued*

Time; State; Military District	Unit Title; Readiness Category	ARMORED RECONNAISSANCE VEHICLES TO&E OT65 Oth	BRDM	BMP	AT5	WUV: (WEI-CW 62)	ARMORED PERS CARRIERS TO&E ARV	APC	WUV: (WEI-CW 36)	SMALL ARMS TO&E	WUV: (WEI-CW 3.3)	UNIT WUV: Division Total
M+55												
USSR												
Carp	66 MR Dv (3)			20	18	2,145				2,309	7,620	23,953
Len	111 MR Dv (3)			20	18	2,145				2,309	7,620	23,953
M+60												
USSR												
Byel	50 MR Dv (3)			20	18	2,145				2,309	7,620	23,953
Len	77 MR Dv i(3)			20	18	2,145				2,309	7,620	23,953
Balt	88 MR Dv (3)			20	18	2,145				2,309	7,620	23,953
Czech												
East	13 Tk Dv (3)			12		710				1,379	4,551	15,580
East	14 Tk Dv (3)			12		710				1,379	4,551	15,580
M+65												
USSR												
Carp	17 MR Dv (3)			20	18	2,145				2,309	7,620	23,953
Balt	26 MR Dv (3)			20	18	2,145				2,309	7,620	23,953
Len	69 MR Dv (3)			20	18	2,145				2,309	7,620	23,953
M+70												
USSR												
Carp	97 MR Dv (3)			20	18	2,145				2,309	7,620	23,953
Balt	44 MR Dv (3)			20	18	2,145				2,309	7,620	23,953
Len	45 MR Dv (3)			20	18	2,145				2,309	7,620	23,953

M+75						
USSR						
Len	45 MR Dv (3)	20	18	2,145	2,309	7,620	23,953
Balt	107 MR Dv (3)	20	18	2,145	2,309	7,620	23,953
M+80						
USSR						
Mosc	13 MR Dv (3)	20	18	2,145	2,309	7,620	23,953
Vol	43 MR Dv (3)	20	18	2,145	2,309	7,620	23,953
Vol	Art A Dv (3)				254	838	26,135
Czech East	15 MR Dv (3)				2,446	8,072	16,718
Pol War	1 MR Dv (3)				2,479	8,181	14,717
M+85						
USSR						
Mosc	32 MR Dv (3)	20	18	2,145	2,309	7,620	23,962
Vol	96 MR Dv (3)	20	18	2,145	2,309	7,620	23,962
Ural	77 MR Dv (3)	20	18	2,145	2,309	7,620	23,962
Czech East	19 MR Dv (3)				2,446	8,072	16,718
Pol War	3 MR Dv (3)						
M+90						
USSR						
Vol	21 MR Dv (3)	20	18	2,145	2,309	7,620	23,962
Ural	MR Dv (3)	20	18	2,145	2,309	7,620	23,962
Czech East	20 MR Dv (3)				2,446	8,072	9,906
Pol War	9 MR Dv (3)						5,474

Table C-12. *continued*

ATTU Units Not Allocated to Central Front
USSR

Time; State; Military District	Unit Title; Readiness Category	ARMORED RECONNAISSANCE VEHICLES TO&E: OT65 Oth	BRDM	BMP	AT5	WUV: (WEI-CW 62)	ARMORED PERS CARRIERS TO&E: ARV	APC	WUV: (WEI-CW 36)	SMALL ARMS TO&E	WUV: (WEI-CW 3.3)	UNIT WUV: Division Total
NW	MR Dv (1)			20	18	2,438				2,649	8,742	35,569
NW	MR Dv (1)			20	18	2,438				2,649	8,742	35,569
NW	MR Dv (1)			20	18	2,438				2,649	8,742	35,569
NW	MR Dv (1)			20	18	2,438				2,649	8,742	35,569
NW	MR Dv (1)			20	18	2,438				2,649	8,742	35,569
NW	MR Dv (1)			20	18	2,438				2,649	8,742	35,569
NW	MR Dv (1)			20	18	2,438				2,649	8,742	35,569
NW	MR Dv (1)			20	18	2,438				2,649	8,742	35,569
SW	MR Dv (1)			20	18	2,438				2,649	8,742	35,569
SW	MR Dv (1)			20	18	2,438				2,649	8,742	35,569
SW	Art A Dv (1)									254	838	23,188
SW	MR Dv (1)			20	18	2,438				2,649	8,742	35,569
SW	MR Dv (1)			20	18	2,438				2,649	8,742	35,569
SW	MR Dv (1)			20	18	2,438				2,649	8,742	35,569
SW	MR Dv (1)			20	18	2,438				2,649	8,742	35,569
SW	MR Dv (1)			20	18	2,438				2,649	8,742	35,569
SW	MR Dv (1)			20	18	2,438				2,649	8,742	35,569
SW	MR Dv (1)			20	18	2,438				2,649	8,742	35,497
SW	MR Dv (1)			20	18	2,438				2,649	8,742	35,497
SW	MR Dv (1)			20	18	2,438				2,649	8,742	35,497
SW	MR Dv (1)			20	18	2,438				2,649	8,742	35,497
SW	MR Dv (1)			20	18	2,438				2,649	8,742	35,497
SW	MR Dv (1)			20	18	2,438				2,649	8,742	35,497
SW	MR Dv (1)			20	18	2,438				2,649	8,742	35,497
SW	MR Dv (1)			20	18	2,438				2,649	8,742	35,497
SW	Tk Dv (1)			12	9	1,347				1,098	3,623	22,210
SW	Tk Dv (1)			12	9	1,347				1,098	3,623	22,210
SW	Tk Dv (1)			12	9	1,347				1,098	3,623	22,210
SW	Tk Dv (1)			12	9	1,347				1,098	3,623	22,210
SW	Tk Dv (1)			12	9	1,347				1,098	3,623	22,210
SW	Tk Dv (1)			12	9	1,347				1,098	3,623	22,210

SW	Tk Dv (1)	12	9	1,347	1,098	3,623	22,210
SW	Tk Dv (1)	12	9	1,347	1,098	3,623	22,210
SW	Tk Dv (1)	12	9	1,347	1,098	3,623	22,210
SW	Tk Dv (1)	12	9	1,347	1,098	3,623	22,210
SW	Art A Dv (1)				254	838	2,600
Hun	MR Dv (1)				2,446	8,072	16,718
Hun	MR Dv (1)				2,446	8,072	16,718
Hun	MR Dv (1)				2,446	8,072	16,718
Hun	MR Dv (1)				2,446	8,072	16,718
Hun	MR Dv (1)				2,446	8,072	16,718
Hun	MR Dv (1)				2,446	8,072	16,718
Rom	MR Dv (1)				2,446	8,072	16,718
Rom	MR Dv (1)				2,446	8,072	16,718
Rom	MR Dv (1)				2,446	8,072	16,718
Rom	MR Dv (1)				2,446	8,072	16,718
Rom	MR Dv (1)				2,446	8,072	16,718
Rom	MR Dv (1)				2,446	8,072	16,506
Rom	MR Dv (1)				2,446	8,072	16,506
Rom	MR Dv (1)				2,446	8,072	16,506
Rom	MR Dv (1)				2,446	8,072	16,506
Bul	MR Dv (1)	12		710	1,379	4,551	15,459
Bul	MR Dv (1)	12		710	1,379	4,551	15,459
Bul	MR Dv (1)	12		710	1,379	4,551	15,459
Bul	MR Dv (1)	12		710	1,379	4,551	15,459
Bul	MR Dv (1)	12		710	1,379	4,551	15,459
S	MR Dv (1)	20	18	2,438	2,649	8,742	35,500
S	MR Dv (1)	20	18	2,438	2,649	8,742	35,500
S	MR Dv (1)	20	18	2,438	2,649	8,742	35,500
S	MR Dv (1)	20	18	2,438	2,649	8,742	35,500
S	MR Dv (1)	20	18	2,438	2,649	8,742	35,500
S	MR Dv (1)	20	18	2,438	2,649	8,742	35,500
S	Tk Dv (1)	12	9	1,347	1,098	3,623	22,644
S	Art A Dv (1)				254	838	15,318

Notes to Table C-12

See the notes to table C-1 for methodology and sources.

This reduction was executed in one stage, with Soviet force levels after the CFE I reductions as the starting point. The alliancewide limit forces the WTO to accept reductions of 8,333 in tanks, 9,901 in artillery, and 11,666 in armored vehicles. Conservatively, it was assumed that one-third of the cuts would be taken by the non-Soviet WTO nations, one-third by non-Western TVD Soviet forces, and one-third by Soviet central reserve forces oriented toward the central front. These groupings were assumed to cut where it would reduce the WEI/WUV score the least and, ceteris paribus, to cut the latest-arriving units first.

TABLE C-13. WTO Weapon Totals and ADE Mobilization Schedule Derived from Table C-12, after CFE II

TANKS

WEAPONS AND CFE II CONDITIONS	TOTAL	Tank: T-34/T-55	Tank: T-64	Tank: T-72	Tank: T-80
ALLIANCEWIDE					
CFE II limit: "Alliancewide"	10,000				
WTO Tanks including spares, "Alliancewide"	20,000				
WTO Tank TO&E "Alliancewide" before reduction	16,667				
Reductions in WTO Tank TO&E "Alliancewide"	−8,333				
WTO Tank TO&E "Alliancewide" after reduction	8,334				
ATTU including spares	10,000				
ATTU TO&E	8,334			5,658	2,676
Central Front including spares	6,644				
Central Front TO&E	5,537			2,861	2,676

ARTILLERY

WEAPONS AND CFE II CONDITIONS	TOTAL	Arty: 122 M-38	Arty: MRL	Arty: 152 D-1	Arty: 122 M74	Mortar: 120MM	Antiarmor: T-21	Antiarmor: 100MM
ALLIANCEWIDE								
CFE II limit: "Alliancewide"	12,000							
WTO Artillery including spares, "Alliancewide"	23,882							
WTO Artillery TO&E "Alliancewide" before reduction	19,901							
Reductions in WTO Artillery TO&E "Alliancewide"	−9901							
WTO Artillery TO&E "Alliancewide" after reduction	10,000							
ATTU including spares	11,998							
ATTU TO&E	9,998		4,093	905	5,000			
Central Front including spares	8,470							
Central Front TO&E	7,058		2,701	743	3,614			

ARMORED VEHICLES

ALLIANCEWIDE

CFE II limit: "Alliancewide"	14,000
WTO Armored Vehicles including spares, "Alliancewide"	28,000
WTO Armored Vehicles TO&E "Alliancewide" before reduction	23,333
Reductions in WTO Armored Vehicles TO&E "Alliancewide"	-11,666
WTO Armored Vehicles TO&E "Alliancewide" after reduction	11,667

	Total	ARV: OT-65	ARV: BRDM	ARV: BMP-R	ARV: BRDM AT5	APC: ARV	APC: APC	IFV: BMP
ATTU including spares	13,996		28	2,372	1,485			7,806
ATTU TO&E	11,663							
Central Front including spares	8,981		28	1,500	774			5,210
Central Front TO&E	7,484							

CENTRAL FRONT MOBILIZATION SCHEDULE AFTER CFE II

Days After M+0	M+1	M+5	M+10	M+15	M+20	M+25	M+30	M+35	M+40
ADE arrival	6.5	6.4	5.0	1.4	1.1	.9	2.4	1.9	1.0
Total ADEs	6.5	12.9	17.9	19.3	20.4	21.2	23.6	25.6	26.5
WUV Arrival	644,676	640,237	493,405	136,594	108,580	84,632	238,806	192,018	95,740
Total WUV	644,676	1,284,913	1,778,318	1,914,912	2,023,492	2,108,123	2,346,930	2,538,948	2,634,688

Days After M+0	M+45	M+50	M+55	M+60	M+65	M+70	M+75	M+80	M+85	M+90
ADE arrival	.2	.2	.5	1.0	.7	.7	.5	1.1	.9	.6
Total ADEs	26.8	27.0	27.5	28.5	29.3	30.0	30.5	31.5	32.4	33.1
WUV Arrival	23,953	23,953	47,906	103,019	71,859	71,859	47,906	105,477	88,603	63,302
Total WUV	2,658,641	2,682,594	2,730,500	2,833,518	2,905,377	2,977,236	3,025,142	3,130,619	3,219,222	3,282,525

Source: Data given in table C-12

Table C-14. **NATO Units, Central Front Arrival Times, and WUV Scores, after CFE II**

STATE; CORPS	DIVISION	BRIGADE	REGIMENT	ORIGINAL LOCATION	CORPS SECTOR	DAY	TANKS TO&E	TANKS WEI	TANKS (WEI-CW 100)	ARTILLERY TO&E	ARTILLERY WEI	ARTILLERY (WEI-CW 92)
Netherlands							CENT — LEO 1			M-108 — 155HOW		
I Netherlands	4th Mech	41,42,43			2	M+5	131	134	13,362	90	75	6,872
I Netherlands	5th Mech	51,52,53			2	M+5	131	134	13,362	90	75	6,872
I Netherlands	1st Mech	11,12,13		Schaarsbergen, NE	2	M+10	132	135	13,464	90	75	6,872
Belgium							CENT — LEO 1 CHIEF			M-108 — 155HOW		
I Belgian	16th Mech	4 mech, 17 Arm		Soest, FRG	4	M+1	11 80	106	10,562	31 18	40	3,682
I Belgian	1st Div	1 mech, 7 mech		Liege, BE	4	M+1	11 40	58	5,842	31 18	40	3,682
I Belgian		10 mech		Zonhoven, BE	4	M+10	0 12	14	1,416	10 7	14	1,301
I Belgian		12 mot		Liege, BE	4	M+10	0 12	14	1,416	10 7	14	1,301
Denmark							CENT LEO 1 CHIEF			M-108 155HOW		
Jutland	Jutland	1, 2, 3 mech inf		Rendsburg, FRG	1	M+15	0 97	99	9,894	121 72	158	14,512
United Kingdom							CENT LEO 1 CHIEF			105MM 155HOW M110		
I British	1 Arm	7, 12, 22		Verden, FRG	3	M+1	0 84	99	9,912	24 12 3	34	3,146
I British	4 Arm	11, 20, 30 Arm		Herford, FRG	3	M+1	0 84	99	9,912	24 12 3	34	3,146
I British	2 Inf	15, 24, 49 inf		York, UK	3	M+1	0 84	99	9,912	24 12 3	34	3,146
I British	Art Div		4 reg	York, UK	3	M+1	0			35 20 12	60	5,492
British		5 Air		Aldershot, UK	3	M+5	0			8	7	633
I British	3 Arm	4 Arm, 6 Arm, 19 inf		Soest, FRG	3	M+10	0 84	99	9,912	24 12 3	34	3,146
UKMF		1 Inf		Tidworth, UK	1	M+10	0			8	7	633
UKMF		Other Btlns		Tidworth, UK	3	M+10	0			8	7	633
Canada							M-48 CENT LEO 1			105MM 155HOW M110		
C. F. Europe	4 Mech			Lahr, FRG	Reserve	M+5	0 45	41	4,050	110 30	121	11,132
Mobile Command	5e Groupe-Brig			Valcar, CA	Reserve	M+10	20 0	18	1,800	10	9	810
Mobile Command	5e Groupe-Brig			Calgary, CA	Reserve	M+25	30 0	27	2,700	10	9	810

France						B2 AMX	CENT	LEO 1	CHIEF			105MM	155HOW	M110		
FAR	4th Air		Nancy, FR	Reserve	M+5		0	0								
FAR	9th lt Arm		Nimes, FR	Reserve	M+5	35	0	0		30	2,996		24		18	1,656
FAR	11th Air		Toulouse, FR	Reserve	M+5		0	0					24		18	1,656
II	3rd Arm		Freiburg, FRG	Reserve	M+10	58	0	0		49	4,909		24		18	1,656
II	5th Arm		Landau, FRG	Reserve	M+10	58	0	0		49	4,909		24		18	1,656
I	1st Arm		Trier, FRG	Reserve	M+10	58	0	0		49	4,909		24		18	1,656
FAR	27th Mou		Grenoble, FR	Reserve	M+10	58	0	0		49	4,909		24		18	1,656
II	15th Inf		Limoges, FR	Reserve	M+15	25	0	0		21	2,104		24		18	1,656
I	12th lt Arm		Saumar, FR	Reserve	M+15	35	0	0		30	2,996		24		18	1,656
I	14th lt Arm		Montpellier, FR	Reserve	M+15	38	0	0		32	3,188		24		18	1,656
III	2nd Arm		Versailles, FR	Reserve	M+15	58	0	0		49	4,909		24		18	1,656
III	8th Inf		Amiens, FR	Reserve	M+15	25	0	0		21	2,104		24		18	1,656
III	10th Arm		Chalons, FR	Reserve	M+15	58	0	0		49	4,909		24		18	1,656
I	7th Arm		Besancon, FR	Reserve	M+20	58	0	0		49	4,909		24		18	1,656
West Germany						M-48	LEO 1	LEO 1	LEO 2			Var	155HOW	MLRS		
I Korps	1st Arm	1, 2 Arm, 3 Inf	Hanover, FRG	3	M+1		6	0	150	189	18,912		54	16	61	5,595
I Korps	3rd Arm	7 A/I,8 Arm,9 Arm	Buxtehude, FRG	2	M+1		5	0	200	249	24,910		54	16	61	5,595
I Korps	6th A/I	16,17 A/I,18 Arm	Neumunster, FRG	1	M+1		5	0	150	188	18,810		54	16	61	5,595
I Korps	7th Arm	19,20 Arm,21 A/I	Westphalia, FRG	3	M+1		5	0	200	249	24,910		54	16	61	5,595
II Korps	4th A/I	10,11 A/I,12 Arm	Regensburg, FRG	8	M+1		5	0	150	188	18,810		54	16	61	5,595
II Korps	1st Mountain	22 A/I,23 mou,24 Arm	Garmisch, FRG	8	M+1		5	0	100	127	12,710		54	16	61	5,595
III Korps	2nd A/I	4,5 A/I,6 Arm	Regensburg, FRG	5	M+1		5	0	150	188	18,810		54	16	61	5,595
III Korps	12th Arm	34 Arm,35 A/I,36 Arm	Garmisch, FRG	6	M+1		5	0	200	249	24,910		54	16	61	5,595
I Korps	11th A/I	31,32 A/I,33 Arm	Oldenburg, FRG	2	M+5		5	0	150	188	18,810		54	16	61	5,595
II Korps	10th Arm	28,29 Arm,30 A/I	Sigmaringen, FRG	8	M+5		5	0	200	249	24,910		54	16	61	5,595
II Korps	1st Air	25,26,27 airborne	Bruchsal, FRG	8	M+5		0	0					54	16	61	5,595
III Korps	5th Arm	14,15 Arm,13 A/I	Sigmaringen, FRG	5	M+5		5	0	200	249	24,910		54	16	61	5,595
Terr Army SH		51 Home Defence	Keil, FRG	1	M+5		0	0				16	18		27	2,464
Terr Army South		56 Home Defence	Munich, FRG	8	M+5		0	0				16	18		27	2,464
Terr Army North		52 Home Defence	Hanover, FRG	3	M+10		0	0				16	18		27	2,464
Terr Army North		62 Home Defence	Hanover, FRG	Reserve	M+10		0	0				16	18		27	2,464
Terr Army North		53 Home Defence	Dusseldorf, FRG	4	M+10		0	0				16	18		27	2,464
Terr Army North		63 Home Defence	Dusseldorf, FRG	Reserve	M+10		0	0				16	18		27	2,464
Terr Army South		52 Home Defence	Mainz, FRG	5	M+10		0	0				16	18		27	2,464
Terr Army South		62 Home Defence	Trier, FRG	Reserve	M+10		0	0				16	18		27	2,464
Terr Army South		55 Home Defence	Stuttgart, FRG	8	M+10		0	0				16	18		27	2,464
Terr Army SH		61 Home Defence	Keil, FRG	Reserve	M+15		0	0				16	18		27	2,464
Terr Army South		66 Home Defence	Munich, FRG	Reserve	M+15		0	0				16	18		27	2,464
Terr Army South		65 Home Defence	Stuttgart, FRG	Reserve	M+20		0	0				16	18		27	2,464

Table C-14. *continued*

STATE: CORPS	DIVISION	BRIGADE	REGIMENT	ORIGINAL LOCATION	CORPS SECTOR	DAY	TANKS TO&E M-48	M-60A1	M-60A2	M-1	WEI	(WEI-CW 100)	ARTILLERY TO&E Var M110	155HOW	GSRS	WEI	(WEI-CW 92)
United States																	
VII US	1st Arm	1,2,3	+ Art	Frankfurt, FRG	7	M+1		0	0	143	187	18,668		72	9	84	7,717
VII US		Art	17,72,210	Stuttgart, FRG	7	M+1		0	0				36	100		137	12,630
V US	3rd Arm	1,2,3	+ Art	Frankfurt, FRG	6	M+1		0	0					72	9	84	7,717
V US		Art: 41,42			6	M+1		0	0	141	185	18,471	36	50		86	7,938
VII /III US	1st Inf	3	11 ACR	Fulda, FRG	6	M+1		0	0	46	60	5,993		25	3	29	2,666
III US	2nd Arm	3		Goppingen, FRG	7	M+1		0	0	61	80	7,958		15	9	32	2,909
VII US	3rd Inf	1,2,3	+ Art	Garstedt, FRG	2	M+1		0	0	46	60	5,993	6	25	3	29	2,666
VII US			2 ACR	Wurzburg, FRG	7	M+5		0	0	164	215	21,517	18	48	3	77	7,088
V US		+ Art		Nuremberg, FRG	7	M+5		0	0	40	52	5,207	16	24		40	3,695
V US	8th Inf (mech)	1,2,3	+ Art	Bad Kreuznach,FRG	Reserve	M+5		0	0	141	185	18,471		72	9	84	7,717
CONUS POMCUS																	
US	1st Inf	1,2		Ft. Riley KS	7	M+10		0	0	122	159	15,917	10	30		51	4,677
III US			3 ACR	Ft. Bliss TX	7	M+10		0	0	40	52	5,207	16	24		40	3,695
III US		Art : 212		Stuttgart, FRG	7	M+10		0	0					54		55	5,067
I US	7th Inf	1,2,3		Ft. Ord, CA	Reserve	M+15		0	0	8	11	1,081	18	48	9	77	7,088
I US	25th Inf	1,2,3		Schofield, HI	Reserve	M+15		0	0	8	11	1,081	18	48	9	77	7,088
III US	2nd Arm	1,2		Ft. Hood, TX	2	M+15		0	0	92	120	11,987		50	6	58	5,332
III US	1st Cav	1,2,155		Ft. Hood, TX	Reserve	M+15		0	0	141	185	18,471		72	9	84	7,717
III US	4th Inf (mech)	1,2,3		Ft. Carson, CO	2	M+15		0	0	141	185	18,471		72	9	84	7,717

Reserve and National Guard

Force	Group	Units	Location	Phase	M+Day	(a)	(b)	(c)	(d)	(e)	Equip	(g)	(h)	(i)	(j)	Pers	Total
III US		Art: 75,214	Ft. Knox, KY	Reserve	M+20			0	0		12,045		36	50		86	7,938
CONUS Res		194 Arm	Ft. Knox, KY	Reserve	M+25			0	20	120	12,045			25	3	29	2,666
CONUS Res		197 mech Inf	MA-CT-SC-RI	Reserve	M+32			20	0	120	22,766	18	18	25	3	29	2,666
NG	26th Inf	1,3,43	PA	Reserve	M+39	100		56		228	12,045			30	9	72	6,624
NG		157 mech Inf	PA-VA-WV	Reserve	M+46			20	0	120	12,045			25	3	29	2,666
NG	28th Inf	2,55,56	IN-IL-PA	Reserve	M+46	100		56		228	22,766	18	18	30	9	72	6,624
CONUS Res		Art: 428,424,479	MA-NY-ME	Reserve	M+53			0				36	36	100		137	12,630
NG		29 Inf	NC	Reserve	M+53	15	20	25	10	57	5,705	10	10			17	1,582
NG		30 Inf (mech)	OH-WV	Reserve	M+53	10	45	20		96	9,575	8	8	8		22	2,017
NG		33 Inf	OH-WV	Reserve	M+60	15	20	60		57	5,705	10	10			17	1,582
NG	107 ACR		NC	Reserve	M+60		60	25	10	127	9,575	16		24		36	3,341
NG		32 Inf (mech)	CO-KS-KY	Reserve	M+60	10	45	75	25	96	12,660	8	8	8		22	2,017
NG	35th Mech Inf	67,69,149	OH-WV	Reserve	M+67	32	150	60		298	9,575	24	24	24	12	66	6,050
NG	116 ACR		MD-VA	Reserve	M+67		60	0		127	12,660	16		24		36	3,341
NG		2,55,56	IN-MI-OH	Reserve	M+67	50	0	75	25	50	4,950	18	18			45	4,129
NG	29th lt Inf	2,46,76	OR	Reserve	M+74	32	150	20		298	29,768	24	24	24		66	6,050
NG	38th Mech Inf	41 Inf	WA	Reserve	M+74	15	20	25	10	57	5,705	10	10			17	1,582
NG		81 Inf (mech)	WI-RI-NC	Reserve	M+74	10	45	60		96	9,575	8	8	8		22	2,017
NG	163 ACR		OK	Reserve	M+74		60	20		127	12,660	16		24		36	3,341
NG		45 Inf	SC	Reserve	M+81	15	20	25	10	57	5,705	10	10			17	1,582
NG		218 Inf (mech)	IN-IL-PA	Reserve	M+81	10	45	60		96	9,575	8	8	8		22	2,017
NG		Art: 45,57,103	TN	Reserve	M+81		0	0			12,660		36	100		137	12,630
NG	278 ACR		FL	Reserve	M+81		60	60		127	12,660	16		24		36	3,341
NG		53 Inf	TN	Reserve	M+88	15	20	20	10	57	5,705	10	10	8		17	1,582
NG		30 Arm	OH	Reserve	M+88	20	45	45		87	8,700	8	8			22	2,017
NG		73 Inf	IN-IL-PA	Reserve	M+88	15	20	20		57	5,705	10	10			17	1,582
NG		Art: 113,115,118	IN-IL-PA	Reserve	M+88		0	0				36	36	100		137	12,630
NG		Art: 135,138,142	AL	Reserve	M+88			0				8	8	100		137	12,630
NG	42nd Inf	31 Arm	NY	Reserve	M+88	20	45	20		87	8,700	8	20	20		22	2,017
NG		1,2		Reserve	M+95	65	65	40	30	213	21,305	50	36			77	7,084
NG		Art: 196,197,209		Reserve	M+95			0					36	100		137	12,630
NG		Art: 147,151,169		Reserve	M+95			0					36	100		137	12,630
NG		Art: 227,163,631		Reserve	M+95			0					24	100		137	12,630
NG	49th Arm	1,2,3	TX-NM	Reserve	M+95	75	150	75	25	340	34,025	50	24	24		85	7,820
NG	50th Arm	1,2,86	NJ	Reserve	M+102	75	150	75	25	340	34,025	50	24	24		85	7,820

Table C-14. continued

STATE; CORPS	DIVISION	TANKS TO&E	TANKS WEI	TANKS (WEI-CW 100)	ARTILLERY TO&E	ARTILLERY WEI	ARTILLERY (WEI-CW 92)
ATTU Units Not Allocated to Central Front							
United Kingdom	Inf	21	25	2,478	16	14	1,266
	Inf	21	25	2,478	16	14	1,266
	Inf	21	25	2,478	16	14	1,266
	Inf	21	25	2,478	16	14	1,266
	Inf	21	25	2,478	16	14	1,266
	Inf	21	25	2,478	16	14	1,266
	Inf	21	25	2,478	16	14	1,266
	Inf	21	25	2,478	16	14	1,266
	Inf	20	24	2,478	16	14	1,266
France	Arm	20	17	1,700	30	48	4,444
	Arm	20	17	1,700	30	48	4,444
Netherlands	Inf	12	12	1,200	13	10	933
Turkey	Mech/Inf	75	66	6,600	68	50	4,629
	Mech/Inf	75	66	6,600	68	50	4,629
	Mech/Inf	75	66	6,600	68	50	4,629
	Mech/Inf	75	66	6,600	68	50	4,629
	Mech/Inf	75	66	6,600	68	50	4,629
	Mech/Inf	75	66	6,600	68	50	4,629
	Mech/Inf	75	66	6,600	68	50	4,629
	Mech/Inf	75	66	6,600	68	50	4,629
	Mech/Inf	75	66	6,600	68	50	4,629
	Mech/Inf	75	66	6,600	68	50	4,629
	Mech/Inf	75	66	6,600	68	50	4,629
	Mech/Inf	75	66	6,600	68	50	4,629
	Mech/Inf	75	66	6,600	68	50	4,629
	Mech/Inf	75	66	6,600	68	50	4,629
	Mech/Inf	75	66	6,600	66	49	4,493
	Mech/Inf	75	66	6,600	66	49	4,493
	Mech/Inf	75	66	6,600	66	49	4,493
	Mech/Inf	75	66	6,600	66	49	4,493
	Mech/Inf	75	66	6,600	66	49	4,493

Greece											
Mech/Inf	58	0	0	51	5,104	100				74	6,808
Mech/Inf	58	0	0	51	5,104	100				74	6,808
Mech/Inf	58	0	0	51	5,104	100				74	6,808
Mech/Inf	58	0	0	51	5,104	100				74	6,808
Mech/Inf	58	0	0	51	5,104	100				74	6,808
Mech/Inf	58	0	0	51	5,104	100				74	6,808
Mech/Inf	58	0	0	51	5,104	100				74	6,808
Mech/Inf	57	0	0	50	5,016	100				74	6,808
Mech/Inf	57	0	0	50	5,016	100				74	6,808
Mech/Inf	57	0	0	50	5,016	100				74	6,808
Mech/Inf	54	0	0	48	4,752	100				74	6,808
Italy											
Mech/Inf		75	0	75	7,500	66	100	50		196	18,201
Mech/Inf		75	0	75	7,500	63	100	50		196	17,997
Mech/Inf		75	0	75	7,500	63	100	50		196	17,997
Mech/Inf		75	0	75	7,500	63	100	50		196	17,997
Mech/Inf		75	0	75	7,500	63	100	50		196	17,997
Mech/Inf		75	0	75	7,500	63	100	50		196	17,997
Mech/Inf		75	0	75	7,500	63	100	50		196	17,997
Mech/Inf		75	0	75	7,500	63	100	50		196	17,997
Spain											
Mech/Inf	41	0	0	36	3,608	50	50	15	15	119	10,920
Mech/Inf	41	0	0	36	3,608	50	50	15	15	119	10,920
Mech/Inf	41	0	0	36	3,608	50	50	15	15	119	10,920
Mech/Inf	41	0	0	36	3,608	50	50	15	15	119	10,920
Mech/Inf	41	0	0	36	3,608	50	50	15	15	119	10,920
Mech/Inf	41	0	0	36	3,608	50	50	15	15	119	10,920
Mech/Inf	41	0	0	36	3,608	50	50	15	15	119	10,920
Mech/Inf	41	0	0	36	3,608	50	50	15	15	119	10,920
Portugal											
Mech/Inf	6	0	0	5	528	10	10	10	10	32	2,975
Mech/Inf	6	0	0	5	528	10	10	10	10	32	2,975
Mech/Inf	6	0	0	5	528	10	10	10	10	32	2,975
Mech/Inf	6	0	0	5	528	10	10	10	10	32	2,975
Mech/Inf	6	0	0	5	528	10	10	10	10	32	2,975
Mech/Inf	6	0	0	5	528	10	10	10	10	32	2,975
Norway											
Mech/Inf		58	0	58	5,800			60	155	241	22,172

Table C-14. *continued*

STATE; CORPS	DIVISION	BRIGADE; OR REGIMENT	MORTARS			ANTIARMOR			INFANTRY FIGHTING VEHICLE			ARMORED RECON VEHICLE		
			TO&E	WEI	(WEI-CW 48)	TO&E	WEI	(WEI-CW 55)	TO&E	WEI	(WEI-CW 69)	TO&E	WEI	(WEI-CW 62)
Netherlands			*120MM M-106*			*LAW GUSTA MAW TOW*			MARDER			*APC ARV M-2*		
I Netherlands	4th Mech	41,42,43	18		864	LAW 210, MAW 90, TOW 60	179	9,834				APC 63, M-2 42	104	6,419
I Netherlands	5th Mech	51,52,53	18		864	LAW 210, MAW 90, TOW 60	179	9,834				APC 63, M-2 42	104	6,419
I Netherlands	1st Mech	11,12,13	18		864	LAW 210, MAW 90, TOW 60	179	9,834				APC 63, M-2 42	104	6,419
Belgium			*60MM 81MM M-107*			*LAW GUSTA MAW TOW*			MARDER			*CVR SCORPN AMX*		
I Belgian	16th Mech	4 mech, 17 Arm	60MM 66, 81MM 42	85	4,074	LAW 600, GUSTA 406, MAW 24, TOW 152	384	21,109				CVR 117, SCORPN 98	193	11,987
I Belgian	1st Div	1 mech, 7 mech	60MM 66, 81MM 42	85	4,074	LAW 600, GUSTA 406, MAW 24, TOW 152	384	21,109				CVR 117, SCORPN 98	193	11,987
I Belgian		10 mech	60MM 33, 81MM 21	42	2,037	LAW 240, GUSTA 162, MAW 10, TOW 46	143	7,857				SCORPN 80	78	4,811
I Belgian		12 mot	60MM 33, 81MM 21	42	2,037	LAW 240, GUSTA 162, MAW 10, TOW 46	143	7,842				SCORPN 80	78	4,811
Denmark			*60MM 81MM M-107*			*LAW GUSTA MAW TOW*			MARDER			*CVR SCORPN AMX*		
Jutland	Jutland	1, 2, 3 mech inf	60MM 66, 81MM 66	104	4,996	LAW 50, GUSTA 100, TOW 70	94	5,192				CVR 16, SCORPN 16, AMX 16	48	2,976
United Kingdom			*51MM 81MM M-125*			*LAW MILAN*			MARDER			*M8 CVR SCORPN SCIMTAR*		
I British	1 Arm	7, 12, 22	51MM 80, 81MM 8	66	3,187	LAW 478, MILAN 54	158	8,711				CVR 25, SCORPN 32, SCIMTAR 40	106	6,560
I British	4 Arm	11, 20, 30 Arm	51MM 80, 81MM 8	66	3,187	LAW 478, MILAN 54	158	8,711				CVR 25, SCORPN 32, SCIMTAR 40	106	6,560
I British	2 Inf	15, 24, 49 inf	51MM 80, 81MM 8	66	3,187	LAW 478, MILAN 100	192	10,533				CVR 25, SCORPN 32, SCIMTAR 40	106	6,560
I British	Art Div	4 reg												
British			*60MM 81MM M-125*			*ATLC GUSTA ATGM*			MARDER			*M8 CVR SCORPN SCIMTAR*		
I British	3 Arm	4 Arm, 6 Arm, 19 inf	60MM 80, 81MM 8	66	3,187	LAW 478, MAW 54	158	8,711				CVR 24, SCORPN 25, SCIMTAR 32	106	6,560
British		5 Air	60MM 26, 81MM 3	22	1,051	ATLC 167, GUSTA 128, ATGM 19	55	3,049				CVR 8, SCORPN 10, SCIMTAR 14	38	2,334
UKMF		1 Inf	60MM 26, 81MM 3	22	1,051	ATLC 167, GUSTA 128, ATGM 20	56	3,088				CVR 8, SCORPN 10, SCIMTAR 14	38	2,334
UKMF		Other Btlns	60MM 26, 81MM 3	22	1,051	ATLC 167, GUSTA 128, ATGM 20	56	3,088				CVR 8, SCORPN 10, SCIMTAR 14	38	2,334
Canada			*60MM 81MM M-125*			*ATLC GUSTA ATGM TOW*			MARDER			*M8 CVR SCORPN SCIMTAR*		
C. F. Europe		4 Mech	60MM 32, 81MM 16	40	1,920	ATLC 128, GUSTA 167, ATGM 24, TOW 149	214	11,758						
Mobile Command		5e Groupe-Brig	60MM 32, 81MM 16	40	1,920	ATLC 128, GUSTA 167, ATGM 24	96	5,284						
Mobile Command		5e Groupe-Brig	60MM 32, 81MM 16	40	1,920	ATLC 128, GUSTA 167, ATGM 24	96	5,284						

Force / Corps	Unit	Divisions	60MM	81MM	120MM	ATLC / LAW		GUSTA	ATGM	TOW		MARDER		M8 VA / SPZ	AMX / ARV	SCIMTAR	
France																	
FAR	4th Air		12														
FAR	9th lt Air			12		23	1,113	20	60	50	2,761			12	36	46	2,857
FAR	11th Air			24		24	1,130	90	72	83	4,584			12	36	30	1,885
II	3rd Arm		12	12	5	23	1,113	20	40	36	1,969			12	36	46	2,857
II	5th Arm		12	12	5	23	1,113	20	40	36	1,969			12	36	46	2,857
I	1st Arm		12	12	5	23	1,113	20	40	36	1,969			12	36	46	2,857
FAR	27th Mou		12	12		23	1,113	20	60	36	2,761			12	36	46	2,857
II	15th Inf		12	12	5	23	1,113	20	60	50	2,761			12	36	46	2,857
_	12th lt Arm		12	12	5	23	1,113	20	40	50	1,969			12	36	46	2,857
_	14th lt Arm		12	12	5	23	1,113	20	60	36	2,761			12	36	46	2,857
	2nd Arm		12	12	5	19	904	20	40	50	1,969			12	36	46	2,857
III	8th Inf		12	12		19	904	20	40	36	2,761			12	36	46	2,857
III	10th Arm		12	12	5	19	904	20	40	36	1,969			12	36	46	2,857
III	7th Arm		12	12		19				36				12	36	46	2,857
West Germany						LAW	GUSTA	ATGM		TOW		MARDER		SPZ	ARV		
I Korps	1st Arm	1, 2 Arm, 3 Inf				51	48	144	143	7,857	80	4,747			13	13	798
I Korps	3rd Arm	7 A/l, 8 Arm, 9 Arm				15	48	144	134	7,343	65	3,857			13	13	798
I Korps	6th A/l	16,17 Arm,18 Arm				51	48	144	143	7,857	80	4,747			13	13	798
I Korps	7th Arm	19,20 Arm,21 A/l				15	48	144	134	7,343	65	3,857			13	13	798
II Korps	4th A/l	10,11 A/l,12 Arm				51	48	144	143	7,857	80	4,747			13	13	798
II Korps	1st Mountain	22 A/l,23 mou,24 Arm				71	68	144	155	8,506	80	4,747			13	13	798
III Korps	2nd A/l	4,5 A/l,6 Arm				51	48	144	143	7,343	65	3,857			13	13	798
III Korps	12th Arm	34 Arm,35 A/l,36 Arm				15	48	144	134	7,857	80	4,747			13	13	798
III Korps	11th A/l	31,32 A/l,33 Arm				51	48	144	143	7,343	65	3,857			13	13	798
II Korps	10th A/l	28,29 Arm,30 A/l				71	68	144	134	7,343	65				13	13	798
II Korps	1st Air	25,26,27 airborne				15	48	200	199	10,940							
III Korps	5th Arm	14,15 Arm,13 A/l				15	48	144	134	7,343	49	2,908			13		798
Terr Army SH	51 Home Defence					15	48	18	34	1,868							
Terr Army South	56 Home Defence					15	48	18	34	1,868							
Terr Army North	52 Home Defence					15	48	18	34	1,868							
Terr Army North	62 Home Defence					15	48	18	34	1,868							
Terr Army North	53 Home Defence					15	48	18	34	1,868							
Terr Army North	63 Home Defence					15	48	18	34	1,868							
Terr Army South	52 Home Defence					15	48	18	34	1,868							
Terr Army South	62 Home Defence					15	48	18	34	1,868							
Terr Army SH	55 Home Defence					15	48	18	34	1,868							
Terr Army South	61 Home Defence					15	48	18	34	1,868							
Terr Army SH	66 Home Defence					15	48	18	34	1,868							
Terr Army South	65 Home Defence					15	48	18	34	1,868							

Table C-14. *continued*

STATE; CORPS	DIVISION	BRIGADE	REGIMENT	MORTARS TO&E 81MM	60MM	M-30	WEI	(WEI-CW 48)	ANTIARMOR LAW	TO&E DRAG	ATGM	TOW	WEI	(WEI-CW 55)	IFV TO&E IFV	WEI	(WEI-CW 69)	ARV TO&E Oth	SPZ	ARV	M-2	WEI	(WEI-CW 62)
United States																							
VII US	1st Arm	1,2,3	+ Art			10	10	480		180		60	191	10,494	190	171	11,799				100	119	7,378
VII US		Art	17,72,210 / + Art																				
V US	3rd Arm	1,2,3	+ Art			10	10	480		180		60	191	10,494	190	171	11,799				150	179	11,067
V US		Art: 41,42																					
VII /III	1st Inf	3	11 ACR	5	15		17	816		60		20	64	3,498							35	42	2,582
			(11 ACR)							263		173	374	20,543							50	60	3,689
III US	2nd Arm	3								100		75	152	8,374							15	18	1,107
VII US	3rd Inf	1,2,3	+ Art / 2 ACR / + Art	18	45		64	3,068		60		20	64	3,498							35	42	2,582
			(2 ACR)						100	50			55	2,998							30	36	2,213
V US	8th Inf (mech)	1,2,3				10	10	480		180		60	191	10,494	190	171	11,799				150	179	11,067
CONUS POMCUS																							
US	1st Inf	1,2	3 ACR	10	30		34	1,632		200		150	305	16,748							24	29	1,771
			(3 ACR)						100	50			55	2,998							24	29	1,771
III US		Art: 212																					
I US	7th Inf	1,2,3		18	45		54	2,588		263		173	374	20,543							25	30	1,845
I US	25th Inf	1,2,3		18	45		54	2,588		263		173	374	20,543							24	29	1,771
III US	2nd Arm	1,2								120		40	127	6,996							65	77	4,796
III US	1st Cav	1,2,155								180		60	191	10,494							55	65	4,058
III US	4th Inf (mech)	1,2,3								180		60	191	10,494							80	95	5,902

Reserve and National Guard

Comp	Division	Units																			
III US		Art: 75,214																				
CONUS Res		194 Arm			20	20	960		60	20	64	3,498	90	81	5,589					35	42	2,582
CONUS Res		197 mech Inf			20	20	960		60	20	64	3,498	90	81	5,589					35	42	2,582
NG	26th Inf	1,3,43	38		30	103	4,959	300	263	173	434	23,843	90	81	5,589					50	60	3,689
CONUS Res		157 mech Inf			20	20	960		60	20	64	3,498	90	81	5,589					35	42	2,582
NG	28th Inf	2,55,56	38		30	103	4,959	300	263	173	434	23,843	90	81	5,589					50	60	3,689
CONUS Res		Art: 428,424,479																				
NG		29 Inf	20	10		38	1,800	100	75	30	105	5,778	30	27	1,863	5	5	5			12	756
NG		30 Inf (mech)	16	8		22	1,056	70	60	8	64	3,535	30	63	4,347	10	10	10			24	1,513
NG		33 Inf	20	10		38	1,800	100	75	30	105	5,778	30	27	1,863	5	5	5			12	756
		107 ACR				19	931		50		55	2,998							30		36	2,213
NG		32 Inf (mech)	20	8		22	1,056	70	60	8	64	3,535	30	63	4,347	10	10	10			24	1,513
NG		67,69,149	40	20		55	2,640	200	180	20	186	10,252	90	189	13,041	35	35	35			85	5,295
		116 ACR				19	931		50		55	2,998							30		36	2,213
NG	35th Mech Inf	2,55,56	40			124	5,940	300	263	82	332	18,287	227	90	4,050					50	60	3,689
NG	29 lt Inf	2,46,76	20	10		55	2,640	200	180	30	186	10,252	270	189	13,041	35	35	35			85	5,295
NG	38th Mech Inf	41 Inf	40	20		38	1,800	100	75	30	105	5,778	30	27	1,863	5	5	5			12	756
NG		81 Inf (mech)	16	8		22	1,056	70	60	8	64	3,535	30	63	4,347	10	10	10			24	1,513
		163 ACR				19	931		50		55	2,998							30		36	2,213
NG		45 Inf	20	10		38	1,800	100	75	30	105	5,778	30	27	1,863	5	5	5			12	756
NG		218 Inf (mech)	16	8		22	1,056	70	60	8	64	3,535	90	63	4,347	10	10	10			24	1,513
		Art: 45,57,103																				
		278 ACR				19	931		50		55	2,998							30		36	2,213
NG		53 Inf	20	10		38	1,800	100	75	30	105	5,778	30	27	1,863	5	5	5			12	756
NG		30 Arm	16	8		22	1,056	70	60	8	64	3,535	90	63	4,347	10	10	10			24	1,513
NG		73 Inf	20	10		38	1,800	100	75	30	105	5,778	30	27	1,863	5	5	5			12	756
		Art: 113,115,118																				
		Art: 135,138,142																				
NG	42nd Inf	31 Arm	16	8		22	1,056	70	60	8	64	3,535	90	63	4,347	10	10	10			24	1,513
NG		1,2	70	20	20	104	4,997	300	150	60	230	12,656	65	59	4,037	10	10	10			36	2,251
		Art: 196,197,209																				
		Art: 147,151,169																				
		Art: 227,163,631																				
NG	49th Arm	1,2,3	60	20		74	3,571	300	180	20	206	11,352	270	189	13,041	35	35	35			85	5,295
NG	50th Arm	1,2,86	60	20		74	3,571	300	180	20	206	11,352	270	189	13,041	35	35	35			85	5,295

Table C-14. *continued*

ATTU Units Not Allocated to Central Front

STATE; CORPS	DIVISION	MORTARS TO&E	MORTARS WEI	MORTARS (WEI-CW 48)	ANTIARMOR TO&E	ANTIARMOR WEI	ANTIARMOR (WEI-CW 55)	IFV TO&E	IFV WEI	IFV (WEI-CW 69)	ARV TO&E	ARV WEI	ARV (WEI-CW 62)
United Kingdom	Inf	26	20	936	100	25	1,375	5			26	29	1,819
	Inf	26	20	936	100	25	1,375	5			30	32	1,965
	Inf	26	20	936	100	25	1,375	5			30	32	1,965
	Inf	26	20	936	100	25	1,375	5			30	32	1,965
	Inf	26	20	936	100	25	1,375	5			30	32	1,965
	Inf	26	20	936	100	25	1,375	5			30	32	1,965
	Inf	26	20	936	100	25	1,375	5			30	32	1,965
	Inf	26	20	936	100	25	1,375	5			30	32	1,965
	Inf	26	20	936	100	25	1,375	5			30	32	1,965
	Inf	26	20	936	100	25	1,375	5			30	32	1,965
France	Arm	12	25	1,197	20	7	385						
	Arm	12	25	1,197	20	7	385						
Netherlands	Inf	20	25	1,197	75	19	1,031				20		
Turkey	Mech/Inf	40	48	2,314	100	28	1,564				83	49	3,036
	Mech/Inf	40	48	2,314	100	28	1,564				88	52	3,219
	Mech/Inf	40	48	2,314	100	28	1,564				88	52	3,219
	Mech/Inf	40	48	2,314	100	28	1,564				88	52	3,219
	Mech/Inf	40	48	2,314	100	28	1,564				88	52	3,219
	Mech/Inf	40	48	2,314	100	28	1,564				88	52	3,219
	Mech/Inf	40	48	2,314	100	28	1,564				88	52	3,219
	Mech/Inf	40	48	2,314	100	28	1,564				88	52	3,219
	Mech/Inf	40	48	2,314	100	28	1,564				88	52	3,219
	Mech/Inf	40	48	2,314	100	28	1,564				88	52	3,219
	Mech/Inf	40	48	2,314	100	28	1,564				88	52	3,219
	Mech/Inf	40	48	2,314	100	28	1,564				88	52	3,219
	Mech/Inf	40	48	2,314	100	28	1,564				88	52	3,219
	Mech/Inf	40	48	2,314	100	28	1,564				88	52	3,219
	Mech/Inf	40	48	2,314	100	28	1,564				88	52	3,219
	Mech/Inf	40	48	2,314	100	28	1,564				88	52	3,219
	Mech/Inf	40	48	2,314	100	28	1,564				88	52	3,219
	Mech/Inf	40	48	2,314	100	28	1,564				88	52	3,219

Greece	50	25	Mech/Inf		60	2,892	160		4	4	40	2,224	5	4	242	55	50			32	2,012
	50	25	Mech/Inf		60	2,892	160		4	4	40	2,224	5	4	242	55	50			32	2,012
	50	25	Mech/Inf		60	2,892	160		4	4	40	2,224	5	4	290	55	50			32	2,012
	50	25	Mech/Inf		60	2,224	160		4	4	40	2,224	5	4	242	55	50			32	2,012
	50	25	Mech/Inf		60	2,892	160		4	4	40	2,224	5	4	242	55	50			32	2,012
	50	25	Mech/Inf		60	2,892	160		4	4	40	2,224	5	4	290	55	50			32	2,012
	50	25	Mech/Inf		60	2,892	160		4	4	40	2,224	5	4	242	55	50			32	2,012
	50	25	Mech/Inf		60	2,892	160		4	4	40	2,224	5	4	242	55	50			32	2,012
	50	25	Mech/Inf		60	2,892	160		4	4	40	2,224	5	4	290	55	50			32	2,012
	50	25	Mech/Inf		60	2,892	160		4	4	40	2,224	5	4	242	55	50			32	2,012
	50	25	Mech/Inf		60	2,892	160		4	4	40	2,224	5	4	242	55	50			32	2,012
Italy	40	20	Mech/Inf	17	48	2,314	100	25	125	25	190	10,450	4	3	193	50	50	25	25	127	7,874
	40	20	Mech/Inf	17	48	2,314	100	25	125	25	190	10,450	4	3	193	50	50	25	25	127	7,874
	40	20	Mech/Inf	17	48	2,314	100	25	125	25	190	10,450	4	3	193	50	50	25	25	127	7,874
	40	20	Mech/Inf	17	48	2,314	100	25	125	25	190	10,450	4	3	193	50	50	25	25	127	7,874
	40	20	Mech/Inf	17	48	2,314	100	25	125	25	190	10,450	4	3	193	50	50	25	25	127	7,874
	40	20	Mech/Inf	17	48	2,314	100	25	125	25	190	10,450	4	3	193	50	50	25	25	127	7,874
	40	20	Mech/Inf	17	48	2,314	100	25	125	25	190	10,450	4	3	193	50	50	25	25	127	7,874
Spain	10	10	Mech/Inf		33	1,589	75	25	50		82	4,524				25	25	25	25	86	5,317
	10	10	Mech/Inf		33	1,589	75	25	50		82	4,524				25	25	25	25	86	5,317
	10	10	Mech/Inf		33	1,589	75	25	50		82	4,524				25	25	25	25	86	5,317
	10	10	Mech/Inf		33	1,589	75	25	50		82	4,524				25	25	25	25	86	5,317
	10	10	Mech/Inf		33	1,589	75	25	50		82	4,524				25	25	25	25	86	5,317
	10	10	Mech/Inf		33	1,589	75	25	50		82	4,524				25	25	25	25	86	5,317
	10	10	Mech/Inf		33	1,589	75	25	50		82	4,524				25	25	25	25	86	5,317
Portugal	5	5	Mech/Inf		8	386	20	10	15	15	43	2,340					5	10		14	880
	5	5	Mech/Inf		8	386	20	10	15	15	43	2,340					5	10		14	880
	5	5	Mech/Inf		8	386	20	10	15	15	43	2,340					5	10		14	880
	5	5	Mech/Inf		8	386	20	10	15	15	43	2,340					5	10		14	880
	5	5	Mech/Inf		8	386	20	10	15	15	43	2,340					5	10		14	880
	5	5	Mech/Inf		8	386	20	10	15	15	43	2,340					5	10		14	880
Norway	25	25	Mech/Inf		40	1,932	200	100	100	150	376	20,653						14	25	44	2,704

Table C-14. *continued*

STATE; CORPS	DIVISION	BRIGADE	REGIMENT	ARMORED PERSONNEL CARRIER TO&E: ARV	M113A1	WEI	(WEI-CW 36)	SMALL ARMS WEI	(WEI-CW 3.3)	UNIT WUV: Division Total
United States				0th						
VII US	1st Arm	1,2,3	+ Art					3,000	9,900	66,435
VII US		Art	17,72,210							12,630
V US	3rd Arm	1,2,3	+ Art					3,000	9,900	69,928
V US		Art: 41,42								7,938
V US			11 ACR					1,000	3,300	18,040
VII /III	1st Inf	3						1,000	3,300	24,464
III US	2nd Arm	3								18,040
VII US	3rd Inf	1,2,3	+ Art					3,600	11,880	67,784
VII US			2 ACR					1,022	3,373	17,486
V US			+ Art							
V US	8th Inf (mech)	1,2,3						3,000	9,900	69,928
CONUS POMCUS										
US	1st Inf	1,2	3 ACR					2,000	6,600	47,344
III US								1,022	3,373	17,043
III US		Art : 212								5,067
I US	7th Inf	1,2,3						3,600	11,880	45,023
I US	25th Inf	1,2,3						3,600	11,880	44,949
III US	2nd Arm	1,2						2,000	6,600	35,711
III US	1st Cav	1,2,155						3,000	9,900	50,640
III US	4th Inf (mech)	1,2,3						3,000	9,900	52,484

260

Reserve and National Guard

Component	Unit	Div	ACR									Total
III US	Art: 75,214						50	50	1,800	1,000	3,300	7,938
CONUS Res	194 Arm						50	50	1,800	1,000	3,300	26,851
CONUS Res	197 mech Inf	26th Inf		60	30		80	109	3,931	3,000	9,900	32,440
NG	1,3,43			60	30		50	50	1,800	1,000	3,300	81,301
CONUS Res	157 mech Inf	28th Inf		60	30		30	109	3,931	3,000	9,900	26,851
NG	2,55,56			60	30		30	109	3,931	3,000	9,900	81,301
CONUS Res	Art: 428,424,479											12,630
NG	29 Inf			25	10	10	10	41	1,467	1,000	3,300	22,252
NG	30 Inf (mech)			20	20	20	20	55	1,994	800	2,640	26,677
NG	33 Inf			25	10	10	10	41	1,467	1,000	3,300	22,252
NG			107 ACR	115	20		118	118	4,250	1,022	3,373	29,766
NG	32 Inf (mech)	35th Mech Inf		20	20	20	55	55	1,994	800	2,640	26,677
NG	67,69,149			55	55	55	152	152	5,485	2,500	8,250	80,780
NG			116 ACR	115	20		118	118	4,250	1,022	3,373	29,766
NG	2,55,56	29th lt Inf		20	100	100	135	135	4,874	3,800	12,540	58,459
NG	2,46,76	38th Mech Inf		55	55	55	152	152	5,485	2,500	8,250	80,780
NG	41 Inf			20	10	10	41	41	1,467	1,000	3,300	22,252
NG	81 Inf (mech)			55	20	20	55	55	1,994	800	2,640	26,677
NG			163 ACR	20	20	20	118	118	4,250	1,022	3,373	29,766
NG	45 Inf			115	10	10	41	41	1,467	1,000	3,300	22,252
NG	218 Inf (mech)			25	20	20	55	55	1,994	800	2,640	26,677
NG	Art: 45,57,103			20	10	10	41	41	1,467	1,000	3,300	12,630
NG			278 ACR		20	20	55	55	1,994	800	2,640	29,766
NG	53 Inf			115	20	20	118	118	4,250	1,022	3,373	22,252
NG	30 Arm			25	10	10	41	41	1,467	1,000	3,300	25,802
NG	73 Inf			20	20	20	55	55	1,994	800	2,640	22,252
NG	Art: 113,115,118			25	10	10	41	41	1,467	1,000	3,300	12,630
NG	Art: 135,138,142											12,630
NG	31 Arm			20	20	20	55	55	1,994	800	2,640	25,802
NG	1,2	42nd Inf		40	25	25	82	82	2,963	2,300	7,590	62,881
NG	Art: 196,197,209											12,630
NG	Art: 147,151,169											12,630
NG	Art: 227,163,631											12,630
NG	1,2,3	49th Arm		55	55	55	152	152	5,485	3,000	9,900	90,489
NG	1,2,86	50th Arm		55	55	55	152	152	5,485	3,000	9,900	90,489

Table C-14. continued

STATE; CORPS	DIVISION	BRIGADE	REGIMENT	ARMORED PERSONNEL CARRIER					SMALL ARMS		UNIT WUV: Division Total
				TO&E			WEI	(WEI-CW 36)	WEI	(WEI-CW 3.3)	
Netherlands											
I Netherlands	4th Mech	41,42,43		AMX	M113A1	APC	102	3,669	2,246	7,412	48,432
I Netherlands	5th Mech	51,52,53				104	102	3,669	2,246	7,412	48,432
I Netherlands	1st Mech	11,12,13				104	102	3,669	2,246	7,412	48,534
						104					
Belgium											
I Belgian	16th Mech	4 mech, 17 Arm		AMX	APC				2,653	8,755	60,169
I Belgian	1st Div	1 mech, 7 mech			ARV				2,453	8,095	54,789
I Belgian		10 mech							981	3,238	20,659
I Belgian		12 mot							981	3,238	20,645
Denmark											
	Jutland	1, 2, 3 mech inf		AMX	ARV	APC 85	77	2,754	2,653	8,755	49,079
United Kingdom											
I British	1 Arm	7, 12, 22		AMX	ARV	APC 30	27	961	2,963	9,778	42,255
I British	4 Arm	11, 20, 30 Arm				30	27	961	2,963	9,778	42,255
I British	2 Inf	15, 24, 49 inf				30	27	961	2,963	9,778	44,077
I British	Art Div		4 reg								5,492
British		5 Air				7	6	224	1,185	3,911	11,203
I British	3 Arm	4 Arm, 6 Arm, 19 inf				30	27	961	2,963	9,778	42,255
UKMF		1 Inf				7	6	224	1,185	3,911	11,242
UKMF		Other Btlns				7	6	224	1,185	3,911	11,242
Canada											
C. F. Europe		4 Mech		AMX	ARV	APC 105	105	3,780	1,384	4,567	37,207
Mobile Command		5e Groupe-Brig				50	50	1,800	554	1,827	13,440
Mobile Command		5e Groupe-Brig				50	50	1,800	554	1,827	14,340

Formation	Unit	Components	AMX	VAB (ARV)	APC (M113A1)			
France								
FAR	4th Air					330	1,089	1,089
FAR	9th lt Air		16	14	518	1,300	4,290	16,192
FAR	11th Air		50	45	1,620	1,300	4,290	15,165
II	3rd Arm		150	135	4,860	1,500	4,950	22,314
II	5th Arm		150	135	4,860	1,500	4,950	22,314
I	1st Arm		150	135	4,860	1,500	4,950	22,314
FAR	27th Mou		15	14	486	1,300	4,290	15,267
II	15th Inf		15	14	486	1,300	4,290	16,159
I	12th lt Arm		15	14	486	1,300	4,290	16,351
I	14th lt Arm		150	135	4,860	1,500	4,950	22,105
III	2nd Arm		15	14	486	1,300	4,290	15,058
III	8th Inf		150	135	4,860	1,500	4,950	22,105
III	10th Arm		150	135	4,860	1,500	4,950	22,105
—	7th Arm		150	135	4,860	1,500	4,950	22,105
West Germany								
I Korps	1st Arm	1, 2 Arm, 3 Inf				3,500	11,550	49,460
I Korps	3rd Arm	7 A/I, 8 Arm, 9 Arm				3,500	11,550	54,053
I Korps	6th A/I	16, 17 A/I, 18 Arm				3,500	11,550	49,358
I Korps	7th Arm	19, 20 Arm, 21 A/I				3,500	11,550	54,053
II Korps	4th A/I	10, 11 A/I, 12 Arm				3,500	11,550	49,358
II Korps	1st Mountain	22 A/I, 23 mou, 24 Arm				3,800	12,540	44,897
III Korps	2nd A/I	4, 5 A/I, 6 Arm				3,500	11,550	49,358
III Korps	12th Arm	34 Arm, 35 A/I, 36 Arm				3,500	11,550	54,053
I Korps	11th A/I	31, 32 A/I, 33 Arm				3,500	11,550	49,358
II Korps	10th Arm	28, 29 Arm, 30 A/I				3,500	11,550	54,053
III Korps	1st Air	25, 26, 27 airborne				2,000	6,600	23,135
III Korps	5th Arm	14, 15 Arm, 13 A/I				3,500	11,550	53,104
III Korps SH	51 Home Defence					1,300	4,290	8,622
Terr Army South	56 Home Defence					1,300	4,290	8,622
Terr Army North	52 Home Defence					1,300	4,290	8,622
Terr Army North	62 Home Defence					1,300	4,290	8,622
Terr Army North	53 Home Defence					1,300	4,290	8,622
Terr Army North	63 Home Defence					1,300	4,290	8,622
Terr Army South	52 Home Defence					1,300	4,290	8,622
Terr Army South	62 Home Defence					1,300	4,290	8,622
Terr Army South	55 Home Defence					1,300	4,290	8,622
Terr Army South	61 Home Defence					1,300	4,290	8,622
Terr Army SH	66 Home Defence					1,300	4,290	8,622
Terr Army South	65 Home Defence					1,300	4,290	8,622

Table C-14. *continued*

STATE; CORPS	DIVISION	ARMORED PERSONNEL CARRIER			SMALL ARMS		UNIT WUV: Division Total
		TO&E	WEI	(WEI-CW 36)	WEI	(WEI-CW 3.3)	
ATTU Units Not Attributed to Central Front							
United Kingdom							
	Inf				800	2,640	10,514
	Inf				800	2,640	10,660
	Inf				800	2,640	10,660
	Inf				800	2,640	10,660
	Inf				800	2,640	10,660
	Inf				800	2,640	10,660
	Inf				800	2,640	10,660
	Inf				800	2,640	10,660
	Inf				800	2,640	10,660
	Inf				800	2,640	10,542
France							
	Arm				700	2,310	10,035
	Arm				700	2,310	10,035
Netherlands							
	Inf				500	1,650	4,814
Turkey							
	Mech/Inf				3,000	9,900	28,043
	Mech/Inf				3,000	9,900	28,226
	Mech/Inf				3,000	9,900	28,226
	Mech/Inf				3,000	9,900	28,226
	Mech/Inf				3,000	9,900	28,226
	Mech/Inf				3,000	9,900	28,226
	Mech/Inf				3,000	9,900	28,226
	Mech/Inf				3,000	9,900	28,226
	Mech/Inf				3,000	9,900	28,226
	Mech/Inf				3,000	9,900	28,226
	Mech/Inf				3,000	9,900	28,226
	Mech/Inf				3,000	9,900	28,226
	Mech/Inf				3,000	9,900	28,226
	Mech/Inf				3,000	9,900	28,226
	Mech/Inf				3,000	9,900	28,090
	Mech/Inf				3,000	9,900	28,090
	Mech/Inf				3,000	9,900	28,090
	Mech/Inf				3,000	9,900	28,090
	Mech/Inf				3,000	9,900	28,090
	Mech/Inf				3,000	9,900	28,090

Greece	Mech/Inf				3,000	9,900	29,182
	Mech/Inf				3,000	9,900	29,182
	Mech/Inf				3,000	9,900	29,230
	Mech/Inf				3,000	9,900	29,182
	Mech/Inf				3,000	9,900	29,182
	Mech/Inf				3,000	9,900	29,182
	Mech/Inf				3,000	9,900	29,230
	Mech/Inf				3,000	9,900	29,182
	Mech/Inf				3,000	9,900	29,094
	Mech/Inf				3,000	9,900	29,142
	Mech/Inf				3,000	9,900	29,094
	Mech/Inf				3,000	9,900	28,830
Italy	Mech/Inf	24	24	864	3,000	9,900	57,296
	Mech/Inf	24	24	864	3,000	9,900	57,092
	Mech/Inf	24	24	864	3,000	9,900	57,092
	Mech/Inf	24	24	864	3,000	9,900	57,092
	Mech/Inf	24	24	864	3,000	9,900	57,092
	Mech/Inf	24	24	864	3,000	9,900	57,092
	Mech/Inf	24	24	864	3,000	9,900	57,092
	Mech/Inf	24	24	864	3,000	9,900	57,092
Spain	Mech/Inf	4	4	144	3,000	9,900	36,001
	Mech/Inf				3,000	9,900	35,857
	Mech/Inf				3,000	9,900	35,857
	Mech/Inf				3,000	9,900	35,857
	Mech/Inf				3,000	9,900	35,857
	Mech/Inf				3,000	9,900	35,857
	Mech/Inf				3,000	9,900	35,857
	Mech/Inf				3,000	9,900	35,857
Portugal	Mech/Inf				3,000	9,900	17,010
	Mech/Inf				3,000	9,900	17,010
	Mech/Inf				3,000	9,900	17,010
	Mech/Inf				3,000	9,900	17,010
	Mech/Inf				3,000	9,900	17,010
	Mech/Inf				3,000	9,900	17,010
Norway	Mech/Inf				3,000	9,900	63,160

265

Notes to Table C-14

See the notes to table C-1 for methodology and the notes to table C-3 for sources.

Under CFE II, each nation is presumed to take a percentage cut equal to the percentage cut imposed on the alliance as a whole. Each nation is assumed to cut where it would reduce the WEI/WUV score the least and, ceteris paribus, to cut the latest-arriving units first.

TABLE C-15. NATO Weapon Totals and ADE Mobilization Schedule Derived from Table C-14, after CFE II

TANKS

WEAPONS AND CFE II CONDITIONS	TOTAL	Tanks: M-48	Tanks: M60A1 CENT LEO 1	Tanks: M-60A2/A3	Tanks: M-1/M1A1 CHIEF LEO 2
ALLIANCEWIDE					
CFE II limit: "Alliancewide"	10,000				
NATO Tanks including spares, "Alliancewide"	20,088				
NATO Tank TO&E "Alliancewide" before reduction	16,740				
Reductions in NATO Tank TO&E "Alliancewide"	−8,137				
NATO Tank TO&E "Alliancewide" after reduction	8,333				
ATTU including spares	9,972	3,155	726	558	3,871
ATTU TO&E	8,310	562	56	558	3,662
Central Front (without CONUS) including spares	5,806				
Central Front (without CONUS) TO&E	4,838				

ARTILLERY

WEAPONS AND CFE II CONDITIONS	TOTAL	Arty: 155 HOW 105MM Var	Arty: M110A1/A2 155HOW	Arty: 155 HOW M110E2	Arty: GSRS	Mortar: 120 MM	Mortar: M-30
ALLIANCEWIDE							
CFE II limit: "Alliancewide"	12,000						
NATO Artillery including spares, "Alliancewide"	17,885						
NATO Artillery TO&E "Alliancewide" before reduction	14,904						
Reductions in NATO Artillery TO&E "Alliancewide"	−4,904						
NATO Artillery TO&E "Alliancewide" after reduction	10,000						
ATTU including spares	11,999	4,356	3,160	1,757	437	59	230
ATTU TO&E	9,999	660	1,840	1,117	102	45	94
Central Front (without CONUS) including spares	4,630						
Central Front (without CONUS) TO&E	3,858						

ARMORED VEHICLES

ALLIANCEWIDE

CFE II limit: "Alliancewide"	14,000
NATO Armored Vehicles including spares, "Alliancewide"	27,955
NATO Armored Vehicles TO&E "Alliancewide" before reduction	23,296
Reductions in NATO Armored Vehicles TO&E "Alliancewide"	−11,596
NATO Armored Vehicles TO&E "Alliancewide" after reduction	11,700

		ARV: M8	ARV: CVR SPZ	ARV: SCORPN AMX	ARV: CFV M2 SCIMTAR	APC: Oth	APC: Oth	APC: AFV, ARV, VAB	APC: M113A1	IFV: MARDER
ATTU including spares	13,990									
ATTU TO&E	11,658	3,451	1,405	1,863	1,470			1,176	839	1,454
Central Front (without CONUS) including spares	7,628									
Central Front (without CONUS) TO&E	6,357	120	725	1,128	1,206			1,176	643	1,359

CENTRAL FRONT MOBILIZATION SCHEDULE AFTER CFE II

Days After M+0	M+1	M+5	M+10	M+15	M+20	M+25	M+32	M+39
ADE arrival	9.22	5.34	3.45	3.74	.39	.73	.33	.82
Total ADEs	9.22	14.55	18.00	21.74	22.13	22.86	23.18	24.00
WUV Arrival	915,411	529,868	342,692	371,081	38,664	72,285	32,440	81,301
Total WUV	915,411	1,445,279	1,787,970	2,159,051	2,197,716	2,270,001	2,302,441	2,383,742

	M+46	M+53	M+60	M+67	M+74	M+81	M+88	M+95	M+102
ADE arrival	1.09	.84	1.38	1.70	1.29	1.13	1.27	1.17	.91
Total ADEs	25.09	25.93	27.32	29.02	30.30	31.44	32.71	33.88	34.79
WUV Arrival	108,152	83,810	137,224	169,006	127,624	112,701	126,573	115,748	90,489
Total WUV	2,491,894	2,575,704	2,712,927	2,881,933	3,009,556	3,122,257	3,248,830	3,364,578	3,455,067

Source: Data given in table C-14.

SENSITIVITY ANALYSIS ON ρ

This appendix presents a sensitivity analysis on ρ, the ground-to-ground casualty-exchange ratio used in the extended adaptive dynamic model employed in this book. A sensitivity analysis, as the name implies, is conducted to gauge the sensitivity of one's conclusions to plausible variations in one's assumptions. A total of 120 runs are presented below, 20 runs for each of five different assumptions concerning ρ. Each run is summarized by a pair of entries. The first entry gives the attrition winner (NATO or the WTO). The second entry gives the total territory sacrificed by NATO, in kilometers.

The scenarios used for analysis are listed down the left of the table. For each scenario the outcomes under different balances are listed from left to right—from the current balance to CFE II.[1] Clearly, the core comparative point of the book is *not sensitive* to these changes in ρ.[2]

---

1. Results for CFE II plus the unilateral US reductions are not displayed since, by design, they closely approximate the outcomes for CFE I over this range of ρ-values.

2. Improvements in the *margin* of victory are not shown in tables D-1–D-6, though they are readily obtained by simulation.

TABLE D-1. **Sensitivity Analysis with ρ = 1.2**

Scenario	1989		Unilateral Cuts		CFE I		CFE II	
1 (perfect dexterity)	WTO	500	WTO	500	NATO	0	NATO	0
4 (perfect dexterity)	WTO	500	WTO	500	NATO	0	NATO	0
1 North (60:40)	WTO	500	WTO	500	NATO	310	NATO	207
4 North (60:40)	WTO	500	WTO	500	WTO	500	WTO	500
Corps Sector 5 (Multi-Sector Feint)	WTO	500	WTO	500	WTO	500	NATO	287

TABLE D-2. **Sensitivity Analysis with ρ = 1.3**

Scenario	1989		Unilateral Cuts		CFE I		CFE II	
1 (perfect dexterity)	WTO	500	NATO	0	NATO	0	NATO	0
4 (perfect dexterity)	WTO	500	NATO	0	NATO	0	NATO	0
1 North (60:40)	WTO	500	WTO	500	NATO	75	NATO	54
4 North (60:40)	WTO	500	WTO	500	WTO	500	WTO	500
Corps Sector 5 (Multi-Sector Feint)	WTO	500	WTO	500	NATO	345	NATO	190

TABLE D-3. **Sensitivity Analysis with ρ = 1.5**

Scenario	1989		Unilateral Cuts		CFE I		CFE II	
1 (perfect dexterity)	NATO	47	NATO	0	NATO	0	NATO	0
4 (perfect dexterity)	NATO	0	NATO	0	NATO	0	NATO	0
1 North (60:40)	WTO	500	WTO	500	NATO	3	NATO	2
4 North (60:40)	WTO	500	WTO	500	WTO	500	NATO	0
Corps Sector 5 (Multi-Sector Feint)	WTO	500	WTO	500	NATO	103	NATO	58

TABLE D-4. **Sensitivity Analysis with** $\rho = 1.85$

Scenario	1989		Unilateral Cuts		CFE I		CFE II	
1 (perfect dexterity)	NATO	0	NATO	0	NATO	0	NATO	0
4 (perfect dexterity)	NATO	0	NATO	0	NATO	0	NATO	0
1 North (60:40)	WTO	500	NATO	3	NATO	1	NATO	1
4 North (60:40)	WTO	500	WTO	500	NATO	0	NATO	0
Corps Sector 5 (Multi-Sector Feint)	WTO	500	WTO	500	NATO	1	NATO	1

TABLE D-5. **Sensitivity Analysis with** $\rho = 2.0$

Scenario	1989		Unilateral Cuts		CFE I		CFE II	
1 (perfect dexterity)	NATO	0	NATO	0	NATO	0	NATO	0
4 (perfect dexterity)	NATO	0	NATO	0	NATO	0	NATO	0
1 North (60:40)	NATO	20	NATO	2	NATO	1	NATO	0
4 North (60:40)	WTO	500	WTO	500	NATO	0	NATO	0
Corps Sector 5 (Multi-Sector Feint)	WTO	500	NATO	182	NATO	0	NATO	0

TABLE D-6. **Sensitivity Analysis with Nonconstant** ρ[a]

Scenario	1989		Unilateral Cuts		CFE I		CFE II	
1 (perfect dexterity)	NATO	0	NATO	0	NATO	0	NATO	0
4 (perfect dexterity)	NATO	0	NATO	0	NATO	0	NATO	0
1 North (60:40)	WTO	500	NATO	52	NATO	2	NATO	1
4 North (60:40)	WTO	500	WTO	500	Stalemate	0	NATO	0
Corps Sector 5 (Multi-Sector Feint)	WTO	500	WTO	500	NATO	63	NATO	29

a. This sequence of runs employs the generalized $\rho(t)$ given in equation (A-8) of Appendix A. For these runs, $\lambda_a = 0.075$, $\lambda_d = 0.10$, and $\rho_0 = 1.2$.

INDEX

ADEs. *See* Armored division equivalents

Air power: in air-to-air combat, 45–46; close air support planes, 5, 8; CFE I agreement on, 45, 82; follow-on forces and follow-on forces attack, 46–47

Armed forces: combat scoring system under CFE I, 40; combat scoring system under current balance, 8, 40; limits on geographical distribution, 65, 67; restructuring, 64–65, 67. *See also* Force-to-space rules

Armored division equivalents (ADEs) score: under CFE I, 40, 42; under CFE II plus U.S. unilateral cuts, 63; under current balance, 8, 24; under WTO unilateral reductions, 30

Army, U.S.: barrier plans, 77–78; Concepts Analysis Agency, 56–57; on obstacle systems, 67, 68–69; on surprise attack, 71

Atlantic-to-the-Urals (ATTU) region: CFE I on armed forces in, 1, 38, 40, 48–49; establishment of zones in, 67; north-south versus east-west dimension, 67; WTO unilateral force reduction in, 30

Attack: counterconcentration in, 14, 18, 24, 72; large-scale offensive, 20; obstacle system to hinder, 69; place of, 14; problem in predicting plan of, 24; reinforcement scheduling and, 24; scenarios under current balance, 12, 15; surprise, 34, 71; time, 12

ATTU. *See* Atlantic-to-the-Urals region

Biddle, Stephen, 57n
Blair, Bruce G., 28n
Blechman, Barry M., 48n, 51n
Boone, Howard E., 72n, 77n, 78n

CAA. *See* Concepts Analysis Agency, U.S. Army

Central Intelligence Agency, assessment of unilateral reductions, 34

Central Region Barrier Agreement, *1979*, 78

CFE. *See* Conventional Forces in Europe

China, Soviet forces opposite, 39, 40n

Communications, theater-level dexterity and, 28

Concepts Analysis Agency (CAA), U.S. Army, 57

Conventional Forces in Europe (CFE). *See* Conventional Forces in Europe I; Conventional Forces in Europe II; Conventional Forces in Europe II plus unilateral U.S. cuts; Current balance in conventional forces; Warsaw Treaty Organization unilateral reduction of

Conventional Forces in Europe I (CFE I): air power under, 45, 82; follow-on-forces and follow-on-forces attack before and after, 46–47, 82; NATO security under, 3, 42, 48, 83; NATO-WTO fully mobilized ADE scores, 40, 42; NATO-WTO ground force balance, 1, 30, 38–39; numerical equality in ATTU, 38, 40, 42, 48–49; opposition to NATO reductions beyond, 51–52

Conventional Forces in Europe II (CFE II): force-to-space requirements, 51–53; minimum consolidation level for military control, 54–55; NATO position under, 3, 51, 83–84; results, 82; restructuring forces under, 64–65; test scenarios to assess, 56–63

Conventional Forces in Europe II plus unilateral U.S. cuts, 49, 51; ADEs at start of